DATE DUE

AUG 07 1990	FEB 08 1996
OCT 2 5 1990	FEB 2 8 1996
APR 9 1992	NOV 05 1997
DEC 1 4 1992	
APR. 1 5 1993	
MAY 1 8 1993	
JUL 3 1 1993	
DEC. 7 1993	
MAR. 9 1994	
OCT. 1 0 1994	
OCT. 2 8 1994	
DEC. 1 1994	
DEC. 1 9 1994	
MAY 3 0 1995	

PANIC
ON WALL STREET

ALSO BY ROBERT SOBEL

The New Game on Wall Street
RCA
Salomon Brothers 1910–1985: Advancing to Leadership
IBM vs. Japan: The Struggle for the Future
Car Wars: The Battle for Global Supremacy
The Rise and Fall of the Conglomerate Kings
ITT: The Management of Opportunity
IBM: Colossus in Transition
The Worldly Economists
The Last Bull Market: Wall Street in the 1960s
The Fallen Colossus: The Great Crash of the Penn Central
Inside Wall Street
The Manipulators: America in the Media Age
They Satisfy: The Cigarette in American Life
NYSE: A History of the New York Stock Exchange
Herbert Hoover at the Onset of the Great Depression
The Entrepreneurs: Explorations Within the American Business Tradition
For Want of a Nail: If Burgoyne Had Won at Saratoga
Money Manias: Eras of Great Speculation in American History
Machines and Morality: The United States in the 1850s
Amex: A History of the American Stock Exchange
The Age of Giant Corporations: A Microeconomic History of the United States
Conquest and Conscience: The United States in the 1840s
The Curbstone Brokers: Origins of the American Stock Exchange
The Great Bull Market: Wall Street in the 1920s
The Big Board: A History of the New York Stock Market
The Origins of Interventionism: The United States and the Russo-Finnish War

PANIC
ON WALL STREET

A Classic History of America's Financial Disasters—
with a New Exploration of the Crash of 1987

ROBERT SOBEL

TT TRUMAN TALLEY BOOKS / E. P. DUTTON / NEW YORK

This paperback edition of Panic on Wall Street
first published in 1988 by E. P. Dutton

Published in the United States by
Truman Talley Books • E. P. Dutton,
a division of NAL Penguin Inc.,
2 Park Avenue, New York, N.Y. 10016.

Published simultaneously in Canada
by Fitzhenry and Whiteside, Limited, Toronto.

Library of Congress Catalog Card Number: 88-50104
ISBN: 0-525-48404-3

10 9 8 7 6 5 4 3 2 1

for Marlene Ritter

CONTENTS

PANIC
ON WALL STREET

INTRODUCTION

Most Americans in their late twenties or early thirties have no recollection of the Great Depression, the last of its kind the nation has endured. Not only have today's college students no memories of the depression, but they have learned about World War II from history books and tales of their parents and friends. These are two of the most important facts of contemporary American life: the nation has produced its first generation with no deep scars of economic or military disaster. To be sure, there were recessions in 1953–54 and 1957–58, but these cannot compare with the tragedies of the late 1830s and early 1840s, the period from 1873 to 1895, or the 1930s. Similarly, more Americans died in the taking of several island chains in World War II than in the Korean War or the Vietnam conflict. This is not to say that recessions and limited wars are a matter for indifference, but rather to place them in proper perspective.

Americans under the age of fifty do not remember the last financial panic clearly, and we are rapidly approaching the time when only Social Security recipients will be able to talk knowingly of what happened in the last part of 1929. It was a dramatic period, from which emerged few victors and a nation of losers. The mythology of the Great Crash has become an important part of America's history, and the depression of the 1930s is considered second only to the Civil War in its impact on American society. There is a major difference in attitudes regarding the two events. Somehow it is possible to view wars as necessary, as semicrusades. Afterward, participants become nostalgic about the period of conflict, hold reunions, and brag of exploits. This is not the case with financial panics and depressions, which all agree bring little good to the nation. Several years ago America was reminded that the last surviving soldier of the Civil War had died; it is doubtful that we will be informed when the last broker or major speculator of the Great Crash breathes his last. Such people and events hardly seem dashing, courageous, or worthy of nostalgia. Yet, his death will be no less important an event than the demise of a drummer boy who entered the Union Army in the final days of the conflict.

In studying wars, we are always concerned with the problems of beginnings, those dramatic moments which seem to initiate the conflict. So it is that we remember the battles of Lexington and Concord, the shelling of Fort Sumter, and the attack on Pearl Harbor. Dozens of books deal with an obscure Austrian archduke whose only claim to fame is that his assassination sparked World War I. Historians realize that although accidents may well change the course of history, much of their impact comes from the setting off of a chain of events in the period that follows, and that no great change in human affairs takes place without some preparation in the social framework. Lexington and Concord capped more than a decade of antagonism between the colonies and the mother country. Friction between North and South did not begin with the shelling of Fort Sumter, or the election of Lincoln some months earlier. The origins of the Pearl Harbor attack can be found as far back as the turn of the century, and to understand it one must first study the Spanish-American and Russo-Japanese wars. Furthermore, these moments of crisis would be of only passing interest were they not followed by great upheavals.

So it is with the present study of financial panics. I have chosen twelve periods of Wall Street history, when the possibility of panic was foremost in the minds of many Americans. Not all were important; not all set off depressions; in fact, several were not panics in the truest sense of the term. Each has been chosen for different sets of reasons, and together they will illustrate the complexity of such moments, and our inability to make more than the vaguest generalizations about them as a group.

The specific panics were selected with care. For example, the chapters on 1914 and 1962 were included to illustrate aborted panics, the former through the wisdom of the New York Stock Exchange, the latter the result of basic strengths of the economy. On the other hand, I have not included chapters on the crises of 1785, 1808, 1819, 1825, 1847, 1860, 1878, 1889, 1903, 1920, 1937, and the few difficult moments preceding World War II and those following the war. There was a panic in 1898 when the battleship *Maine* was sunk. The market fell 16 percent during the next four weeks, but recovered the loss the following month. The market declined 25 percent in the twenty-six days after France's collapse in 1940; it sank 7 percent on Eisenhower's illness in 1955 and 4 percent when Kennedy was assassinated in 1963. None of these events are covered in the present work.

These twelve episodes in Wall Street history were chosen with four criteria in mind. In the first place, although not all were of major importance, each had a great impact on Americans of the time. Secondly, each may be used to illustrate several points I hope to make about the nature of panics. Next, all twelve were dramatic, and drama is present in most important events in history. We had economic disasters in 1819 and 1937, but in both instances this element was absent. The Kennedy slide of 1962 was dramatic; the Johnson erosion of 1966, though in most respects more severe, was not. Finally, I was drawn to each of the twelve panics as a result of what I believe has been neglect on the part of others. In some cases I have relied on familiar sources which needed reinterpretation; other chapters deal with men and happenings well known to contemporaries but half-forgotten due to a scarcity of historians interested in such matters. In about half the chapters I have found material which, for one reason or another, has led me to new interpretations of what in some cases are major, and in other, minor events and individuals.

Viewed as a whole, the book has no hero, villain, or victim, although J. P. Morgan was the hero of several panics and U. S. Grant was victimized in others. More accurately, one may say that Wall Street and the public have been, at once, heroes, victims, and villains of all the panics.

Financial panics are unusual phenomena; anyone who has lived through one never forgets it. On the other hand, such a person might find it difficult to differentiate between that panic and "bad moments," which he would not label as panics. Is it the severity of the decline that makes for a panic? If so, why do we consider the Northern Pacific conflict of 1901 a panic and not the decline of 1966? Securities prices dropped further in the latter year than in the former, but although 1966 was uncomfortable on Wall Street, there was no panic.

Perhaps the severity of the crash is not as important as the length of time in which it occurs. We may say, keeping 1966 in mind, that short dips may be termed panics while long, regular declines are not. This leads to other problems, however, since the nation's most destructive panics—such as those of 1837, 1873, and 1929—were long-lived, while the sharp collapses of 1869 and 1901 were not nearly as important.

For that matter, there is no universally accepted definition of a panic. Most economists agree that they occur after periods of crisis, but do not tell us how to differentiate them from other climaxes that conclude crises. Others say that a panic is really psychological in nature. William Graham Sumner wrote that it is "a wave of emotion, apprehension, alarm. It is more or less irrational. It is superinduced upon a crisis, which is real and inevitable, but it exaggerates, conjures up possibilities, takes away courage and energy." Sumner concludes that while crises are real, panics are irrational. Should the economy be faced with a crisis, only prompt actions would serve to overcome difficulties. But since panics are psychological, they may be corrected only through the use of reason. "A panic can be partly overcome by judicious reflection, by realization of the truth, and by measurement of facts."

Of course, Sumner did not live to see the 1929 panic, a time when no amount of reason would have been effective, if indeed a reasonable man could have gained an audience. One need only read the speeches and statements of President Hoover in late 1929 and early 1930 to see the impact of reason; each time the President spoke, the market seemed to slide another few points. Writing in 1867, John Stuart Mill said "Panics do not destroy capital; they merely reveal the extent to which it has been previously destroyed by its betrayal into hopelessly unproductive works." Reasonable men like Sumner and Mill would have been astonished by the prevalence of irrationality in the twentieth century, but it may be argued that had they known more of the panics of their own times, they might have been less sanguine about the use of reason. Indeed, some of the most reasonable presidents—Washington, Van Buren and Cleveland, as well as Hoover—were unable to cope with such events.

Is there a pattern to panics? Will we have another such crisis as that of 1929? How can we prevent panics? Such questions come to mind when reading about this subject. Clearly, the author has some reflections on them, which are best discussed in the conclusion, after the reader has traversed twelve of the most harrowing moments in American history. There is, however, one thought to keep in mind before turning to the study of William Duer and the first major panic on Wall Street. That is, far more time and effort have been spent on the study of war than on the study of panics. Do we know more about wars now than we did a century ago? Is there a pattern to wars? Will there be a World War III? How can we prevent wars? One may have ideas and thoughts about these questions, but the answers, unfortunately, have yet to be found.

Alexander Dana Noyes and Frederick Lewis Allen, two great financial historians now deceased, inspired this book, as they have many others in the field of stock market history. Mr. Peter Ritner of The Macmillan Company suggested the possibilities of such a work, and I am grateful for his assistance at every stage of its development. Mr. Ray Roberts of Macmillan was a most meticulous editor and went over the final manuscript with a magnifying glass tempered by a sense of humor. My wife put up with me during the writing of the book and was especially kind when I became depressed at the thought of all those moments of grief I was studying. Miss Elsie Reynolds of the Hofstra University Library spent a good part of many days in obtaining rare books and ordering many periodicals for my use. My students at New College may have grown tired of hearing tales of the various panics, but they were polite enough not to say so. Finally, several brokers told me of their recollections of the panics of 1914, 1929, and 1962, and one remembered the panic of 1907. They asked not to be quoted or mentioned, insisting only on a complimentary copy of this work in payment for their efforts. I hope they are pleased with the result.

1.

WILLIAM DUER AND
THE PANIC OF 1792

The city of New York was covered with snow in early January of 1790, but the life of the municipality continued. Men and boys fished from the Hudson piers at Rector Street, and reported good catches of lobster and crab. Couples skated at the Collect Pond, located above Chambers Street, or took sleigh rides on Bowry Road past the Negro Burial Ground on Rivington Street. The city seemed clean and fresh compared to what would come a few decades later. Its population—33,131 in 1790—made it the largest city in the United States, but the municipal sanitation department, composed of thirty-five scavengers and a host of pigs who roamed the streets, did their jobs well.

At the close of Washington's first administration, New York seemed to be a new city. There had been a fire in 1776, which destroyed all the houses between Broad and Whitehall Streets and along both sides of Broadway as far north as Rector Street. Cheap frame structures had been erected to take the place of the charred hulls, but by 1790 these had been replaced by neat brick homes. There were some five thousand dwellings in the city proper, and more than eight hundred houses were being built each year. The city moved north rapidly; some predicted that within two generations there would be homes on the treed meadows on Houston Street. Bunker Hill, off Broadway on Grand Street, was used for bull-baiting and other sports best indulged in away from the city; Mayor Richard Varick thought the area might have to be relocated when the population reached that point.

New York was a bustling port, passing Philadelphia in total

tonnage by 1794. Boasting the finest harbor in America and fed by a satisfactory road system and the Hudson River, it was natural for New York to become the commercial center of the North. Skiffs from the upper Hudson would unload at Rector Street or at any of the many docks along Washington Street on the west side. The major land route was along Bowry Road. Drovers would stop at the Bull's Head Tavern on Bayard Street for a last drink before entering the city proper, and then continue on to Chatham Street, which slanted across the island until it merged with Broadway. This was one of the busiest intersections of the city, with St. Paul's Church on one side of the street, a theater and park on the other, and the almshouse, municipal jail, and city hospital within close range. Behind St. Paul's on Church Street was a row of boardinghouses frequented by students of Columbia College.

The drovers would then continue down Broadway for seven blocks until they reached the Trinity Church, at Wall Street. Should they turn left, they could walk past the City Hall, rows of banks and mercantile establishments, and many taverns and inns. The Merchants' Exchange and the Government House were below Wall Street, but this narrow lane was the center of the city in 1790.

Wall Street was also the seat of American government. Alexander Hamilton, the Secretary of the Treasury, resided at the corner of Wall and Water Streets, in a small house not far from the Coffee House Slip on the East River. The City Hall, renamed Federal Hall, was the temporary center of government. Washington's original New York residence, Number 3 Cherry Street, was in Franklin Square, then a fashionable section not far from Wall Street. The city's social elite were clustered in mansions around Bowling Green, but the men could usually be found at noontime two blocks farther north, on Wall Street.

The city's inns were the location of much government business as the new administration established itself. But this was temporary, since all knew that Washington and his retinue would soon move to more permanent quarters in Philadelphia. When the government left New York in the summer of 1790, activities were barely slackened. The President departed by means of a barge moored on the Hudson, at McComb's Wharf; as he bade farewell, other ships were being unloaded on the East River side of Manhattan.

The East River wharfs were quiet on Sundays, but busy at all other times. Shipments of coffee, chocolate, tea, molasses, sugar, nuts, fruits, candles, spices, indigo, cotton, and other American or foreign products were unloaded either for local use or, more often, transshipment. The inns on the east end of Wall Street hummed with activity, as bills of lading, merchants' acceptances, notes, and checks were passed back and forth throughout the day and into the night. Small old coffeehouses were torn down to make room for larger ones. For a while, the Merchants' Coffee-House was the center of activity, not only in mercantile bills but in the transfer of stocks and bonds as well. Early in 1792 some merchants decided to erect their own building, the Tontine Coffee-House, not far from Hamilton's New York residence on Wall Street. Membership would be restricted to dealers and traders; in effect, the Tontine would be an American version of Lloyd's of London. The Tontine would be used primarily for business transactions, but social activities would also be permitted. Many of the meetings called to discuss plans for the Tontine ended with a toast to the health of Secretary of the Treasury Hamilton, the hero of the New York business community and the city's most prominent resident.

Hamilton was not the only New Yorker in a powerful position in the new government. Samuel Osgood, related by marriage to the powerful Livingston clan, was postmaster general, and John Jay was the first chief justice of the Supreme Court. Hamilton's chief aide at the Treasury, the assistant secretary, was a man well known at the time but forgotten today. His name was William Duer.

Portraits of William Duer show a slight man with sharp features, a receding hairline, and the air of confidence so often present in the faces portrayed in paintings of the period. It is the face of a man who realized that he was important, having the elegance of one who "had arrived."

In 1790 Duer was one of the social and economic arbiters of American society. It was Duer who found the house that Washington occupied in New York, and he also arranged terms for its lease. It was Duer who helped organize the ill-fated but spectacular Scioto Company, which planned massive speculations in western lands. He controlled the destinies of Parker & Duer, Duer & Parker, William Duer & Co., and other firms engaged in speculations in land, international trade, currency, stocks, and whatever else seemed to offer a rich return. More than any American, save Robert Morris, Duer was known in European banking circles as a master of finance. He was one of Hamilton's closest friends, and had been mentioned with asperity in many of Jefferson's and Madison's letters. Duer was a former member of the Continental Congress and was married to socially promient Kitty Sterling (the daughter of Revolutionary General Lord Sterling).

An Englishman by birth, Duer joined the Revolutionary forces early in the war, abandoning his many commercial interests for the time being. In his capacity as deputy adjutant general for the New York militia, he secured stores for the troops when none seemed available. He became an intimate of the circle which surrounded George Washington, and was one of those who helped foil the Conway Cabal, which had been organized to depose the General. Later on, Duer entered into commercial dealings with the French and facilitated the shipment of foreign goods to the American army. After the war, he joined with Hamilton to work for a stronger union, and was one of those asked by Hamilton to contribute to the *Federalist Papers* when passage of the new Constitution by the New York Convention seemed in doubt. Duer wrote several articles in favor of the Constitution, and although he did not join with Hamilton, Madison, and Jay in the writing of the *Federalist*, he was given much credit for swaying votes in favor of the new government. It was only natural, then, that Duer be asked to take a high post in the government. At the time, it seemed that no position the nation could offer him would be beyond his ambition.

But more than anything else, William Duer was a speculator, a description he himself would not deny. However, the term meant something quite different in 1790 than it does today. At that stage of capitalist development, dealings in land, bills, or joint stock companies were considered legitimate enterprises for a gentleman. There were few banks and no "blue chip" bonds and stocks at the close of the eighteenth century, and so speculation was the only means by which a person of wealth might invest his surplus funds. Washington, Hamilton, Jefferson, Madison—almost all the founding fathers—were engaged in land ventures at one time or another in their careers, and this did not detract from their reputations for probity.

While accepting the situation, Jefferson and his circle drew a distinction between *types* of speculation. Investments in land, commerce, or joint stock companies were fine, they said, for such activities enable the community to increase its store of wealth, and so benefit all. These were not only acceptable, but participation in them was the duty of gentlemen who wished to aid in the nation's development. On the other hand, speculation in securities was frowned upon by this group. If a man purchases a piece of paper representing ownership in an enterprise, after that enterprise has commenced activities, the paper benefits no one. Should the paper increase in value and then be sold for a profit, the speculator gains, but society does not. Should funds be drawn out of society for such activities, then useful enterprises would be stunted, and society would actually suffer. Thus, Jefferson would accept the land companies of the Virginia aristocracy but would condemn the "paper speculations" of men like William Duer.

Of course, Jefferson and his circle could do little to curb the paper speculations of the period. Ever since the first years of the Revolution, there were dealers in Continental currency, bonds, and other obligations of the new nation. The speculations increased during the Confederation period, as American obligations rose and fell rapidly on the performance of the new government. State obligations were also bought and sold, as were bonds and stocks of local corporations and banks. Should the new nation fail, these papers would be almost worthless; should it succeed, they would increase in value. What better avenue of speculation could there be? The European securities were relatively stable, and offered few opportunities for killings. Thus, foreign syndicates sent their money to the United States, and by the late 1780s, according to some sources, the American markets were dominated by European interests. Willinks & Stadinski of Amsterdam was one outlet for such funds. Étienne Clavière, a noted French banker, was another. The Société Gallo-Américaine of France was a third. And there were others, representing almost all the countries of Europe. Some bought and sold through their own nationals, who were sent to America for that purpose. Others used the talents of native speculators.

Andrew Craigie of Boston moved from that city to New York to engage in this business. After serving as apothecary general in the Continental Army, Craigie became interested in securities. In 1787 he visited London to make the proper contacts for investments. Craigie then returned to New York, where he met Daniel Parker and reestablished relations with his old friend William Duer. Shortly thereafter, Craigie began to funnel foreign funds into American securities, and most of the investments were handled by Parker & Duer.

The Philadelphia convention of the summer of 1787 added to the speculative activities. Should a strong new government be established, one of its first acts would have to be that of establishing national credit. This could be accomplished only by guaranteeing in one form or another the obligations of the Confederation. Prices of and activities in the Confederation's obligations rose as the meetings continued, and they were followed with great care by the Europeans. They had always been aware of the great potential of the new nation; now it might be realized. There was land speculation, the China trade, and the possibilities of manufactures. The wheat trade alone offered tremendous profits, not to mention tobacco and possibly cotton. Most important, however, were public securities. If purchased and sold at the right times, they could offer great rewards with few risks. Inside information was needed for this. Accordingly, Van Staphorts & Hubbard of Amsterdam joined with Willinks & Stadinski and Clavière in sending Brissot de Warville to America to gain such information. Find a good situation, wrote Clavière. "Study it, and if at first view it looks romantic, find the means of saving it from that objection; converse upon it with intelligent persons; find such as are sufficiently attached to great objects, to be willing to concur in them with zeal, when they are designed for the aid and consolation of humanity."

Brissot arrived in America early in 1788, as the new Constitution was making the rounds of the states. In gathering information for his syndicate, he met William Duer, and they soon became fast friends. Duer led Brissot into several land and trade speculations, and as the new government took shape, they began to discuss securities as well. Brissot was convinced that Duer was the best man to aid the group in its American dealings, a conviction that was fortified when his friend gained a major post at the Treasury. In writing of Duer, Brissot was ecstatic. "It is difficult to unite to a great facility in calculation, more extensive views and a quicker penetration into the most complicated projects. To these qualities he joins goodness of heart; and it is to his obliging character, and his zeal, that I owe much valuable information on the finances of this country, which I shall communicate hereafter." In October 1788, Brissot suggested that his group and Duer's might enter into an agreement regarding investments in America, working for closer ties between their nations—and speculation. In effect, Brissot and Clavière of France would form a combine for land and securities speculations with Duer and Craigie of the United States. There was no doubt as to who would dominate the combine: Clavière, Brissot, and Craigie were each to receive one fifth of the profits, while Duer was to receive two fifths for himself. Brissot left America on December 4, pleased with his work and confident that the combine was in good hands.

The Americans had every reason to exude optimism. They realized that the new government would take action on the public debt, and that they would be in positions to receive privileged information. Craigie made no attempt to hide his confidence. Duer was a rising star in the Federalist camp, and seemed certain to gain high office in the government, from which he would obtain government secrets. After all, wrote Craigie, the main reason he had purchased shares in the Scioto Company was to gain Duer's friendship and confidence. Now everything seemed to be falling into place. "The public debt affords the best field in the world for speculation," he wrote, "but it is a field in which strangers may easily be lost. I know of no way of making safe speculations but by being associated with people who from their official situation know all present and can aid future arrangements either for or against the funds."

French and Dutch funds continued to flow to America—much of it through Duer and Craigie—during 1789. News of Washington's inauguration on April 30 was greated by the speculators as a sign of stability, which would result in a rise in prices. On September 2, the act establishing the Treasury Department was passed, and shortly thereafter Hamilton—the friend of business—was named Secretary of the Treasury. Within a few days Duer accepted the post of Assistant Secretary, assuring inside information for the combine. Duer did not make his business dealings secret; Hamilton and others knew of them and did not require him to relinquish outside affairs. Letters of the period indicate clearly that Duer was not above speculating on his privileged information and for his own good. Duer would make his purchases and then let news stories "leak" to the public, so as to cause a rise in price. Noah Webster, writing to a Dutch friend, described the growth of speculation in America. There was news, he indicated, that the public debt would soon be funded; "this is the outdoor talk of Colonel Duer, the Vice-Secretary." Nor was the combine unaware of this. Theophile Cazenove, an ally of the Clavière group, made ready to come to America to aid in the dealings. Brissot wrote of this to Duer, and after congratulating him on his appointment, asked the Assistant Secretary to make Cazenove at home in New York. "I am sure, knowing your obliging temper you'll give him good information about his speculations; and I'll be much obliged to you to do it and to introduce him to your acquaintances."

Meanwhile, debates on funding measures began. Hamilton was intent on establishing the national credit by calling in old obligations of the Confederation and exchanging them for new issues. With Washington's prestige and support, Hamilton was able to gain passage of the Funding Act of 1790, which provided for the issuance of federal bonds in exchange for Confederation and Continental debts. The Act authorized the issuance of three types of securities: 6 percent bonds that bore interest from date of issue; 6 percent bonds that would not pay interest for the first ten years; and 3 percent bonds. A similar arrangement was made for the assumption of state debts after Hamilton and Jefferson came to an understanding on the issue. By the end of 1790, the new government had a domestic debt of $62,650,000, largely as a result of these measures.

Hamilton's next program involved the establishment of a Bank of the United States, which would, in effect, guarantee the public credit. The bank bill was passed, through the intercession of Washington and despite Jefferson's opposition, in February, 1791. The BUS (as the bank came to be called) was capitalized at $10 million (25,000 shares of $400 par value), of which the government was to subscribe one fifth. The other sales were to be made to the public, with the limitation that no subscription could be for more than 1,000 shares. Payment was to be made through submission of 25 percent of the price in gold and the rest in 6 percent government bonds.

In order to pay for its share of stock, the government floated a new bond issue overseas. The issue was handled by Hope & Co. of Amsterdam, and in the next six years, this firm would take more than $7 million in federal bonds. Some of the government's subscription payment was met through a loan from the Bank of North America, a private bank which had been chartered in 1781 and which opened its doors the following year.

Hamilton's financial program gave new confidence to both American and European speculators. Bonds, stocks, and other obligations were still low; they were bound to rise when the Hamiltonian measures were put into operation. Naturally, the soon-to-be-issued stock in the BUS was the center of activity early in 1791. Daniel Crommelin & Co. of Amsterdam sent over $1 million to its American correspondent, Watson & Greenleaf, to be used in speculations. Daniel Parker established sales outlets in London to better distribute American securities in Britain. Cazenove arrived in New York and immediately plunged into the securities markets. The credit of the United States government itself was placed behind speculations. Believing that United States obligations were selling at too low a price, and eager to have such bills at par with their foreign counterparts, Hamilton began buying bonds as early as September 1790, and he continued such purchases into 1791. Treasury purchases were limited to the 6 percents, the deferred 6 percents, and the 3 percents; speculators were interested in all three issues, but also in stocks of private banks, the "when issued" stock of the BUS and, by early 1791, almost any American obligation that showed promise of a rise.

The sustained bull market led to the development of new forms. Speculators would borrow stock from its holders, paying a fixed amount of money for the privilege and promising to return it within a fixed number of months. The borrowed stock would be sold, and the funds gained used to purchase other issues. When the due date arrived, the borrower would sell out his position, and repurchase the borrowed stock. If the latter rose more slowly than the former (taking interest into account) he made money; if not, he lost. "Wager stock" was an important factor in the bull market, and it served to intensify dealings and increase prices. Similarly, stock was purchased for delivery within from three to six months. If the stock rose in this period, then the purchaser could immediately sell it and pocket the difference between the contract price and the final quotation; if not, he would lose the difference. The seller received a guaranteed price—in the bull market higher than the immediate delivery price—and the purchaser gained the opportunity to speculate. Dealings in credit abounded before the end of the year, and buyers and sellers alike sought means of intensifying the gambling mania. Volume increased sharply, and speculators quickly recognized the need for a centralized market for securities.

By the late autumn of 1790, several brokers opened daily auctions in their offices, and there was talk of establishing a central securities market for the city. M'Evers & Barclay, which sold $180,000 worth of securities in July 1791, demanded such a market, as did Pintard & Bleecker and others. The new race of specialized brokers in securities—none had existed prior to this period in America—and the increasing number of securities speculators began negotiations for what would become the forerunner of the New York Stock Exchange.

The key to this great increase in speculative interest was the subscription to stock in the BUS, which took place early in July 1791. Although shares were high in price, the entire issue was taken within the first hour; indeed, the BUS issue was 20 percent oversubscribed. Few purchased the stock for investment; most of the buyers paid with IOUs, and only $675,000 in cash went into the bank's coffers. Within a week "half-shares" of bank stock were traded in New York, and its price rose regularly throughout the summer and autumn.

The BUS issue was reported in all the New York newspapers, which noted that "scrip" was the topic of the day.* Such words as "scriptomania," "scripponomy," "scriptophobia," and "stock-jobbing" became commonplace in the *New York Daily Gazette*, the *New York Journal and Patriotic Register* and the *Daily Advertiser*. Few thought the bull market would last. "The Scriptophobia is at full height," reported the Journal. "It has risen like a rocket—like a rocket it will burst with a crack—then down drops the rocket stick. What goes up must come down." "The cry is—what can be the reason of this strange and astonishing rise of the American stocks! O that I had but cash—how soon would I have a finger in the pie!" This, from the reader of the *Journal* early in August; at the time BUS stock had risen thirty points, and showed no sign of a decline. Could it last? There was a slight dip on August 11 and 12, and a *Journal* reader with the pseudonym of I———c Dipdeep wrote, "The Bubble is Burst! Wanted immediately, the advice of a *honest* Stock Jobber, how to dispose of about three hundred Bank Scripts, purchased at two hundred and fifty dollars per script, so as not entirely to ruin the present holder." If "Dipdeep" had held onto his stock for another week, he would have seen it rise to new heights, as the fever continued to grip the population. James Madison, writing to Jefferson of the mania, noted that "stock and scrip the sole domestic subjects of conversation . . . speculations . . . carried on with money borrowed at from two and a half per cent a month to one per cent a week." Madison's words were echoed by the *Advertiser*. "The National Bank stock has risen so high, so enormously above its real value, that no two transactions in the annals of history can be found to equal it." The newspapers even published poems about the mania. The *Gazette* of August 13, 1791, printed the following:

---

* The term "scrip" was derived from "subscription stock," which at the time referred to equity ownership in an enterprise as distinct from bonds, or other debts.

Speculation

What magic this among the people,
That swells a may-pole to a steeple?
Touched by the wand of speculation,
A frenzy runs through all the nation;
For soon or late, so truth advises,
Things must assume their proper sizes—
And sure as death all mortal trips,
Thousands will rue the name of SCRIPTS.

"Where will it end?" asked a reader of the *Journal*. "What is the role of the government in all this?" asked another. The answer seemed clear to all those involved in the speculations. Prices would rise indefinitely, and the Treasury (Hamilton) was supporting the prices.

Hamilton saw no inconsistency in continued Treasury purchases of bonds. The bull market was good for business, attracted foreign capital to America, and gave the new government an aura of confidence and success. Nor was he concerned about the obvious speculations of his friends and past associates at the Treasury. Rufus King and others informed the Secretary that Duer was occupied in heavy speculation, and Hamilton did warn Duer not to get too involved in the market. Duer—who had left his post at Hamilton's side early in 1790 when the government moved to Philadelphia—defended himself before his friend and former associate. Hamilton replied on August 17, at a time when the mania seemed at full tide. He noted the speculation and fever it brought in its wake, and assured Duer that he realized his former associate was an honest man. But consider your fortunes and reputation, requested Hamilton. Do not be too sure of yourself, for such self-confidence may bring a fall. "I feared lest it might carry you further than was consistent either with your own safety or the public good. My friendship for you, and my concern for the public cause, were both alarmed." Notwithstanding this, Hamilton agreed that the prices of stocks should continue their rise. The Secretary of the Treasury, in writing to a leading speculator, concluded, "I do not widely differ from you about the real value of bank scrip. I should rather call it about 190 to be within bounds, with hopes of better things, and I sincerely wish you may be able to support it at what you mention." What was the reason for this encouragement of Duer's purchases? "The acquisition of too much of it by foreigners will certainly be an evil." Did Hamilton realize that much of Duer's support came from Amsterdam and London? The letters of the time give no answer to this question, but we do know that Duer was acting for foreign interests throughout this period.

The bull market of 1791 was made to order for a man of Duer's talents. Those who had purchased shares with IOUs had invested $25 in cash in single shares; by late August the price of such scrip was $185. Although it did decline in September, the price never went below $130; by late October, it was back to $170. Duer bought and sold shares, making profits from both the declines and rises; he was clearly the king of the speculators—the man who called the tune. Should a stock dealer stand on good terms with Duer, his fortune was made; if not, he could count on eventual failure. This was not a conspiracy; even the newspapers carried stories of Duer's power. The *Journal* of September 14 noted that some were attempting to escape from Duer's control, showing that his grip was tightening. A poem composed at the time indicated his power:

> The Scrips Legislature, or the Old Saw Verified, of
> Honor Among Thieves

> At Jonathan's, y'clept of late,
> Where scrip-mongers of every rate,
> From Billy, of a thousand less-one
> To him of humble half a dozen—
> Have, for a moon, gulled half the world,
> And thousands to perdition hurled;
> A puny duckling quit the phalanx,
> And left behind a gently balance—
> This roused the honor of the Co.
> And every bull and bear cried "ho!"
> By show of hands they fixed this rule.
> Henceforth a statute in their school,
> That every duck that drops a feather,

Or strays an inch beyond his tether;
Or does what other birds would scorn,
Though on a dirty dunghill born,
Shall posted be, with horrid charcoal,
And stand eternal on the black-rolle.
Which done, a Philadelphia blue,
Whom late they plucked from hat to shoe,
By honorable oaths of lies,
That scrip in York were on the rise,
Burst in a fury towards the wall,
And cried, "by heaven, here's post you all!"

But Duer was more than a mere speculator, although his reputation was made in this area. His ambitions included control of a manufacturing complex, commercial connections with Europe, and a permanent organization for land speculation. Had he succeeded in all of these activities, he would have emerged as the most important businessman in America, and its most powerful until the days of J. P. Morgan.

Needless to say, all of this would take large amounts of money, in comparison to which the European funds used by Duer and Craigie seemed piddling. The best source of funds would be banking, and so Duer needed control over one or more banks, whose deposits would be used to finance his other dealings. Accordingly, Duer maintained a strong position in the stock of the Bank of North America and other institutions. But to purchase such stocks money would be needed, and this had to come from speculation. By late December Duer had his plans formed: he would make a fortune in speculations, invest it in more productive enterprises, and then go on to greater fame, wealth, and glory.

New York prepared for the new year in a flush of optimism. The government was stable; Indian problems seemed on the decline; trade was booming, and the city would receive more than its share of the business; construction and other activities were satisfactory; the poorhouse was able to report that its numbers had diminished during the past year; and good crops seemed to assure a fine year for 1792. The social season had been a success, stilling fears that the removal of the capital to Philadelphia would make New York a "dead city." True, there were still slave hunts, as Negroes continued to elude their masters, and almost each issue of the newspapers carried reward notices for escaped slaves. But this had always been the case, and did not merit the attention of men of affairs.

Alexander Macomb, a land speculator, trader, and businessman, was one of the richest and most highly respected citizens of the city. He was invited to all the balls, and his own home at 39 Broadway had been occupied by Washington himself just before the President moved to Philadelphia. Macomb knew all the right people, and was on good terms with William Duer.

During the last week of 1791, Duer and Macomb met to form a combine for dealings in securities. On December 29, two days before the New Year celebrations would begin, the two set their names on a secret agreement. During the next twelve months they would unite to speculate in stocks and bonds, especially those of the BUS and the Bank of New York. All purchases would be made in Macomb's name (apparently to mask the fact that master speculator William Duer was in the combine), and all securities would be held in Macomb's name. The agreement would run until December 31, 1792, at which time it would be dissolved and profits distributed. Although the agreement makes no mention of shares, it appears that they were to be divided evenly between the two men. Macomb was to gain the advice and connections of the more astute Duer, while Duer would be able to draw upon the Macomb fortune.

But what of Duer's connections with Clavière and the Dutch group? There is no mention of this in Duer's papers or other collections of important figures of the period, but we do know that Duer did not end his relationship with the foreigners. On the other hand, both Duer's and Craigie's papers contain letters and documents relating to Duer's relations with another group at this time. Duer had a warm friendship with Walter Livingston, a member of the state's most prestigious clan. Brockholst Livingston and J. R. Livingston also seemed involved in one way or another in this group, as was Edward Livingston, who had been in speculations before. The papers are spotty and incomplete; perhaps we shall never know what transpired between the Livingstons and Duer with any degree of accuracy. It is known, however, that while

Duer and Macomb were committed to purchasing shares and were acting on the bull side of the market in 1792, the Livingstons were selling securities early in 1792, apparently in the expectation of a bear market. And one of the contracts entered into by the Livingstons provided for the delivery of almost all the stock in the Bank of New York to William Duer.

This seems clear-cut on the surface: Duer was purchasing Bank of New York stock, expecting it to rise, while the Livingstons sold the stock, expecting a fall. Macomb probably assumed that Duer was acting on inside information from the Treasury. There were rumors that the BUS would take over the Bank of New York and make it a branch. If this were true, then the Bank of New York stock was due for a rise; if not, it would decline. On the other hand, the Livingstons also had sources of information in Philadelphia. To the casual onlooker it appeared as though it was a battle between insiders.

But when we look beneath the surface, other factors begin to cloud the situation. Duer and Macomb purchased 290 shares of Bank of New York stock within days after signing their agreement, and shortly thereafter bought an additional 110 shares. But at the same time, Duer owned for his own account some shares of the bank. He sold these privately while he purchased others publicly. Then he notified Walter Livingston to sell short an additional hundred shares. Thus, Duer was acting on both sides of the market at the same time! His agreement with Macomb provided for the union of his advice with Macomb's money; he would give bad advice, and the Duer-Macomb combine would lose money—with Duer parting with nothing but his reputation for picking stocks. At the same time, his short sales of Bank of New York stock would bring him a small fortune. It was all based on the merger. In his public dealings, Duer stated that the BUS-Bank of New York merger was inevitable; privately, he was betting against it. And all the while, he used Craigie, Clavière, and the Dutch group to aid in the creation of this private fortune.

During late 1791 the speculation in New York was centered in United States debts, and so the title "scriptomania" was justi- fied. When the several Duer groups began their activities in Bank of New York stock, interest switched from debts to banks,

and scriptomania disappeared from the newspapers, to be replaced by "bancomania." For the first time in American history,
the nation was witness to mass incorporations throughout the
land. The business activity of early 1792 was not to be duplicated
for another two generations.

Macomb's and Duer's activities in Bank of New York stock
set the stage for the bancomania; talk of incorporating the Million Bank of the State of New York raised the curtain. The new
bank—true to its name—was to be capitalized at $1 million, with
2,000 shares at $500 each. The proposal was announced on Jan-
uary 16 by its subscribers, which included Brockholst Livingston,
John M'Vicar—and Alexander Macomb. It was to operate in-
dependently, but its charter was to contain provisions for incorpo-
ration into the Bank of New York within nine months if the
directors of both banks agreed. To the average speculator, the
meaning was clear: The Bank of New York would merge with the
Million Bank prior to being taken over by the BUS. The shares
of all three institutions were bound to rise. Accordingly, Macomb
and his associates were mobbed by subscribers on the first day
of offerings, and the capital was raised within a few hours. By the
end of the week, the price of Million Bank scrip had risen over
100 percent, while rights to purchase stock at the offering price
sold for $92 cash. Stocks in other banks also rose, reaching new
highs on January 18.

The Tammany Bank, capitalized at $200,000, was announced
that day, and its 4,000 shares were offered to the public; subscriptions for 21,740 shares were quickly recorded. Those unable
to purchase Tammany shares were taken care of by promoters of
the Merchants' Bank, capitalized at $1 million. Other promoters
hastened schemes for new banks, as newspapers wailed that the
city now had more banks than it needed. Writing in the *Advertiser*, "Banco" claimed that " More banks may certainly assist
gambling, and enable adventurers the longer to swim on the
fluctuating waves of speculation." "A Speculator" worried on the
pages of the same newspaper that interest would lag in the BUS.
He had shares in that institution, and thought that speculative
interest in other areas might cause a decline in BUS shares. "Many
large stockholders in the National Bank reside in this city. . . .

No less than seven hundred shares were purchased payable May next. Now would it not be an extreme hardship on such men who have such a fondness for this stock to have purchased it at a rate which cannot yield 4 per cent per annum to be under a necessity of parting with it at a loss in consequence of [the setting up of rival banks]."

Even Hamilton, who had done his part in encouraging speculation, was fearful of its results. Writing to William Seton, cashier of the Bank of New York, on January 24, he complained of "these extravagant sallies of speculation," which "do injury to the government, and to the whole system of public credit, by disgusting all sober citizens, and giving a wild air to every thing." Three new banks in the city would create much artificial credit, lead to increased speculation, the creation of a "bubble," and ultimately disaster when the burst came. Wishing to maintain sound banking in New York, Hamilton expressed the hope that Seton would do all in his power to prevent an alliance between the Bank of New York and the new institutions. Most importantly, he promised aid to the Bank of New York; it would "continue to receive deposits from the Collector, in the paper of the Bank of the United States, and that they may also receive payments for the Dutch bills in the same paper." Significantly, no mention was made of a merger between the two institutions. Duer the short seller had been correct! Duer the partner of Macomb had been wrong! Duer the private individual stood to be a rich man once this news broke.

Meanwhile, the battle between opponents and supporters of the new banks continued in the press, as prices of all shares rose. We have no clear idea of Duer's purchases and sales in this period—for any of his many groups or for himself—but the private papers of Craigie seem to indicate that Duer was both buying and selling the same issues. Whether he was trying to shift with the changing prices, manipulate them, or double-cross one set of partners or another is not clear—perhaps he was doing all three! In any event, Duer was at the center of the market every day, and his actions on the buy or sell side were duplicated by a host of followers in January and February. All of his activities were ostensibly secret, but the public discovered them in one way or another and followed him with ready funds and credit. And all the while Duer maintained his interests in land speculation (Scioto Company), manufacturing (Society for Useful Manufactures), and commerce (the French and Dutch correspondents).

Engaged in several major projects, all of them apparently successful, and making a fortune through securities speculations, Duer was giddy with success. He had a seemingly bottomless purse, and could have invested his own money and that of his supporters in safe projects. But the rapid rise in stock values was too great a temptation for him. Sometime early in March 1792, Duer began to purchase huge amounts of stock on a deferred basis. In effect, he contracted to buy bank and debt securities at the market, promising to pay within a fixed number of days, usually two weeks. Duer expected prices to rise, so that he would hold securities worth far more than the contract price at the time he had to pay for them. There is no way of finding out how much money he committed at this time, or who was in the speculation with him. Duer borrowed more than $203,000 from Walter Livingston early in March, employed funds from the S.U.M. and Scioto schemes, and entered into arrangements with others of the Livingston clan, John and Nicholas Roosevelt, Isaac Whippo, John Pintard, Leonard Bleeker and other social and business leaders of the community. Macomb was included in the speculation, as Duer honored his agreement with that businessman, but Craigie and the French-Dutch group were excluded.

Had prices risen in March, Duer might have emerged as the wealthiest man in America. But they did not. Undergoing what today would be called a "correction," prices fell slightly during the first two weeks of the month. On March 6, the 6 percent debts sold for 24 shillings, 4½ pence; by March 15, the price had declined to 21 shillings, 4 pence. Other debts followed in the decline, as did the bank stocks. Money dried up on Wall Street and elsewhere, and Duer was unable to borrow funds to cover his obligations.

At the same time, Duer's past caught up with him. Discrepancies were uncovered in his books, and Comptroller of the Treasury Oliver Wolcott informed the harried Duer that he owed the government almost a quarter of a million dollars in shortages from his period as Assistant Secretary. Duer busied himself with writing letters to all concerned, promising to make good in short order, while at the same time he attempted to borrow funds to cover his market obligations. The master speculator was willing to pay any interest demanded, but he appeared to have lost the golden touch; no one would lend him money. New York and Philadelphia buzzed with rumors that Duer would not be able to make good on his notes, and other obligations were presented to him for payment. In desperation, Duer wrote to Hamilton, pleading for aid. But the plea was too late, for even if Hamilton had been able to offer assistance, it could not have reached New York in time. On March 22, Duer assured the troubled Walter Livingston that all was well. "I am now secure from my enemies, and feeling the purity of my heart I defy the world." Within twenty-four hours, the master speculator would be taken to debtors' prison.

The news of Duer's incarceration sent a wave of panic across the Wall Street area. The respected John Pintard fled the city. Walter Livingston rushed from door to door declaring his solvency. Pierre de Peyster, who owned a Duer note, rushed to the prison and confronted Duer with a brace of dueling pistols. Pay me now, he shouted, or prepare to defend your honor. Duer paid the $1,500 note, and the challenger left.

Twenty-five failures were reported the next day, with more to come. Duer wrote to Livingston and Macomb, begging for aid. Neither was equipped to help Duer, even if they had desired to do so. Livingston discovered that Duer had committed him to some speculations without his knowledge. He was short some $100,000 which he could not raise. Walter Livingston, a member of one of the state's first families, declared his insolvency. As for Macomb, he went under early in April. Commenting on Macomb's subsequent incarceration, a writer in the *Advertiser* noted that "The failure of Mr. Duer has laid the foundation for others, which affect the community in a manner never experienced in the country before. The fulfilment of individual engagements is not only suspended, but private and public confidence has received such a blow as may eventually stagger the stability of the government." Judge Thomas Jones of New York, writing to an out-of-town friend, said practically the same thing. "Colonel Duer has failed for they say three million dollars, and has taken in almost every person in the city, from the richest merchants to even the poorest women and the little shopkeepers. . . . How it will end God only knows; it has put a stop to general business and money is so exceedingly scarce that his runners go about with his printed notes indorsed and signed, but no sum inserted, and if they could find a lender, they give four percent a month and put it in the note." Jefferson took notice of the panic. "At length our paper bubble is burst," he wrote to Thomas Randolph. "The failure of Duer in New York soon brought on others, and these still more, like nine pins knocking one another down, till at that place the bankruptcy is become general, every man concerned in paper being broke, and most of the tradesmen and farmers, who have been laying by money, having been tempted by speculators to lend it to them at an interest of from 3 to 6 per cent a month, have lost the whole." Jefferson thought the total losses in New York alone were around $5 million. Since the property of the city was estimated at about that sum, he compared the panic to what might have occurred if the city had been leveled.

Jefferson exaggerated the losses, but not the impact of the panic upon those directly involved. Another correspondent noted that the talk of the town in February was the new banking structure, with all rushing to buy shares in the Million, Tammany, and Merchants' banks; now these institutions were no longer mentioned except when accompanied by a curse. They too were victims of the panic, and would never open their doors.

Yet, with all this dislocation and news of failures, security prices did not fall below the mid-March figures for most issues. Volume did rise, and this resulted in the establishment of a stock exchange, but prices quickly firmed. As a result, those who gambled on a rise suffered, but those who owned securities outright lost little or nothing.

The reason for this unusual phenomenon was not hard to find: it was Alexander Hamilton.

March 1792 was not an easy period for Hamilton. While still

the key man in the Administration, he was forced to deal with the husband of his mistress, who was engaged in blackmailing him. Many of his close friends and associates were involved in the securities speculations, and he had warned them of the consequences while at the same time he was delighted with the rise in American securities. The market rise aided the BUS and the Bank of New York, which pleased him. But it also resulted in the organization of other banks, which he opposed.

When Hamilton learned of Duer's imprisonment and its results, he was both saddened and pleased—saddened that his friend was suffering, but pleased that the situation was on the way to stabilization. Government actions had provided the securities which made speculation possible; now the government would move to correct the abuses of men like Duer.

In 1791, Hamilton had acted to purchase government securities so as to raise their prices. Now he repeated the operation. As early as March 19, three days before Duer's failure, he ordered his aides to buy securities on the Philadelphia market to give "a new face to things." With Duer's failure in New York, Hamilton directed his friend Seton to begin purchasing the 6 percent bonds to maintain their price above par. Seton was authorized to invest $50,000 initially in the project. Seton was to use his judgment as to when, how, and how much to buy at any one time, but all should be informed that he was acting for the government, and he should give the appearance of willingness to support the market indefinitely. If necessary, he could release the news that a new loan had been floated for the government, with Amsterdam lending the United States 3 million florins at 4 percent interest. "Why then so much despondency among the holders of our stock? When foreigners lend the United States at 4 per cent, will they not purchase here upon a similar scale, making reasonable allowance for expense of agency, etc.? Why then do individuals part with so good a property so much below its value? Does Duer's failure affect the solidity of the government?" Thus, Hamilton instructed Seton to imply the existence of huge amounts of Dutch money, prepared to purchase American securities at low prices to make a killing. To complete Seton's arsenal, he was authorized to have the customhouse accept sixty-

day notes rather than cash payments for the time being, so as
to alleviate financial distress among importers.

Seton began his purchases, and the word of Hamilton's support gave heart to some. But after a brief rally, prices declined
once more. Again, Hamilton instructed Seton to purchase $50,-
000 worth of United States securities, pledging an additional
$100,000 if it became necessary to do so. But even this amount
would not help, and Macomb's failure in mid-April added to the
gloom. Seton wrote to Hamilton, indicating that the worst was
yet to come. The Secretary replied quickly, disagreeing with his
friend. All those who had speculated unduly had been punished;
if a man were in an extended position, this would already have
been made known. In other words, Hamilton believed the shake-
out was over, and the bottom of the slide was in sight. Further,
he indicated that the government's strong role in supporting its
securities would enhance its reputation both at home and among
foreign lenders. To be sure, Hamilton was charged with all sorts
of crimes by his detractors. Some said he entered the arena to
help his friends, while others claimed that he made a fortune
on speculation in this period. The Secretary was able to refute all
of these charges, but the dirt was never completely washed from
his image.

By April 16, it appeared that conditions had returned to normal.
The government paid its interest on the debt, and this was a
bullish sign. Many who had fled the markets in March now
reconsidered their position; gold which had been shipped abroad
in fear of financial collapse now returned, along with more to
be used for investment purposes. By midsummer the markets were
up again, investment easy, and prospects optimistic. Road and
turnpike companies, small manufacturers, and commercial firms
reported little difficulty in raising funds. New York resumed its
growth, and a housing boom developed as immigrants poured
into the city. The new stock exchange on Wall Street operated
efficiently; the city hoped it could take much business away from
the Philadelphia Exchange. The *National Gazette* of June 18 reported that there were few traces of the March disaster to be
found in America. "The shock at the time was very severe, but of
short continuance. Credit is again revived—and prosperity once
more approaches in sight."

Much of the human wreckage was out of sight. Pintard returned from his flight, to become one of the city's leading lights. Macomb and others recovered; the French-Dutch combine and Craigie continued their activities in land and business investments. Some losers left the city, and a few were unable to recover. One of these was William Duer.

Duer remained in jail but was able to conduct business enterprises from there. He would take meals at a local tavern, entertain visitors, and write long business letters. For the rest of his life he tried to put his house in order through land and business ventures, some of them involving large sums of money. But he was never able to clear his name or pay off his debts. Duer died in prison on May 7, 1799, ending the career of the nation's first major securities speculator, and the chief victim of the first financial panic in the young nation's history.

2.
THE CRISIS OF JACKSONIAN FINANCES: 1837

"In the fashionable world Mr. Hone held a high rank in the prime of life, being always considered a leader of the *ton*. Indeed, it has been said that if an order of nobility had existed in this country, Mr. Hone would have claimed the right of being numbered in their ranks." Thus, the *New York Herald* disposed of Philip Hone in May 1851, soon after that prominent New Yorker died. Hone would have appreciated the tone of the obituary; a prudent Whig who had opposed most leveling movements, he certainly identified himself with America's men of quality.

In 1820, at the age of forty, Hone left a profitable auction business and set out for Europe, the first step toward entering the political, literary, and artistic worlds which he so admired. Philip Hone was not a very successful politician. He was elected assistant alderman in 1823 and 1824, but lost the race for alderman the following year. Nonetheless, Hone was chosen mayor by the Common Council in 1825, the result of a split between supporters of two other candidates. He stepped down in 1826, and although Hone ran for other offices, he was never again elected. Still, for the rest of his life, Hone gave advice to the powerful and circulated at times in the inner circles of the Whig party. He also presided over one of the most charming salons in New York, meeting that city's social elite on equal terms. Thus, Hone was able to fulfill some of the promises he made to himself in 1820; he was well known in politics and society. His literary ambitions were disappointed, however; Hone never wrote the great epics and histories he dreamed of in his youth. Instead, he set down his thoughts and reflections in a diary. Today it is Hone's sole claim to immortality, and one of the best sources for happenings in the Jacksonian era.

"My birthday; I am 55 years of age. My health tolerably good, my facilities unimpaired, my mind capable, I believe as ever it was, but less disposed to exertion. My temper, I fear, a little more irritable than it should be, and I cannot jump so high, nor run so fast, as I did twenty years ago, but on the whole I have not much reason to complain, and am better off in all respects than I deserve to be." Thus, Philip Hone began his diary entry for Monday, October 25, 1835.

It was an exciting year for New York and the nation. The city was struck by a fire in early August, which wiped out part of the business district. Then, on December 16, the greatest fire in the city's history began, and before it was quenched, 648 buildings were destroyed together with other property; the total loss was reckoned at more than $18 million. New York had always suffered from fires, and usually they were blamed on one group or another among the city's newcomers. This one was no exception; some of the New York newspapers hinted that the abolitionists, whose speeches and demonstrations were daily occurrences, were behind the tragedy. The nation was in the grip of a wave of violence, complained the *Herald,* and the *Times* concurred. On January 30, an attempt had been made on the life of President Jackson himself! In November, Osceola, leader of the Florida Seminoles, began a new war against Americans of the Southwest. Reverend Charles Giles observed that 56,000 people were killed annually by demon rum, while the nation contained more than a half million drunkards; his solution was simple: prohibition. And while the prohibitionists and abolitionists vied for control of the streets, Chief Justice John Marshall died. On July 8, as the Liberty Bell tolled for his death, it cracked badly. It seemed an evil omen.

Philip Hone was not as happy on his fifty sixth birthday as he had been on his fifty fifth. He had lost more than $11,000 in fire-insurance stock as a result of the Great Conflagration, and he was disturbed by the "lawlessness" of the abolitionists and the seeming inability of government troops to deal with Osceola and the Seminoles. More important, however, was the failure of the Whigs to capture the Presidency in the elections of 1836. Martin Van Buren was a friend of the Hones, and certainly no wild man of the Jacksonian stripe. He had defeated a Whig coalition which included Hugh White, Daniel Webster, Benjamin Harrison, and a scattering of other Whig and third-party candidates. Now it appeared that Jackson would get what his opponents called his third term. To Hone and his friends, such a period might see the end of the republic, and they prayed Van Buren would temper the Jacksonian policies. The most important of these were the outgoing President's views and actions in matters concerned with currency and banking. Unless a change was forthcoming in these areas, said many Whigs, the difficulties with Osceola and the abolitionists would seem tame. Riots would erupt throughout the land as a result of the business paralysis caused by what they considered insane notions of the deranged former general. Jackson knew nothing of banking, charged the Whigs; now the entire nation would pay for his lessons.

Actually, the problems were more complex than the Whigs believed them to be, and in some ways more dangerous. Their struggle with Jackson had been distilled into a single episode: the matter of the Second Bank of the United States. This had been the key issue of the 1832 Presidential campaign, in which Jackson promised that if he was returned to Washington, he would prevent the bank from receiving a new charter. Jackson won the election, thus dooming the institution.

The Bank War was one of the most inflammatory events of the Jackson Administration, and Nicholas Biddle, the BUS president, one of Jackson's bitterest enemies. Biddle is generally considered among the half dozen or so greatest bankers produced in the United States. He had become president of the BUS in 1823, at the age of thirty-six. Prior to that time he had served as a member of the bank's board of directors, where he was considered the foremost expert on the institution's structure and operation. Biddle was called a genius by many of his contemporaries even then. He had completed all the work for his degree at the University of Pennsylvania by the time he was thirteen years old. When that school refused him a diploma because of his youth,

Biddle went to Princeton, and two years later won his B.A. with honors, being elected class valedictorian. Biddle's family was a leader in Philadelphia society, and he later married Jane Craig, the daughter of the city's wealthiest man. In 1832, then, Biddle was a brilliant businessman and banker, with all the right connections and necessary capital for an illustrious career. He was handsome, well-spoken, and tactful. A trip to Greece had left Biddle with a consuming interest in Hellenic civilization, and he could converse on classical themes with any scholar in the nation. An aristocrat by birth, a businessman by choice, and a politician by endowment and training, Biddle's future seemed unlimited. He had already been a member of the Pennsylvania legislature, and now he was the most important banker in the land.

Biddle inherited a bank whose previous leaders had proved incapable of their tasks. William Jones, the first president, had served as Secretary of the Navy and Secretary pro tem of the Treasury. Jones had been a political choice; he was a man who knew nothing of banking, and to make things worse, was venal as well. During his years as president, the bank caused distress in all parts of the country through speculation on the part of its leaders (including Jones himself) and unwise loan policies. After a Congressional investigation, Jones resigned, and was replaced in 1819 by Langdon Cheves of South Carolina, the former Speaker of the House of Representatives. Cheves was determined to put the BUS's affairs in order, and to do so called in many loans and advances. The result was a general straightening out of a messy situation, and the abrupt end of a period of wildcatting led by Jones and his friends. On the other hand, Cheves acted quickly and without sensitivity; as a result, several banks were forced to close their doors. Taken together with worldwide financial problems, the Cheves program helped cause the brief but painful panic of 1819.

This was the situation Biddle inherited in 1823. Within a few years he had reorganized the BUS, acted responsibly to assure the country of a stable currency, and had restored confidence in the central bank. By 1828, he had political as well as financial powers of great magnitude, and some thought that Biddle, although a Democrat himself, might one day hope for the White House. All of this helped bring out a natural arrogance in the man which, together with his ideas on banking, turned Jackson against the BUS and all other similar schemes.

In vain Biddle's supporters attempted to gain recharter, and in the process simplified still further the basic monetary problems the nation faced in the 1830s. If recharter were won, they claimed, the BUS would continue its management of the currency, assuring stability and respectability to the dollar. Its paper was acceptable in all parts of the United States; its branches worked to bind the nation together. Should Jackson have his way, then central banking was doomed, and would be replaced by hundreds of small banks, each with limited resources and no relationship to the others. Paper from the Carolinas would not be so easily negotiable in New York or, for that matter, within a hundred miles of the issuing bank. The result would be financial paralysis, an end to most commerce, and panic.

The Jacksonians responded by saying that the BUS had aided only a few important merchants and foreigners at the expense of most Americans. Through its manipulations, it enabled directors and their allies to stifle the economy when it suited their ends, and free it when they desired a change in policy. Jackson himself favored an end to all paper money and the establishment of a simple gold standard, which would end speculation and provide the nation with the only currency he believed had intrinsic value: gold. Jackson never trusted banks, which he felt caused depressions and disasters. Necessarily, the bigger the bank, the more evil its actions. Thus, the fight against the BUS had become a moral as well as economic contest for the general.

The BUS charter ran until March 1, 1836. After its defeat in Congress, Biddle attempted to gain a new charter from Pennsylvania. Although he had many friends, Biddle's struggles with Jackson had also increased the number of his enemies, which now included those who felt he had manipulated the currency in 1833–35 to win support. Still, he managed to win a charter on February 18, 1836, thus establishing the Bank of the United States of Pennsylvania. Biddle's allies, who viewed him as their champion against a power-crazed Jackson, rejoiced. Philip Hone celebrated the event in his diary.

Mr. Biddle has foiled his implacable enemy, Gen. Jackson. The United States Bank has been incorporated in the State of Pennsylvania. Every effort was made to defeat it and the stale charge of bribery brought against some of its friends; but it passed both houses, and the Governor, Rittner, having signed it, "the monster" is on its legs again, and the President must seek his retreat "in the deserts of Arabia," where he swore he would go whenever the bank was incorporated.

Obviously, the new bank would not be as powerful as its predecessor. Deposits fell off considerably, as did activities. Still, it was the largest bank in the state, and one of the most influential in the nation.

STATISTICS FOR THE BANK OF THE UNITED STATES, 1834–1837

Year	Loans	Deposits	Circulation	Specie
1834	$54,911,461	$10,838,555	$19,208,379	$10,039,237
1835	51,808,739	11,756,905	17,339,797	15,708,369
1836	59,232,445	5,061,456	23,075,422	8,417,988
1837	57,393,709	2,332,409	11,447,968	2,638,449

Source: Conant, *History of Modern Banks of Issue*, p. 355

The transfer from federal to state charter had been accompanied by much fanfare, and predictions of disaster proved unfounded. Still, a major bulwark against a financial crisis had been removed. In times of panic the BUS could have acted as a calming influence. Now, as leader of a large Pennsylvania bank, Biddle had less power. The engine of the economy was still surging forward, but some of the brakes were jettisoned.

Philip Hone celebrated Biddle's victory in Philadelphia on February 19. Four days later he wrote of another, seemingly unrelated happening: the sale of some property in New York. Hone was amazed at the prices the land obtained, and he speculated as to its meaning.

Twenty lots in the "burned district," the property of Joel Post, deceased, were sold at auction this day, by James Bleecker & Son, at most enormous prices, greater than they would have brought before the fire, when covered with valuable buildings. This, at least, is the

opinion of the best judges of the value of down-town property. The
settlement of the French question has had much to do in producing
this result, aided by the spirit of speculation and the sanguine hopes
of the merchants of a great business this year. The lots were formed
principally out of the property bought by Mr. Post from the guardians
of Mr. Coster's children, for which he gave $93,000. . . . The whole
brought $765,000.

Prices of most goods had risen sharply during the preceding
year, in part a result of expansion of state banking following
Jackson's victory over Biddle. These new institutions—known as
"pet banks" by the Whigs—were usually poorly organized, in-
adequately capitalized, and led by men of dubious backgrounds
and uncertain skills. Between 1830 and 1837, 347 new banks
were chartered, 249 of which were in the East.

BANKING STATISTICS, 1829–1837

Year	Number of Banks	Capital	Circulation (millions of dollars)	Loans
1829	329	110.2	48.2	137.0
1834	506	200.0	94.8	324.1
1835	704	231.2	103.7	365.2
1836	713	251.9	140.3	457.5
1837	788	290.8	149.2	525.1

Source, Dewey, *Financial History of the United States*, p. 225

Few of these institutions could be classified as conservative; in
1837, Pennsylvania banks were issuing ten paper dollars for every
silver one held in reserve, and a few banks admitted to issuing
thirty paper dollars for every cartwheel. In Michigan, a new state
banking law made it possible for almost anyone to set up a
bank. During the last nine months of 1837, forty-nine banks
were opened in the state, with a nominal capital of $3.9 million,
but with actual reserves of less than $1.8 million. Some of the
new banks in the West did business, transacted loans, and
printed currency with no initial reserves.

Most of the new institutions expected to benefit from federal
deposits withdrawn from the Bank of the United States. And

when these deposits were made, the raw bankers went wild, issuing paper money with abandon. Currency in circulation, which had risen from $59 million in 1832 to $94 million in 1834, reached $140 million by 1836. The nation thus embarked on a new wave of inflation, which resulted in higher prices for almost all American goods. Inflation attracted speculators, who in turn created still higher prices and further speculation. Land, canals, manufacturing establishments—all gained investors. By 1835 the nation had taken on the aura of boom; the prosperity seemed limitless and without a flaw. It was in this atmosphere that the BUS closed its doors, and it was for this reason that even its supporters were forced to admit that its destruction would not result in the end of the American nation. Together with the Democrats, Whigs joined the speculative mania which had gripped the nation, and which Hone noted in the aftermath of Biddle's defeat at the hands of the Jacksonians.

In retrospect, it can be seen that the 1836 boom had its origins in 1831, when rising cotton prices and the development of the internal market led to an economic revival. For a while this expansion was not considered very remarkable. Prices remained constant, since the expanded industries and commerce absorbed the many thousands of jobless, and bank policies maintained close coordination between currency and economic expansion. Then, when bank wars and related matters resulted in dislocations, inflation struck, and Europeans, especially the English, began to take note of opportunities in America. Canals and railroads appeared interesting, but much of the money went into that favorite American speculative vehicle: land.

By mid-1836, new land companies had sprung up in all parts of the nation. Public sales in 1834 had been 4.7 million acres; in 1835, they reached 12.6 million, and rose to a spectacular 20 million acres in the boom year 1836. The land was paid for with paper money, a fact which angered the bullionist in Jackson. "The receipts from the public land were nothing more than credits on the bank," he complained. "The banks let out their notes to speculators, they were paid to the receivers, and immediately returned to the banks to be sent out again and again, being merely instruments to transfer to the speculator the most valuable public

lands. Indeed, each speculation furnished means for another."
Jackson issued broadsides against the speculators, to no avail.
Lots in Bangor, Maine, which had sold for $300 in the early
part of the decade, now brought upward of $1,000; New York
real estate was at record highs, as was land in Boston and Philadelphia. What was true in the West and East also held for the
South. Within a few months land in Pontotoc, Mississippi, rose
from $1.25 an acre to $2.50, the result of speculation between
land companies. Banks accepted land as collateral for loans,
issued paper money based on land, which was then used to buy
more land, repeating the cycle again and again. Fears of panic
were drowned in a flood of paper from the pet banks and older
institutions.

By this time money had arrived in great quantities from
Europeans eager to make quick profits. Samuel Jaudon of the
United States Bank carried $20 million worth of securities to
London in the late spring of 1836, in addition to bonds exchanged

STATISTICS ON FOREIGN INDEBTEDNESS, 1831–1837

Year	Aggregate Foreign Indebtedness (millions of dollars)	Interest and Dividends on Foreign Debts (millions of dollars)
1831	89.0	4.1
1832	95.7	4.9
1833	109.2	5.3
1834	128.0	6.0
1835	158.1	7.0
1836	220.3	8.7
1837	242.9	8.8

Source: North, *Economic Growth of the United States*, pp.
237–38

for a gold loan of $2 million. Such trips were unusual, but not
unexpected, during the boom year. Nor did it matter that American prices were rising so rapidly as to force American goods out
of the world markets.

The nation had had a chronic balance-of-payments difficulty earlier in the century, especially in the aftermath of the War of 1812
and the depression following a panic in 1819. In 1816, for ex-

ample, the trade deficit reached the previously unheard of figure
of $58.1 million. All such records were eclipsed during the 1830s.
In the year ending September 30, 1836, imports exceeded exports
by $52 million, the result of American inflation and prosperity.
Yet so great was the inflow of funds from Europe that the nation

RESIDUAL BALANCE OF PAYMENTS, 1831–1837

Year	Balance (millions of dollars)
1831	−14.1
1832	− 6.8
1833	−13.5
1834	−18.0
1835	−30.0
1836	−62.2
1837	−22.6

Source: North, *Economic Growth of the
United States*, p. 238

actually imported gold in this period. In part, at least, America's
prosperity was being financed by European investments. During
the three years beginning on January 1, 1834, the nation imported
$43 million in gold while exporting only $11 million. Early in
1837, Andrew Jackson estimated that foreign investments in the
United States approximated $200 million. As usual, the President
tended to exaggerate foreign influence in America. Nonetheless,
some $130 million in European funds, the largest amount being
English, were invested in American businesses at the time. American canals, turnpikes, and later on, railroads, were financed in
part by sales of securities overseas. The Barings of London employed Thomas Ward as their American representative, and he
scoured the countryside, sending reports of interesting new
ventures and attractive securities to the home office. The Barings
began their purchases of canal stock in 1823, in that year taking
almost a quarter of a million dollars' worth of New York canal
securities alone. Other London banks joined the parade of firms
with American agents, and by the end of the decade the Paris
house of Hottinguer had its aggressive agents in New York,

Philadelphia, Boston, and Charleston. The London Rothschilds waited until the 1830s to begin their activities, but by 1833 seemed destined to become the biggest single factor in the American canal and railroad market.

London experienced a panic in 1825 but recovered quickly, and the markets, led by American shares, began to rise. Within three years, more than a quarter of all securities traded on the London Exchange were American, and agents were encouraged to ship still more securities to England. Rhode Island's Blackstone Canal was capitalized at $500,000; it received bids for more than $1.5 million, much from Europeans. The Morris Canal & Banking Company, a well-publicized firm, tried to raise $1 million on the capital markets and received offers of $20 million; again, Europeans led the way. Similar occurrences marked most other offerings of the period, as Europeans sparked the bull market.

European money brought prosperity to American bankers. Samuel Gurney of Philadelphia and Joshua Bates, a managing partner for the Barings, made substantial sums from their European dealings, as did Prime, Ward & King and Alexander Brown & Sons of New York, important Baring contacts. Fitch Brothers & Co. was formed through connections with the Hottinguers and other French banks. Thomas Biddle & Co. of Philadelphia, organized by the brother of the famed banker, corresponded with the Barings, while S.V.S. Wilder & Co. of New York, led by men with BUS ties, dealt with Hottinguer. Former BUS men were involved with such Europe-oriented houses as the Codmans of Boston and Robert Gilmore & Co. of Baltimore. Little wonder, then, that the Jacksonians identified American bankers as agents of foreign powers, not to be trusted. A half-century later a Wall Streeter would say, "When London sneezes, New York catches cold." In 1833 a Jacksonian member of Congress observed that "the barometer of the American money market hangs up at the stock exchange in London."

European domination of American capital markets enabled worthwhile enterprises to be carried out, but also resulted in the bilking of foreign investors. Many questionable firms were financed through securities sales to Europeans, with the rest being distributed to a scattering of American investors and the various governments involved. Indeed, by the late 1820s, during John Quincy Adams' administration, Washington had become a prime source for capital investment, and although Jackson had reversed this trend, state and local governments continued to purchase large blocks of securities from new firms organized within their boundaries. The flow of easy money from American governments and European banks led to the construction of many worthless canals and to huge amounts of waste, as well as providing the nation with an adequate transportation network.

Another byproduct of the canal and railroad mania was large state debts, which became staggering by the mid-1830s. By then, many municipalities and some states were obliged to go to the capital markets to obtain money with which to pay interest on old debts. Sudden bankruptcies in Europe, or federal actions to

STATE DEBTS FOR CANALS, RAILROADS, AND BANKS, 1837

State	Debts (millions of dollars)
Alabama	7.5
Louisiana	15.0
Maryland	3.0
New Jersey	3.5
New York	2.0
Ohio	5.0
Pennsylvania	20.0
Tennessee	2.0
District of Columbia	3.0

Source: *New York Herald*, February 14, 1837

hinder the capital flow, could easily cause the bankruptcy of several states and cities.

Such a situation developed in 1834, when the Rothschilds stopped buying stocks. Other British houses found Spanish and Portuguese bonds more attractive than American railroads, as the bank wars in America unsettled all predictions. At the time, the Rothschilds alone owned some $5 million in American securities, and that firm's absence from the market caused several American issues to go unsold. The Bank of England, formerly interested in American securities, also looked elsewhere. "This immense engine of finance is now so intimately connected with monetary matters in our own country that the slightest throb of its quickening pulse has a controlling influence on movements in State or Wall Street." So wrote an American observer in 1834.

A wave of bankruptcies swept the nation, and securities fell sharply in all the American markets. When Philadelphia learned that the Rothschilds had returned a batch of American securities as "quite unsalable," the stock exchange of that city experienced its worst decline since its founding, and repercussions from Philadelphia had their effects on New York, where the markets were already suffering a slump of moderate proportions.

PRICES OF SELECTED ISSUES, 1833–1834

Issue	Aug. 1833	Closing Prices Dec. 1833	Jan. 3, 1834	Jan. 17, 1834
Mohawk & Hudson R.R.	136	101¼	80	94
Delaware & Hudson Canal	125	99	91	73
Boston & Providence R.R.	111¼	92	90	89
Saratoga R.R.	128	108½	105	103

Source: Medbury, *Men and Mysteries of Wall Street*, p. 294

Since his veto of the Bank Bill on July 10, 1832, Jackson had warned that foreigners had gained control of much of America's business and banking and that measures should be taken to reverse this tendency. By 1835, Jacksonians could point to the impact European bankers had on the country earlier that year as proof their leader was correct. Whigs responded, as did Philip Hone and others, by saying that without foreign investments the nation could not have developed, and that a withdrawal of European funds would bring an end to the great expansion for which the Jacksonians had wrongly taken credit. The nation was prosperous in 1836, despite Jackson's victory over Biddle; Democrats rejoiced and saw further progress to come under Van Buren. Whig leaders, on the other hand, had grave misgivings. In retrospect, we can see that both were correct, in different ways and for different reasons. The inflation resulting from the disestablishment of the BUS had indeed provided a spark for expansion, but without the fuel gained from overseas, a panic might easily ensue. Jackson had warned of European power; in 1837, that power was to be exercised, in part the result of fears of Jacksonian practices harbored by many Europeans.

Most observant Americans of 1836 were aware of the possibilities, dangers, and problems besetting the economy that election year. Whig and Democrat alike knew the BUS had been capable of positive actions to prevent monetary collapse as well as abuses of power. The Whigs would correct abuses by establishing a new central bank, while Democrats called for an end to all paper money. Van Buren and Senator Henry Clay of Kentucky realized that Europe's banks had an important role in America's prosperity and growth, but while the Democrat feared London's influence, Clay welcomed it. Amid the differences between the parties and individuals in 1836 was a general agreement as to the nature and magnitude of the forces in operation. Although their goals differed, both Democrat and Whig recognized that a financial crisis was in the making.

Philip Hone was personally aware of the problems. In searching for a site on which to build his new home, he found a seller's market in real estate. "Everything in New York is at an exorbitant price," he wrote on March 12, 1836. "Rents have risen 50 per cent for the next year. I have sold my house, it is true, for a large sum; but where to go I know not. Lots two miles from the City Hall are worth $8,000 or $10,000. Even in the eleventh ward, toward the East River, where they sold two or three years ago for $2,000 or $3,000, they are now held at $4,000 and $5,000." Hone finally purchased a lot on the corner of Broadway and Great Jones Street from Samuel Ward on March 24; the price was $15,000 for a plot measuring 29 feet by 130 feet. Ward made a large profit from the transaction but was doing even better at his brokerage and bank, since Europe's investors were once again demanding American securities.

As Hone and Ward concluded their business, Congress debated the nation's financial problems. It had been estimated in early 1835 that Treasury receipts would total $20 million; due to the high tariff and continued land sales, actual receipts reached $35 million. At the same time, federal expenditures remained steady, as Jackson refused to invest funds in the internal improvements schemes of various states and municipalities. Since 1817, when the national debt had declined from $127 million to $123 million, government bonds were redeemed at a greater rate than they were issued. It was evident that within a short period the entire debt would be liquidated, at which time funds would pile up in the Treasury and so be removed from circulation. This alone would cause a commercial paralysis, and by 1836, when the debt was almost completely paid off, Congress was forced to act.

DECLINE IN THE FEDERAL DEBT, 1825–1835

Year	Gross Debt
	(thousands of dollars)
1825	$83,788
1826	81,054
1827	73,987
1828	67,475
1829	58,421
1830	48,565
1831	39,123
1832	24,322
1833	7,021
1834	4,760
1835	38

Source: *Historical Statistics of the United States, 1789–1960*, p. 721

At the same time, Jackson grew increasingly concerned with the papermania and abuses of the pet banks. As early as April 6, 1835, the Treasury had refused to accept bank notes in denominations below $5, and Senator Thomas Hart Benton of Missouri, the foremost defender of a gold standard and opponent of all paper, suggested the establishment of a schedule by which, eventually, the Treasury would accept only gold in settlement of debts. Early in 1836, he put forth the following timetable: after March 3, 1837, the Treasury would no longer accept bills less than $20. Then the denominations would rise.

No bills less than $50 after March 3, 1838
No bills less than $100 after March 3, 1839
No bills less than $500 after March 3, 1840
No bills less than $1,000 after March 3, 1842
No paper at all after March 3, 1942

The plan was rejected, but Benton grew in stature as the leader of gold forces in the Senate.

Jackson's hatred of banks, Benton's gold mania, abuses of the pet banks, and the problem of the Treasury surplus resulted in action in July 1836. Early in that month the President learned that the banks held less gold in their vaults than had been deposited in them by the Treasury; in other words, paper-money issuance had reached the stage where the banks were extremely vulnerable to runs and closures. Total deposits on June 1 were

CONDITION OF THIRTY-SIX DEPOSIT BANKS, JUNE 1, 1836

Assets (millions of dollars)		Liabilities (millions of dollars)	
Loans and discounts	108.5	Public deposits	41.0
Real estate	1.9	Other deposits	16.0
Due from banks	17.9	Circulation	29.0
Bank notes	11.0	Due to banks	17.1
Specie	10.5	Capital	46.4
Other investments	12.6	Other liabilities	13.8
	162.3		162.3

Source: Dewey, *Financial History of the United States*, p. 283

$57 million, while the banks held only $10.5 million in gold.

On July 11, Jackson ordered Secretary of the Treasury Levi Woodbury to issue the Specie Circular, which had been largely based on a Benton draft. Under its terms, after August 15 the government would accept only gold, silver, and in special cases, Virginia scrip, in payment for public land sales. However, paper would still be accepted from bona fide settlers until December 15 for land parcels up to 320 acres. The Circular was issued "in consequence of complaints which have been made of frauds, speculations, and monopolies, in the purchase of public lands, and the aid which is said to be given to effect these objects by excessive bank credits. . . ." Woodbury's proclamation concluded:

The principal objects of the President in adopting this measure being to repress alleged frauds, and to withhold any countenance or facilities in the power of the Government from the monopoly of the public lands in the hands of speculators and capitalists, to the injury of the actual settlers in the new States, and of emigrants in search of new homes, as well as to discourage the ruinous extension of bank issues, and bank credits, by which those results are generally supposed to be promoted, your utmost vigilance is required, and relied on, to carry this order into complete execution.

Jackson believed the Specie Circular would force the banks to call in land loans and, in general, disengage from speculative activities. He hoped paper money issues would be cut back, and that eventually gold coins would become the sole standard of value and exchange. In practice, however, the banks were placed in a position where rapid contraction was necessary, but not possible without panic, foreclosure, and deflation.

The banks might have been able to bear the Specie Circular were it not followed by additional problems emanating from the surplus. By January 1, 1836, this amounted to $26.7 million and was growing rapidly. The Jacksonians wanted to lower the tariff, in this way decreasing revenues. But Clay and the Whigs would not hear of tampering with the Tariff of 1833, and under their leadership, Congress passed the Deposit Act, a plan to distribute the surplus to the states. Grudgingly, Jackson accepted the measure.

Under the new legislation, $5 million of the surplus was to remain in the Treasury while the rest would be given to the states in proportion to their Congressional representation. The first of the quarterly distributions would take place on January 1, 1837; the government would withdraw some $9 million from the pet banks every three months and give it to the states. These withdrawals, coupled with the Specie Circular, were more than the banks could bear. Beginning in September 1836, several collapsed, and along with them, dependent mercantile houses. Western banks rushed to convert their paper into gold, and a flight from paper began in earnest. Since land speculation was fueled by currency, gold tended to flow from East to West, where it was used to purchase land from the government. The Treasury then redeposited this gold in Western banks, which feared to use it, since they knew that on January 1 the huge federal withdrawals would begin, and gold would become scarce once again. This was further complicated by the fact that Woodbury had decided to withdraw almost the entire $9 million from Northeastern banks in order to reduce "the excess in certain banks in certain states, and place it in the states where it would be paid next year and where before they had not an equal portion of the public money." Biddle protested; such a move would strip the East of currency and so stifle credit in that section and cause a financial crisis. Redeposits in the West, on the other hand, would only serve to intensify speculation in that already overheated area. Woodbury's move may have made sense politically, but it contained economic dynamite. It was evident that a panic was in the making; the storm clouds were present for all to see.

Philip Hone laid the cornerstone for his new house on June 30, and soon after went to Europe to visit his daughter. He returned in October and was shocked to learn that the great inflation that had existed prior to his departure had ended abruptly. On November 12, he wrote:

Hard Times. There has been for some time past a severe pressure for money, which continues, and I feel the effects of it. Stocks have fallen very much. Delaware & Hudson, which was above par when I went abroad, has been as low as 60 and is now selling at 72. Boston & Providence Railroad, which was 120, is not worth now above par, and all others in proportion. The best mortgages cannot be converted into money without a sacrifice of 20 per cent, and undoubted business paper is selling in Wall Street at a discount of three per cent a month. Real estate is a drug. The price of houses and lots is not much lower nominally, but there are no sales, there is no money to pay for it, and nobody wants bonds and mortgages which cannot be converted into cash. . . .

Hone bemoaned his fate, which he blamed on the Democrats. "Immense amounts of specie have been transferred to the West to pay for the public lands, for the government refuses any other kind of payment; although that part of the country is deeply indebted to us, and it must all come back. But Gen. Jackson will pursue his course if every merchant in New York shall be ruined by it." Like other Whigs, Hone hoped the situation would be remedied by Van Buren, but he doubted whether the "Little Magician" would veer from Jacksonianism. Clay, Webster, and other Senators would do their part, but in the end, only one man could save the country: Nicholas Biddle. "If any man in the United States has reason to be proud of his standing in the community, it is Nicholas Biddle." So wrote Philip Hone on December 14. "Assailed as he has been by the malice and ignorance of unworthy men in high stations, he had performed his course with dignity and forebearance, illuminating his official path as by a sunbeam, and without the exultation of little minds, overcoming and placing under his feet all his opponents."

The new year arrived auspiciously, with riots in several cities and foreclosures and bankruptcies reported in all parts of the country. On January 2 the first transfer under the distribution program—$9 million—was made, and almost all of this money came from federal withdrawals from Eastern banks. The *Herald* saw hope for the city but disaster for the nation.

From this day forward we begin a new year, and a new era in the money market, business, exchanges, and Wall Street. Commencing with the great fire, and the embarrassment in trade, both in this country and in Europe, New York has passed through scenes during the last year beyond parallel in the history of commerce. Within the last few months failures have taken place in every important point of the commercial world, but we believe New York has escaped with fewer than any of her sisters or compeers. Interest has risen from 7 per cent a year to 2 and 3 per cent a month—domestic exchanges from 1 to 6 and 7—and yet the merchants have weathered the storm.

The city was struck by a series of bankruptcies in February, and so joined the ranks of the unfortunate. A mob gathered near City Hall on February 13 to protest the lack of work and high food prices. The day was cold, with the worst winds in memory, and yet thousands appeared at the rally. Food shops were broken into; for a while it appeared that all order had vanished. In the end, the Mayor called upon the militia, and the mob dispersed,

but not before looting dozens of shops and razing others. *Niles'*
Weekly Register reported the mob action and called for calm.
"Now is the time for people to thank God and take courage.
Down with the panic makers, and down with the prevailing
distrust. . . . A bright sun will soon dispel the remaining darkness,
and days of prosperity and glory will be ours."

While the mob did its work, and Niles called for calm, Van
Buren busily organized his new government and planned for his
inauguration. James Gordon Bennett, who had opposed Van
Buren in the election but still hoped he would act sanely, wrote
an editorial expressing his fears on February 7.

The great inquiry which is now made in the streets is, "what course
will Mr. Van Buren pursue?" "Will he continue the financial system
of the present executive?"—"or will he not create an entire revolution
in the action of the government?" These questions are of the highest
importance. Legislative bodies are so subject to caprice and secret
causes that no dependence can be placed on their action. No government in the world possesses such an overwhelming power in the
monetary concerns of the country as ours does. This power it possesses,
through the medium of the Surplus Revenue—the present tariff law,
and the general land system. . . . The State governments are powerless.
They are all, more or less, in debt. They are in the hands of the banks,
and are wielded entirely by bank directors. Not so the general government. The Executive in Washington controls the banks—controls the
currency—controls the exchanges—and exercises an influence that is
felt throughout the commercial world. . . . In less than one month
Mr. Van Buren will be this Executive and will then possess more
power than any potentate in Europe or America ever did before his
day. How will he use it?

Benton viewed the scene, and like Bennett realized that the
nation faced a major panic unless something was done to relieve the banks. The Senator invited the President-elect to his offices and began to warn him of impending problems. Van Buren
interrupted: "Your friends think you a little exalted in the head
on that subject," he observed. Benton fell silent, but as the two
left the room, the Senator thought, "You will soon feel the
thunderbolt."

Philip Hone and others felt the thunderbolt in the days that followed. On March 4, as Jackson prepared to leave office, Hone wrote that future generations would wonder "that such a man should have governed this great country. . . ." Hone had reason to be bitter.

This is a dark and melancholy day in the annals of my family. Brown & Hone stopped payment to-day, and called a meeting of their creditors. My eldest son has lost the capital I gave him, and I am implicated as endorser for them to a fearful amount. The pressure of the times, the immense amount they have paid of extra interest, and the almost total failure of remittances have been the causes of their ruin. This is a heavy blow for me, and added to the difficulty I experience in raising money on my property to meet my own engagements, almost breaks me down, but I have the consolation to know, and the public cannot fail to know it also, that the good name which it has been the object of my life to establish, cannot be compromised in this matter.

But the moment belonged to the Jacksonians. William Leggett, the Democrat writer, thought that "this day completes a period that will shine in American history with more inherent and undying lustre, than any other which the chronicler has yet recorded, or which perhaps will ever form a portion of our country's annals." Jackson and Van Buren rode together to the capitol, and at noon the two men appeared on the east portico, where Chief Justice Roger Taney waited with the inauguration party to swear in the new President.

Van Buren's speech was undistinguished except for several comments on slavery and sectionalism, both of which he deplored. As for banking, currency, and economic problems, he remained silent. The day would not pass without some reference to these key aspects of the Jacksonian era, and, fittingly, the general himself spoke of the issue. In his strongly worded farewell address, Jackson warned the nation once more against banks, paper money, and speculation.

The paper system being founded in public confidence, and having itself no intrinsic value, it is liable to great and sudden fluctuations, thereby rendering property insecure, and the wages of labor unsteady and uncertain. The corporations which create the paper money cannot be relied upon to keep the circulating medium uniform in amount. . . . Recent events have proved that the paper money system of this country may be used as an engine to undermine your free institutions. . . .

Whigs noted that Van Buren sounded much more moderate than Jackson, and they hoped he would listen to reason. On the other hand, Van Buren indicated a continuity in policy by keeping all the old Cabinet members save one, and by appointing Jacksonians to other important positions. There may well be a change in style, thought James Gordon Bennett, but there will be "no change in the policies of the new government."

Like Jackson, the new President thought the economic dislocations were caused by the end of wild speculation that followed the closing of the BUS. Van Buren was saddened by the suffering of the innocent but certain that the depression was felt most severely by bankers, businessmen, and speculators who had hoped to make fortunes through control of a government-banks nexus. Now that they knew such profits were no longer possible, they were withdrawing from unstable enterprises. There may be suffering, thought Van Buren, but in the end the nation will be more secure in the hands of the people.

Whether or not Van Buren's analysis was correct, it made sense to the Jacksonians and hard money men in general. When asked to repeal the Specie Circular, and so bring a halt to the growing depression, Van Buren put forth ten reasons for maintaining his predecessor's policy. He observed that land sales to *legitimate* purchasers had not been affected by the Circular; the only sufferers were speculators. Although repeal would indeed increase government revenues, the new money would be in the form of bank credits, which according to Jacksonian dogma was not real money. Repeal would also lead to a flow of gold from the West to the East, and so weaken the Western institutions. And in the end, he thought, the gold would wind up in the usual place; repeal would "aid them to get gold from the West to New York, and thence to Liverpool." Thus, Van Buren proved himself a good Jacksonian in his fear and distrust of foreigners who would control the veins and arteries of the American financial structure.

Hope lingered that the new President would moderate this Jacksonian stand. John Forsyth, who remained as Secretary of State, was a personal friend of Nicholas Biddle, as was Joel Poinsett of South Carolina, who replaced Benjamin F. Butler at the War Department. For a while Biddle believed he could sway Van Buren; he had gone so far as to send him a message in early March asking "whether the Specie Circular will be rescinded, and when it will be rescinded." By the end of the month, however, it was evident to all that the new President had no intention of changing his predecessor's program.

Within a short time Van Buren would learn what most American bankers had realized for two decades: that the morality of foreign investments aside, America was linked inextricably to the European money markets. Van Buren thought London's discomfort was America's gain; New York bankers knew that a tightening of credit overseas could destroy American business and commerce.

The situation in London was such as to concern American bankers. Gold exports, which had become chronic in the early part of the decade, expanded in 1836, and in the second half of the year British reserves declined from £7.4 million to £4.25 million. It was common knowledge on Lombard Street that a good part of this gold had gone to America, drawn out by the Specie Circular, purchases of American securities, and new money to finance the Bank of the United States of Philadelphia. On July 21 the Bank of England was obliged to raise its rediscount rate to 4½ percent, and a few weeks later it went to 5 percent. These moves were popular, not only for their impact on gold exports, but in the hope that they would help end a banking expansion program which had worried England's conservatives for the past decade. On the other hand, tighter money caused grave concern among the Anglo-American merchants, especially those who needed low-cost money to finance the cotton trade.

While London debated the merits of the higher rate, a run developed at the Northern & Central Bank, which closed its doors in late November. The Bank of England investigated the matter, and after saving the institution's depositors, decided it would close the N & C for good on February 18, 1837. The problems at Northern

& Central soon spread to other banks, and in late 1836 and early 1837, Britain found itself in the midst of a monetary panic. In March several Anglo-American banks failed, among them Wildes, Wiggins, and Wilson, known in the city as the "Three W's." In the end the London money market managed to pull itself together, and few other failures were listed. The 1836–37 "pressure" was over and almost forgotten by early summer. Its repercussions, however, were still being felt in America.

Most American bankers were aware of these difficulties in 1836, and knew Britain would have to take steps to correct them. In an open letter to John Quincy Adams on November 11, Biddle warned that the increased money rates in London would inevitably result in fewer and smaller investments in America and would end in the paralysis of several important projects in need of finances. The *Herald* of January 2, 1837, wrote that although London's official rate was still 5 percent, "we learn by private advices that what we call street loans are as high as 10, 12, and 15 per cent. . . . The specie of the Bank of England is still in a state of diminution."

Britain's higher interest rates attracted those investors who otherwise might have purchased American securities, and at the same time the American inflation led to a falling off of Europe's purchases in America. Both these forces were maturing and already in effect as Van Buren took his oath of office. By the end of his first week as President, currency shortages were being reported in all parts of the nation. New Orleans banks in particular were in bad straits. In response to the Specie Circular, Westerners had turned their paper back to the issuing institutions to be redeemed for gold. Since New Orleans had provided much of the paper for the Mississippi Valley, that city was naturally the first to feel the impact of the return to gold. To further complicate matters, the price of cotton was declining rapidly, leading to the failure of several important mercantile houses. In early March, some New Orleans banks admitted their inability to honor gold drafts from the interior. Then Herman, Briggs & Co., a leading mercantile firm, announced its insolvency, suspending payments with liabilities of more than $4 million. This lead to a wave of failures throughout the Mississippi Valley. John Somerville of the Union

Bank of Tennessee wrote Nicholas Biddle, pleading for him to "again save the people from a . . . state of distress." Apparently addressing itself to J. & S. Joseph & Co., a New York house with intimate connections with Herman, Briggs, the *Herald* wrote on March 5 that "We are in the commencement of a fresh panic. The only question is, 'how long will it last, Joe?' Stocks fell yesterday—every stock—the list came tumbling down like Joseph's new banking house." That day the Josephs, whose clients included not only Herman, Briggs, but the Rothschilds as well, announced its closing. Others would soon follow, as Wall Street faced its worst moments since the founding of the Exchange.

The New York Stock and Exchange Board was a flourishing though troubled institution during the early 1830s. The panic of 1819 had almost destroyed the market; a short-lived boom in 1826–27 led to the establishment of rival institutions. It appeared that both good and bad times would threaten the Board's existence, while "normal" activity made it unnecessary. So it seemed, at least, during the first years of the Jacksonian Presidency.

Then, in 1830, a change took place. The seventeen-mile-long Mohawk & Hudson Railroad obtained listing at the Board, and it was called regularly at the auctions. This marked the beginning of a railroad mania on Wall Street, as other lines petitioned for admission to the list. Business boomed; by early 1835, 5,000 share days were considered normal, and on June 26 the *Herald* reported "heavy trading" of 7,875 shares. This increased business enabled the Board to raise its initiation fee from $100 in 1827 to $150 in 1833.

Judging from the incomplete records available today, the Board's list in early 1835 consisted of thirty-eight bank stocks (twenty-two of which were New York City institutions), twenty-one railroads, thirty-three insurance companies, and the securities of seven firms engaged in "mixed" ventures, such as New Orleans Canal & Banking, Morris Canal & Banking, and Manhattan Gas. None of these ninety-nine companies could be categorized as "industrials" by today's standards. They included such familiar names as the Dry Dock Bank, the Manhattan Bank, the Long Island Railroad, the New Haven Railroad, Aetna Insurance, and American Fire Insurance, along with such now defunct firms as the Leather Manufacturers'

Bank, Butchers' and Drovers' Bank, and Phenix Insurance. Some of these companies listed securities and then within a short time declared bankruptcy, leaving no other trace. Business was chancy in the 1820s and 1830s, and survival possibilities slim. Stock Exchange records for May 1832, for example, tell of a wash sale in Catskill Rail Road stock. Fifty shares were traded between two brokers by prearranged signals in order to create an illusion of activity and interest. The Catskill went bankrupt soon after and was forgotten. The two brokers received temporary suspensions, and this too would have been ignored by today's historians were it not for the fact that one of them disclosed that he was the agent in the transaction for Alexander Hamilton, the son of the former Secretary of the Treasury, who had become the "patron saint" of Wall Street.

Jackson's reelection in 1832, the formation of pet banks, Britain's contractions in the early part of 1834, together with the continued canal mania and the young railroad boom, led to violent cross-currents at securities auctions in New York, Boston, Philadelphia, and Charleston. By the end of the year, however, most recognized that the New York market had become the dominant auction in the nation, as Philadelphia, having lost the prestigious BUS, declined to second place. Indeed, some went so far as to claim that Van Buren had worked for the destruction of the BUS in order to please his New York friends, many of whom now entered the speculative world of Wall Street.

Bull and bear cliques were quickly organized, and fixed upon one or another security which they rode up and down in the fluctuating markets. Samuel J. Beebe, J. W. Bleecker, and Jacob Barker made fortunes and reputations as wild speculators in those days. Barker in particular was considered a notorious and canny financier. In 1825 he had managed to gain control of some fourteen banks and insurance companies in New York "as if by the wand of a magician." The directors of the local BUS branch thought Barker's ambitions were boundless, and that he and his group "will not stop till they get the United States Bank, and I really do not see but they may do it." Biddle counterattacked, and as Barker put pressure on the BUS, Biddle attacked his institutions. The conspiracy collapsed in the fall of 1826, ending another major clash between the New York and Philadelphia financial communities. But by the early 1830s Barker was back on Wall Street, engaging with gusto in the new bull market.

Barker was not the district's most respected trader; that title belonged to Jacob Little, known as "the Great Bear of Wall Street." Little was wealthy by 1834, having cleaned up on corners, pools, and manipulations of earlier days. Now, as prices began to rise sharply in late 1834 and early 1835, Little formed bull pools in key issues. Little's most successful manipulation occurred when

SECURITIES PRICES, 1834–1835

Issue	Nov. 25, 1834	April 25, 1835
Morris R.R.	70	200
Harlem R.R.	64	105
Dry Dock Bank	118	145
Delaware & Hudson Canal	72	113

Source: Medbury, *Men and Mysteries of Wall Street*, p. 294

he gained a corner on Morris Canal & Banking in late December 1834. Before the bears realized what had happened, Little demanded delivery of shorted stock. Morris Canal rose from a low of 10 in December to almost 185 in late January, making still another fortune for Little and his friends.

The Morris Canal corner was followed by more speculations. Harlem Railroad had a total capitalization of 7,000 shares; by September 1835, a bull ring had accumulated 64,000 shares, almost all of which, of course, were sold for future delivery. Then the bulls began to squeeze, in the process raising the price from 60 to 195 in a matter of weeks. The Harlem corner trapped several prominent individuals in its web. The cashier of the Albany Commercial Bank defaulted to the extent of $130,000, and Benjamin Rathbun of Buffalo, one of the state's most important businessmen, declared his bankruptcy with liabilities of more than $3 million. A London speculator fled New York with $45,000 worth of Harlem stock, and there were at least four suicides resulting from the corner. An investigation followed, which ended in the expulsion of a state senator.

Scandal could not end the bull market of 1835. The demand for stocks continued, and issues from all over the country were sent to New York, where they found ready customers. One newspaper protested that "Pearl Street is nearly impassable by reason of the quantities of boxes [of securities] on the sidewalks. So is Wall Street by the groups of brokers."

Along with the rest of the city, Wall Street was almost leveled by the fire of December 1835. The Merchants' Exchange Building was destroyed, and the Tontine Coffee House gutted. Not even this tragedy could stop the auctions, which continued in the apartment of an important broker, John Warren, who for a while ran the Exchange as though it were a floating crap game. Warren took the auction to Howard's Hotel a few days later and then shifted to several other locations. Finally, Howard and a committee found a suitable place at 43 Wall Street, where trading was still taking place in a suite of rooms when Andrew Jackson left the White House.

Securities prices drifted lower in late 1835 and throughout 1836, the result of papermania, inflation, the surplus, and uncertainty regarding the future of American banking and European invest-

SECURITIES PRICES, 1836–1837

Issue	Dec. 31, 1836	Jan. 13, 1837
United States Bank	119	115
Delaware & Hudson R.R.	86½	87
State Bank of New York	106½	109
Morris Canal	96	98¼
Ohio Trust	112	114⅛
Harlem R.R.	62¼	87
Utica R.R.	118	125
Mohawk R.R.	78	88
Farmer's Loan Co.	104	106

Source: *New York Herald,* January 13, 1837

ments. By early 1837, declines were almost daily occurrences, as volume at the action remained high, reaching 7,000 shares regularly. The city's newspapers printed daily warnings of panic and depression, but the Exchange, not yet a mirror of the economy but rather the reflection of momentary whims and personal pressures, did not show large declines; nor did brokers and speculators expect stock prices to parallel any major economic dislocation that might occur in the future. Although more important than it had been in the days of William Duer, the securities markets handled only a minute part of the nation's business, and its rises and declines had little but passing interest for the vast majority of businessmen. In early January, for example, as warnings of financial panic increased, with gold being drained from New York to the West and Europe, prices on Wall Street advanced over their December closings.

On January 17, in what *Niles' Weekly Register* considered an average day on Wall Street, the auction handled 6,671 shares, with the largest sale being 900 shares of New Orleans Gas Company, a transaction worth $92,475 plus commissions.

SALES AT THE STOCK EXCHANGE, JANUARY 17, 1837

Issue	Terms	Price
United States Bank		
50	regular	115¾
50	regular	116¼
City Bank		
100	regular	120
Delaware & Hudson Canal		
50	Feb. 7	88½
50	regular	88
50	regular	88½
50	30 days	90
50	cash	89
50	next week	89
50	next week	89
50	next week	89
50	next week	89
50	next week	89
100	next week	89
100	next week	89
100	next week	89
50	10 days	88½
25	regular	88¾
50	regular	88¾
50	next week	88¾

SALES AT THE STOCK EXCHANGE, JANUARY 17, 1837

Issue	Terms	Price
50	next week	88¾
50	next week	88¾
50	next week	88¾
50	regular	88¾
50	regular	88¾
Boston & Worcester		
50	regular	95½
50	60 days	96
50	60 days	96
Utica Railroad		
50	60 days	125
50	60 days	125
50	cash	124
50	cash	124
100	cash	124
25	regular	124
50	regular	124½
50	10 days	124½
50	2 weeks	125
Long Island Railroad		
300	regular	72½
50	regular	72¼
50	regular	72¼
Butchers' and Drovers' Bank		
50	regular	119
Bank of State of New York		
20	3 days	111
5	regular	111
50	regular	111
50	4 months	113½
Atlantic Bank		
17	regular	102
Morris Canal Co.		
50	regular	99
50	regular	99
50	15 days	100
50	next week	100
50	next week	99¾
50	next week	99¾
50	90 days	101
25	regular	99
100	45 days	100

SALES AT THE STOCK EXCHANGE, JANUARY 17, 1837

Issue	Terms	Price
New Orleans Mechanics' & Traders' Bank		
10	regular	98½
10	regular	98½
Vicksburg Bank		
25	30 days	97½
200	60 days	97½
Planters Bank, Tennessee		
100	April 5	108½
Kentucky Bank		
25	regular	90
15	regular	93
Planters Bank, Mississippi		
50	regular	127½
New Orleans Gas Company		
300	30 days	102¾
Farmers Trust Co.		
50	Jan. 30	108
50	Jan. 30	108
100	90 days	110
100	regular	108½
50	60 days	110
50	60 days	110¼
100	90 days	111
Ohio Life & Trust Co.		
50	Jan. 20	114¼
50	Jan. 20	114¾
50	Jan. 23	114¾
Mohawk Railroad		
29	cash	88
50	next week	89
50	cash	88½
50	cash	89
50	2 weeks	89
50	2 weeks	89
Paterson Railroad		
50	regular	78
Harlem Railroad		
20	regular	83½
100	regular	83½
35	regular	83¾
25	regular	83¾

SALES AT THE STOCK EXCHANGE, JANUARY 17, 1837

Issue	Terms	Price
65	regular	83¾
40	30 days	85
15	30 days	85
50	regular	83½
50	30 days	85
150	30 days	85
Boston & Providence Railroad		
10	regular	105¾
50	10 days	106
50	10 days	106
100	2 weeks	106
100	2 weeks	106
New Jersey Railroad & Transportation Co.		
20	regular	104¾
10	regular	104½
50	2 weeks	104
25	30 days	105¼
50	60 days	106
50	2 weeks	104
50	2 weeks	104
100	30 days	106
50	10 days	104½
Stonington Railroad		
25	regular	80

Source: Eames, *New York Stock Exchange*, pp. 32–33

Prices continued their slow decline in late January, and they drifted lower in February. In early March, as bankruptcies increased and the heritage of Jacksonian finances became more evident, stocks dipped sharply, though irregularly, and on several days volume at the auctions reached the 10,000-shares level. Then, in mid-March, Wall Street learned of further financial problems in London, which would affect the American cotton prices. "The reaction in Europe is going on as in this country," wrote the *Herald*. "Prices are gradually declining, particularly in American cottons and other staples. The embarrassments of the commercial community are so great that the Bank of England has adopted a

DECLINE IN SECURITIES PRICES, MARCH 1837

Issue	March 1, 1837	March 29, 1837	Decline
United States Bank	119½	118	1½
Delaware & Hudson	92	73	19
Mohawk R.R.	84⅛	69⅛	15
Harlem R.R.	77	62	15
Boston & Providence R.R.	104½	95½	9
Utica R.R.	120	114	6
Long Island R.R.	78	64	14
Morris Canal	96	80	16

Source: *New York Herald*, March 30, 1837

bold measure—that of advancing their paper in exchange for internal bills of exchange in order to relieve the business of the country. . . . " The *Herald* concluded that London would be saved through these efforts.

But what of the United States? The decline in cotton prices had wrecked whatever remained of public confidence, and there was no Bank of the United States to restore credit as had the Bank of England. Two days later, editor Bennett went still further: "The United States were never in such a perilous condition as they are at this moment. We are in the midst of a commercial panic which threatens to break up all the business of society—to ruin whole States—to lay waste to large districts—to sweep half our banking institutions from the land—to excite the most inflammable passions, and to create a revulsion that will retard the country for years."

Fate was unkind to Wall Street. At a time when money was going into hiding, several states were obliged to come to New York to refinance their bonds. Ohio required $5 million for this purpose and to complete already committed projects. New Jersey attempted to sell $1.5 million worth of bonds, and other states sought similar amounts. None were taken, as the gold drain to the West continued.

Philip Hone deplored the conditions of late March, which he had sorrowfully predicted. "The prospects in Wall Street are getting worse and worse," he wrote on March 20. Three days later a fire at the American Academy of the Arts destroyed several valuable paintings; Hone considered it a bad omen. Clearly the business community could expect little help from Washington; Van Buren had proven as reckless as Jackson as far as Wall Street

STATISTICS FOR NEW YORK CITY BANKS, 1837

	January 1, 1837	April 1, 1837
Bank notes in circulation	$8,155,803	$7,500,000
Deposits of United States	7,176,021	8,500,000
Individual deposits	11,180,310	12,500,000
Specie	3,854,452	2,800,000

Source: *New York Herald*, April 7, 1837

was concerned. Realizing that only a strong man could save the situation, as Hamilton had in 1791—and knowing that such a man existed and was eager to play his part—Hone and his friends sent an urgent appeal to Nicholas Biddle, asking him to "step forward in this most appalling crisis and save the financial community of New York." Biddle responded with alacrity, and in the last days of March came to Wall Street to consult with leading New York bankers.

Biddle was followed from door to door by an entourage, which cheered him as he went. "Did ever man enjoy so great a moral triumph?" wrote Hone. The New York bankers asked Biddle to assist them by sending gold from the Philadelphia banks, and Biddle agreed. Furthermore, Biddle promised to recommend to his directors that the Philadelphia bank issue $4 million in one-year bonds, payable with interest in Europe, to be used as a substitute for foreign bills of exchange. He would also release $4 million in notes for use in America. These two issues would ease the money squeeze developing from the Specie Circular and the Deposit Act. Finally, he agreed to use his influence in Europe to save the city's banks from a liquidity crisis. Word soon reached the streets, and more cheers were raised. The *Journal of Commerce* thought that "The past week will long be remembered . . . as the crisis of the great financial troubles that have been gathering for more than a year from the combined influence of speculation, the surplus revenue, bad government. . . . "

It was a glorious time for panic makers, croakers, and assassins of credit . . . when by a concerted movement between the United States Bank and our local institutions, measures were adopted for the relief of the community; and from that moment the state of the money market had been evidently improving.

Bennett outdid himself in writing of the event in the March 30 *Herald:*

Nicholas Biddle is the Napoleon of finance. He is twice as great as Henry Clay—twice and a half as great as Daniel Webster—and eight or ten times as great as Martin Van Buren. "I would sooner be Nicholas Biddle in Wall Street," said our ex-Mayor, "than any potentate in the world." Nicholas Biddle walks around the street like a spirit from heaven—saying to the hurricane of commerce, "peace"—and telling the storm of speculation, "be still." He is the genius—the impersonation of the "calm summer morning." As he entered or emerged from this bank or that bank, people gazed, gazed and gazed.

Biddle's visit had no impact at the auctions, however, as prices continued their declines with no bulls in sight. And, despite his

PRICES OF SELECTED ISSUES, FEBRUARY–APRIL 1837
Closing Prices (fractions rounded off)

Issue	Feb. 2	March 4	March 20	March 27	March 28	April 14
Long Island Railroad	71	79	66	66	65	64
Mohawk Railroad	78	75	74	71	70	67
Ohio Life & Trust	113	111	n.t.	107	105	106
Utica Railroad	119	120	118	115	114	113

Source: *New York Herald,* February 3–April 15, 1837

efforts, the business failures continued. Hicks, Lawrence & Co. closed its Wall Street office, the first of a long line of houses to suspend. "Money is exorbitantly dear," wrote Philip Hone. "The blood-suckers are beginning to be alarmed, and keep their unholy treasures locked up." And on April 1, another $9 million left the banks as the distribution program continued.

The situation worsened in April. Distress sales were reported in all the large cities; bank runs were daily occurrences. As businesses were forced to shut down, swelling the unemployment rolls, protest meetings were organized. More than 50,000 unemployed workers attended one in Greenwich Village in mid-April and threatened to march on the banks unless given work. An unofficial survey estimated that some 200,000 New Yorkers were without adequate means of support. Riots erupted in Boston and Philadelphia; charitable organizations reported their inability to provide food for the poor and predicted widespread suffering unless conditions were bettered before winter.

Stock prices fell sharply on Wall Street, as gold seemed to vanish. The banks remained weak, with the Bowery, The Greenwich, and the Bank for Savings near collapse. On April 21 George Templeton Strong, then a student at Columbia College, reported: "Wall Street. The blackness of darkness still hangeth over it. Failure on failure. . . . " The next day he wrote of the city's elite. "Philip Hone has gone to the d———l, figuratively speaking, having lost pretty much everything by his son, by Scheck & Co. (of Matteawan factory) and by some speculation moreover, all of which have eased him out of not much below $200,000. What will become of his sons now? For they have nothing to prop their conceit but their father's cash, and now that that is gone, what will become of them?"

"No man can calculate to escape ruin but he who owes no money," lamented Hone the previous week. "Happy is he who has little and is free from debt."

Almost all the city's gold had gone into hiding by early May, and the few banks that remained open were in serious trouble. The Dry Dock, considered the city's strongest, was faced with a run on May 7 and stopped payments the following day. Ironically, the Dry Dock was the leading pet bank in the city. John Fleming, president of the Merchants' Bank, fell dead at his desk, starting a new run on the remaining liquid institutions. As the Dry Dock closed, stock in the United States Bank fell far below par for the first time in twenty years. The bank runs continued on May 8 and 9. The next day all banks in the city suspended operations, and trading at the auctions fell to a new low point. With this, commercial paralysis set in. Bank of America, Merchants', and Man-

hattan tried to work out formulas by which limited specie payments could be made, but on May 10 they too were obliged to
close. In a matter of days, most of the nation's banks were unable
to meet obligations in gold.

As expected, the Whig papers blamed the crisis on the Jackson
and Van Buren policies, especially the Specie Circular, the distribution of the surplus, and most importantly, the bank wars. The
Commercial Record, one of the few Democrat organs in the city,
retorted that Whigs had caused the bank closings. "This course
was forced on the banks by the unrestrained run upon them
for specie, not only by bill holders, but depositors," wrote the
newspaper on April 11.

We do not wish to indulge in any unnecessary animadversions on the
conduct of any party, but it cannot be denied that the whigs were the
principal cause of the demand for specie. No man can say Loco Foco-
ism had any thing to do with it. Most of the withdrawals were in
checks, for large sums, and in many instances the specie was sold to
brokers for a large premium.

Both Whig and Democrat were correct. Clearly Jacksonian
monetary ideas had unsettled the business community and economy. Together with international and foreign difficulties, this led
to the specie shortage in March and bank failures in April. On
the other hand, Whig depositors, seeing the opportunity to
speculate on the price of gold, did so in early April. Jacksonian
policies were a major underlying cause for the panic; the general's
inability to understand financial problems caused more havoc than
any other failing he may have had, and did much to mar the
otherwise progressive accomplishments of his eight years as President. The Whigs, however, could scarcely claim to have acted
responsibly in the dark days of early April.

Strangely enough, suspension ended rather than began the
period of panic. The moment had been expected, so that when it
came, businessmen were able to make new plans on what existed
rather than what might happen. Business continued, on a barter
basis or with bills of credit and letters of exchange. Stock prices,
which had fallen throughout the late March and early April
auctions, actually rose sharply on April 10 and then rallied for

SALES AT THE STOCK EXCHANGE, APRIL 10, 1837

Issue	Terms	Price
United States Bank		
100	cash	100
20	cash	100
100	this week	101
100	next week	101
150	this week	101
Delaware & Hudson Canal Co		
50	cash	67
Morris Canal & Banking Co.		
10	cash	45
10	cash	44
5	cash	51
Farmers Loan & Trust Co.		
10	cash	80
Ohio Life & Trust Co.		
20	cash	95
105	cash	100
50	30 days	97½
Howard Insurance Co.		
10	cash	100
New York Insurance Co.		
10	cash	85
Harlem Railroad Co.		
180	cash	55
10	cash	53
25	cash	52
Boston & Providence Railroad Co.		
15	cash	95
50	cash	98
50	4 days	99
New Jersey Railroad Co.		
60	cash	84
50	cash	85
Long Island Railroad Co.		
100	cash	60

Source: *New York Herald*, April 11, 1837

the next four sessions. As for Wall Street itself, the scene was calm, with little business being transacted and no brokers in sight except during midday and afternoon meetings at the coffeehouses and auctions.

In the months that followed, a special session of Congress took up banking problems but failed to resolve them. Van Buren held the view that he had no responsibility for the panic and depression: "The less government interferes with private pursuits," he said, "the better for the general prosperity." Still, Congress provided for the issuance of one-year Treasury notes, which helped ease the money situation. When Congress realized the depression would not end quickly, a second issue was made, and then, between 1838 and 1843, six more, for a total of $47,002,900 in Treasury notes. More than any other action, their issuance helped salvage whatever confidence remained in American currency during the year following suspension of specie payments.

Van Buren had less success for his proposed Independent Treasury, which in any case would have done little to help conditions during the depression. In all, he did what precedent dictated a chief executive should in such a situation: nothing. Inheriting a depression born in the Jackson Administration, Van Buren was President during four years of stagnation and economic decline. For this reason and others, he was turned out of office in 1841, the first President other than the Adamses to lose a bid for a second term.

As for Nicholas Biddle, his attempts to save the banks were doomed, although he appeared successful in a bold experiment at cornering the cotton market and then issuing currency against the crops. At the same time, Van Buren's program for establishing a subtreasury system failed, and the government was forced to use the Bank of the United States of Philadelphia as a depository. Biddle was delighted, and he considered the President's action a capitulation. He dined with Van Buren in February 1839 and assumed a condescending attitude toward that harried man. Biddle resigned his post a month later, and was praised by the bank's directors as one who had "performed so much so faithfully," and who had left the bank "prosperous in all its relations . . . and secure in the respect and esteem of all who are connected with it in foreign or domestic intercourse." He was then given a gold service by the Philadelphia banking community and was wished a long and happy life.

The cotton syndicate collapsed; Biddle lost his investment and those of his friends. His reputation, once the highest in banking circles, now sank to near zero. Shortly thereafter he was sued by his stockholders for a quarter of a million dollars, charged with financial crimes and criminal conspiracy, and arrested. Philip Hone remained true to his hero; he wrote that the banker had been charged with "high crimes and vulgar misdemeanors by a secret conclave of greasy householders. . . ." Biddle was freed, but other litigation followed, and would plague him until he died on February 27, 1844, of bronchitis complicated by dropsy. At the time Nicholas Biddle was fifty-eight years old.

While Biddle speculated in cotton, Albert Gallatin, Jefferson's Secretary of the Treasury who had become president of the National Bank of New York, took up the task of resuming specie payment. Gallatin's position was somewhere between that of Jackson and Biddle. Although philosophically sympathetic with Jackson's policies, he nonetheless recognized the need for a central bank. Thus, in 1836, he had urged his fellow bankers to organize a convention "for the purpose of agreeing on a uniform course of measures and on the time when the resumption should take place." Gallatin attempted to prevent the panic, in so doing assuming leadership of the New York banking community.

Gallatin continued his work after the collapse of 1837. He organized a committee of New York bankers, which contacted their counterparts in other cities with the goal of resuming gold payments. He soon found himself in conflict with both Van Buren and Biddle. The Administration position was that only specie should be acceptable for the payment of debts, while Gallatin desired the acceptance of paper with the understanding that it would be fully convertible to gold or silver on demand. Biddle objected to resumption on the grounds that hundreds and possibly thousands of businessmen had been saved by the suspension of gold payments, since they were not obliged to honor debts falling due after the suspension had gone into effect. Should resumption take place prior to a return to liquidity, then the entire commercial and industrial structure of the nation might well collapse. Furthermore, Gallatin's success would inevitably result in benefits to New York and the corresponding loss of power in Philadelphia.

Gallatin's committee succeeded in its attempts, and resumption took place on May 10, 1838, more than a year after suspension had been announced. With this move, New York's domination over the nation's financial affairs was assured.

By early autumn of 1837, nine tenths of the Eastern factories were closed, and Horace Greeley estimated that "one fourth of all connected with the mercantile interests are out of business, with dreary prospects for the coming winter." In New York, five hundred persons answered an advertisement for twenty day laborers to work for $4 a month plus room and board. Conditions were slightly better in 1838, but declined once again in 1839. By then it seemed the depression had become a permanent part of the American scene.

The panic and depression led to the revision of many state constitutions, including that of New York, and the new documents contained far more lenient bankruptcy provisions than the old. In addition, a federal bankruptcy law was passed, and through its use some $450 million in debts affecting one million creditors were wiped out. The nation's credit was gone as far as domestic businessmen were concerned. The governor of Pennsylvania was said to have recommended the construction of a special railroad to take defaulters to Texas; only in this way could Americans once again trust one another. As for Europeans, they could not have helped America had they wished, since Britain and France were having their own difficulties during what came to be called "the Hungry Forties." Furthermore, the wave of bankruptcies soured most foreign banks on American securities. British investors had lost approximately $130 million in the American crash, and they had no desire to be burned again. The London *Times* spoke for thousands when it wrote, "The people of the United States may be fully persuaded that there is a certain class of securities to which no abundance of money, however great, can give value, and that in this class their own securities stand pre-eminent. The Paris Rothschilds wrote Duff Green, "You may tell your government that you have seen the man who is at the head of the finances of Europe, and that he has told you that they cannot borrow a dollar, not a dollar." By 1841, American trade, manufacturing, and general economic conditions reached new lows, as did securities on the Board.

PRICES OF SELECTED ISSUES, 1837 AND 1841

Issue	1837 High	Nov. 25, 1841
United States Bank	122	4
Vicksburg Bank	89	5
Kentucky Bank	92	56
North American Trust	95	3
Farmers' Trust	113	30
American Trust	120	0
Illinois State Bank	80	35
Morris Canal	75	0
Patterson R.R.	75	53
Long Island R.R.	60	52

Source: Pratt, *Work of Wall Street*, p. 13

The economy and the securities markets did not recover fully from the 1837 panic until 1844, when trade revived, the effects of the liquidations had been absorbed, and expansion into the West accelerated once more. The Mexican War and gold discoveries in California gave a further fillip to the economy, as did the banking and tariff reforms of the Polk Administration. By that time, Europeans had forgotten their vows of 1837–41, and resumed their purchases of American securities. A boom was on, one which would not end before America had become an important power. By that time the securities markets were far more reflective of the national economy than they had been in 1837.

The problems of the mid-1830s seemed remote in 1844. Although several attempts had been made to establish a new national bank, none succeeded, and by 1844 the issue no longer dominated congressional debates on financial matters. Two years later a Democratic Congress passed the Independent Treasury Bill, which was signed by President James K. Polk, called "Young Hickory" by his admirers. Except for a series of changes made during the Civil War, this device functioned as the closest equivalent the nation would have to a central bank until the establishment of the Federal Reserve System. The Independent Treasury system proved inadequate for the tasks assigned it, and its failures were responsible for more than one panic in the next seventy years.

INDEX OF RAILROAD STOCK PRICES, 1837–1844 (BASE: 1834–1842)

Year	Jan.	Feb.	March	April	May	June	July	Aug.	Sept.	Oct.	Nov.	Dec.
1837	118	118	108	99	95	91	104	100	100	103	103	99
1838	96	92	87	86	92	99	97	103	105	97	97	94
1839	99	104	99	100	103	99	95	92	90	86	81	83
1840	87	86	83	86	85	85	85	83	86	92	91	88
1841	86	85	78	81	85	85	86	85	81	79	81	77
1842	64	62	59	60	65	68	65	63	65	63	60	60
1843	58	60	60	60	69	74	73	76	77	76	81	92
1844	91	95	96	104	113	113	110	114	115	118	114	112

Source: Smith and Cole, *Fluctuations in American Business*, p. 183

In 1837 the budget showed its first deficit since 1824, and for the next few years they continued. This was caused in large part by declines in tariff receipts and sales of public lands, and in-

FEDERAL RECEIPTS AND EXPENDITURES, 1832–1842

Year	Receipts	Expenditures	Surplus or Deficit
		(millions of dollars)	
1832	31.9	17.3	+14.6
1833	34.0	23.0	+10.9
1834	21.8	18.6	+ 3.2
1835	35.4	17.6	+17.9
1836	50.8	30.9	+20.0
1837	24.9	37.2	−12.3
1838	26.3	33.9	− 7.6
1839	31.5	26.9	+ 4.6
1840	19.5	24.3	− 4.8
1841	16.9	26.6	− 9.7
1842	20.0	25.2	− 5.2

Source: U.S. Treasury, *Annual Report*, 1941, pp. 412–17

creases in federal expenditures, as the central government took over obligations of the states during the depression. The debt rose to $66.2 million in 1851 before declining once more to reach a low of $28.7 million in 1857, when gold piled up at the Treasury. Tight money again plagued the nation, and a new panic seemed in sight.

Philip Hone lived to see the recovery of the mid-1840s. The 1837 panic had ruined him, through no fault of his own. George Templeton Strong's comments on Hone proved correct: through injudicious advances to his sons and friends, he found himself in 1838 with less than half the money he had in 1836. The years of high living seemed over, as Hone was obliged to seek employment, first as a New York postmaster and then as president of the American Mutual Insurance Company. For a while conditions appeared to be righted, but Philip Hone, whose life was punctuated by disastrous fires, was once again brought low by conflagration; on July 19, 1845, several fires that resulted in large policy payments caused American Mutual to fail. By this time, however, both the economy and Hone were in healthy financial condition, and the diarist was able to spend the rest of his life in travel, politics, and the arts. He remained a leading municipal figure and spent much time attacking Democrats, praising Whigs, reflecting on old age, and wondering about the future financial condition of the nation.

On February 3, 1851, Hone noted that "there has been of late a great rise in the value of real estate," and that his holdings had increased substantially. Several days later he fell ill, and his diary entries became irregular and shorter. On Wednesday, April 30, he noted that only four more pages remained in the journal, and the sick and weary Philip Hone wondered if he should go on, since he was "feeble beyond description, destitute of appetite, with no strength in my limbs." Six days later Philip Hone, at the age of seventy, died.

3.
THE WESTERN
BLIZZARD OF 1857

The depression ushered in by the panic of 1837 still numbed the country five years later. But there were signs of a turn. Grain and cotton exports were rising, the infant industries of New England and the middle states were seeking capital, and foreign investors once again considered the economic potential of America favorably while trying to forget the frivolity of the nation's bankruptcy laws. Senator James Buchanan of Pennsylvania, a solid Democrat and an aspirant for the Presidency, who nonetheless supported some aspects of Clay's American System, thought the nation on the threshold of a great step forward. He applauded the growth of cotton culture along with the productivity of wheat farmers of his own state, believing the farms to be the keys to future development. At all times he tried to protect farmers from their enemies, among whom he numbered railroad promoters who sought special privilege from government. Early in 1843, Buchanan rose to deliver a broadside against these "leeches."

If you defeat them at this session, they will be here in greater force than ever at the commencement of the next. Their importunity will never cease whilst the least hope of success shall remain, and we have learned from our experience that they have both the ability and the will to select shrewd and skilful agents to accomplish their purposes before Congress.

Enough congressmen and senators were impressed by the dangers of a new business-government coalition to heed such

Jacksonian warnings and to present a front against the railroads, but not enough to prevent grants from being voted. State and local governments joined to promote the roads, which were considered by some a panacea for prosperity. Although only one of several forces leading the nation out of the depression, railroads were easily the most dramatic. Foreign investors sought new lines and pushed their funds upon them. Land companies combined with them or organized "paper railroads" to enhance the value of their holdings. The lines attracted foreign labor and helped alleviate unemployment. Railroad securities led the New York and other stock exchanges out of the bear market of 1836–43.

The four-year return to prosperity was shattered in 1847, as the combination of European disorders and financial confusion, a severe depression in central Europe, and the Mexican War caused uncertainty. But the fears of late 1847 were dispelled by mid-1848 by three events.

In Europe, bad harvests and revolutions caused a sharp increase in grain imports from the United States, bringing new prosperity to farmers, who now could afford to purchase farm implements from Northern factories. Britain's repeal of her Corn Laws of 1846 had little effect that year or the one following, but in 1848 "hard times" in England and Ireland resulted in new demands for American grain, while at the same time Europe exported workers who were attracted by the American boom. Thus, war and depression overseas provided American farmers with markets, and American railroads and factories with laborers.

In February 1848, the United States and Mexico signed the Treaty of Guadalupe Hidalgo, ending the Mexican War. California, New Mexico, and parts of present-day Nevada, Arizona, Utah, and Colorado were added to the nation, in return for $15 million and the assumption of debts owed Americans by Mexico. The uncertainties of war were thus replaced by the promise of expansion into the new territories.

On January 24, 1848, a week before the treaty was concluded, a New Jersey mechanic named James Marshall discovered gold at a sawmill owned by Johann Sutter in the lower Sacramento Valley in California. For a while Marshall kept the news to himself, but it soon leaked to the community, and by early February all of California learned of the gold strike; within a few months all the world knew about what had been found at Sutter's Mill.

These three events converged in late 1848. Europeans left their troubled homelands for the prosperous United States, and many hoped to go to California and pick nuggets out of the sand. The agricultural boom encouraged speculation, and Americans too joined in the gold rush. At the same time, the import balance of trade, combined with California gold, transformed America from a beggar country into a rich one. Europeans who had hesitated to invest in America in 1843 now pleaded with their New York correspondents for securities. The most popular of these were the rails, the key to western settlement and the California bonanza. Cotton prices, which had lagged at first, went up in 1849, bringing prosperity to the South. In 1850 the United States and Britain signed the Clayton-Bulwer Treaty, promising to cooperate in the building of a canal across the Isthmus of Panama; some began to speak of an American empire in the Caribbean. Nothing seemed capable of preventing this; nothing could stand in the way of the nation's progress.

Not even the growing dissent from Abolitionists in the North and "Fire Eaters" in the South could cast a cloud on the optimism of the period. In 1850 moderates from both the Democratic and Whig parties united to steer the "Compromise of 1850" through

GOLD PRODUCTION, 1847–1856

Year	Production (1,000 fine troy ounces)
1847	43
1848	484
1849	1935
1850	2419
1851	2661
1852	2902
1853	3144
1854	2902
1855	2661
1856	2661

Source: *Historical Statistics*, p. 371

Congress, and when the bills were signed by President Fillmore, many hoped the slave question would recede and become less a topic of controversy between the sections.

The period from 1850 to 1856 was one of unbroken prosperity. Almost any set of statistics shows the remarkable growth of the United States and supports the high hopes of 1850. Gold production rose sharply, reaching a plateau in 1854 and not declining until the Civil War. Total railroad mileage grew from less than 8,000 miles in 1846 to more than 30,000 in 1860. The growth in railroads and

RAILROAD MILEAGE, 1850–1856

Year	Mileage
1850	9,021
1851	10,982
1852	12,908
1853	15,360
1854	16,721
1855	18,374
1856	22,076

Source: *Historical Statistics*, p. 288

agricultural equipment led to an increase in demand for pig iron and an increase in its price, and requirements of both the iron and railroad industries caused rapid increases in the production of coal, which further stimulated railroad growth and

PIG IRON PRODUCTION AND PRICES, 1850–1856

Year	Shipments	Price/Long Ton
	(1,000 short tons)	
1850	63	$20.87
1851	N.A.	21.37
1852	560	22.62
1853	N.A.	36.12
1854	736	36.87
1855	784	27.75
1856	883	27.12

Source: *Historical Statistics*, p. 366

provided a market for picks, axes, and other mine equipment. The tremendous expansion in capital investment was made pos-

COAL PRODUCTION, 1850–1856

Year	Bituminous Production	Anthracite Production
	(*1,000 short tons*)	(*1,000 short tons*)
1850	4.0	4.3
1851	4.6	5.8
1852	4.9	6.4
1853	6.1	6.7
1854	7.4	7.7
1855	7.5	8.6
1856	8.0	9.0

Source: Historical Statistics, pp. 357, 359

sible by California gold, an increase in the use of notes, and foreign investment, which reached a high point in 1853, when

CAPITAL TRANSFERS TO THE UNITED STATES, 1850–1856

Year	Net Flow
	(*millions of dollars*)
1850	29
1851	6
1852	16
1853	56
1854	42
1855	15
1856	12

Source: *Historical Statistics, p. 565*

the nation's balance of trade showed a deficit of $37 million. Indeed, for four of the seven years of this period, imports exceeded exports. Thus, foreigners not only made up the deficit in trade by purchasing American securities but also provided additional millions of dollars for investments in American enterprises.

In 1850, some $318 million was invested in American railroads. This figure rose to $764 million by 1855, and over $1 billion by

BALANCE OF TRADE, 1850–1856

Year	Total Exports	Total Imports	Balance
	(millions of dollars)		
1850	152	178	−26
1851	218	216	2
1852	210	213	− 3
1853	231	268	−37
1854	278	305	−26
1855	275	261	14
1856	327	315	12

Source: *Historical Statistics*, p. 538

the end of the decade. Much of this money came from Britain, France, and other European nations. Foreigners were attracted by promises of huge profits and the sound condition of the dollar

AGGREGATE FOREIGN INDEBTEDNESS, 1847–1857

Year	Indebtedness
	(millions of dollars)
1847	193.7
1848	196.0
1849	193.2
1850	221.1
1851	229.6
1852	245.8
1853	301.3
1854	343.3
1855	356.3
1856	366.9
1857	383.3

Source: Douglass North, *The Economic Growth of the United States 1790–1860*, p. 238

after 1849. The federal budget was balanced easily in spite of a low tariff, and in every year from 1850 to 1857 showed a surplus which was used to pay the national debt. Nor did the repayment of the debt result in the kind of money shortage that had bedeviled Jackson and would cause anguish to Grover Cleveland.

FEDERAL FINANCES, 1850–1857

Year	Receipts	Expenditures	Surplus	Gross Debt
	(millions of dollars)			
1850	43.6	39.5	4.0	63.5
1851	52.6	47.7	4.9	68.3
1852	49.8	44.2	5.7	66.2
1853	61.6	48.2	13.4	59.8
1854	73.8	58.0	15.8	42.2
1855	65.4	59.7	5.6	35.6
1856	74.1	69.6	4.5	32.0
1857	69.0	67.8	1.2	28.7

Source: *Historical Statistics*, p. 711

California gold plus credit assured a plentiful supply of currency. On the other hand, prosperity also resulted in the worst inflation since the Confederation era.

Although undesirable, inflation seemed a small price to pay for the many economic benefits of the period. When James Buchanan finally became President in 1857, he could say, "No nation has ever before been embarrassed from too large a surplus in the Treasury." Buchanan's inaugural address in March stressed the power and wealth of the country. He proposed to extinguish the debt, strengthen the army and navy, expand the nation's boundaries, and build a rail connection to the Pacific. By then, however, the slavery question had come to dominate

COST OF LIVING AND WHOLESALE PRICE INDICES, 1850–1856

Year	Cost of Living Index	Farm Products	Manufactured Goods	All
	(1913 = 100)	(1910–1914 = 100)		
1850	54	71	147	84
1851	60	71	141	83
1852	60	77	144	88
1853	64	83	186	97
1854	64	93	191	108
1855	67	95	176	110
1856	68	84	174	105

Source: *Historical Statistics*, pp. 115, 127

politics and economic thinking. The new President tried to dismiss the problem as being "happily a matter of but little practical importance," but few would agree with this diagnosis.

Ironically, the same forces that made possible the impressive growth of the 1850s also brought into sharper focus the problems which now threatened the Union. A decade earlier it had been hoped that territorial expansion would be relatively slow and that adjustments between the sections would be possible. The Compromise of 1850 was an attempt to align political to economic and sectional realities, and for a brief period it appeared to work. By 1852, however, sectional ties were disintegrating rapidly. The fugitive-slave issue, the growing popularity of moral crusades in both North and South, publication of *Uncle Tom's Cabin,* together with the rapid rise of new free-soil-oriented parties in the elections of that year, were signs of growing discontent. Compromisers like Senator Stephen Douglas of Illinois applauded the "Young America" movement as an attempt to draw the nation's attention to other matters. George Francis Train called upon Americans to forget their differences and unite in a great colonizing effort, which he thought would prevent a sectional struggle. But this was not to be.

Douglas sponsored and Congress passed the Kansas–Nebraska Act in 1854, designed to settle both the question of slavery in new territories and that of a transcontinental railroad. Under his plan, Kansas was to enter the Union as a slave state and Nebraska as free. Bloody fighting erupted soon after in Kansas, which in 1855 seemed to threaten the future of the nation. By 1856 President Franklin Pierce's attempts to moderate the issue had failed, John Brown terrorized slaveholders in southern Kansas, while "border ruffians" killed free soilers in the northern part of the territory.

On March 6, 1857, the Supreme Court, in the Dred Scott decision, held that Congress was prohibited by the Fifth Amendment to legislate slavery out of the territories. Now the Kansas–Nebraska Act was a dead letter, as was the earlier Missouri Compromise. To many, the decision, along with what had preceded it, spelled the end of the nation.

As Buchanan delivered his inaugural address in 1857, both North and South believed they could triumph in any conflict between the sections, and each claimed the right to the dominant voice in national affairs.

Southern leaders observed that cotton was the nation's leading product. In 1856 the value of America's exports was $281.2 million; over $128.3 million of it came from cotton. Total exports from 1846 to 1856 were $1,986 million, and cotton accounted for $917 million. America was prosperous, and many credited the nation's wealth to California gold. America could survive without gold, however, as long as cotton exports continued. But not even the total production of the Western mines could save the country if cotton exports ceased. According to the section's leaders, this fact alone should entitle the South to national leadership. If war between the states did erupt, the loss of this vital commodity would bring the North to financial ruin in a short period.

Northern leaders replied that their section's factories were growing at a more rapid rate than Southern plantations, and while cotton dominated the export trade, Northern goods were more important in national trade. Furthermore, through an alliance with the West, the North controlled grain production, which after the repeal of the Corn Laws was becoming increasingly important to Europe. The North had shown that even with low tariffs it could compete on the world market. While the South believed Europe would come to its aid to save its cotton source, the North thought England and France would remain neutral in order to prevent a wheat embargo and to protect their sizable investments in Northern and Western railroads.

The matter of which side was right was the leading economic question of 1857, and it dominated politics as well. There seemed no way of resolving differences, and no method of deciding which section had more power. But within a year of Buchanan's inauguration, Southern leaders thought they had the answer to the second question: in a war between the states, they would be an easy victor. This answer did not come from Washington; nor was it derived from production figures, cotton exports, gold production, or the like. Instead, the South received its sign from Wall Street in New York.

Securities dealings on Wall Street fell off after the 1837 panic; business life in the district was dominated by merchants, lottery-ticket dealers, and tradesmen rather than stockholders. The Stock and Exchange Board met daily except Sundays at the old Jauncey Building at 43 Wall Street until 1842, when it moved into a large hall over the reading room at the Merchants' Exchange Building on William Street. The New Board, or "Bourse," a rival organization, occupied rooms in the same building, and for a while threatened the existence of the "Old Board." The revival of interest in securities led to a search for more spacious quarters, and in 1854 still another move was made, this time to the top floor of the Corn Exchange Building on William and Beaver Streets. Oppressive heat and cramped rooms resulted in a shift to Lord's Court, on 25 William Street, in the summer of 1856.

These moves did not interrupt business at the Exchange, since on a typical day in the early 1850s only 7,000 or so shares might be traded, while an additional 40,000 could be sold at the curb markets.

Although the financial district prospered during the period following the Gold Rush, the institutional structure of the Exchange was much the same as it had been a generation earlier. Clearings were still cumbersome, petty thievery the rule, and three-day weekends in the summer normal for partners in trading houses. In 1855, when the bull market was at its height and the subject of discussion in all the newspapers, the Stock and Exchange Board regularly traded shares in approximately forty railroads, ten canals, eight coal and mining companies, three gas lighting companies, and four banks, as well as a variety of bonds. The Exchange still used the auction system. There were two sessions, the first at 10:30 A.M. and the second at 2:45 P.M. Sellers would deposit their slips with the president prior to the "calls," while buyers would straggle into the room a few minutes before the gavel was sounded. Then the list was called, the bonds first, and next the bank, canal, coal, shipping, and rails stocks in turn. Between calls brokers and buyers would congregate in the streets or coffeehouses, and on busy days go to one or another of several private stock auctions held on Wall Street. Even though volume picked up in 1856 and 1857, the same pattern persisted. Trading for July 13, 1857, a day newspapers called normal, was reported in this fashion by the *New York Herald:*

FIRST BOARD

$11,000	Tenn. 6's	82
38,000	Mo. 6's	77¼
3,000	" "	78
1,000	Cal. 7's	53
1,000	Erie R.R.	100
1,000	Lake Erie & Western	47
3,000	Buffalo & St. Louis 7's	90
8,000	Terre Haute 2nd mortgage	63
5 sh.	Hanover Bank	93
60	Del. & Hudson Canal Co.	117
100	Cumberland Coal	16½
100	" "	17
20	La Crosse & Milwaukee R.R.	38
160	" " " "	36
30	" " " "	36
20	Pacific Mail Steamship Co.	74¼
30	" " " "	74
5	New York Central R.R.	81
550	" " " "	80¾
50	" " " "	80¾
200	" " " "	80½
10	" " " "	80⅝
1100	" " " "	80¾
60	Erie R.R.	27⅞
50	" "	27¾
200	" "	27¾
260	" "	28
100	" "	28
125	" "	28
150	" "	28¼
210	Harlem R.R.	16½
40	Harlem R.R. pfd.	23
10	" "	23⅛
50	Galena & Chicago R.R.	91⅛
100	" " "	92⅛
57	Mo. Southern & Nashville R.R.	47⅛
100	" " " "	47⅛
400	" " " "	47¾
5	" " " "	48
100	" " " "	45
100	" " " "	44
100	Illinois Central R.R.	120
100	" " "	118
100	Cleveland & Toledo R.R.	58

FIRST BOARD

300	" " "	57¾
50	" " "	57⅛
100	" " "	57⅜
200	Chicago & Rock Island R.R.	91½
210	" " " "	91
200	" " " "	90¾
200	" " " "	90
10	Milwaukee & Mississippi R.R.	52
50	" " "	51½
150	" " "	51¾
150	" " "	50⅛
6	Panama R.R.	87¾

SECOND BOARD

$1,000	Lake Erie & Western R.R.	47
3,000	" " " "	46
2,000	Michigan Southern R.R.	50
10 sh.	Park Bank	102
20	Metropolitan Bank	106
100	Erie R.R.	28⅜
250	" "	28¾
100	" "	28
100	" "	28
100	Michigan Southern R.R.	44½
64	" " "	47½
100	Cleveland & Toledo R.R.	57¼
600	" " "	57¼
100	" " "	57⅛
25	Milwaukee & Missouri R.R.	51⅛
100	" " "	51
50	La Crosse & Milwaukee R.R.	35
50	" " " "	35
50	" " " "	35
50	" " " "	35¼
25	Stonington R.R.	50
50	Delaware & Lackawanna R.R.	50
38	New York Central R.R.	81¼
50	" " " "	81⅛
25	" " " "	81½
500	Reading R.R.	78
200	" "	77¾
200	Cleveland & Pittsburgh R.R.	39
50	Galena & Chicago R.R.	92⅛

During these two sessions, $72,000 worth of bonds were sold, and 9,490 shares of stock, of which all but 345 shares were of railroads. The "volume leader" on that date was New York Central, which traded 2,028 shares and closed unchanged from the previous day.

Since the market was so small, it was easily manipulated and attracted speculators and raiders. To be sure, most talented rogues were busier in more lucrative fields, such as land speculation, railroads, and commodities, but the bull market following the gold rush did attract new men to Wall Street. Writing of them, an old banker said:

One had acquired wealth by selling dry goods, and therefore he was fit to be a bank president; another had been equally successful in making shoes; another had been a ship chandler, and made a fortune in the schooner coasting-trade; another had been a stage-driver; not a few were men of the narrowest minds, wholly lacking in mercantile education and without the ability to conduct the simplest commercial correspondence. It is due to some of these gentlemen to say that, if they were ignorant in the beginning, they have improved by close attention to practical duties, and that for general intelligence they are not far below their contemporaries in office. They have yet to learn, however, that it is one thing to be a bill broker and a shrewd calculator of balances, and quite another to understand the principles of true economy in finance.

Few such individuals were able to gain admittance to the Stock and Exchange Board, however. The Board was still dominated by older men, who frowned on the newcomers and forced them to curb trading or seats on the Bourse. Among the older speculators of note, only Jacob Little remained from previous bull markets, and he was less active than he had been earlier. The Board was dull, conservative, and secure when the bull market began—an accurate reflection of the New York financial community. Then, as money began to flow, some of it stuck to the fingers of the respectable.

As president of both the New Haven and the Harlem railroads and grandson of Revolutionary War General Philip Schuyler, Robert Schuyler was one of the most powerful as well as high-

ranking members of the New York elite. In July 1854, several
directors of the New Haven made a regular examination of the
books and found several small irregularities. While this was going
on, Schuyler's brokerage house failed. Several friends, including
Commodore Vanderbilt, offered assistance, but Schuyler assured
them that all was well. Then the directors reported huge shortages at the New Haven, and within hours Schuyler was on his
way to Canada to escape the law. Subsequent investigations disclosed that he had privately printed 20,000 shares of bogus New
Haven stock, which he sold for $2 million, and had deposited
the money in his private account. In addition, he had borrowed
$600,000 from Vanderbilt, leaving as security his pledge for other
faked shares. Neither Schuyler nor the money were ever recovered.

Other disclosures followed. Alexander Kyle, Jr., secretary of
the Harlem, admitted having forged more than 5,000 shares of
that line's stock and then swapped them for securities in the New
Haven—also forged. He had helped Schuyler misappropriate
$200,000 in Harlem bonds, and had even aided in picking an
apartment for Schuyler's mistress. Wall Street was shocked by
the forgeries and thefts, while the city's social set was stunned
when it learned that Robert Schuyler had lived a double life
for years, fathering a family under the assumed name of Spicer.

Nor was this the end of the scandals. The Board of Directors
at the Parker Vein Coal Company issued five times as much
stock as was authorized, sold it, and pocketed the money. Edward Crane, head of the Vermont Central Railroad, sold some
10,000 shares of the line's stock which, like Schuyler's, was
forged. Simon Draper, Jr., an important banker, was caught over-
drawing on his accounts. Henry Dwight, Jr., prominent at the
Chicago & Mississippi Railroad, was charged with malpractice
and forced to resign. Then came the robbery of $14,000 from
August Belmont. William Paul, Belmont's cashier, described the
thief to the police; a search was begun, and then stopped when
Paul admitted having stolen the money himself. The teller at
the Ocean Bank took $50,000 from that institution, another
teller, at the National, stole $70,000, while a third took $25,000
from the Market Bank. Benjamin Brotherson, bookkeeper of the

Union Bank, fled the city after it was learned that he had stolen $200,000 from the bank and had forged his balances for months. The financial district was in a state of near-panic. Securities trading fell sharply and prices gyrated wildly, rising and then falling as rumors showered the financial district. Writing in his diary, Philip Hone said:

One of those astounding Wall Street revolutions has occurred which are occasionally gotten up by gamblers, and by which the turn of a day makes nabobs and beggars, and unsettles the minds of men who watch the brokers' books with anxiety equal to that which the old attended the developments of the sibylline leaves. Within the last week many descriptions of what are called "fancy stocks" were inflated, by the progress of bubble-blowing, to prices double and quadruple those of the previous week. . . . This inflated state of things lasted three days, and then came the reverse which always follows these high pressure operations. All of a sudden stocks fell back nearly to the place where the speculation found them; the sellers became buyers, pocketed their gains, and laughed at their dupes.

For a while it seemed that the bull market would be ended by this loss of confidence, but as business conditions improved, and grain exports increased to make up Europe's losses due to the Crimean War, prices steadied and began to rise once more.

The bull market was able to continue because the economy appeared sound, with both railroads and agriculture in good condition and expanding. On the other hand, the banking situation was as bad as it had been during the past twenty years. Structurally speaking, the United States had one of the worst systems in the Western world.

In 1844 an agrarian-controlled Congress passed, and the President signed, a bill establishing the Independent Treasury System, which remained the basic national banking law until passage and implementation of the Federal Reserve Act almost seventy years later. The agrarians distrusted banking and banks, and were determined to prevent the growth of powerful central banking of the type supported by Nicholas Biddle and many Eastern Whigs. Under the new law, government funds would be kept in a series of subtreasuries in various key cities, and debts owed the national

government were payable in gold or Treasury notes. The financial
needs of the private sector were left to state banks, the number
of which rose from 696 in 1844 to 1,562 in 1856. The states passed
banking laws far stricter than those of the late Jacksonian period,
but notes were still not accepted at par with gold, and the banks
continued to expand more than did their resources. From 1844 to
1856, state bank capital doubled from $210.9 million to $421.9
million, while loans rose more rapidly, going from $264.9 million
to $691.9 million. State bank notes, as before, were readily accept-
able in areas close to the issuing bank, but sold at progressively
higher discounts as the distance from the bank increased. Forged
banknotes were commonplace and currency expansion difficult;
up to 1857, it was legal to settle debts in foreign currency in most
states of the Union.

As the national economy grew, so did the banking network.
Local banks filled most needs, but farmers shipping goods hundreds of miles and merchants engaged in inter-regional trade
demanded a more stable and uniform currency. Many Western
banks had deposited parts of their reserve in New York since the
early 1840s, so as to assure merchants that their bank notes would
be redeemable in that city. In 1840, bankers' balances held by
New York banks were calculated at almost $8 million; by 1850
the figure was $17 million, and in early 1857 estimates of balances
held in New York varied from $30 million to as high as $50
million. New York had become central banker for the nation, and
its heart. "Every beat of this great financial organ is felt from
Maine to Florida, and from the Atlantic to the Pacific," wrote
the *Louisville Courier* that year. Foreign capital flowed to America
through New York, and foreigners bought and sold stocks and
bonds on the New York Stock and Exchange Board, and other of
the city's markets. A majority of the nation's railroads floated their
securities with New York banks; Southern cotton and Western
wheat used the city's financial resources.

This ad hoc central bank seemed to work well. Defenders
claimed it had all the benefits of Biddle's bank and none of its
liabilities. Critics charged the system had weaknesses. The banks
were undercapitalized and uncoordinated. Bank clearings were
irregular until the Clearing House was established in 1853, and

even then inter-bank relations were inefficient. When supporters noted that the greatest economic boom in the nation's history had taken place under the Independent Treasury system, opponents responded that the expansion was due to increases in gold, and not to any wisdom of New York bankers. At no point did bank notes sell at par with gold; even at the height of the boom, market prices showed distrust of paper money. The economy was healthy, so it seemed, and there was more money about than ever before, but this did not indicate a papermania such as had existed in 1836. Not until 1856 did the use of paper money grow rapidly, and even then it did not seem dangerous. In 1845,

AMERICAN CURRENCY, 1840–1857

Year	Total Gold	Gold in Circulation	Bank Note Circulation	Total Currency
		(millions of dollars)		
1840	83	47	107	154
1842	80	49	84	133
1845	96	45	90	135
1850	154	90	131	221
1855	250	155	187	342
1857	260	159	215	374

Source: William Schultz and M. R. Caine, *Financial Development of the United States*, p. 256

the per capita money in circulation was $6.79; by 1855, the figure had risen to $12.55. At this time gold, not paper, sparked the economy. The 1855–57 period, when the bull market took hold and the use of credit expanded, saw per capita money rise from $12.55 to $12.93—not as rapidly as it had in the preceding period. It could not be claimed, then, that the banking system in 1857 was as vulnerable as it had been twenty years earlier, or as reckless.

This is not to say that the system was stronger. For if the flagrant abuses of 1836–37 were missing, so was the comparatively primitive economy of the earlier age. The growth of inter-regional trade, especially in agricultural goods, put severe strains on the system. In late summer and early fall, during the planting and harvesting seasons, depositors in the South and West withdrew their funds from local banks, which responded by drawing upon their accounts in New York. The money would return in the late fall as farmers were paid for their produce and redeposited their money. But from August to October, the flow of money from the East to the South and West was great, and would usually cause the collapse of several small banks. The New York banks were indispensable to the national economy, and for the most part did their jobs satisfactorily. In 1857, however, they remained a weak link, and should pressures mount in the city, causing the downfall of one or more major institutions, repercussions would be felt throughout the nation.

Critics believed the system could collapse as a result of an unfavorable trade balance, causing widespread economic losses. As large gold shipments left America, hoarding would begin, and paper would lose its value. Such a situation seemed possible in 1854, when the nation had its third consecutive year of import balances. Then came the Crimean War, followed by British military campaigns in China and Persia, culminating with an Indian mutiny in 1857. At the same time France conducted operations in Algeria and elsewhere. Europeans needed American grain more than ever before, and this shifted the trade balance in America's favor.

On the other hand, the wars cost money, and deficit spending in Europe led to sharp rises in the interest rates. As the rates rose in England and on the Continent, Europeans began to purchase bonds issued by their own countries, and their demands for American securities were slaked. Capital transfers to the United States, which reached a high of $56 million in 1853, dropped to $12 million three years later. The rather abrupt end of a great investment period led to a decline at the New York exchanges and caused concern in those banks and insurance companies whose assets were in stocks and bonds. Just as Europe's problems had aided the agrarians, so they caused difficulties for urban bankers.

All of these questions were discussed fully in the city's newspapers, which were numerous and contentious. On July 4, the

New York Herald, the City's foremost sensationalist paper, carried the following headline:

GREAT QUESTION OF THE DAY
THE KANSAS CONTROVERSY
The North No-Slavery and the South Pro-Slavery Factions
Speech of Senator Trumbull of Illinois, Nigger Worshiper

Trumbull spoke strongly against those Southerners who would force slavery on Kansas, while his opponents charged bad faith regarding the Kansas-Nebraska Act. Clearly conditions in the West were worsening.

The *Times*, more conservative than the *Herald*, also spoke of the Kansas controversy and predicted a showdown between the sections, while the *Tribune* concentrated on the laying of the Atlantic cable, which promised almost instantaneous communication with Europe. In future editions, the *Times* and *Tribune* would both attack the *Herald* as an inflammatory sheet, and each other as not recognizing the true problems of the nation.

Most newspapers of the period reflected the personality of a single man. Henry Raymond of the *Times* hoped to present a paper which would print "whatever has interest or importance for any considerable portion of the community," without "being objectionable on the ground of morality." Horace Greeley meant the *Tribune* to mirror his personal beliefs and idiosyncrasies regarding any and all topics. James Gordon Bennett of the *Herald* was a muckraker before the term was used. "Until this epoch of the world the daily newspaper press has been a mere organ of dry detail—uninteresting facts—political nonsense—personal squabbles—obsolete rows—tedious ship news—or meagre quotations of the market. I have changed all this." So wrote Bennett in 1837. He instituted a Wall Street column by young Jay Cooke, ran more detailed crime reports than the city had ever known before, and was a crusader for many causes and a bitter enemy of some.

Bennett was a Democrat with strong pro-Southern proclivities, one who distrusted Wall Street and believed the nation's prosperity and future lay with workers and farmers, not with businessmen and bankers. In early spring of 1857 he met young Leonard Jerome, a Wall Street speculator whose place in history is assured more by his being the grandfather of Winston Churchill than by several daring bear raids of the 1850s and 1860s. Jerome wanted prices on Wall Street to fall in order to squeeze the bulls, while Bennett would print any item critical of finance. They combined against the bull speculators. Beginning in June, the *Herald* became the organ of bearishness on Wall Street. As was his wont from time to time, Bennett adopted a puritanical tone in his editorial of June 27.

What can be the end of all this but another general collapse like that of 1837, only upon a much grander scale? The same premonitory symptoms that prevailed in 1835–6 prevail in 1857 in a tenfold degree. Government spoilations, public defaulters, paper bubbles of all descriptions, a general scramble for western lands and town and city sites, millions of dollars, made or borrowed, expended in fine houses and gaudy furniture; hundreds of thousands in the silly rivalries of fashionable parvenues, in silks, laces, diamonds and every variety of costly frippery are only a few among the many crying evils of the day. The worst of all these evils is the moral pestilence of luxurious exemption from honest labor, which is infecting all classes of society. The country merchant is becoming a city stockjobber, and the honest country farmer has gone off among the gamblers in western land. Thus, as this general scramble among all classes to be rich at once, and by the shortest possible cut, extends and increases, our rogues, defaulters and forgers are multiplied. The epidemic and its attending evils must run their course.

The *Times* and the *Tribune*, both of which were bullish as well as opposed to Bennett's style of journalism, charged the *Herald* with distortions and exaggerations. Bennett answered their accusations and continued to preach panic and depression.

Wall Street's optimism was not shattered by Bennett's gloomy predictions. There was bad news from Kansas, where the civil war continued, and from Utah, where a fight with the Mormons loomed. The Crimean War had ended, and there were reports of record European crops which would surely depress world prices and American exports. But not even these stories caused prices to fall on Wall Street. Rather, the first important blow to confidence came from civil insurrections in New York City.

During the decade of the forties more than a million and a half Europeans came to America, and the majority of them arrived in New York. Some moved on, but most remained in the city to take low-paying jobs, live in East Side slums, and make New York the most cosmopolitan city in America. Lower Manhattan was dotted with immigrant quarters, the largest and most notorious of which were Irish. By the end of the decade organized gangs roamed the streets, making some neighborhoods unsafe even in daylight. Mike Walsh's Spartan Band and the Empire Club vied for the West Side, while the Dead Rabbits and the Bowery Boys sought to control the entire city. The Astor Place riots of 1849 involved many of the gangs, fire departments, and individual citizens. Other outbreaks occurred in the next few years. Then, on July 4, 1857, trouble appeared in lower New York.

At first, it seemed part of the Independence Day celebrations, but by noon the city learned of pitched battles between members of the Dead Rabbit Club and their rivals. The police were called in and were able to force a retreat. Then the Dead Rabbits counterattacked, and the police commissioner was obliged to ask the militia for help. Before anything could be done, the Five Pointers entered the battle, erecting barricades and shooting at the Dead Rabbits. The fighting ended shortly thereafter, but then erupted once more. On July 13 some five hundred gang members attacked the police with pistols and knives, causing them to withdraw and killing several. Not until August would the rioting cease, and then it would stop due to boredom with violence, and not to police and militia efficiency.

Bennett deplored the riots, as did Greeley and Raymond. But he went further. To him, they were symptomatic of a general breakdown in American life, and could be viewed as a lower-class version of what was going on in Wall Street. Just as the Bowery Boys and Dead Rabbits had no respect for law or morality, so the bulls and bears, the railroad promoters and stockjobbers were indecent parasites draining the nation's vitality. Bennett peered into the future and saw disaster. The railroads were overcapitalized and under-utilized. Good crops in

Europe and the drying up of London and Paris capital would force many railroads into bankruptcy. Poorly capitalized banks would follow, dragging down others as they fell. Street riots such as those of July would be followed by a general insurrection. Aided by Leonard Jerome, Bennett began to catalogue those railroads in difficulty, concentrating his fire on the Michigan Central, a line whose stock Jerome had sold short. The *Tribune* attacked Bennett for his recklessness, but by mid-July wrote of flaws in the economy. The *Times*—despite the fact that Jerome owned one-quarter of its stock—issued optimistic statements almost daily.

Stock prices, which had been falling since the first riots, remained fairly stable, and some issues rose in the face of all these difficulties and charges.

PRICES OF SELECTED ISSUES, JULY 1857

Issue	Closing Prices (fractions rounded off)				
	July 3	July 10	July 17	July 24	July 31
Erie R.R.	27	28	32	35	35
Illinois Central R.R.	116	120	119	117	119
Michigan Central R.R.	81	82	83	79	85
New York Central R.R.	80	80	83	85	83
Pennsylvania Coal	91	92	96	92	87
Reading R.R.	72	78	78	74	72

Source: *New York Herald*, July 4–August 1, 1857

N. H. Wolfe & Co. failed on August 11. The oldest flour and grain company in the city, and a conservatively run concern, its bankruptcy shook confidence on Wall Street. The *Times* remained hopeful. "Our present impression is, that without reaching to the high prices of 1853, our leading railway funds will gradually recover in public appreciation to at least a more creditable standard than by comparison with the banking and mercantile interests they occupy at present." Referring to Bennett's crusade against the Michigan Central, the *Times* was "content to abide patiently the coming of such a reaction, rather than join in the hue and cry of the Stock Exchange against this property, or add to the general distrust, and thus hasten 'a crisis' of our own imagination by wild and wicked prognostics of 'convulsion and ruin' to banks and merchants, as well as railroads." The *Herald's* reaction was short and to the point. "The stock market is decidedly sick. There is no health in it. The supply of weak, sickly stock securities pressing for sale is very great, and there are no buyers, no demand from any source. . . ."

Financial and monetary statistics, which appeared weekly in all the New York papers, seemed to bear out Bennett's gloom. Bank loans, gold in circulation, deposits—all fell in August. The *Times* noted that the declines were due to the usual seasonal shrinkages, as Western farmers called in their deposits. The *Herald* was silent on this point, but Bennett knew August had always been a month of low liquidity. All the same, the banking system was more vulnerable by mid-month than it had been all year.

FINANCIAL CONDITION OF NEW YORK BANKS, AUGUST 1857

Week Ending	Loans	Gold	Circulation	Deposits
August 8	$122,077,000	$11,737,000	$8,982,000	$67,372,000
August 15	121,241,000	11,361,000	8,780,000	66,815,000
August 22	120,140,000	10,097,000	8,694,000	64,241,000
August 29	116,589,000	9,241,000	8,671,000	60,861,000

Source: *New York Herald*, August 9–30, 1857

On August 19, Edwin C. Litchfield, president of the Michigan Central, resigned, "in order to spend more time on personal matters." Securities prices had been drifting downward since the beginning of the month. Now, as Bennett's predictions came true, prices began to tumble. Again the *Times* argued that the economic situation was bright. Bennett responded on August 23, stating flatly that "in all human probability, every railroad in the United States will become bankrupt in the course of the next six or eight years. There may be a few exceptions; but they will be uncommonly few." The following morning, President Charles Stetson of the Ohio Life & Trust Company announced that the New York branch of his firm had suspended payments.

Ohio Life & Trust specialized in placing Eastern and foreign

PRICES OF SELECTED ISSUES, AUGUST 1857

Issue	Closing Prices (fractions rounded off)		
	August 7	August 14	August 21
Erie R.R.	34	32	28
Illinois Central R.R.	120	117	113
Michigan Central R.R.	85	84	79
New York Central R.R.	83	81	76
Pennsylvania Coal	84	81	73
Reading R.R.	72	69	67

Source: *New York Herald*, August 8–22, 1857

funds in Western investments, especially land, railroads, and commodity futures. Its failure reached into all sections of the country; as Bennett and others had predicted, the web of credit was about to collapse. Prices fell sharply on Wall Street that morning, but recovered some of the loss in the afternoon auction. The decline continued steady and regular for the rest of the week, as news of more failures appeared daily. The Michigan Central was

PRICES OF SELECTED ISSUES, AUGUST 22–29, 1857

Issue	Closing Prices (fractions rounded off)						
	Aug. 22	Aug. 24	Aug. 25	Aug. 26	Aug. 27	Aug. 28	Aug. 29
Erie R.R.	28	25	no trade	23	20	22	21
Illinois Central R.R.	112	112	104	100	99	92	90
Michigan Central R.R.	75	76	76	71	75	69	67
New York Central R.R.	77	75	74	74	73	74	74
Pennsylvania Coal	69	68	64	60	63	64	66
Reading R.R.	68	63	61	61	61	60	58

Source: *New York Herald*, August 23–30, 1857

struck down on August 25th, the result of overcapitalization and speculation more than manipulations by Jerome and his friends. The *St. Louis Intelligencer* was quoted approvingly on the subject by the *Times*:

And all this ruin of families and fortunes has been brought about by the unprincipled course of a set of stock gamblers in Wall Street, New-York, who probably never owned, legitimately, one-thousandth part of stock in the road they ruined. They have sold the stock, *to be delivered at a future date*, and then set about inventing the most atrocious and rascally lies in regard to the road and its management; and in the *New York Herald* they found a willing instrument to circulate their falsehoods and thus, finally, after six months of desperate detraction, they have accomplished their work, and brought ruin and distress on thousands of orphans, widows, and aged persons, who have no hope of recovery.

Like most national papers, the *Intelligencer* blamed the crash on Wall Street speculations, and not on weaknesses in the economy. In late August, the panic was believed by most to be a local, transitory phenomenon. "A financial crisis in Wall Street, which seems to have run its course and terminated in convalescence much sooner than the Bear predicted"—thus George Templeton Strong dismissed the panic when writing in his diary of August 30. Attempting to see the failures as isolated events, the *Times* asked, "Why push it to extremes because the Ohio Trust Bank has suspended payments? Does everything in the way of securities go to pieces because one concern has been mistaken or unfortunate in selecting its borrowers?" Henry Raymond blamed the Wall Street speculators for the crash in values. "The Stock Exchange, as at present managed, is very little more than an enormous gambling establishment—and the whole scale of its operations is quite as ruinous, quite as infamous, as any of the Broadway hells which have recently enjoyed the attention of the Metropolitan Police." Greeley's *Tribune* called for action, saying that Raymond was doing little more than asking for public prayers while Bennett predicted the end of the world. "It is absolutely necessary that men and institutions which have means and influence should exert themselves in calming the public mind; in checking the progress of the present crisis; and in restoring as much as possible, public confidence in the general soundness of the country." To which Bennett, reporting the securities dealings of August 25, wrote, "Wall Street was in a fever of excitement throughout the day. We have not seen for years anything like it. The panic was deep and widespread; the decline in railroad stocks and in stock securities generally ranged from three to seven per cent."

Bennett was closer to the truth than his rivals. Panic had developed and new failures were announced hourly. De Launay, Iselin & Clark, private bankers, suspended operations on August 25, along with E. S. Monroe and John Thompson, who were described as "speculators." E. A. Benedict and E. F. Post, also speculators, were unable to meet their obligations the following day; the former had been bullish on Illinois Central, while Post was a leading owner of Ohio Life common. Jacob Little, most famous of Wall Street figures, went under on the 27th. Ironically, Little failed not through betting the wrong way, but rather because those who owed him stock and money were unable to deliver. In writing (with errors) of the event, the *Times* pontificated:

There was another *crack* in Wall-Street yesterday. Jacob Little faded again, and his example was imitated by several others. They were all, however, of the fraternity of Stock Gamblers, and failed mainly because they found it more convenient to do so than to pay their losses and fulfil their contracts. These contracts were for the delivery of stocks on time, and as they were not recognized in law it is for those who make them to fulfil them or not as they may see fit. These debts are, like those of other gamblers, debts of honor;—and it is getting quite fashionable among our Stock Exchange speculators to consider the *honor* involved merely a matter of convenience.

The Wall Street collapse had been caused in part by banking weaknesses, speculation, and overexpansion, but the lack of a strong force in the district was also to blame. Even so, the worst was over insofar as securities prices were concerned; while the newspapers wrote of panic, stocks firmed on the Exchange.

The first bank failures appeared in early September. A closing in one city would result in several elsewhere, and these in turn to still more. Runs on New York banks became commonplace, and the Hanover, Metropolitan, and Bank of Commerce suffered. The Mechanics' Banking Association closed, as did a score of other minor organizations. Gold started to go into hiding or was sent overseas for safekeeping. Thinly capitalized railroads fell—in September the Delaware, Lackawanna & Western, the Fond du Lac, and several smaller roads went into receivership. New York banks

PRICES OF SELECTED ISSUES, SEPTEMBER 1–12, 1857

| Issue | Closing Prices (fractions rounded off) | | | | | |
	Sept. 1	Sept. 2	Sept. 3	Sept. 4	Sept. 5	Sept. 7
Erie R.R.	20	22	24	24	22	22
Illinois Central R.R.	90	95	110	99	93	96
Michigan Central R.R.	64	63	66	66	64	67
New York Central R.R.	72	73	76	77	76	72
Pennsylvania Coal	68	69	72	75	74	75
Reading R.R.	53	53	56	52	52	50

Issue	Sept. 8	Sept. 9	Sept. 10	Sept. 11	Sept. 12
Erie R.R.	21	21	20	20	20
Illinois Central R.R.	91	90	95	93	92
Michigan Central R.R.	64	64	66	64	64
New York Central R.R.	73	71	70	70	70
Pennsylvania Coal	71	69	70	69	70
Reading R.R.	50	43	44	45	48

Source: *New York Times*, September 2–13, 1857

which had railroad securities in their portfolios faced large losses, which compounded the problems of seasonal withdrawals. Despite this, no major institution was obliged to declare bankruptcy during the first half of the month. Considered by many the weakest link in the economy, the banking system showed surprising strength in late August and early September. Despite runs and shortages, most key institutions held fast.

Expectation of a large gold shipment from California, due sometime in late September, helped bolster confidence and provided hope of an eventual recovery. But nature conspired against this. On September 12, the steamer *Central America*, with $1.6 million in California gold in its hold, sank in a hurricane off Cape Hatteras. The gold was lost, along with the lives of more than four hundred passengers and crew. Gold production had been low since January, but in the past had provided psychological support for the economy. News of the sinking reached New York shortly thereafter and precipitated a new wave of panic as well as failures among the major banks. Institutions in Philadelphia and Baltimore were forced to stop gold payments on September 25, and it seemed only a matter of days before New York followed their lead.

Previous Presidents had done little to stem panics, and had Buchanan remained quiet few could have criticized him. On the other hand, Secretary of the Treasury Howell Cobb saw a way to restore confidence while at the same time preserving the appearance of aloofness. The Treasury still had a substantial gold balance, which could easily be coined and put into the monetary system. Cobb began purchasing state bonds, redeeming paper with gold, and in other ways sending the yellow metal to the public. For a while the scheme worked, but a flood of redemptions quickly dried out the gold supply. The October shipment of California gold temporarily bolstered confidence, but on October 13, Cobb was forced to stop redemptions of paper and disbursement of gold, and news of this led to new panic in the cities.

The Atlantic Cable, which had become a symbol of a more optimistic America, broke down in the first week of the panic; the *Tribune* thought it an evil omen. Nonetheless, London and Paris quickly learned of what had happened on Wall Street, and Lombard Street and the Bourse were to feel the effects of what had been dubbed "The Western Blizzard." More than a third of all foreign securities traded in these capitals were American, and their collapse affected the entire list. On October 12, the Bank of England asked its agent to practice "guarded caution" regarding the tense market situation. The next week London learned of a fresh wave of bank failures in the American West. The Bank of England's money rate began to rise sharply, reaching 8 percent on October 8, after an unprecedented rise of 3 percent in less than a month. Failures were reported shortly thereafter, and only prompt and effective actions by the Bank of England prevented widespread damage.

The American panic was more harmful to Paris, where the Credit Mobilier bubble was about to burst. There was a sharp decline on the Bourse in early October, adding to Louis Napoleon's already growing list of problems. Exchanges in central Europe were also affected, in what was soon recognized as the first international panic of modern times. As Disraeli later put it, "All the bubbles, blunders, and dishonesties of five years' European exuberance and experimentations in credit were tested or revealed."

Meanwhile, the chain of failures grew in America. The Erie and Pittsburgh and the Fort Wayne & Chicago went bankrupt in October, as did the Reading and Illinois Central. Bennett's prediction that eventually all lines would be in receivership seemed possible in late October. George Strong, who little more than a month earlier thought the panic a local matter, was deep in gloom by this time.

We seem foundering. Affairs are worse than ever today, and a period of general insolvency seems close upon us. People say, "we must reach the bottom soon," but the bottom has certainly come out. Depression and depletion are going on without any sign of limit and promise to continue till we reach zero point or universal suspension. This attack is far more sudden, acute and prostrating than that of 1837. Will the banks stand it? I think *not*, and predict their downfall within ten days.

More banks did fall, as waves from the West reached New York and then rebounded to wipe out more Western institutions. William Herndon, Lincoln's partner, thought "The most of us are determined to stand firm," while William Tecumseh Sherman wrote from St. Louis that "You can have no idea of the troubles here." Late in December U.S. Grant, no longer in the Army, pawned his watch for $22 in order to buy Christmas gifts for his children. In New York Mayor Fernando Wood promised economic aid but added that none would be given to slackers. Wood also attacked the city's rich. Most New Yorkers, he said, "labor without income while surrounded by thousands in selfishness and splendor who have income without labor." New riots erupted; more misery was felt.

New York financial leaders met to discuss means of ending the panic. Without sound banks, recovery would be impossible, and so they would attempt to salvage their institutions. Early in September some suggested ending gold payments until the crisis passed. This would put a stop to the bank runs, and preserve gold for foreign dealings. The idea was quickly rejected; such a move would destroy whatever confidence remained in the dollar. Nonetheless, by early October it seemed the only solution. In any case, suspension was inevitable, since few New York banks had gold left in their vaults. On October 13, after learning of the end of Treasury gold support, some banks announced suspensions, and others followed the next day. From October 13 to October 15 there were tremendous runs on these institutions. "Wall Street blue with collapse. Everything limp and flaccid like a defunct Actina," wrote George Strong on October 15.

Strong's forebodings were not based on the irrational fears seen on Wall Street and elsewhere, but rather on the banking statistics in the newspapers each week. They showed, to the practiced reader, that despite a continuation of contraction in September and a fall in deposits, there were no signs of bank runs in New York. Not until mid-October did the New York banks suffer a truly sharp drop in deposits and gold. These statistics illustrate that the week of October 19 was the worst point of the panic in terms of the banking situation. In the following weeks, confidence returned and an upswing developed.

Deposits rose, in part as a result of the normal return flow to

**FINANCIAL CONDITION OF NEW YORK BANKS, SEPTEMBER–
DECEMBER, 1857**

Week Ending	Loans	Gold	Circulation	Deposits
September 5	$112,221,000	$10,228,000	$8,673,000	$57,261,000
September 12	109,986,000	12,182,000	8,322,000	57,334,000
September 19	108,777,000	13,556,000	8,074,000	57,852,000
September 26	107,791,000	13,327,000	7,838,000	56,919,000
October 3	105,935,000	11,400,000	7,916,000	52,798,000
October 10	101,917,000	11,476,000	7,524,000	49,745,000
October 17	97,246,000	7,843,000	8,087,000	42,696,000
October 24	95,593,000	10,411,000	6,884,000	47,873,000
October 31	95,317,000	12,883,000	6,334,000	51,583,000
November 7	95,866,000	16,492,000	6,434,000	56,424,000
November 14	95,239,000	19,451,000	6,258,000	60,601,000
November 21	95,375,000	23,167,000	6,283,000	64,917,000
November 28	94,963,000	24,303,000	6,520,000	64,307,000
December 5	96,333,000	26,069,000	6,555,000	64,444,000
December 12	96,526,000	26,058,000	6,348,000	62,908,000
December 19	97,211,000	27,957,000	6,309,000	63,710,000
December 26	97,902,000	27,142,000	6,352,000	65,239,000

Source: *New York Herald*, September 6–December 27, 1857

New York after the crops were sold. Gold reserves increased sharply, an indication of public confidence in the banks after mid-October. But loans and money in circulation remained stable and depressed, a sign that economic activity had not as yet begun to pick up significantly.

Prices on Wall Street also reached their low points in October, and then began to rise slowly but without conviction. A careful analysis of the trading indicates that there was no pattern insofar as a "general movement" was concerned. Instead, each issue moved up or down as specific news was released, or when a bull or bear group selected it for speculation. Wall Street was considered by many the symbol of the depression, but price movements and volume figures show clearly that the Exchange was not yet as powerful or indispensable as Bennett and his group thought it to

PRICES OF SELECTED ISSUES, 1857

Issue	Jan.	Feb.	March	April	May	June
			End of Month Closing Prices (fractions rounded off)			
Bank of Commerce	104	105	106	106	107	108
Pennsylvania Coal	100	94	95	93	94	90
Pacific Mail	66	68	70	74	71	74
Erie R.R.	62	57	54	42	38	27
New York Central R.R.	91	90	89	88	87	76
Reading R.R.	81	81	79	81	81	69
Panama R.R.	95	95	94	95	95	90
Michigan Central R.R.	96	96	95	95	94	81
Illinois Central R.R.	129	136	132	135	139	127

	July	Aug.	Sept.	Oct.	Nov.	Dec.
Bank of Commerce	105	100	82	76	92	100
Pennsylvania Coal	87	69	62	61	60	68
Pacific Mail	74	66	60	74	68	66
Erie R.R.	34	21	11	13	16	18
New York Central R.R.	86	76	60	65	74	74
Reading R.R.	73	59	32	30	54	55
Panama R.R.	95	82	71	72	87	94
Michigan Central R.R.	84	66	43	40	54	53
Illinois Central R.R.	110	86	84	81	94	88

Source: *New York Times*

be, or as important a litmus as it would be later on. Prices moved upward in December, for example, but in that month the situation became critical in several large cities, as mobs broke into coalyards to steal fuel and into stores for Christmas gifts which no longer could be afforded. New York suffered more from the December riots than did any other city. Crowds gathered in Tompkins Square nightly to protest, to hear radical solutions for the nation's ills, and then go on to riot elsewhere. The crime rate rose, and murders led the list. Emboldened by success, the Dead Rabbits entered City Hall, threw out the municipal administration, and held the center of government for more than an hour before leaving.

Stock prices rose as a result of the resumption of gold payments on December 12, but this did not mean the panic and depression were over. Indeed, in early January economic conditions seemed worse than they had appeared in October. As business and political leaders seemed unable to end the crisis, religious sects called for appeals to God. A Dutch Reformed minister, Reverend Lamphire, thought an hour of prayer each day might help distraught businessmen. Others followed his lead, and several churches opened in the business district, to excellent attendance. Throughout the nation thousands went to tent meetings or joined urban congregations to ask forgiveness for sins, real and imagined. The movement—called "The Great Revival"—had its beginnings before the panic of 1857, but the Western Blizzard was the catalyst that brought many to the churches, where they prayed for an end to bloodshed in Kansas, civil strife in the cities, and a return to prosperity. The usually staid *Journal of Commerce* thought prayer might be the answer, and asked its readers to

> Steal awhile away from Wall Street
> and every worldly care,
> And spend an hour about mid-day
> in humble, hopeful prayer.

Statistics indicate that the worst of the depression was over by late 1858. In that year, for the first time in a decade, foreign sales of American securities exceeded investment by the impressive figure of $23 million. The tide turned in 1859, as $26 million flowed back to America. Pig-iron production fell from 883,000 tons in 1856 to 798,000 in 1857, and then to a low of 705,000 tons the following year. There was substantial recovery late in 1858, however, and in 1859 production reached 841,000 tons, going on to a new high of 920,000 tons in 1860. This did not mean prosperity for the ironmongers, however, as the price of their product fell from $27.12 a ton in 1856 to $22.75 in 1860. But lower prices allowed American iron to compete overseas and gave stimulation to the industrial sector of the economy. Similarly, the price of American cotton goods fell from 1856 to 1860, but production

ALL-INCLUSIVE INDEX OF RAILROAD STOCK PRICES: MONTHLY, 1850–1860

Year	Jan.	Feb.	Mar.	April	May	June
1850	80	79	82	81	84	86
1851	94	95	94	96	95	96
1852	89	89	94	96	98	98
1853	105	104	103	102	105	104
1854	94	94	98	96	93	93
1855	67	74	76	76	76	77
1856	68	68	72	73	72	70
1857	71	71	71	68	68	63
1858	49	52	61	55	58	56
1859	56	54	54	51	50	47
1860	48	48	50	55	59	61

Year	July	Aug.	Sept.	Oct.	Nov.	Dec.
1850	83	84	85	90	91	95
1851	93	87	88	89	91	92
1852	99	101	102	103	106	110
1853	103	98	96	95	89	96
1854	85	79	74	77	74	67
1855	80	79	78	75	66	68
1856	71	71	68	68	68	71
1857	58	61	52	39	42	49
1858	53	56	55	54	56	56
1859	47	48	49	48	47	50
1860	61	67	70	74	66	57

Source: Smith & Cole, *Fluctuations in Business*, p. 184

rose significantly, as America continued to invade England's markets for cheap textiles. Coal production rose quickly after the short depression, and railroad mileage reached new highs, even in the worst days of the panic. In 1856, the nation had 22,076 miles of track; by 1860, the figure was 31,286 miles. Federal deficits persisted, giving the economy an aura of depression, and prices at the Exchange remained low, reinforcing the gloom.

Every part of the nation suffered from the panic and depression, with the exception of California, where gold production provided a note of optimism. New York and Boston were hard hit, but so were Indianapolis and St. Louis, New Orleans and Charleston. The East suffered the most, but its recovery was rapid, as most statistics indicate. Still, the gloomy atmosphere so evident in Eastern cities in 1858 was not dispelled two years later. The economic aspects of the depression were over, but psychological scars remained.

Southern leaders looked at the statistics for cotton and saw that it remained a major product throughout the period. American cotton worth $128 million had been exported in 1856; in 1857, the value was $132 million, despite a decline in shipments from 1.4 million pounds to one million pounds. In 1860 cotton brought $192 million to America, as exports reached a new high of 1.8

COTTON PRODUCTION, 1850–1859

Year	Production (1,000 bales)
1850	2.1
1851	2.8
1852	3.1
1853	2.8
1854	2.7
1855	3.2
1856	2.9
1857	3.0
1858	3.7
1859	4.5

Source: *Historical Statistics,* p. 302

million pounds. Cotton production had not been affected severely by the depression, and it continued to grow even more rapidly in the depression period. Whatever difficulty the South had in 1857 was blamed on the North. On October 14 the *Charleston Mercury* asked:

Why does the South allow itself to be tattered and torn by the dissensions and death struggles of New York money changers? Why not trade directly with our customers? What need is there for this go-between to convey to the markets of the world our rich products, for which the consumers stand ready, gold in hand, to pay the full value.

Southern banks had failed, but in smaller numbers than those of the North and West. The *New Orleans Picayune* declared with pride:

In the process of healthy reaction, the banks are stronger than they were when the northern suspensions alarmed the sensitive billholder, and caused that senseless run which produced so much mischief. The steadiness with which these banks sustained themselves against the shock, and the strength with which they have righted themselves so speedily, are proofs of the intrinsic excellence of the principles upon which they are organized; and the endurance and success with which the commercial community stood up under the intense pressure which these curtailments called for, are titles to confidence of inestimable value to their future prosperity and that of the city.

The cause for this happy situation was the nature of the Southern economy. "The wealth of the South is permanent and real, that of the North fugitive and fictitious. Events now transpiring are exposing the fiction as humbug after humbug explodes." So wrote *DeBow's Review* in December 1857. Senator James Hammond of South Carolina, a firebrand who nonetheless had counseled moderation in the past, was now convinced that cotton had saved the national economy. Speaking to his Northern colleagues, he said:

Cotton is king! Who can doubt it that has looked upon recent events? When the abuse of credit annihilated confidence . . . when you came to a deadlock and revolutions were threatened, what brought you up? Fortunately for you it was the commencement of the cotton season and we have poured upon you one million six hundred thousand bales of cotton just at the crisis to save you.

Many Northerners tended to agree, and echoed the belief that cotton was vital to the economy, while the loss of money earned through its export would ruin the nation. "There is no disrupting the fact that the southern portion of the Confederacy is in a highly prosperous condition," wrote the New Orleans correspondent of the *Times* on March 25, 1859.

Of all the great staples produced, the crops during the past year have been abundant, sales active, and prices high. No species of property has felt the effect of this state of affairs more sensibly than the negroes. The average price of field hands may be stated at $1500 and the tendency is upward. A-1 niggers sell for $1750 to $2000. These rates were never reached but once before, and that was during the speculative times of 1836. The South is getting out of debt and beginning to accumulate surplus capital.

To which the pro-Southern *Herald,* in its January 13, 1859 edition, added:

We have not thought it necessary to go over Southern states seriatim as we have done with the West. The comparative prosperity prevailing there, the general healthy tone of business, and the absence of excessive and wild speculation, have rendered it in our judgement unnecessary. . . . The accounts from all parts of the South, except portions of Virginia, are uniform in their testimony that trade is in a healthy condition.

Three months later, the correspondent of the *Commercial Advertiser* wrote that the "unexampled prosperity" of the South was intact, and that a friend who had just returned from that section "after spending several of the winter months in New Orleans informed us that he has seldom witnessed such evidence of prosperity and rapidly accumulating wealth."

Prior to the panic of 1857, many Southern leaders who harbored hopes of secession believed an independent Southern nation might not be able to survive and could not withstand pressures

from the North. Events of 1857 and 1858 caused them to re-
assess the situation. The North is paralyzed, thought Governor
Herschel Johnson of Georgia, while the South "stands calm and
unmoved, poised upon the consciousness of her capacity to out-
ride the tempest." Senator Hammond added that while the panic
and depression had cost the North and West $142 million,
Southern losses were less than $17 million. New Orleans and
Charleston banks seemed in better shape than those of Philadelphia and New York. Western railroads had fallen in the
depression, while those of the South were barely touched. To such
men, the Southern economy appeared far stronger than that of
any other section. The South could survive without the North or
West, but without cotton the other sections would be doomed.

Looking at prices on Wall Street, Southern leaders concluded
that the Northern economy was still shaky and would collapse
quickly in time of war, as would the Northern banking structure.
The riots of 1857 led them to believe that in a civil war Northern
workers would rise in revolt and become their allies. James
Bennett observed that the black slaves of the South were being
fed, while 200,000 workers had lost their jobs in the North. "In
view of these . . . facts," wrote Bennett on September 29, 1857,
"how can any candid, common sense man profess the belief that
slavery is a horrible, atrocious, accursed, God-defying sin?" If
slaves hated their masters, so out-of-work laborers would have
all the more reason to wish to overthrow their former employers.
This they would do in case of civil war. But Bennett thought the
panic and depression would prevent such a conflict. "The nigger
question must give way to the superior issues of a safe currency,
sound credits, and solid and permanent basis of security upon
which all the varied commercial and business interests of the
country may repose." Slavery would recede into the background,
and the nation would unite to bring about recovery. Unless
Americans turned their thoughts from the slavery issue, thought
Bennett, war would erupt, and with it the triumph of the South.

Utah remained a smoldering area of potential danger; the
North would have to send armies there if war erupted. Washington was unable to put down an insurrection in Kansas; how could
it deal with a larger one involving the entire South? England and

France, which viewed their financial difficulties as having their roots in the Western Blizzard, could be counted upon to have Southern sympathies—which would be added to their obvious dependence upon Southern cotton. In such circumstances, secession became not only feasible but also an almost riskless venture.

The panic of 1857 was the worst collapse up to that time, and so its effects were exaggerated by the imaginations of individuals in all parts of the nation. It led to despair in the North and optimism in the South, months after recovery could be discerned by businessmen and bankers, planters and factors. On Wall Street it wiped out a generation of conservative, old-fashioned bankers and brokers, and made it possible for younger, more daring speculators to take their places. By 1860, the fruits of the panic could be seen in preparations for Southern secession in Washington and Charleston, and the beginnings of a new era of speculation on Wall Street.

4.
THE CIRCUS COMES
TO TOWN: 1865–69

The war wrought a physical transformation on Wall Street. The financial district and its environs had undergone their most hectic period up to that time, one which saw the opening of several rival exchanges, the introduction of around-the-clock trading in hotel lobbies, and the rapid construction of an intelligence network better than that used by either the Union or Confederate governments. Most of the stables and the many taverns that had dominated the landscape since the colonial era were torn down and replaced by brokerages, insurance offices, and banks. Real-estate values had increased sharply, and eating places had to move to the west side of Broadway or uptown, while the stables expanded outward to form a ring around the district. Now the runners and clerks had to go to Trinity Place and Cedar Street for lunch. During the war a dozen or so small restaurants appeared there, and they catered to young men who had just begun their careers in business. The most popular of them, Fred Blacke's, served a large slice of brown bread and a bowl of milk for ten cents.

Senior clerks and junior brokers congregated at Henry Cunningham's Bar & Grill on Broadway near Eighth Avenue, where they rubbed shoulders with actors and artists. Others went to Thomas Stewart's horseshoe bar, which featured an impressive collection of paintings and prints and soon became the stamping ground for junior partners. The heads of large houses, bankers, and the *nouveaux riches* could be seen at Delmonico's, which had a room on William Street and another at Chambers Street and Broadway.

Rudolph Staudinger's, a fine restaurant located at Pine and Wall Streets, was considered the best eating place near the Exchange.

The Wall Street area had jelled, taking on that essential form of a banking-insurance-brokerage complex which characterizes it today. Then, as now, one could find sharpers, plungers, and eccentrics. But men like Henry Clews, a pillar of his church, a person of eminent respectability, a chatty social climber, and a shrewd analyst, made up the large majority of those who worked in the financial district. An upright Victorian, Clews was considered a broker of honor and integrity, which meant that he would participate in raids, pools and corners but did not associate with known criminals. The public morality was high, even though the private left something to be desired. This type of integrity might be illustrated by noting that the robberies of gold which had led to the formation of the Exchange Bank came to an end, and the honor of the Street returned. By the late 1860s gold was transported openly, carried by messengers in heavy canvas bags. From time to time one of the bags would burst, and its contents—usually $5,000 in coin—would scatter in the street. The custom on these occasions was for a crowd to form a circle around the area, not moving until the messenger had picked up all the coins. Anyone who stooped to take a gold piece would receive a boot in the rear.

This is not to say that all those who worked on Wall Street were honest: pickpockets, petty thieves, and confidence men could always be found in the district. For a while, Captain Sampson of the New York Police kept a special force in the area on the lookout for irregularities. One patrolman, Phil Farley, was particularly adept at spotting thieves, earning himself the title of "the Sherlock Holmes of the Financial District."

Late in the war, orators made a practice of setting up shop near the Subtreasury, where they spoke throughout the day, but especially during lunch hour. Henry Smith, who for some reason was called "the Razor Strop Man," used to attract crowds numbering in the hundreds. He was eventually barred from the district for inciting to riot, but his descendants can be found at his old spot today, exorting Wall Streeters to renounce their love of Mammon, stop drinking and smoking, and ban nuclear war.

The Street was full of characters who would entertain onlookers and panhandle at the same time. One, called "the Frenchman," who wore several decorations which he claimed had been awarded him by Napoleon I, would sing patriotic French and American songs for pennies and nickels. Former speculators who had lost all their winnings on unsuccessful raids and corners could be seen there. Lower Broad Street had many pawnshops where they hocked their clothes, jewelry, and everything else that had been bought in lush times. These "spouts" were the busiest in the city during sharp rises and falls at the Exchange; some did a greater volume of business than many medium-size brokerages. "I have learned my lesson," said one speculator, "and though X, Y or Z, the spout holders, have my money, I have been taught that legitimate business is better than feverish speculation." William Worthington Fowler, a grandson of Noah Webster, wrote of the Street during this period in a florid fashion. He reflected that "some delve in the broad prairies, some plow the main, some go back to their ancestral farms, or their avuncular merchandise." Fowler called the pawnshops "living museums" of the Civil War boom.

Civil War speculation hastened the retirement of many older men who had remained after the 1857 panic to protest the new styles on Wall Street, and it brought replacements from all parts of the nation. These new men quickly threw up leaders whose exploits seemed as daring as those of Grant and Lee. The lure of quick money attracted them. According to one contemporary source there were approximately twenty millionaires in America in 1843. By the middle of the war there were more than one hundred in New York alone. This increase was both a cause and result of the new glamour of high finance.

One of these new men was Anthony Wellman Morse, a short redheaded speculator whose boldness and nerve amazed Wall Streeters during 1863 and 1864. Morse had come to New York from New Hampshire in 1851, when he was seventeen years old. After working for several concerns, he settled down as chief clerk for Corning & Co., which fell during the 1857 panic. Morse then formed a partnership with Edward Wolf, but the firm of Morse & Wolf collapsed early in the war. Undaunted, he organ-

ized a new company with his brother, and at the beginning of
the next bull market, in 1862, was a member of the Board with
offices at 24 William Street.

Morse's specialty was the bull corner in rails, and on at least
five occasions during the war he managed to fight almost the
entire Open Board to win his point. Relying upon private messengers, he learned of the Confederate victory at Chancellors-
ville in 1863 and went long on gold before the news hit Wall
Street. When it did, prices rose rapidly. Morse covered his
contracts and made a profit of over $200,000 on this one deal.
He could not go wrong in the months that followed; other
brokers were fearful of Morse's apparent clairvoyance in matters
of the markets. Once he openly bid for the entire capital stock
of Pittsburgh Railroad, then selling for 80, offering 100 "for the
whole lot or any part." Anyone who wished could have bought
the stock and sold to Morse, making a profit. The scheme seemed
too good to be true, however, and not trusting the uncrowned
King of Wall Street, the brokers bought all they could on margin,
paying well over 100 for the contracts. If Morse was buying at
100, they reasoned, it must be because he knew the price would
go over that bid. At the end of the day the brokers learned that
they had bought Pittsburgh shares from Morse himself, who
realized the stock was not worth more than 80 but had counted
on their belief in his omniscience to bid the price up more than
twenty points. When the brokers discovered that Morse had not
really meant to buy at 100, they sold heavily at the evening exchanges. Morse then stepped in and picked up the dumped stock
at below 80, selling it at a profit a few days later. Thus he made
a killing twice on the same ruse. His charge for this skillful lesson
in speculation came to over $500,000.

Morse's great moment of glory came in early April 1864, when
he caused sharp rises in Rock Island, Erie, Fort Wayne, Pittsburgh, and Ohio and Mississippi by buying a few hundred shares
of each. Several bear rings were formed in an attempt to beat the
prices down, but they failed, and fortunes were lost by those
who opposed Morse. His fall came when he tried to bull Fort
Wayne to new heights, at a time when practically all other Wall
Street concerns were turning bearish. Morse and his friends lost

hundreds of thousands of dollars when the market fell on April 16 and 17. On the next day shares broke downward sharply, and Morse was almost wiped out. When the evening sessions saw a further decline, the firm of Morse & Co. was obliged to declare bankruptcy. A few months later the King of Wall Street died in a shabby rooming house. Because he was behind on his rent, the landlady refused to surrender the body to his family until the debt was paid. A few old friends redeemed the corpse.

One of those Morse had defeated in several bull raids was John W. Tobin. Coming to Wall Street in 1862 with a total capital of five hundred dollars, Tobin bluffed the speculators into believing he was worth hundreds of thousands of dollars. He dropped hints of secret connections with Commodore Vanderbilt, whom he didn't know at that time. Thus, whenever he bought or sold, the brokers assumed he was acting for or with the all-powerful Commodore. When Tobin was introduced to Vanderbilt the two hit it off; together they engineered several of the largest coups of the period. The bear brokers learned of the deception only many years later.

Tobin's greatest success came in 1864, when he gained a corner in Harlem Railroad. Through spies, he had learned that the Common Council of New York City would favor that line over Commodore Vanderbilt's Broadway Railroad in some contract awards. When the news broke and Harlem stock rose sharply, Tobin was able to sell shares that had cost him $40 for $164.

The following year Tobin once more scored heavily with Harlem, on this occasion working with Vanderbilt. At that time the Council had decided to revoke the road's grants. Several members of the city government entered the market and sold Harlem short, in expectation of a decline when the news was made public. Knowing of this scheme, Tobin and Vanderbilt began buying every share they could find, running the price up from 80 to 285. When word of the contract revocation hit Wall Street, panicked sellers found that the two men were willing to buy their shares at the same high level as before. As a result Harlem did not fall, and the Council members were obliged to cover their short sales with purchases at a far higher price than that at which they had sold. The only people on Wall Street from whom they could buy were Tobin and Vanderbilt, who had cornered Harlem. Several brokerages fell as a result of this trick, the councilmen were publicly embarrassed, and the two conspirators made a net profit of $3 million.

Addison G. Jerome, "the Napoleon of the Open Board," had his day in the sun in 1863, when through a series of raids he became the most feared man on Wall Street. Within the first nine months of the year the shrewd speculator made over $3 million. Jerome had a fine mentor for his spectacular debut; his brother Leonard, mentioned in a previous chapter, had made several killings on the Street. Leonard had quit while he was ahead. Leaving Wall Street, he went to Paris, where he lived a long and affluent life. Addison was not so fortunate. After successfully cornering four railroads, in this way making his reputation and fortune, he lost everything in an attempt to manipulate Pacific Mail and Old Southern. Addison died of a heart attack in 1864, ending a brief but exciting career. This colorful grand-uncle of Winston Churchill would have been destitute were it not for a birthday present of several hundred thousand dollars he had given his wife in lusher days.

Addison Jerome was defeated by Henry Keep, who was rumored to have been born in a poorhouse. A quiet man who distrusted everyone on Wall Street, he was known as "Henry the Silent." Keep was the first master of the "pool," in which several speculators combined their assets to manage a corner and then divided the profits or losses according to the proportion of investments. Pools had been used prior to Keep's day, but he refined and polished the technique. So clever was he that the members trusted Keep to run the first of the "blind pools." In this operation each member paid a certain amount of money to the manager, who would use it for a speculation. So as to prevent any one member from using information gained during the meetings to secretly work against his fellows at the market, no one was to know when the stock would be bought or sold, how the corner would be accomplished, or even which stock was chosen for the manipulation. Keep considered it a great honor for his colleagues to have given him so much latitude. He never betrayed a confidence, and as his reputation grew, so did the length of the list of men willing to join his blind pools. At the height of his career, Keep could raise a million dollars in less than a week.

Keep's most famous pools were in Michigan, Southern Railroad and Cleveland & Ohio. His operations in Chicago & Northwestern earned him over $1.5 million in eight months. Rufus Hatch, who went along in one blind pool, made $2,185,000 on an investment of $100,000 because of Keep's good judgment. Henry the Silent died wealthy, leaving an estate of $4.5 million in 1869.

Tales of other Wall Streeters active in this period could be told almost indefinitely. William H. Marston's pool in Prairie du Chien raised the price of that obscure rail from 60 to 250 in one week. W. S. Woodward, said to have bought and sold more shares than anyone else during the war, ran pools in five rails simultaneously and won in all. Addison Cammack, who left his Kentucky plantation for Wall Street just before the attack on Fort Sumter, made a fortune in gold contracts by betting on Confederate defeats. A mild man with pleasant manners, Cammack was one of the few who spared his victims; he would take payment up to the point of bankrupting the losers, but not beyond. This kindness was returned when Cammack had his back to the wall. His thirty-five-year career in finance was a happy exception to the cutthroat activities of other speculators.

Finally, there was David Groesbeck, known to his friends as "Grosy," who had been schooled by the master, Jacob Little. Groesbeck was Little's last partner, and he helped support the old man after his final bankruptcy. Like Cammack, Groesbeck was a quiet man, with limited ambitions. In 1864 he opened a broker's office, promising to handle other people's money and never to speculate with it on his own. Groesbeck's fortune was made in commissions, since many of the greatest plungers used his rooms as headquarters for their pools, giving him business in payment. He probably knew more about the financial district than any other Wall Streeter of his day. Unfortunately for historians, Groesbeck was able to keep secrets; unlike other brokers, from whose works many of these incidents have been taken, he never wrote his memoirs.

Men of this stripe were powers in their own right during the war. They entered Wall Street with the air of a leading man in a play, and like actors, they were always aware that every eye in the audience was on them. When they clashed, others stood by like hyenas, waiting to scavenge around the dead loser. Pools, raids, wash sales, and corners were common occurrences in the 1860s, and the men who ran them were viewed by their colleagues and by interested onlookers as gallant highwaymen. But as important as men like Jerome, Morse and Tobin were, they did not occupy the center of the arena. That place was reserved for four of the wildest, most improbable characters in the history of American finance: Cornelius Vanderbilt, Daniel Drew, Jay Gould, and James Fisk.

Daniel Drew's preparations for his Wall Street career began early in life. In 1814, at the age of seventeen, he sold himself as a military substitute for one hundred dollars. After a few months in camp he decided that military life was not for him, and he deserted. Backed by the bounty money, Drew entered the illegal "bob veal" business. He would buy newborn calves and rush them to market if they seemed sickly and not likely to survive. The rest were raised and sold as cows and steers. Farmers who supplied the calves complained that Drew didn't meet his bills, and butchers said that the calf flesh was so loose that "it could be sucked through a quill."

Facing bankruptcy, Drew left the bob-veal business and joined a circus. One night he went to a revival meeting after the tents closed, and there he heard an itinerant preacher warn of hellfire and damnation, which awaited all who sinned. Drew was impressed. He marched down the aisle and told the congregation that the spirit of Jesus had entered his soul; henceforth he would lead the good life.

Drew quit the circus a few months later. He became a drover, taking cattle from Pennsylvania to the New York markets in lower Manhattan. It was then that Drew began "watering stocks." He would allow the beasts no water until just before they were to be sold. Then he would feed them salt and let them drink their fill. Since cattle sold by the pound on the hoof, his price was always higher than the thirsty cattle would ordinarily have brought. The butchers—led by Henry Astor, John Jacob's brother

—soon got wise to this trick, but by then Drew was busy planning new methods of hoodwinking them.

This was young Daniel Drew—part circus clown, part religious zealot, but primarily shrewd speculator. By the late 1830s he had already acquired the characteristics that would make him the most audacious fraud of his time, and one of the most colorful figures in the history of Wall Street.

Drew left the drover's trade to become proprietor of the Bull's Head Tavern in the Third Avenue meat-packing district. For a while he continued speculating in cattle, but he soon branched out into money-lending, charging exorbitant rates for short-term loans. Then he perceived the future of steamships, especially those which plied the Hudson. Fighting the established interests, he managed to control one of the largest lines on the river. When the Hudson River Railroad was completed, Drew's business was in trouble. "You might as well hang up your fiddle," said President Boorman of the Hudson. "We've got you whipped. Own up. Your steamships can't hold out against these things that go along the rails thirty miles an hour like a streak of lightning. Give up the boat business. Boats can't live on the Hudson River any longer."

Drew took this advice. He had already begun speculating in railroad stocks at the auctions, but now he turned to Wall Street in earnest. As the head of Drew, Robinson & Co., he participated in most of the exciting bull and bear raids that preceded the 1857 panic.

Drew was one of the first to realize how direct control of a road would aid the speculator in his market operations. Prior to his time there had been many businessmen who speculated; he was the first major speculator who went into business. Drew knew that if he controlled a railroad, manipulation of its securities would be a simple matter. He could bear its stock, and then when delivery was called for, could go to the company printing press and turn out all the shares needed to cover contracts. In addition, the railroad's treasury would be his plaything.

The road Drew fastened upon was the Erie, a great trunk line which was nearly five hundred miles long. In its early years the Erie had shown promise, but by the 1850s was run down, dilapidated, and poorly financed. Drew knew this, but the road's condition caused him no concern. Erie was a speculative favorite on Wall Street, and that was all that mattered. He began his campaign by giving preferential rates on his steamers to other railroads. Drew next took control of the Lake Erie ships on which the road depended for water transport; he also bought out the Buffalo and the State Line Railroads, Erie's primary feeders. Thus he completely encircled his prey. Drew's price for relenting was the post of treasurer of the Erie, which he assumed in 1854. Then he endorsed several loans, taking a mortgage on all the road's property. Drew could have taken control of the Erie, but this was not his goal. Instead, he started speculating in its shares, making his first killing late in 1854.

Erie was financially ruined in the panic of 1857. Although Drew had lost a fortune during the decline, he managed to scrape up $1.5 million to lend the company in return for which he received another chattel mortgage. Now he had complete control, and Drew began to use and reuse the Erie, which came to be called "the Scarlet Woman of Wall Street."

Drew had become a familiar sight in the financial district by the time of the attack on Fort Sumter. His appearance alone would have assured him of notice. Drew always dressed in black and carried a furled umbrella. With his lanky body and cadaverous face, he resembled a small-town undertaker. One writer said that he appeared to the onlooker like a dishonest Abraham Lincoln. Drew was a suspicious, ruthless market operator, and although he was not as yet a major figure, he had been marked as a man to watch.

Drew's chief antagonist and sometime partner was "Commodore" Cornelius Vanderbilt, who could generally be counted on to bull those shares that Drew beared. When seen together, the two seemed like some rustic vaudeville act. The Commodore was tall and aristocratic in his bulky fur coat and top hat. He had a large nose, piercing eyes, and an expression of utter contempt on his face that frightened friends as well as enemies. When he spoke, a stream of colorful, profane language would emerge from imperious lips. Vanderbilt had the body and face of a patrician, combined with the mind of a businessman and the upbringing of a wharf rat. He was not the sort of man that one crossed twice. Vanderbilt had his wife committed to an insane asylum when she protested his move to a Washington Square address. His son William was exiled to a Staten Island farm until he was able to prove that he could outwit the Commodore.

Vanderbilt was born in 1794—three years before Drew. As a boy he was drawn to water transportation; his early youth was spent as a Staten Island ferry hand. Later Vanderbilt owned several sailing vessels. When the steamship came along he sold his clippers and concentrated on paddle-wheelers. Vanderbilt soon became the dominant factor in American shipping, controlling a good deal of the coastwise, California, and transatlantic business. During the gold rush of 1849, Vanderbilt moved more men to the fields than any other individual, and he nearly succeeded in building a canal across Nicaragua. By then he was probably the most important American businessman, and certainly the most enterprising. Vanderbilt's success may be attributed to the right combination of vision and ruthlessness. When several associates tried to profit from his absence to take control of some Vanderbilt property, the Commodore wrote:

Gentlemen:

You have undertaken to cheat me. I will not sue you, for law takes too long. I will ruin you.

Sincerely yours,
CORNELIUS VAN DERBILT

On his return, this promise was kept.

Since both Vanderbilt and Drew were operators of Hudson River lines, it was inevitable that the two would clash. Drew's *Water Witch* charged lower rates than the Vanderbilt ships, although it lost money at the rate of $10,000 a year. "Uncle Dan'l" was willing to take this loss, hoping the Commodore would eventually buy him out at a large profit. Drew told shippers that he was charging normal rates and received a good return on his investment. By charging higher rates, his competition was actually robbing them. Vanderbilt was obliged to capitulate to

Drew, and he bought the *Water Witch* for a handsome price.
Thus, Uncle Dan'l won the first encounter. The Commodore was
not as angry as might have been expected, however. Drew
fascinated him, and a few years later the two jointly owned
the steamer *North America,* a leaky old craft that returned large
dividends.

By all rights Vanderbilt should have retired around 1857. He
was then sixty-four years old, a millionaire, and at the top of his
field. There seemed few new lands for the Commodore's shipping
lines to conquer. But he was not quite through; as a matter of fact,
the most important years lay in the future. In the early 1850s he
perceived the future of the railroad and began neglecting his
shipping interests for selected Eastern rails. The first of his lines
was the New York & Harlem. Buying depressed shares at 8,
Vanderbilt pushed them to 50, making a profit and establishing
his reputation as Wall Street's leading bull. He then bribed
members of New York's Common Council to grant Harlem a
franchise within the city. The stock moved up, making new
millions for Vanderbilt and, as we have seen, establishing John
Tobin and others as important Wall Street figures. Now Vanderbilt was considered a leading operator in Eastern rails.

By this time Jay Gould was also making a reputation on Wall
Street as a rail manipulator. Gould was born in Roxbury, New
York, in 1836, when Vanderbilt had already established himself
in sailing ships and paddle-wheelers. During his youth Gould
worked as a surveyor, bookkeeper, and clerk, taking any jobs
that would give him enough money to get by. He was always
sickly and later on suffered from neuralgia and tuberculosis.
Gould was little more than five feet tall, stooped and unpre-
possessing. One would scarcely have chosen him as the future
champion in battles with the hale and hearty Commodore.

The turning point in Gould's early career came when he promoted and sold a better mousetrap, which had been invented by
his grandfather. By 1857, having marketed several other devices,
he was worth $5,000. At that time he was part owner and manager
of a leather business. Gould used company funds to finance an
attempted corner of the hide market, which fell through during
the panic of 1857. His partner, Charles Leupp, committed suicide
shortly thereafter, and for the rest of his life Gould would be

charged with the responsibility for this tragedy. His touch, it was said, brought death.

Gould entered the stock markets as a rail speculator. Within a year he had learned all the tricks of the trade, and, as one of his biographers noted, "Gould could use them as a dentist uses a drill, or as a butcher uses a cleaver." By the time of the Civil War he was a familiar Wall Street figure, respected as a cool operator, and one of the most devious men in the district. Henry N. Smith, who later became Gould's partner, claimed that he was the poorest judge of the market he had ever known, while a close friend, Charlie Osborne, said that Gould would go into a funk when faced with reverses. Still, word that Gould was involved in one or another new venture would cause ripples to run up and down the Street.

Gould would go to the exchanges in the morning, remain all day, and then return home, pain-wracked by his afflictions, late at night. His only joy, other than speculation, came from flower arrangements, of which he was considered an expert. As Daniel Drew once put it, "The difference between Jay and me is, I have more trouble to get my dinner than to digest it, and Jay has more trouble to digest it than to get it."

One could hardly imagine a person more different from Gould than James Fisk, who was his partner in some of the most audacious schemes of the period. While Gould was small and nervous, Fisk was large and calm. Gould reminded onlookers of a bearded dark ferret, while Fisk gave the appearance of a blond peacock. Gould was a family man. Fisk, though married, kept his wife in Boston while he cavorted with ladies of the street in New York. Gould was able to concoct ingenious campaigns; Fisk had the knack of knowing how to carry them out. The two men, with so many disparate characteristics, were perfectly mated.

Jim Fisk once worked as a Vermont peddler, a job his father had before him. Born on All Fool's Day in 1835, he was a wild clown who loved coming to town with his wagon and being the center of attention in the frontier settlements. Later on he found an even more natural showcase as ringmaster of a one-tent circus. Fisk, who liked to call himself a "Green Mountain Boy," looked upon those days as being the happiest of his life.

When the Civil War began, Fisk was quick to see opportunities for profit. He ran contraband cotton and became a commission agent for the firm of Jordan, Marsh & Company in Boston. Fisk came to Wall Street just before the war ended. He opened a brokerage on Broad Street and loudly predicted that within a short time he would rule the district. Fisk's first success involved selling Confederate bonds on the London market before the English had learned of the South's defeat. He did this by chartering fast boats which arrived in London before the mail ships. The timidity of his partners limited his gains, but Fisk made a sizable killing. All this was lost in the next few months, however, as the Wall Streeters, recognizing Fisk for the rube he then was, took him for all his winnings plus the original capital. Fisk was bankrupt, but he vowed to come back, "and if I don't make things squirm I'll eat nothing but bone soup till Judgment Day."

Fisk returned to Wall Street late in 1865 and set up the firm of Fisk & Belden. At this point he met Drew and, having learned of the old man's circus days, called on him to reminisce about grease paint and pratfalls. Early in 1866 he worked with Drew in bearing Erie, thus reestablishing himself on the Street. Fisk also met Gould, then the guiding force behind Smith, Gould & Martin. From the first, a strange chemistry seemed to unite these two, and along with Drew, they began plotting ways of milking the Erie of every penny in its purse.

In 1866 there were three great railroad systems that tied the North to the Midwest. The Pennsylvania, tightly held by Thomas Scott and a group of Philadelphia businessmen, was the best run and also the most conservative. The Erie, controlled by Drew since 1854, had decayed into "two thin streaks of rust." It was a profitable operation, however, primarily due to the large oil traffic which had come in from the Pennsylvania fields after 1862. By the end of the war the line's future seemed bright, despite the fact that many of its facilities were unimproved and accidents were common. The third of the routes was the New York Central, headed by Henry Keep, who was acting for Vanderbilt. The Commodore, with all his faults, had proven a masterful rail tycoon. Unlike Drew, he was genuinely interested in his roads. When he purchased lines he would build them up, and only then water the stock. Soon after, the road would declare a large dividend, which would send the shares up on the Exchange, thus enriching the Commodore. Vanderbilt planned the same course of action for the Central. He always made a fortune when he took over a road, but the Commodore left it in good running condition as well.

Vanderbilt began buying shares of Erie in 1866. He later said that he had no desire to speculate or to control the company. Rather, he bought the stock to please friends. This overlooks the fact that Vanderbilt had endorsed Drew's Erie notes as early as 1854, and in 1866 had been a director of the road for more than seven years. It is probable that the Commodore hoped to take over completely, forcing out the Drew group, and then merge the Erie into the Central. By the winter of the year Vanderbilt believed that he had enough shares to gain control. It was then that Drew counterattacked, opening the first chapter of the Erie war.

Uncle Dan'l had foreseen the possibility of such a move and planned to use it as part of a bear raid. He loaned the road $3.5 million, in return for which he received 28,000 shares of unissued and unregistered stock. In addition he held $3 million of convertible bonds, whch were kept in reserve.

Vanderbilt began to buy at 80, and in short order had pushed the price to 95. Although he didn't know it then, many of his holdings had come from Drew, who had sold heavily and at the same time had gone short on several large contracts. The Commodore got an inkling of what had happened when he discovered that he had bought more Erie shares than had been registered. His first reaction was that of joy; Vanderbilt believed the bears had sold shares they hadn't yet bought in the hope of picking them up when the price dropped. As Uncle Dan'l had once said:

> He who sells what isn't his'n
> Must buy it back or go to prison.

Now Drew moved in on the kill. He dumped 58,000 shares on the market at once, 30,000 of which came from his convertibles. Erie dropped from 95 to 50, wiping out the bulls as the bears danced on the floor of the Exchange. Vanderbilt's losses ran in the millions, while Drew measured his gains in terms of the

Commodore's fall. Both men began buying the loyalties of local judges. Injunctions were issued against each, with little effect. The antagonists knew that the real power lay in control of Erie, and they prepared for the showdown.

Vanderbilt won the first round. He contacted the directors of the Boston, Hartford & Erie, a small, almost bankrupt line, which owned a sizable block of Erie stock. The Commodore promised to merge the two roads if the B. H. & E. would cooperate in forcing Drew from his post as treasurer of the Erie. The directors agreed, thus giving Vanderbilt the support he needed. Next, the Commodore had his judge issue an injunction against Drew, forbidding him from voting converted shares at the coming election.

Uncle Dan'l was panic-stricken for the first time in his life. He visited Vanderbilt and pleaded for mercy, also pointing out that there was plenty of loot for both of them if they would only work together. Vanderbilt consented to spare his opponent, perhaps reasoning that Drew would be a useful tool on the board should the B. H. & E. men get out of hand. Uncle Dan'l agreed to end his bear raids on Erie and to cooperate with the Commodore in future bull operations.

According to plan, Drew was ousted from his post at the stockholders' meeting of October 17, 1867. Vanderbilt representatives took over, a clear sign to the public that a bull movement was in the making. Shares went up on the news, but they fell when, a few days later, the new treasurer resigned and Drew, as per agreement, got back his old position. He rejoined his two friends Fisk and Gould, who had been elected directors at the October meeting.

In November the Commodore began buying shares, hoping to bull Erie to a new high. The price rose, but not as fast as it should have. Vanderbilt smelled a rat; investigation showed that Drew, Fisk and Gould were bearing Erie contrary to agreement. Thus there were now three groups struggling for control of the road: the Commodore's, led by brokers Frank Work and Richard Schell; Drew's, which included Gould and Fisk; and the Boston group, which was in the middle. When Vanderbilt tried to merge Erie into the Central, the two other factions joined forces to prevent him. Like the enraged bull that he was, the Commodore turned on the alliance and prepared to destroy it with a show of brute force.

Vanderbilt instructed his broker, William Heath, to start buying Erie on the open market. At the same time he began a campaign to win independent shareholders to his banner; New York newspapers wrote that should they "give their proxies before the next election to Mr. Vanderbilt, Erie will be a 10 percent dividend paying stock very soon." In February he had Frank Work gain a temporary injunction from Vanderbilt-controlled Judge George Barnard, forbidding Drew and his cohorts from selling any more stock or convertible bonds, and preventing Erie from paying interest on the $3.5 million it owed Drew. A few days later Barnard issued another injunction, this one temporarily suspending the treasurer from the Board. Drew promptly bribed Judge Ransom Balcom to set aside the injunction. Then Gould called a meeting of the executive committee to discuss improvements to be made in rolling stock and rails. Under his direction, $10 million of convertible bonds were authorized to sell at not less than 72½, then the market price of Erie. Half the issue was taken up by David Groesbeck, who acted for Drew. They were quickly converted and dumped on the market. Other brokers allied to Gould bought the rest and prepared to sell them at the Exchange.

Vanderbilt knew of the bond offering and, working quickly, had Judge Barnard issue an injunction against its conversion into common stock. He then returned to Wall Street, where, aided by John Tobin, he continued to buy Erie. The Commodore bought all the floating supply of stock, and had taken the first 50,000 shares which Groesbeck had converted before he suspected that Drew had violated the injunction. Even then, Vanderbilt took no action, for since the shares had been distributed through several brokers, he assumed that no central selling was taking place. The Commodore was confident as Erie reached 80 on March 10. Then the second batch of shares gained through bond conversions hit the market, and since these were signed by Fisk, there was no doubt that the injunction had been violated. Now Vanderbilt was in trouble. The price of Erie fell to 71, but it steadied as the Commodore bought every share offered at that level. The total value of Erie stock declined over $8 million, and most of this was absorbed by Vanderbilt, who was scraping the bottom of the barrel in terms of cash. When he tried to borrow money on those Erie shares he already owned, the bankers told him that they would only lend on his Central holdings. The Commodore replied that unless they gave him the money on his conditions, he would dump Central on the Exchange, thus wrecking a large part of the financial community, including them. Vanderbilt received his loan the next day, and continued to support Erie against Drew and the bears. He was now the undisputed hero of the Wall Street bulls. But he had been forced to buy 150,000 shares of Erie without having gained control. And 100,000 of them had come from Drew's convertibles, which due to Barnard's injunction were legally worthless!

Vanderbilt vowed revenge. Calling in the hapless Barnard, he had the judge issue an arrest warrant for Drew, Gould and Fisk. The conspirators got wind of the order before it could be executed, and, hastily packing Erie's records into cases and the $8 million of profits in valises, they set out for the ferry and the safe confines of Jersey City. Headquarters were established in Taylor's Hotel—which the press soon called Fort Taylor—and a publicity war began, with broadsides crossing the Hudson almost daily. Vanderbilt charged the fugitives with legal and moral crimes and put a price on their heads. Fisk responded piously that "this is a battle between right and wrong, and we have no fears as to which will win." Gould was concerned about the situation, which showed no signs of being resolved, but Fisk was in his element. After bribing the Jersey City police to provide protection, he settled down to a life of luxury. His mistress, the buxom Josie Mansfield, came when sent for, and life was sweet for "Jubilee Jim," with parties and good times continuing around the clock.

Drew did not approve of such wild goings-on. Not only was he shocked by Fisk's behavior, but he was also homesick for Wall Street. Looking across the river, he realized that the Commodore was busy consolidating his position, thus assuring Uncle Dan'l of what seemed to be a permanent exile in New Jersey.

Hoping to outflank Vanderbilt, Gould packed a carpetbag full of thousand-dollar bills and set off for Albany, where he planned to bribe the state legislature to legalize the bond conversions. His agents, led by a shifty character named John Develin, offered $1,000 a vote to the legislators, and were turned down as being cheap. Running the Vanderbilt forces was Boss William Tweed of New York City, who was also a state senator. Tweed spent over $180,000 of Vanderbilt's money in buying votes, and more was ready if needed. The Commodore sent one lobbyist to Albany with $100,000. Gould offered him $70,000 if he would disappear with the money. The man left Albany shortly thereafter, never to return. Still, Gould was unsuccessful in this first bid to gain vindication from the Assembly; on March 27, the report legalizing his actions failed of passage.

The exiles threw everything they had into the battle, making the bribes of the first period seem like penny ante. Senator A. C. Mattoon received a bribe of $20,000 from one side and $15,000 from the other. Gould took full command of the campaign and met with success; in mid-April the Senate legalized the actions of the previous month, and Gould emerged as an important figure in his own right. The *Herald* reported that "The Erie men have succeeded admirably under Jay Gould, who had undone the bungling work of John A. Develin and his coterie, who came here to direct the first Erie campaign." Now he, and not Drew, was recognized as the leader of the Erie group. Vanderbilt capitulated before the resolution reached the Senate. As a sign of this, he closed his liquor dispensary, which previously had served as a meeting place for his forces. Gould added a rider to the resolution forbidding interlocking directors between the Erie, the Central, and the Harlem, in a move to prevent further action by the Commodore. The bill then passed the Senate by a large margin and was signed into law by Governor Fenton, who may have been bribed by Gould along with the majority of the legislators.

Vanderbilt still controlled New York through Boss Tweed. Now Fisk entered the fray, bribing Tweed with promises of money and favors. Victory seemed complete, but the conspirators knew that real peace was not possible until the Commodore laid down his arms.

The first move toward a negotiated settlement came when Vanderbilt contacted his old nemesis, Drew. In a characteristic note, the Commodore said:

DREW: I'm sick of the whole damned business. Come and see me.
VAN DERBILT

The two met at the Commodore's Washington Square mansion without the knowledge of Fisk and Gould. Although his position was the superior one, Drew played the role of suitor; he was homesick and appalled at the antics of Fisk and his friends. Drew spoke of the good old days when he and Vanderbilt had been river comrades and rivals. He noted, as he often did on such occasions, that his son William had been named after the Commodore's son. Drew wheedled and whined, begging for a settlement. Then Vanderbilt set his terms. The ringleaders, operating through the Erie treasury, would purchase 50,000 shares of his stock for 70, paying the Commodore $2.5 million in cash and the rest in Boston, Hartford & Erie bonds. In addition, Vanderbilt would grant them an option on an additional 50,000 shares, which the ring could buy at 70, for the consideration of another million dollars. Since Erie was then selling below that figure, and would sink lower when the public realized that the Commodore had been ousted, the option was actually worthless. Frank Work and Richard Schell, Vanderbilt's lieutenants, were to receive $429,250, which equaled the amount they had lost while speculating in Erie. Thus the victims would be reimbursed for their losses in the March speculations. The victors would lose nothing, for the ransom was to be paid from the Erie treasury; the price was met through an informal levy on the road's shareholders.

The terms were accepted, and peace was declared. Drew was found out by his two friends, who considered his meeting with Vanderbilt a stab in the back. Gould was named president of Erie, and Fisk a director. The former began scheming stock-market raids as soon as he returned to Wall Street. On his part, Fisk bought an opera house, a regiment, and a small navy, which were paid for by legal thievery of the Erie exchequer.

Gould attempted his first post-Vanderbilt raid early in 1868. Aided by a board of directors which now included Boss Tweed, and a complaisant Judge Barnard, who had been bribed to do for him what he had previously done for the Commodore, Gould raised the capital stock of Erie from 165,000 shares to 700,000. He dumped the new securities on the Exchange, after first entering into bear contracts. The price fell from 68 to 35, making millions for Gould and Fisk. Then, using Erie treasury funds, the two bulled the price to 62, again cleaning up. Among their victims in the second move was Drew, who went bearish at the wrong time. Uncle Dan'l was wrecked, and he sadly relinquished his post as the Street's leading conniver to Gould, who received the nickname of "Mephistopheles of Wall Street."

Having rid themselves of both the Commodore and Drew, the two leaders of Erie began to clash with other rail tycoons who stood in their way. At that time the Albany and Susquehanna competed with Erie for the coal business of Pennsylvania. The A. & S., led by Joseph H. Ramsey, was in control of the fields in mid-1868; Gould challenged its position by entering into agreements with coal producers in the region, while at the same time buying A. & S. stock on the market in an attempt to take over from Ramsay. The directors of the A. & S. called for help in the form of young J. P. Morgan. After a flurry of injunctions, which in those days usually marked the beginning of a raid, Morgan and Fisk locked horns. Each man bought an army; Fisk's was recruited from the notorious Five Points district of New York's lower West Side, while Morgan's came from the Bowery and included some of the Dead Rabbits. In a series of battles, culminating in a wild free-for-all during which each group tried to take possession of a station in Binghamton, the Morgan forces proved superior, and Fisk returned to New York, remarking that "nothing is lost save honor." The Erie directors had met their first defeat, and J. P. Morgan had made an auspicious debut in the big leagues of high finance.

Gould rebounded with ease, and in the fall of 1868 took over the moribund Wabash Railroad, which he hoped to consolidate with the Lake Shore. Before this could be accomplished, Gould was forced to borrow heavily and wager on a rise in Wabash earnings to recoup his investment. Since the Wabash was primarily a grain carrier, any increase in wheat sales was bound to affect its earnings.

It was at this point that Gould began to formulate the most audacious plot in American financial history: he would corner the nation's gold supply. The nation's financial policies in 1869 made such a dream possible.

The United States had issued millions of dollars of paper money —greenbacks—during the Civil War. Since this money was not redeemable in gold, people began to hoard the metal, which soon became scarce. Within a matter of weeks after the first greenback issue, gold sold at a premium on Wall Street. Should an individual wish to purchase one hundred dollars in gold, for example, he might have to offer one hundred and twenty dollars in greenbacks. Since foreigners would not accept greenbacks in settlement of debts, the gold market was frequented by merchants, and since the gold price fluctuated with the fortunes of the Union armies, it soon attracted speculators as well. Should the North win the Civil War, then it could be expected that greenbacks would, eventually, be redeemed in gold at face value. If, on the other hand, the South won the war, then Union finances might collapse, in which case greenbacks could be worthless.

Early in April 1862, several speculators joined to form what would soon become the wildest exchange in the nation—Gilpin's Gold Room. Only one commodity was traded—gold—and those seeking quick action soon flocked there. In April the price was 120, but after the North's defeat at Fredericksburg it rose to 134, and a month later to 150. The high point, reached in 1863, was 287, but after Gettysburg it fell back once again. In fact, the gold speculators learned of Confederate withdrawals before Lincoln did. By then, Wall Streeters had private wires to the battlefield and spies in both Confederate and Union camps to report on happenings. "What do you think of those fellows in Wall Street who are gambling in gold at such a time as this?" Lincoln asked Governor Curtin. "For my part, I wish every one of them had his devilish head shot off." Lincoln attempted to curb speculation, and Congress passed laws forbidding it. But trading merely went underground; nothing could stop the speculators from attempting to win quick profits. All Congress could do was to close Gilpin's Gold Room. When the closure was rescinded late in 1864, the brokers and speculators regrouped, opening the New York Gold Exchange, in October 1864. Writing in 1866, Horace White described the new Gold Room:

HIGHEST AND LOWEST PRICES OF GOLD, 1862–1868

Year	High	Low
1862	134	—
1863	172½	122⅛
1864	287	151½
1865	233¾	128⅝
1866	167¾	125
1867	145⅝	132
1868	150	133¼

Source: Francis Eames, *The New York Stock Exchange,* p. 120

Imagine a rat-pit in full blast, with 20 or 30 men ranged around the rat tragedy, each with a canine under his arm, yelling and howling at once, and you have as good a comparison as can be found in the outside world of the aspect of the Gold Room as it strikes the beholder on his first entrance. The furniture of this room is extremely simple. It consists of two iron railings and an indicator. The first railing is a circle about four feet high and ten feet in diameter, placed exactly in the centre of the room. In the interior, which represents the space devoted to rat killing in other establishments, is a marble cupid throwing up a jet of pure Croton water. The artistic conception is not appropriate. Instead of a cupid throwing a pearly fountain into the air, there should be a hungry Midas turning everything to gold and starving from sheer inability to eat.

The other railing is a semicircle 20 to 30 feet from the central one. On the outer rail fences are the "lame ducks" and "dead beats," men who have once been famous at the rat-pit, but have since been cleaned out. Solvency is the first essential of the Gold Room. . . . The indicator, which is the third piece of furniture in the room, is a piece of mechanism to show the changes in the market. It is something like an old fashioned Dutch clock, 7 or 8 feet high, with an open space at the top, disclosing three figures and a fraction, as 141½.

On a normal day the Gold Room might transact $50 million worth of trades, of which only $5–$6 million represented purchases or sales for commercial accounts, and the rest the buying and selling of speculators, hoping to make money on the rise or fall of a quarter-point in the price of gold. Should important news be received at the Room, or a new bull or bear move take form, trading would become hectic. William Worthington Fowler, describing the Room after the Civil War, had this to say of it.

The Gold Room was like a cavern, full of dank and noisome vapors, and the deadly carbonic acid was blended with the fumes of stale smoke and vinous breaths. But the stifling gases engendered in that low-browed cave of evil enchanters, never seemed to depress the energies of the gold-dealers; from "morn to dewy eve" the drooping ceiling and bistre-colored walls re-echoed with the sounds of all kinds of voices, from the shrill, piping treble of the call boys, to the deep bass of R.H.———, J.R.———, L.J.———, etc., etc., while an up-reared forest of arms was swayed furiously by the storms of a swiftly rising and falling market.

Fowler, White, and other observers considered the Gold Room a place for little else but gambling and believed its main economic importance was to provide a quick market for gold. Conservative businessmen who had never been to the Room and would shy from trading there, and farmers with knowledge of what happened to their crops after they left the fields, told a different story. To them, transactions at the Gold Room made possible the nation's prosperity.

The United States was the world's leading grain-producing nation in 1868; grains occupied an important position in the export market, earning foreign exchange which served to keep trade in balance. Should the sales abroad be cut drastically, and the return flow of foreign capital cease, then America would suffer a severe financial shock, followed by a disastrous depression. This fear haunted many businessmen in 1868, as they knew that costs of ocean transportation, combined with the high price of domestic labor, could force American wheat off the world market. To these men the Gold Room represented a vital part of the nation's defense against depression.

Foreigners purchased American wheat with dollars, often selling gold to acquire them. When the gold price was high, foreigners could get more dollars; when it fell, they received fewer. Translated into terms the farmers and exporters could understand, a low gold price meant expensive wheat. A rise in the price, which would make dollars cheap, would have the same effect on grains and other exports. The gold premium, then, was an important concomitant of the nation's prosperity.

A high price would lead to prosperity for all, and especially would benefit Jay Gould's Wabash Railroad, whose earnings would rise as more grain was shipped to the East for transshipment overseas. If Gould could purchase gold at low prices and then force it upward, he would make two fortunes—one in currency speculation, the other in railroads. And all this could be accomplished in the name of patriotism!

Only one man stood between Gould and the realization of his plan: President Ulysses S. Grant. On July 1, 1869, the Treasury had at its disposal $79.7 million in gold. Grant was considered a "sound money man," which meant that should the price of gold rise precipitously, he might sell Treasury gold to bring it down to "normal," which at that time was around 130. But if Grant could be convinced that a higher price would be beneficial to the nation, then he might withhold gold from the market, thus insuring Gould's success.

Gould's campaign to win Presidential support began in June, when Grant was scheduled to open the great Peace Jubilee in Boston. The President went to the festivities aboard the *Providence*, flagship of the Narragansett Line, which was owned by "Commodore" Jim Fisk. The garishly dressed Fisk invited Cyrus Field, William Marston, and other leading citizens to join in the voyage, and even arranged for the famous Dodsworth Band to entertain along the way. Naturally, Jay Gould was also invited, and Fisk made certain Gould would dine alone with the President.

Gould spared no effort to make his dinner with Grant a success. Earlier he had arranged to meet Abel Rathbone Corbin, an aged speculator and lobbyist whose only distinction was the fact that he had married Grant's sister. Gould had had occasion to deal with Corbin in the past, but until then they were only casual acquaintances. As a result, Corbin was puzzled at first when the prestigious Jay Gould confided his belief that gold would go higher. This was especially surprising, since Wall Street assumed the price would fall. Gold had not risen as much as had been expected in early June, and was due for a fall when Europeans paid for their wheat exports in September. Such had been the pattern for the past few years, and there seemed no reason to expect a change. But change there would be, said Gould to Corbin, hinting broadly that he would bring the President's brother-in-law into the syndicate in return for "cooperation." Corbin eagerly indicated his willingness to go along with Gould in the scheme.

At first it appeared that Corbin's aid plus the natural simplicity of the President would be enough to swing Grant to the Gould position. At dinner on June 15, Gould spoke of the importance of a high gold price to farmers, and Grant listened carefully, nodding his head from time to time. All that would be needed, said Gould, was for the Treasury not to sell gold while the price rose. If this were done, prosperity would continue; if not, there might be a panic.

At this point the President indicated his wish to be heard. "It seems to me that there's a good deal of fiction in all this talk about prosperity," he said. "The bubble may as well be pricked one way as another." This, at least, was Fisk's later report of the conversation. In any case, Grant refused to go along with the scheme, and it appeared as though a gold corner would not be possible.

Jay Gould was not a man to be easily discouraged. If he could not bull gold with Treasury aid, he would do it without help from that quarter. First, he would have to test his strength, and the key here was Abel Corbin. If Corbin could prevent Grant from acting promptly when gold rose, perhaps the corner could be carried off after all.

Corbin's first task was to plant an editorial in *The New York Times* on the President's financial policy. This was done on August 5, when the newspaper printed a story which indicated that Grant had become a fiscal expansionist. Next, Gould asked Corbin to have Robert Catherwood, Gould's son-in-law, named Assistant Treasurer in New York. Corbin was on the point of success when Catherwood indicated his unwillingness to co-operate, and Gould quickly substituted the name of General Daniel Butterfield, a more compliant individual. Within days Butterfield was named to the post. Finally, Gould asked Corbin to see to it that the President came to his home. The meeting was arranged for early September, when Grant would be in New York for the funeral of Secretary of War John Rawlins. Gould wanted the meeting less for the purpose of convincing Grant that gold should be withheld than for impressing Wall Streeters with his power in the Administration. The meeting was held, and the impression made. Now Gould was certain that he controlled a key point in the Treasury, and at the same time he knew that Corbin had power over Grant.

The next step was for the Treasury to stop gold sales. On September 1, Grant told Secretary of the Treasury George Boutwell to end the regular gold auctions. Gould was delighted, as were others in the group. The financier purchased $2 million in gold at 133 and assigned it to Corbin, telling him he would not have to pay for it until later. Similar steps were taken to reward others, including Horace Porter, Grant's secretary, who was to receive $500,000 in gold under the same arrangement. Although Porter declined the bribe, money was given Butterfield and others. With all the pieces in place, Gould began his corner in gold.

The stock market was in a slump in late August, with prices and volume at their usual seasonal lows. Brokers and speculators had fled New York for the summer, as was their custom, and few

PRICES OF SELECTED ISSUES, JULY–AUGUST 1869

	Closing Prices (Fractions rounded off)					
Issue	July 24	July 31	Aug. 7	Aug. 14	Aug. 21	Aug. 28
Adams Express	60	59	60	59	58	56
Cleveland & Pittsburgh R.R.	109	108	108	106	105	107
Hudson River R.R.	190	187	187	186	181	184
New York Central R.R.	216	215	209	210	200	202
Pacific Mail S.S.	84	85	86	83	80	81
Reading R.R.	97	98	97	96	96	96

Source: *New York Times*, July 25–August 29, 1869

expected much activity until mid-September, when they would return. Activity was brisk at the Gold Exchange, however, with bull and bear pools forming, dissolving, and then re-forming. Such action too was customary on Wall Street, as the harvests and foreign purchases made late summer and early autumn one of the busiest periods at the Exchange. Prices fluctuated daily, but in general traded within a narrow range throughout July and August, with a peak in late July when a particularly strong bull pool managed to push the price past 140 for a short time. By early September, the gold price was steady at around 134, after a spirited

CLOSING PRICES AT THE GOLD ROOM, JULY–AUGUST 1869

Date	Last Sale	Date	Last Sale	Date	Last Sale
July 12	137⅛	July 29	136¼	Aug. 17	133
13	137½	30	136¼	18	133
14	137	31	136¼	19	133½
15	136⅝	Aug. 2	136	20	132⅜
16	135⅞	3	135¾	21	131⅝
17	135¾	4	135¾	23	132
19	135⅞	5	136½	24	132⅞
20	135⅜	6	136¼	25	133½
21	135⅛	7	136⅛	26	134
22	135½	9	135⅞	27	134⅜
23	135⅜	10	135¾	28	134
24	136½	11	135¼	30	134½
26	137½	12	134¼	31	134½
27	140	13	134⅛		
28	135⅞	16	134¼		

Source: *New York Times*, July 13–29, 1869

attempt on the part of the bulls to pull off one more coup before what most Gold Room veterans assumed would be the September decline. With Wall Street believing that conditions were normal, Gould began his purchases.

At first all went well. Gould's associates, brokers Arthur Kimber and W. S. Woodward, bought gold from eager sellers, who could not believe that prices would not fall. Although the scheme was a closely guarded secret, such massive purchases could not help being noticed. On September 3, the *Times* wrote that "a very decided, and in point of wealth strong *Bull* movement was inaugurated in the Gold-Room today, and advanced the price of Gold by main force." The price did indeed rise, and it appeared that Gould was about to accomplish his task with ease. But then the bears counterattacked, selling heavily to force the price downward. Gould panicked, but maintained his order to buy. As long as Butterfield kept Treasury gold off the market, he was safe. Bear speculators were selling gold they did not own, going short in the expectation of a drop in price, which would enable them to cover their sales at large profits. According to Gould's plan, the price would be forced ever higher, squeezing the shorts who would have to buy gold to honor their contracts, and in so doing help Gould in his work.

As usual, James Gordon Bennett's *Herald* was the keenest observer of Wall Street happenings. On Sunday, September 12, Bennett noted that the New York bank statement of the previous day showed a loss of $4 million in legal tender and of $2.5 million in gold. Yet, deposits were off by only $1.25 million. It was evident that someone was draining gold from New York banks. "Who is drying up money?" asked the *Herald*. The unspoken answer was: Jay Gould.

By mid-month the carefully laid plan seemed stalled. The price of gold was rising, but not fast enough to swing the corner. The closing sale on August 31 had been at 134½; by September 14, gold was 136½. Gould had contracts for more than $50 million, and unless the price rose soon, he would be in trouble.

The steadiness of gold was only one of Gould's problems.

CLOSING PRICES AT THE GOLD ROOM, SEPTEMBER 1–15, 1869

Date	Last Sale
Sept. 1	133¼
2	135¼
3	136¾
4	137¼
6	137¼
7	136½
8	135¼
9	135¼
10	135¼
11	135¾
13	135⅞
14	136½

Source: *New York Times,* September 2–15, 1869

Woodward reported that his friend thought the Treasury would soon sell gold in New York and depress the price. At that time he was responsible for $12 million in contracts. Now, at mid-month, he notified Gould he was leaving the syndicate and liquidating his holdings. Kimber was also uneasy about Treasury policy, and when he learned of Woodward's action, he too left the syndicate, selling his contracts, which amounted to an additional $12 million.

Gould was clearly in deep trouble as his enterprise began to crumble. What he now needed was a dramatic event or person who could create a panic situation and so send gold skyward. Gould knew of such a man, of course: he would call on Jim Fisk.

Fisk had assumed that Gould had abandoned hope of a corner when Grant refused to cooperate. Now he learned otherwise. Gould pleaded with him to take charge of buying operations on the floor. Fisk was assured the plot was complete—Gould hinted that the President and Mrs. Grant were aware of what was going on and were being taken care of. "Oh, this matter is all fixed up," he said. "Butterfield is all right. Corbin has got Butterfield all right, and Corbin has got Grant all right." Now the syndicate needed the master touch. Gould flattered Fisk, and Jubilee Jim finally agreed to take command of operations at the Gold Room.

The next day Fisk entered the Room with a great flourish and placed large orders for gold, making certain all saw what he was

CLOSING PRICES AT THE GOLD ROOM, SEPTEMBER 15–23, 1869

Date	Last Sale
Sept. 15	138
16	136½
17	136⅜
18	136⅝
20	137⅜
21	137½
22	141½
23	143⅜

Source: *New York Times*, September 16–24, 1869

doing. He would shout commands, whisper to a confederate, wink, and follow this with a poke in the side and a loud guffaw. The bears were puzzled, and as Gould had predicted, began to panic. The gold price rose sharply, leveled off, and then rose again.

By Thursday evening, September 23, Gould had accumulated some $40 million in gold contracts, twice the available supply in the city. Some of the money came from his own pocket, but most from railroad treasuries and banks controlled by the Gould forces. On that day the corner was completed. Price fluctuations toward the close seemed to confirm this fact, and within a half-hour of the last official trade, corner brokers were quoting gold at 144½.

PRICES AT THE GOLD ROOM, THURSDAY, SEPTEMBER 23, 1869

Time	Price
10:00 A.M	141⅝
10:14	141⅛
11:00	142
12:00	142⅞
1:00 P.M.	143¼
2:00	143½
2:17	144¼
3:00	143⅛
4:00	143
5:30	143⅜

Source: *New York Herald*, September 24, 1869

Now, as Gould was on the brink of victory, more loose ends began to appear in his carefully woven fabric. The syndicate had purchased more gold than ever before in American—perhaps world—history. If the corner carried, then its members would make millions of dollars, but should it fail, all would be lost. Far too much depended upon the Treasury, Grant, and Corbin, to suit Gould and Fisk; as far as they could judge, none of these factors could be relied upon. Fisk asked Corbin to write a letter to Grant asking his brother-in-law to keep gold off the market. Secretary of the Treasury Boutwell had been in New York on September 15 to investigate the gold markets, and although nothing resulted from the trip, Gould was visibly worried, and he approved the Corbin letter.

Corbin's letter was carried to the President by one of Fisk's men. At the time Grant was on vacation near Pittsburgh. He read the letter carefully and did not like its tone. Corbin seemed much too eager to keep gold off the market. Apparently the nature of the conspiracy had finally dawned on the stolid Grant. He sent for his wife and asked her to write a letter to Mrs. Corbin telling Abel to get out of the market if he was in it, and to keep away from the Gold Room under all circumstances.

Meanwhile Fisk's messenger dashed to the telegraph office to inform his employed that Grant had been contacted. He wired his chief: "Letter delivered all right." But the message was garbled in transmission, and Fisk received the following instead: "Letter delivered. All right." Fisk now assumed Grant had accepted Gould's proposals and would withhold gold from the market. As a result, he and Gould proceeded to act with more assurance than ever before.

In the meantime, Mrs. Grant's letter made its way to Mrs. Corbin, who gave it to Abel. As soon as he read it, the old swindler ran to Gould's headquarters and showed the letter to his partner. Corbin demanded that Gould sell his holdings; he wanted a check for $100,000, his profit on the $2 million in gold which Gould was holding for him. Both men realized that it was only a matter of hours before Grant would sell Treasury gold in New York, bringing prices down and ending the corner.

Gould allowed Corbin to leave the pool, but only on condition that he keep his letter private. Then Gould prepared to switch to the bear side of the market and sell while he could. This would be difficult, for once Fisk stopped buying, the bears would realize that the Treasury was on its way with the gold. Purchases at the artificially high price would end, and gold would return to normal before Gould had sold out. There was only one way out for Gould. He told Fisk about the letter, but instructed him to continue his purchases nonetheless. He would sell, while Fisk, his partner, continued to buy!

Fisk marshaled his forces outside the Gold Room on the morning of Friday, September 24. William Belden, his former partner, was there. Belden had been "let in" on the ring, in return for which he was to share in its risks. Now the entire Belden organization, plus all its resources, went behind the bull push. Smith, Gould, Martin & Co., the Gould-Fisk firm, would lead the buying, and Belden would follow. E. K. Willard was put in charge of lending gold to harrassed shorts attempting to cover; he was to squeeze every cent he could out of them. Albert Speyers was assigned the task of bidding gold as high as he could. Gould was supposedly in close communication with Washington; he would warn the group if any change of policy seemed imminent at the Treasury. Fisk was to maintain an air of optimism and do all he could to raise prices and panic fever.

Trading opened with a roar, as the bears quickly learned that Fisk was prepared to purchase gold at any price and was predicting its eventual rise to more than 200. The market opened at 143½, but within minutes Speyers was bidding 145 and taking all he could get. This price was reached in a matter of minutes, and Fisk hiked the price to 150, and then 155. Speyers was attacked by enraged bears, but he stood firm, and purchased all the gold offered. The Room was the scene of the wildest trading any exchange would witness in the century. Traders fainted; ambulances carried victims to nearby hospitals; there were rumors that Grant and his entire administration had organized the bull syndicate; suicides were reported among the city's elite. Fisk chortled, while Gould sat nervously in his office or paced the floor, holding his churning stomach. While Jim Fisk was buying all the gold he could, thus rocketing the price, Gould's men were selling on the other side of the Room. Later on it was learned that a pattern had developed around 9:30 A.M. Fisk would lift the price, frightening the shorts, who would then buy gold from E. K. Willard to cover their contracts. The money for these purchases came from nearby banks, whose resources were seriously strained and who raised the loan rate at a dizzying pace. The only question in Gould's mind, however, was whether he could clean out his holdings before the Treasury announced gold sales. Just before noon, it appeared that he could.

Meanwhile, prices on the Stock Exchanges plummeted, as speculators sold their securities to gain funds for short covering at the

Gold Room. Commodore Vanderbilt was livid; he had to pour over one million dollars into the market to support the price of New York Central. He and others sent messages to Washington, demanding quick action. The Exchange group noted that several banks were on the verge of failing, and with their fall would come the disintegration of the entire financial structure. Before an answer could be received, several runs developed. Lockwood & Co., a small but old brokerage, declared itself insolvent, and other firms also closed their doors. Solomon Mahler, known as a tight conservative, committed suicide. Now the entire district was in a state of pandemonium.

Meanwhile, Speyers continued to push gold higher. The price reached 160 at noon, with no sellers. Speyers then bid 161, and all were shocked when no one appeared to take the bid. Then he lifted the bid by fractions, first to 161⅛, then 161¼, and finally 161⅜. At this point he found a response. James Brown, a Scots banker who was known to represent several European groups, sold Speyers one million dollars in gold at that price. The Fisk combine was stunned, and lowered the bid to 161. Again Brown took the offer. The tide had turned.

Later on, some who were there on "Black Friday" claimed that these two purchases turned the market in favor of the bears. The Room buzzed with the news that a gigantic bear syndicate, organized in Europe, was prepared to dump tens of millions of dollars in gold in New York. Speyers was besieged with offers to sell, most of them coming from individuals who seconds earlier believed Fisk's prediction of $200 gold might well come true.

Shortly thereafter news reached the Gold Room of events outside. Grant had ordered Secretary Boutwell to sell gold, and Boutwell sent a telegram to Butterfield, telling him, in effect, to purchase $4 million in bonds with gold, thus putting the metal into the financial stream. Future President James Garfield was sent to the financial district to spread the news. He mounted the steps of the Subtreasury and shouted, "Fellow citizens, God reigns and the government in Washington still lives! I am instructed to inform you that the Secretary of the Treasury has placed ten million in gold upon the market!"

This news reached the Gold Room while Speyers was still bidding for gold at 160, probably at the moment Brown (who may have had his own pipeline to Washington) took the bid. The price broke downward immediately, but so great was the confusion that on one end of the Room the bid was 135, while at the other it was still 160. But the word spread quickly, with Speyers one of the last to learn that the gold ring had been smashed. Black Friday was over.

Although gold returned to normal, ending trading that day at 131¼, the shocks caused by the corner continued to be felt. Gould had made a fortune, and when some of his victims attempted to prosecute him for breaking contracts, he obtained twelve injunctions and court orders from his "captive judges," which shielded him from legal actions. Belden and his group went bankrupt; since all sales had been made in their name, and they could not possibly cover them, they took legal steps to avoid settlement. Fisk was unaffected by the fact that he had purchased some $60 million in gold and then refused to accept his obligations. All the buying had been done in the names of others; he could not be touched. Of course, he had reason to protest Gould's double-dealing in not telling him of his gold sales, but his hurts were salved when Gould gave him a share of the profits. In addition, Fisk, who had been charged with delivering Corbin's $100,000 check, conveniently forgot to send it to the speculator, and now he ripped it up. Corbin emerged with nothing for his efforts, as did others of the Grant circle.

A Congressional investigation followed, and the entire affair was exposed. As expected, Fisk was the star of the inquiry, admitting all and refusing to accept responsibility for failures of others. The ebullient Fisk complained, "A fellow can't have a little innocent fun without everyone raising a halloo and going wild." Gould was more serious about the matter. He brushed aside those who said his group had made $40 million on the corner, although the estimate seems reasonable. "I regret very much this depression in financial circles," he said, "but I predicted it long ago. I was in no way instrumental in producing the panic."

The full measure of the panic of 1869 cannot be had by studying the gold corner alone; its impact was felt for the rest of the year and well into 1870. Prices on the Stock Exchange fell throughout

September, in the worst month since the war. Most of the losses came in the final week of September, and the decline continued

DECLINES ON THE STOCK EXCHANGE, SEPTEMBER 1869

Stock	Sept. 1 Price	Sept. 29 Price	Decline
New York Central	205¼	145	60¼
Hudson River R.R.	187½	128	59½
Harlem R.R.	160	117	43
Erie R.R.	35	27	8
Cleveland & Pittsburgh R.R.	108	82	26
Chicago & Northwest R.R.	86¼	62	24¼
Chicago & Rock Island R.R.	115¼	101	14¼
Milwaukee & St. Paul R.R.	79½	59½	20
Michigan Central R.R.	106¼	74½	31¾
Reading R.R.	97½	90	7½
New Jersey Central R.R.	107	96	11
Pacific Mail S.S.	80¼	55	25¼

Source: *New York Herald*, September 30, 1869

into 1870, although economic news was good and the currency situation well in hand. But, as the investigating committee concluded, "for many weeks the business of the whole country was paralyzed," and the "foundations of business morality were rudely shaken."

The price of gold continued to decline, and when economic conditions improved, it settled down at around 120. Speculation diminished gradually as attention turned to the Stock Exchange in the early 1870s. In 1877 the Exchange took over the Gold Room, and it continued operations as a subsidiary organization. This occurred on May 1, at which time the old Gold Room was ripped down and its assets distributed among its four hundred and eighty-six members. Each received $260.72. The fountain and Cupid disappeared and were never recovered.

In time Black Friday and the Gold Ring would pass into legend, with Fisk and Gould appearing more the inventive creations of tall-story tellers than real people. The exploits of these two, together with Vanderbilt and Drew, make up the wildest chapter in Wall Street history. These men may not have caused

the most severe panics on the Street, but they were responsible
for more crises than any other quartet the financial district has
ever known. The tales told of them are sometimes humorous, but
their impact was not, especially on those foolish enough to fall in
their webs. One of these, broker Albert Speyers, the man in charge
of pushing gold to new highs, went insane as a result of Black
Friday, and never recovered. Young E. C. Stedman, a poet as well
as a broker, immortalized Black Friday the next day, helping to
perpetuate the legend of the greatest corner in Wall Street history.*

Israel Freyer's Bid for Gold

Zounds! how the price went flashing through
Wall Street, William, Broad Street, New!
All the specie in the land
Held in one Ring by a giant hand—
For millions more it was ready to pay,
And throttle the Street on hangman's day.
Up from the Gold Pit's nether hell,
While the innocent fountain rose and fell,
Louder and higher the bidding rose,
And the bulls, triumphant, faced their foes.
It seemed as if Satan himself were in it:
Lifting it—one per cent a minute—
Through the bellowing broker, there amid,
Who made the terrible, final bid!
　　High over all, and ever higher,
　　Was heard the voice of Israel Freyer—
A doleful knell in the storm-swept mart—
"Five Million more! and for any part
　　I'll give One Hundred and Sixty!"

Now through his thankless mouth rings out
The leaguers' last and cruelest shout!
Pity the shorts? Not they, indeed,
While a single rival's left to bleed!
Down come dealers in silks and hides,

* Stedman writes of Israel Freyer, not Albert Speyers, but the two are the
same. The change of name was made, apparently, as a reflection of anti-
Semitic sentiments roused by the corner, some of which were also directed
against Gould—who, however, was not Jewish.

Crowding the Gold Room's rounded sides,
Jostling, tramping each other's feet,
Uttering groans in the outer street;
Watching, with upturned faces pale,
The scurrying index marks its tale;
   Hearing the bid of Israel Freyer—
   That ominous voice, would it never tire?
"Five Millions more!—for any part,
(If it breaks your firm, if it cracks your heart,)
   I'll give One Hundred and Sixty!"

One Hundred and Sixty! Can't be true!
What will the bears-at-forty do?
How will the merchants pay their dues?
How will the country stand the news?
What'll the banks—but listen! hold!
In screwing up the price of gold
To that dangerous, last, particular peg,
They had killed their Goose with the Golden Egg!
Just there the metal came pouring out,
All ways at once, like a water spout,
Or a rushing, gushing, yellow flood,
That drenched the bulls wherever they stood!
Small need to open the Washington main,
Their coffer-dams were burst with the strain!
   It came by runners, it came by wire,
   To answer the bid of Israel Freyer,
It poured in millions from every side,
And almost strangled him as he cried—
   "I'll give One Hundred and Sixty!"

Like Vulcan after Jupiter's kick,
Or the aphoristical Rocket's stick,
Down, down, down, the premium fell,
Faster than this rude rhyme can tell!
Thirty per cent the index slid.
Yet Freyer kept making his bid—

"One Hundred and Sixty for any part!"
The sudden rush had crazed *his* heart,
Shattered his senses, cracked his brain,
And left him crying again and again —
Still making his bid at the market's top

(Like the Dutchman's leg that never could stop,)
"One Hundred and Sixty—Five millions more!"
Till they dragged him, howling, off the floor.
  The very last words that seller or buyer
  Heard from the mouth of Israel Freyer—
A cry to remember as long as they live—
Were, "I'll take Five Million more! I'll give—
  I'll give One Hundred and Sixty!"

5.
CRISIS OF THE
GILDED AGE: 1873

Fisk and Gould went their separate ways after dividing the profits from Black Friday. Gould turned increasingly to Erie and other railroads. For him Black Friday marked a way station in his drive for national power, which in the end he attained. Within a few years the vaguest hint that Jay Gould was "interested" in one situation or another would be enough to send tremors up and down Wall Street. In 1870, the *Herald* thought the best way to prevent any future panic would be to ship Gould off to Europe and keep him there, by force if necessary. The sickly, ferretlike Gould would never inspire admiration, but for the next generation he was the most respected force in the financial district.

Fisk was of a different type. His showmanship and shrewdness might have served to gain him power, had he desired it, but Jubilee Jim was more interested in gaudy trappings than true substance. He had his opera house, steamships, and resplendent uniforms. These, and his mistress, Josie Mansfield, were enough to satisfy him. From time to time he would dabble in local politics, enter special situations on Wall Street, and play the hero to old friends from New England. Never again would he gain the eminence he once had, while associated with Jay Gould.

Fisk's desire for the good life was fulfilled, but not for long. Shortly after Black Friday Josie became enamored of socially prominent Edward Stokes, a handsome young man who made his living through taking money from Josie and through blackmailing acquaintances. In 1871 he began to blackmail Fisk, using the financier's letters written to Josie. Stokes threatened to expose Jim as an unfaithful husband, and worse, a cuckold.

For a while Fisk paid whatever Stokes asked, gaining a measure of revenge by involving him in speculations through which much of the money was lost. Then he announced that he was through paying. Stokes promptly released the letters, initiating the case of Mansfield vs. Fisk in November. The *Herald, Times* and *Tribune* anticipated the trial with delight, for it promised not only lurid revelations of the private lives of Fisk and those around him, but also new information regarding the machinations of Wall Street speculators. Even Gould was concerned; he dropped Fisk from the board of Erie Railroad and brought in such eminent individuals as John Jacob Astor, Levi P. Morton, and August Belmont to give the line an aura of respectability, in the hope that some would rub off on him and so protect the Gould interests from any mud that might come his way.

Readers of the city's newspapers were not disappointed. Josie testified on what the *Herald* called Fisk's "oriental tastes and desires," and spoke candidly of her relations with both him and Stokes. Fisk became the laughingstock of New York, while Stokes would thereafter be shunned in the city's social circles.

On the evening of January 6, 1872, Fisk entered Pike's Opera House and bid his last farewell to Erie Railroad, whose offices were established over the stage. Next he went to the Grand Central Hotel on Fourth Street, where he entered with a flourish of his cape, and then began to ascend the stairs. Stokes awaited him at the first landing. Enraged by what had happened in court and determined to destroy the man who had wrecked him, Stokes fired at Fisk, hitting him in the body, while he screamed, "Now I've got you!" A second shot struck Fisk in the arm. Jim fell, asking, "Will nobody protect me?" A crowd rushed to his side, and the blood-spattered body was carried upstairs to a room. Within a few hours, Jim Fisk was dead.

As might be expected, the newspapers had a field day over the affair. All dredged up stories of Fisk's escapades and printed elaborate tales of railroad manipulations and the gold conspiracy. Interestingly enough, Fisk emerged from these articles a hero; in the end, his daring and style eclipsed his thievery and flaunting of the law. Ordinarily, Stokes might have gained sympathy by killing a man of Fisk's reputation—the classic case of a young aristocrat striking out at an evil, gross villain delighted theatre audiences of that day. Instead, he was roundly condemned and quickly arraigned for murder. Stokes' first trial ended in a hung jury. He was found guilty at the second and sentenced to death by hanging, but the conviction was set aside by the Court of Appeals. Stokes then underwent a third trial. This time he was convicted of manslaughter and sentenced to six years in Sing Sing. Released in 1876, he first entered the restaurant business and then began to speculate once more on Wall Street. Exposed on several occasions as a cheat and liar, Stokes was forced to leave the district and take up new employment. Wherever he went, he would insist on a night light while he slept. It was said that Stokes feared retribution from Fisk's ghost.

Gould and Drew were silent regarding Fisk's death, as was Commodore Vanderbilt. There is no direct evidence that any of them thought much about their former comrade and foe. Twenty years later, however, it was learned that Commodore Vanderbilt, a long-time believer in ghosts and fortune-tellers, hired a medium in 1873 to attempt to contact the spirit of Jim Fisk, in order to get information and advice on the stock markets from beyond the grave!

Vanderbilt had reason to seek advice early in 1873. The economy appeared strong, the currency situation in hand, and stock prices due for a rise. These bullish signs were balanced, however, by equally strong arguments supporting the bears, such as continued governmental scandals, tremors following an English collapse in 1866, the difficult tasks of reconstruction in the South, overbuilding in some areas of the economy, and fears of currency manipulation that remained after Black Friday. As a result, the market was irregular in January and February of 1873, so leading the Commodore to try to contact Jim Fisk's ghost.

If statistics alone were to guide market operators at that time, they would all have been bulls. Railroads, considered the nation's economic bellwether, were expanding rapidly, penetrating the West and making possible a truly national economy, with Eastern

RAILROAD MILEAGE AND TOTAL INVESTMENT, 1865–1873

Year	Total Mileage	Miles Constructed	Total Investment (thousands of dollars)
1865	35,085	819	N.A.
1866	36,801	1404	N.A.
1867	39,050	2541	1,172,881
1868	42,229	2468	1,869,529
1869	46,844	4103	2,041,226
1870	52,922	5658	2,476,893
1871	60,301	6660	2,664,628
1872	66,171	7439	3,159,423
1873	70,268	5217	3,784,543

Source: *Historical Statistics*, p. 427, 428

manufactured goods carried West, while on the return trip the locomotives would carry grains and other foodstuffs on a seasonal basis. To be sure, the new Western roads faced major problems. The territorial markets were still not large enough to enable the lines to use their rolling stock efficiently, and during most of the year they ran at a loss, hoping to make up deficits when shipping foodstuffs to markets after harvests. Railroaders could note with satisfaction that American grain production was increasing rapidly, and they hoped that still larger shipments would soon make their lines economical. On the other hand, grain prices tended downward after the war, making it difficult for the lines to charge

WHEAT PRODUCTION, 1866–1873

Year	Acreage Harvested (1,000 acres)	Wheat Production (1,000 bushels)
1866	15,408	169,703
1867	16,738	210,878
1868	19,140	246,273
1869	N.A.	287,746
1870	20,945	254,429
1871	22,230	271,881
1872	22,962	271,482
1873	24,866	321,931

Source: *Historical Statistics*, p. 297

higher rates which would enable them to service their debts. For their part, the wheat farmers were trapped in that familiar circumstance of being forced to overproduce when grain prices fell, so as to receive sufficient funds to pay off bank mortgages. Increased production resulted in still lower prices, and the cycle then repeated itself.

WHOLESALE PRICES OF WHEAT AND STEEL, 1865–1873

Year	Wheat (bushel)	Steel Rails (100 pounds)	Whole Price Index (1910–14 = 100)
1865	$2.10	N.A.	185
1866	2.95	N.A.	174
1867	2.84	$166.00	162
1868	2.54	158.50	158
1869	1.65	132.25	151
1870	1.37	106.74	135
1871	1.58	102.52	130
1872	1.78	111.94	136
1873	1.78	120.58	133

Source: *Historical Statistics*, pp. 115, 123

The downward spiral was also evident in the prices of steel rails, the basic constituent of railroad building. Since rail construction was not dependent upon the agricultural cycle and since it ex-

COST OF LIVING INDEX, 1865–1873 (1913 = 100)

Year	Index
1865	102
1866	103
1867	102
1868	98
1869	95
1870	91
1871	89
1872	90
1873	88

Source: *Historical Statistics*, p. 127

panded more regularly than wheat or other crops, the drop in the price levels for steel rails in the postwar period was a still more striking indication of the general deflationary tendencies of the period.

Other constituents of the economy were affected. Although employment was obtained easily in most parts of the country and for most occupations, wages tended lower after the Civil War, a factor which was balanced, however, by the general decline in the cost of living. As a result, the laboring classes were not severely affected by the deflation.

Holders of fixed obligations, such as bonds, did well as interest rates declined, while debtors suffered in having to service heavy obligations at a time when money was becoming dearer. The two largest debtor classes in the nation were the farmers and the railroads. Each was in constant danger of bankruptcy should the monetary noose tighten; each was forced to gamble yearly on easy money; each felt the other was preying upon it and—in part at least—was responsible for its difficulties. It was during this period that farmers became inflationist, supporting legislation to expand the supply of greenbacks and later on, silver, so as to make money more plentiful. Most railroaders were of two opinions on the subject. As businessmen they recognized the need of a sound dollar to maintain commercial equilibrium, but as debtors they were attracted by inflationary schemes.

From the end of the war until 1870, farmers, railroaders, and steel producers expanded their operations in order to maintain net profits in the face of falling prices. This was a period of unreal and often unwise growth, when hopes for the future obliterated realities of the present. On the surface all seemed well, and observers noted with pride the great vigor of the economy. Had they dug deeper, they might have recognized that this growth was cancerous and, had it continued along the same lines for much longer, might have resulted in economic paralysis.

This was not to be, fortunately, for in 1870 the price levels stopped declining and then began to rise.

There were many reasons for this rise—shortages of grain overseas and war preparations abroad were factors—but a leading domestic reason was the temporary settlement of the currency problem. In 1868 greenback contraction ceased, and fears of the inflationists that President Grant would make good his promise to restore a gold standard seemed ended. Two major setbacks followed. Black Friday unsettled conditions the next year, and in 1870 the Supreme Court decided, in Hepburn vs. Griswold, that greenbacks need not be accepted as legal tender. In 1871, the court reversed its stand in Knox vs. Lee, stating that Congress had the right to determine how debts should be met. Stabilization of the greenbacks and Knox vs. Lee were considered important expansionist victories, and so the tendency of the economy turned; in early 1873 inflationary forces appeared stronger than those of the sound dollar.

Economic growth had to be financed, and this could be accomplished by several means, among them reinvestment, inflation, borrowing, and the diversion of earnings from one sector of the economy to others.

Reinvestment seemed out of the question. By 1869, some 129 million acres had been granted the transcontinentals by Washington, while the states added 52 million more. In addition, the federal government made loans of almost $65 million to the six transcontinentals alone. Almost 40 percent of all construction cost prior to 1870 were borne by local, state, and federal governments. Still, in 1869, the year the Union Pacific was completed, the line showed profits of only $2 million, barely enough to pay for improvements and repairs in 1870, when the line had to go to the capital markets for additional funds. The American economy was capital-hungry, and would remain so for decades. Although earnings were plowed back into large enterprises, they were inadequate for the tasks ahead.

As had been indicated, inflation was another path, but the best that could be expected, given the power of the opposition, was the kind of compromise arrived at by 1871. Some hoped earnings from the agrarian sector would balance deficits in the industrial, but in the decade following the Civil War the nation had a chronic balance of international payments problem, and so that avenue was also closed, especially when deficits mounted in the early

BALANCE OF INTERNATIONAL PAYMENTS (millions of dollars)

Year	Exports	Imports	Deficit
1865	279	343	64
1866	481	572	91
1867	401	550	149
1868	428	505	77
1869	395	567	172
1870	507	608	101
1871	603	704	101
1872	576	824	248
1873	675	856	181

Source: *Historical Statistics*, pp. 562–63

1870s. The only recourse left was the utilization of European banks for the flotation of American stocks and bonds.

In this period London was the key capital market. Great advances in transportation which had taken place earlier in the century were now accelerated. The Suez Canal was completed in 1869, facilitating trade with the Orient and leading to renewed interest in ocean transportation. Throughout the world nations embarked on ambitious railroad schemes. Austria tripled her total mileage in eight years, and Russia constructed a 12,000-mile system in four. Argentina and other Latin American nations went to London, Paris, and Amsterdam to borrow money for rail ventures, as did the United States.

Prior to the Civil War, American entrepreneurs had gone to London for capital and had usually found interest there for securities. After the shock waves caused by the 1857 panic disappeared, London banks began to look favorably at American securities once more, and during the Civil War plowed millions of pounds into new lines. The London crash of 1866 led to a temporary contraction, but toward the end of the decade flotations increased in size and number, reaching what were considered astronomical heights in the early 1870s. In 1853 foreigners had owned $51.9 million in railroad securities, then, as later, the single most important investment category. By 1869, the figure was $243 million. Four years later the figure was still higher. Clearly, America's economic boom had its motor in London and other European capitals. Undercapitalized American railroads with large debts could easily collapse should this flow of funds cease. A momentary shudder in London or another important capital could lead to panic and destruction, not only in America but throughout the world. And in May 1873, panic struck in Berlin and Vienna, starting a chain of contraction in Paris, Amsterdam—and London.

In 1873, then, the rapidly expanding American economy was

FLOTATIONS OF AMERICAN RAIL SECURITIES IN LONDON, 1860–1873
(millions of pounds sterling)

Year	U.S. Rails	Total Foreign Investment
1860	1.0	6.7
1861	—	4.8
1862	—	7.4
1863	.2	12.9
1864	1.3	14.2
1865	2.7	20.9
1866	2.0	11.0
1867	1.0	6.5
1868	1.6	9.7
1869	1.8	8.8
1870	3.9	9.8
1871	6.1	15.3
1872	12.0	31.2
1873	14.3	29.8

Source: Leland Jenks, *Migration of British Capital to 1875*, p. 426

showing signs of strain, and the fabric could easily be rent in several places. An unexpected increase in demand for funds could lead to a breakdown of an already tight monetary situation. Political scandals could result in an erosion of confidence—and this was the age of corruption, both in Washington and in local and state governments. Slight declines in rail shipments might lead to bankruptcies on key lines, which could spread rapidly to other roads, banks, insurance companies, and the like. Gold shipments, necessary to service European debts could—when combined with seasonal outflows in late summer and early autumn—result in a liquidity problem. Should London find it necessary to call in American loans, or for some reason alter its relationship to American companies, it could wreck the nation. Any of these situations would be serious in terms of ending the façade of prosperity which existed early in 1873; a combination of them could result in the worst panic and depression in the nation's history.

Such matters as railroad overconstruction and the condition of the London market were of major importance for investment bankers, but Wall Street speculators considered short-run factors and special situations more important in terms of making their fortunes. The fluctuating markets of the postwar decade led to regular bull and bear drives on the Street, and scarcely a week passed without several new pools being formed. The smaller fry would switch from one side to the other with amazing alacrity—understandable, considering that shifts were so rapid that failure to move could easily result in disaster. Speculators would rush to and from the Open Board, the Petroleum and Mining Board, the Gold Room, and the half-dozen other markets that had sprung up during the war, usually ending up at the Exchange in the attempt to unravel the mysteries of the doings of the mighty.

Most of the speculation and manipulation was carried on by the younger element, while the exchanges were controlled by the more established brokers. The latter group organized against the speculators, passing resolutions against shady deals and forcing those who transgressed from exchange memberships. Some smaller exchanges closed their doors, and in 1869 the New York Exchange and the Open Board merged, forming what today is the leading Wall Street market and was to become the stage for most great manipulations and panics of the future.

Transactions were still carried on by the old auction methods, but the list grew longer each month, and volume increased rapidly. As a result, continuous trading was permitted before and between the morning and afternoon sessions. Finally, in 1882, the auctions were abandoned, and continuous trading became standard. On a busy day in 1873, however, the calls for an active stock like Western Union might last for a quarter-hour in the morning and the same amount of time in the afternoon. Volume on a busy day could reach 50,000 shares for a single issue, and the norm for the entire list was well over 100,000 shares a day that year.

Most speculative moves after Black Friday hinged on dramatic, exterior events. In 1870 stocks fluctuated sharply on reports of new gold and silver strikes in the Far West, and on rosy news of railroad futures. Speculation in rails reached a climax the following year, straining credit facilities and causing brokers to work weekends and holidays to catch up on their bookkeeping. By early October, several large banks were obliged to call in loans to maintain their liquidity, and the money rate began to rise sharply. Then came news of the Chicago fire. Wall Streeters knew this would hit insurance companies especially hard and would draw tens of millions of dollars out of New York. Stocks broke downward, leading to new fortunes for the bears and panic among the bulls. Jay Gould, who was becoming a symbol of bearish influence, made millions on the decline, while Vanderbilt, known as a bull, lost heavily when his railroads led the way downward. The situation was reversed in November and December, however, as stock prices rallied surprisingly and forced the bears to the wall. A similar development occurred before, during, and after the Boston fire of late 1872, after which Gould cornered several key stocks, reaped new fortunes, and almost had to face a trial for criminal practices, prevented only after he agreed to return some of his profits. In addition, Gould was obliged to leave the Erie. Wall Street was relieved, but at the same time concerned. A person with Gould's background could hardly be counted on to quit the scene. The speculator was searching for new "opportunities," and this quest led to several minor panics, as various roads were rumored to have fallen under his control.

Scandal added to the general uneasiness of the early 1870s. There was widespread belief that the Gold Ring could never have operated without important aid from the Grant Administration. New York legislators were involved in the many maneuvers of Erie, "the Scarlet Woman of Wall Street," and the Tweed Ring was famous for its use of political influence in business dealings. Charles Yerkes, a leading Philadelphia stockbroker, embezzled fortunes before being discovered, and, as we have seen, his crimes were duplicated with regularity on Wall Street. Then, in January

1873, the public learned of the greatest scandal of them all. The Crédit Mobilier, which had constructed the Union Pacific Railroad, was shown to have milked that line dry. This could not have been done without the aid, or at least acquiescence, of Washington. Before the investigation was over, a score of statesmen were implicated. Their names sounded like a roll call of the politically potent. Grant's first Vice President, Schuyler Colfax, was implicated, along with future President James Garfield. John Bingham, high in GOP circles, made a fortune on his holdings, as did William (Pig Iron) Kelley and Oakes Ames. Democratic Congressman James Brooks of New York was given a share of the profits, and Republican Senator James Patterson of New Hampshire likewise—the corruption was as bipartisan as it was gigantic. Then, while Wall Street attempted to digest the many implications of Crédit Mobilier's actions, news of another scandal hit the district, this one involving the Pacific Mail Steamship Company, run by Alden Stockwell and made highly profitable by the placing of several lucrative government contracts with the line. Stockwell greased many Washington palms from 1871, when he gained control of Pacific Mail, to 1873, when he was undercut by Jay Gould. By then corruption had become an accepted fact of financial, economic, and political life, and Stockwell's stoic reaction was not unusual. He had attained his post through devious methods, and he lost it the same way. Speaking to reporters, he cheerily summarized his career.

When I came to New York and bought stock by the hundred shares they called me Stockwell. Then I began buying in larger amounts, and they called me Mr. Stockwell. By the time I was trading in thousand-share lots, I was known as Captain Stockwell. They promoted me to Commodore Stockwell when word got around that I had gained control of Pacific Mail. But when Jay Gould got after me and booted me out of the concern all they called me was "that red-headed son-of-a-bitch from the West."

Crédit Mobilier, the Pacific Mail scandals, tales of embezzlement, forgery, deceit, and double-dealing, the many manipulations at Erie—all led to increased bull and bear activities on Wall

Street. To the financial district's regulars the key to most happenings remained Jay Gould, and behind him the "money king" of America, Russell Sage. On September 1, 1873, the *New York World* wrote of them, along with others, in an article entitled "Wall Street Kings": "There is one man in Wall Street today whom men watch, and whose name, built upon ruins, carries with it a certain whisper of ruin. He is the last of the race of kings." The man, of course, was Jay Gould.

There is one whose nature is best described by the record of what he has done, and by the burden of hatred and dread that, loaded upon him for two and one-half years, has not turned him one hair from any place that promised him gain and the most bitter ruin for his chance opponents. They that curse him do not do it blindly, but as cursing one who massacres after victory.

Unquestionably Jay Gould was considered the most powerful Wall Street influence of the time. His activities could and did cause stocks to rise or fall, and he was responsible for several serious Wall Street crises. But Gould lacked the power to bring on a truly serious economic panic and depression, such as those of 1837 and 1857. His influence was on Wall Street and among certain important companies. He lacked the kind of position and influence that could paralyze the entire nation; not even his worst moments with Erie and gold had caused serious difficulties in the countryside. The power to wreak this kind of havoc rested with others—the men who controlled investment and maintained the vital economic ties with Europe. Less flamboyant and more responsible, such individuals belonged to a social elite that Gould, Sage, and their fellows could not enter. Their scope was the world, their collaborators men like the Rothschilds and Barings, and not the Stockwells and Drews. Conflicts between them involved entire countries and, by comparison, made the Erie wars seem skirmishes in the backwoods.

These men—the key investment bankers—were capable of forceful moves, but these were carried out with a sense of aristocratic honor and openness foreign to Jay Gould. Their power was greater than that of Gould, but it was exercised with far more responsibility and caution. Were this not so, the nation's existence, and not merely the price of Erie, would have been endangered. In 1873, the leader of this group in America was Jay Cooke, and his most serious rival was J. P. Morgan.

Cooke was the most inventive banker of his era, as well as the most important. Prior to the Civil War he had pioneered in the distribution of securities, selling them in the countryside to individuals who had never before owned stocks or bonds. Most earlier offerings had been sold locally or taken by a few domestic and foreign groups. Cooke thought there was a huge market among those who would buy small amounts of shares, and he sold his securities in all parts of the nation. His most important issue was a $500 million government loan floated in 1861 and 1862. Cooke had formed a selling group which included most of Wall Street's major houses, had organized a sales force of 2,500 subagents, and was able to distribute the bonds efficiently, gaining the needed funds while at the same time tying thousands of small investors to the Union cause. The financier was applauded by the press as "a savior of the nation" and warmly thanked for his services by President Lincoln.

Cooke's firm continued to thrive after the war. He handled the largest share of the government's refinancing operations, maintained close connections with the Rothschilds and other leading European firms, and became interested in several railroads, especially the Northern Pacific. Cooke seemed more powerful than ever in early 1873. Actually, however, he was in deep trouble.

Cooke's major problem was the Northern Pacific. He had become that road's financial backer in 1869, at a time when the nation was entranced with the transcontinentals. Cooke sold $100 million in bonds for the yet-to-be-built line, buying newspapers, bribing both foreign and American politicians, and in other ways conforming to the morality of American business at the time. Money was loaned to James Blaine and Schuyler Colfax—to anyone whose powers could be used in Cooke's behalf. He hired a newspaperman, Sam Wilkerson, to spread idyllic stories of the land along the route. Horace Greeley received stock in the line, and he began to print the Wilkerson stories of a "vast wilderness waiting like a rich heiress to be appropriated and enjoyed." Rutherford B. Hayes, a future President, spoke well of the line, as did Secretary of the Treasury Hugh McCulloch and preacher Henry Ward Beecher, all three of whom had shares of Northern Pacific.

With all this backing, however, Cooke still lacked sufficient funds for construction. The railroad ran into unexpected difficulties— storms, roadbeds that washed out, bridges that collapsed—and needed a continual flow of new money. In 1870 Cooke's congressional friends pushed a new Northern Pacific bill through the legislature, which provided for additional governmental support and made Cooke the line's sole agent. War was brewing in Europe, and the Rothschilds doubted whether new American issues could be distributed. But Cooke's men did their jobs well, selling bonds not only to European investors but also convincing European workers that they should come to America to live along the Cooke road. Wilkerson called one proposed city "Bismarck," to attract Germans who might come to a city with that name. Newspapers ran prominent advertisements to draw settlers.

Prosperity, Independence, Freedom, Manhood in its highest sense, peace of mind and all the comforts and luxuries of life are awaiting you. . . . Throw down the yardstick and come out here if you would be men. Bid good-by to the theater and turn your backs on the crowd in the street!

How many regret the non-purchase of that lot in Buffalo, that acre in Chicago, that quarter section in Omaha? A $50 lot may prove a $5,000 investment.

Wilkerson did a magnificent job of selling lots, convincing settlers to come to the Northwest, and in general promoting an atmosphere of enthusiasm regarding the railroad. Duluth, then a small town, was called the "Zenith City of the Unsalted Seas," and similar descriptive phrases were used for other barren spots. In time even those who were in on Wilkerson's plans began to believe the propaganda.

To be sure, there were those who knew better and said so. Most of these were Cooke's enemies, supporters of the rival Union Pacific, and others with special reasons to desire continued problems at Northern Pacific. Mark Twain was not one of these. Genuinely disturbed by a railroad boom built on hopes and little else, he and a friend, Charles Dudley Warner, began to write a book dealing with the problem. The work, called *The Gilded Age,* was begun in February 1873, and much of it was written during the great Northern Pacific boom. In it Colonel Berea Sellers, a typical tycoon-promoter, spoke glowingly of his new line, attempting to calm his wife, who feared "we live in the future much too much."

"Aha, my girl, don't you see? Things ain't so dark, are they? Now *I* didn't forget the railroad. Now just think a moment—just figure up a little on the future dead moral certainties. For instance, call this waiter St. Louis.

"And we'll lay this fork (representing the railroad) from St. Louis to this potato, which is Slouchbourg:
"Then with this carving-knife we'll continue the railroad from Slouchburg to Doodleville, shown by the black pepper:
"Then we run along the—yes—the comb—to the tumbler—that's Brimstone:
"Thence by the pipe to Belshazzar, which is the salt-cellar:
"Thence to, to—that quill—Catfish—hand me the pincushion, Marie Antoinette:
"Thence right along these shears to the horse, Babylon:
"Then by the spoon to Bloody Run—thank you, the ink:
"Thence to Hail Columbia—snuffers, Polly, please—move that cup and saucer close up, that's Hail Columbia:

"Then—let me open my knife—to Hark-from-the-Tomb, where we'll put the candlestick—only a little distance from Hail Columbia to Hark-from-the-Tomb—downgrade all the way.

"And there we strike the Columbus River—pass me two or three skeins of thread to stand for the river; the sugar-bowl will do for Hawkeye, and the rat-trap for Stone's Landing—Napoleon, I mean —and you can see how much better Napoleon is located than Hawkeye. Now here you are with your railroad complete, and showing its continuation to Hallelujah, and thence to Corruptionville."

Colonel Sellers admitted that the cities and the railroad were still in the planning stage, but he had no doubt they would soon be ready for many settlers. Each town was capable of supporting large populations, having good soil and easy access to the line. Sellers seemed particularly partial to "Corruptionville, the gaudiest country for early carrots and cauliflowers that ever—good missionary field, too. There ain't such another missionary field outside the jungles of Central Africa. And patriotic?—why, they named it after Congress itself."

The Northern Pacific, which resembled the Sellers line in many respects, was still in difficulties at the time of Twain's writing. A section of its tracks sank into a lake; the line was overdrawn $1.6 million; its bonds were selling at large discounts, and new issues could not be marketed. Northern Pacific had to pay its workers in scrip, and many left rather than work under such conditions. The *Philadelphia Ledger* called the Northern Pacific an American version of the South Sea bubble, and predicted its early bankruptcy. The Crédit Mobilier scandal on the Union Pacific was the talk of Wall Street, and some observers thought a new series of revelations was due—this time for the Northern Pacific. The *Ledger* spread such rumors, going so far as to indicate that Cooke had always been a thief and should be charged with criminal acts. Later on it was discovered that G. W. Childs, owner of the newspaper, was under the control of J. P. Morgan.

By the early 1870s Morgan was prepared to challenge Cooke's domination of American finance. He was allied with Anthony Drexel of Philadelphia, second only to Cooke as a power in that city, and with the influential J. S. Morgan & Co. of London. Levi P. Morton of New York was in the Morgan camp, as were other smaller houses in the Wall Street area which had been elbowed out of flotations by the Cooke forces in the past. All had reason to desire Cooke's downfall, but only Morgan could expect to replace him.

The Morgan forces managed to take a portion of a new $200 million Treasury issue from Cooke in 1871. The following year Cooke attempted to win sole control of a $600 million Treasury flotation, but was stymied when the Morgan group protested that no single house should have so much power. Then, in 1873, Morgan was able to win a share of new flotations awarded early in the year. It was decided that Jay Cooke & Co. would receive half of a

$300 million issue, while the Morgan group would take the rest under the same terms granted Cooke. Since the domestic market was already glutted, most of the bonds would have to be distributed overseas, where money was also tight due to war conditions. Morgan's European allies were the Barings, J. S. Morgan, and Morton, Rose & Co., while Cooke's English house joined with the Rothschilds to compete for sales.

The $300 million issue was to be sold by December 31, 1873, and the two groups would split a commission of $150,000. This was a small amount, to be sure, but the contract also stated that neither house would have to deliver the returns to the Treasury until the last day of the year. In other words, should the bonds be easily sold, Cooke and the Morgan group would have the $300 million for almost a year. And Cooke needed the money desperately. Northern Pacific was on the brink of ruin, and the use of some $150 million, interest-free, might be sufficient to tide it over until conditions improved, hopefully, toward year end.

Morgan realized that Cooke was in a difficult situation and that, unless the bonds were sold quickly, he might fall. We may never know whether Morgan attempted deliberately to destroy Cooke, but that summer the bonds sold very slowly, under orders from the Morgan syndicate. Members of the group later claimed that Cooke's typical rapid-selling techniques could not work in Europe, especially when conditions there were so tight. And each day Cooke's resources dwindled.

Cooke's liquidity could be preserved and his ventures salvaged if more Northern Pacific bonds were sold. But new Crédit Mobilier revelations, scandals involving the Southern Pacific, the usual summer money shortages, and open knowledge of the line's difficulties made such sales almost impossible. Some of Cooke's congressional allies began to worry about their investments, and the banker hastened to soothe their fears. The *Philadelphia Ledger* made the situation worse by discussing Cooke's problems almost daily, while on January 14, 1873, Bennett's *Herald* wrote of "Financial Embarrassment of Northern Pacific R.R." Cooke responded that such charges were "malicious and untrue," as were those which claimed that he was making a large personal fortune by bleeding the line. On January 7 he had his secretary write the following to an aged minister who wanted to know whether Northern Pacific's securities were appropriate for one in his modest circumstances:

Your letter to Washington City has been forwarded here for reply. You are a splendid writer for an old gentleman of sixty-four. Mr. Cooke desires me to say in reply that his advice always is not to put all the eggs in one basket, however good it may be. He has perfect confidence in the Northern Pacific bonds. They are receivable for lands at any moment at ten per cent. better than you can buy the said lands for greenbacks. Your own good sense will show you that a bond thus secured and thus receivable cannot be a bad investment even though the skies should fall. If you have but a small amount of money, you should, in the exercise of common prudence, put a portion into something else. Mr. Cooke himself personally would not hesitate to put all that he has in the world into Northern Pacifics, although he dont [sic] advise any one else to do this.

And two months later, Cooke wrote in answer to a similar inquiry that "If you are able to run the risk of $10,000 in any one investment we should certainly say that you could not do better than to take $5,000 more of the Northern Pacific." "There is not the slightest probability of there being any cessation in the legitimate demand for lands unless the world comes to an end," he told another writer. "The progress of empire is westward." But at the same time Cooke began to press his political friends for payments on stock delivered them earlier. Vice President Colfax asked for a delay, writing, "Unfortunately, I am 'short' just now, as my salary don't [sic] pay my expenses," and most others begged off for the moment. "Blaine will be a hard nut to crack," wrote Cooke, as the Senator refused to pay anything for his shares.

Cooke was in deep trouble by late August. American bonds could not be sold in Europe, said the German correspondent of one newspaper, "even if signed by an angel of Heaven." Cooke was equally unable to sell Northern Pacifics domestically. News that Jay Gould was busy forming a new gold ring on Wall Street served to unsettle things further, and money began to go into hiding. To some, conditions seemed ripe for panic. All the elements were there: speculation, overbuilding, tight money, the seasonal pull of currency to the farm areas, and news of corruption all made it appear feasible that Wall Street might expect troubles.

As usual, the *Herald* printed more stories than most newspapers on Wall Street topics. Its writers agreed that problems existed but thought that institutional safeguards would prevent a repetition of 1837 and 1857.

But for the fact that mercantile borrowers have to a considerable extent anticipated and prepared for the autumn condition, the stringency already foreshadowed would doubtless prove more difficult to contend with than it is in fact likely to be. True, some great event may prick the commercial bubble of the hour suddenly, and create convulsions; but while the Secretary of the Treasury plays the role of banker for the entire United States it is difficult to conceive of any condition of circumstances which he cannot control. Power has been centralized in him to an extent not enjoyed by the Governor of the Bank of England. He can issue the paper representatives of gold to the amount of a score or more of millions, and count it as much as the yellow metal itself. He can put forth $44,000,000 of greenbacks and win distinction in the West at the same time that he seemingly averts one phase of impending trouble, and altogether exercise for good or evil a greater influence than is possessed by all the banking institutions of New York.

Thus, on September 1, 1873, the *Herald* believed the power of central government could be used to avert any panic which might develop. Secretary of the Treasury Richardson was considered the strong bulwark against bears, plungers, and the wave of liquidations which could easily follow the fall of any important financial institution—such as Jay Cooke & Co.

Bankers Magazine, on the other hand, was less certain that panics were a thing of the past. High interest rates obtainable in New York, the result of speculative activities, had drawn surplus funds from all parts of the country. What would happen if one or more major New York institutions failed? Repercussions from such closings would echo throughout the nation. In May of 1873, the journal warned:

Is it surprising that capital concentrates here from the wilds of Maine, the recesses of Connecticut, the prairies of the West, or the tobacco fields of the South, to be used at one or two percent per month, in-

stead of six percent at home. . . . ? We caution our country bankers
to keep a healthy reserve at home, and not to trust too large a fund
in Wall Street on 'call.'

Such advice went unheeded; by 1873, New York was the financial hub of the nation.

On August 28, the *Times* and *Tribune* noted that some railroads were in financial difficulties. The St. Joseph & Denver was
mentioned as one of these, and the New York, Oswego & Mid-
lands another. Neither was large or important, but if they were in
trouble, it could be a sign that other, more important ones were
having similar problems. Traffic on these two lines was considered
better than normal, and rates sufficiently high to return handsome
profits. Both roads had gone to the capital markets in midsummer
to refinance old issues, and neither had been able to sell their new
bonds. As a result, bankruptcy seemed the next step.

Such news did not disturb traders at the Exchange, however.
Although prices fell slightly the first week in September, there
was no sign of large bull or bear pools, and volume remained
average. This was surprising, since the price of gold dropped

PRICES OF SELECTED ISSUES, SEPTEMBER 1–6, 1873

	Closing Prices (fractions rounded off)					
Issue	Sept. 1	Sept. 2	Sept. 3	Sept. 4	Sept. 5	Sept. 6
Erie R.R.	60	59	59	59	59	58
Harlem R.R.	130	130	131	130	130	129
New York Central R.R.	105	105	105	105	104	104
Pacific Mail S.S.	43	43	43	44	43	43
Rock Island R.R.	109	109	108	108	108	107
Union Pacific R.R.	26	27	27	26	26	26
Western Union	92	92	92	91	90	90

Source: *New York Times*, September 2–7, 1873

steadily as a result of activities of a Gould bear pool in that metal.
The weeknd newspapers gave little indication of any expectations
of disaster, although all three of the major journals continued to
report on gold speculations and currency tightness, and printed.

tales of corruption. The city's newspapers carried stories of bond forgeries to the extent of $800,000, and of malfeasance in Buffalo, Boston, and other cities. Forged shares in Erie and New York Central were being wholesaled; brokers and customers were warned to "know your source" when dealing in many issues.

The *Herald*, always on the prowl for scandals and possible weaknesses in the economic fabric, told of increased activity in Wall Street bucket shops, and thought a severe economic contraction was taking place. Although this was the season when money habitually went West, New York reserves were at a dangerously low point even for the season. Unless this trend were reversed, liquidity pressures would develop.

The first sign of trouble appeared on Monday morning, September 8. The New York Warehouse & Security Company, whose most important business was in factoring and commercial loans, admitted to being insolvent, and it suspended operations. President H. A. Johnson was asked the cause, and he replied:

This company has loaned money and its notes to railways and construction companies and individual railroad builders in the South and Southwest, some of whom are not able to respond. For the money and paper loaned the company has what its managers consider ample security in the shape of collaterals and endorsements.

Johnson believed the suspension temporary; once the money situation eased, New York Warehouse would reorganize. He voiced continued optimism in the economy and the future of the nation's railroads. It was no secret that the firm's major defaulter was the Missouri, Kansas & Texas Railroad, which apparently was in serious trouble. Other Wall Street houses with large railroad loans outstanding began to make inquiries, and some attempted to call in loans. There were no more major failures the next few days, however, and the markets remained calm, with prices trading in a narrow range. Some stocks fell slightly on Monday, Tuesday, and Wednesday, while a Thursday-afternoon rally wiped out most losses. Saturday was a calm day, but toward the end of the session, brokers learned that Kenyon, Cox & Co.—Daniel Drew's firm—had suspended. Wall Streeters did not have to be told the reason:

FINANCIAL CONDITION OF NEW YORK BANKS, AUGUST–SEPTEMBER 1873

Week Ending	Loans	Gold	Circulation	Deposits	Legal Tenders
August 9	$293,758,100	$29,820,000	$27,223,500	$ 27,123,100	$49,002,300
August 16	292,614,000	27,644,100	27,222,700	24,857,300	47,540,100
August 23	289,931,800	25,144,200	27,214,400	227,691,300	45,532,400
August 30	288,883,000	23,095,200	27,281,800	220,399,300	44,729,300
September 6	288,374,200	21,767,000	27,355,500	212,772,700	38,679,900
September 13	284,536,200	20,442,300	27,383,400	207,317,500	36,717,200

Source: *New York Herald*, September 15, 1873

Drew had made a $1.5 million loan to the Canada Southern and had attempted to call it in earlier in the week. The Kenyon, Cox failure could only mean that the line, like so many others, was insolvent.

The markets opened quietly on Monday, September 15, which was a dull day considering the news of the previous Saturday. Wall Street buzzed with rumors of new insolvencies, including that of George Opdyke & Co., which had been involved in several recent bond flotations, but prices held steady nonetheless. On Tuesday came news that the New York, Oswego & Midland had

PRICES OF SELECTED ISSUES, SEPTEMBER 8–13, 1873

Issue	Closing Prices (fractions rounded off)					
	Sept. 8	Sept. 9	Sept. 10	Sept. 11	Sept. 12	Sept. 13
Erie R.R.	59	58	59	59	59	59
Harlem R.R.	129	129	129	129	129	129
New York Central R.R.	104	104	103	103	103	103
Pacific Mail S.S.	42	43	41	42	44	43
Rock Island R.R.	108	107	106	107	107	105
Union Pacific R.R.	26	26	25	25	25	25
Western Union	91	90	89	88	91	90

Source: *New York Times*, September 9–14, 1873

suspended; the line was small but well known to Wall Streeters. The market shuddered, fell, but recovered before the close. Just before the last call, the Eclectic Mutual Life Insurance Company announced its insolvency. Like the New York, Oswego & Midland, the Eclectic was a minor company. It had the reputation of extreme conservatism in management and portfolio selection, however, and its decline indicated that less prudent insurance companies might soon follow it into bankruptcy.

The first signs of panic appeared Wednesday morning, September 17, although there was no major item of bad news to cause the decline. Volume picked up as stocks declined throughout the day. The *Herald* reported that market insiders seemed to expect a major news item to shake the market and were unloading so as to be prepared to pick up bargains later on. Short selling was on the rise, another indication of bearish sentiment.

That night brokers and speculators gathered at their usual
haunts in the lobbies of lower Manhattan hotels to swap rumors
and plan strategy for the next day. The general belief was that
the decline would continue until whatever news was being held
back was known. The bears appeared to control the market, but
there was some bullish talk as well. There had been a brief rally
Tuesday afternoon, which led some to believe that buying groups
had been formed to support the prices of several key stocks. Commodore Vanderbilt was mentioned as the key to the situation.
New York Central, the pride of his empire, was one of the few
stocks that had held firm. If it were to remain strong, the entire
list might have to receive assistance. Vanderbilt had the money
and influence for the task. The only question was, did he plan to
save the market?

Vanderbilt was not the person to watch that evening, however;
nor was the future of the decline to be decided in the financial
district. Rather, its fate would be determined at "Ogontz," where
Jay Cooke was entertaining President Grant at dinner. The huge
castlelike mansion, named after an Indian chief, was deep in the
Chelten Hills. Grant had come to Philadelphia to place his son,
Jesse, in a nearby private school, and he met with Cooke before
returning to Washington. That night Cooke received news, by
private wire, of difficulties in New York and Philadelphia. Conditions appeared serious but not critical. The next morning Grant
left Ogontz for the Capital, and Cooke set out for Philadelphia,
hoping to set things right in that city.

Meanwhile, the New York market opened lower on heavy
volume. There was no indication of organized support from Vanderbilt or anyone else. Rumors of runs at several key banks filtered
into the Exhange. The Fourth National, one of the favorites of
several important speculators, was under pressure, as was the
Union Trust, which had been used by the Vanderbilt group to
control Lake Shore Railroad. At the offices of Jay Cooke & Co.,
H. C. Fahnstock, the New York partner, attempted to borrow
funds from several sources in order to maintain operations. Fahnstock dumped blue-chip securities on the market, approached the
city's key bankers, and shortly after 10 A.M. called a meeting at
his offices which was attended by several of Wall Street's major

figures. All this availed nothing. An hour later, Fahnstock was forced to announce the closing of the New York office.

The news hit Wall Street like a thunderbolt. It had all happened so suddenly! While Fahnstock read the notice, Jay Cooke was still busily occupied in Philadelphia; so rapidly had everything transpired that the head of the firm learned of his insolvency after messengers on Wall Street knew of it. Resigned to his fate, Cooke closed the Philadelphia office, and shortly after, the Washington branch and its ally, the First National Bank of Washington, D.C., suspended operations. The seemingly impregnable edifice of America's leading banking house crumbled in less than an hour. "No one could have been more surprised," wrote the *Philadelphia Inquirer*, "if snow had fallen amid the sunshine of a summer noon." The Exchange was in an uproar; the *Tribune* reported that "dread seemed to take possession of the multitude," as the few remaining bulls lost all hope and began selling stocks helter-skelter. Western Union fell ten points in a series of rapid trades, and others followed. Jay Gould, leader of the bears, jubilantly viewed the disaster. According to one source, he made more than $500,000 in the decline that September 18. And as Gould watched, brokers were trampled in the panic, dragged away, and taken to hospitals. When news of the failure of Cooke's Philadelphia office reached the floor, "a monstrous yell went up and seemed to literally shake the building in which all these mad brokers were for the moment confined." Prices were battered mercilessly, and Vanderbilt was the biggest loser of them all. Although able to maintain the price of New York Central, his other interests, especially the Lake Shore Railroad, fell sharply. Despite this, distraught bulls hoped their leader would take command of their forces. "Vanderbilt is the only man who can come to our rescue and re-establish confidence," said one harried speculator. "I hope from the bottom of my heart that he will come down to-morrow, as he did on the occasion of Black Friday, when New York Centrals were depreciated from 190 to 145, throwing ten millions of money on the market. . . . "

Many stocks sold at bargain prices, and others fell without finding purchasers. Money seemed to evaporate, and the rate on Wall Street mounted to ½ percent per day, plus the usual legal rate of 7 percent. Not even Vanderbilt was able to save the situ-

ation; toward the end of the day Robinson & Suydam, a firm in
the Vanderbilt constellation, declared its insolvency, and this was
followed by the bankruptcy of Richard Schell's brokerage, known
as a principal Vanderbilt house. That night the irate Commodore
was asked to comment on the happenings on what was already
being called "Black Thursday."

There are many worthless railroads started in this country without any
means to carry them through. Respectable banking houses in New
York, so called, make themselves agents for the sale of the bonds of
the railroads in question and give a kind of moral guarantee of their
secureness. The bonds soon reach Europe, and the markets of the
commercial centres, from the character of the endorsers, are soon
flooded with them. The roads get into difficulties and bad language
is heard all around.

Clearly, Vanderbilt was referring to Cooke and the Northern
Pacific. But that house and line were not the only ones responsible
for the crash.

These worthless roads prejudice the commercial credit of our country
abroad. Building railroads from nowhere to nowhere at public expense
is not a legitimate undertaking. I might make allusions to Texas, Midland and other new railroads, but you must excuse me, for I am a
friend of the iron horse, and like to see it stretching to every corner
of the United States. They help to develop our commerce and civilization, and ought to be encouraged. All I have to say is, when railroads
are to be built, don't victimize the public to build them.

Vanderbilt then called a secret meeting with his allies and began
to plan for the next day. Their task would be difficult, since most
of their banks were in danger of closing, and they lacked the funds
for a broad buying campaign.

All eyes were on Vanderbilt brokers Friday morning, September
19. It was felt that this was the right time for them to step in and
save the market, turn it around, and save the day for the bull
forces. On the other hand, it was expected that Gould and his men
would fight them and attempt to batter stocks to lower levels.

Prices fell from the opening, as the Vanderbilt group lacked the resources to take all stocks dumped on the market. Western Union and Lake Shore led the decline, and although the Commodore was able to support New York Central, that seemed the only one of his holdings secure from raiders. Fisk & Hatch announced its suspension, followed by Henry Clews & Co. and George Bolton Alley & Co.—all Vanderbilt allies. Union Trust was in trouble, along with a string of other Vanderbilt banks. It was apparent that the Commodore could not aid the bulls.

But aid did arrive—and from unusual sources. Hetty Green, the eccentric "Witch of Wall Street," arrived soon after the opening and went directly to broker John Cisco's office. The richest woman in America and a ruthless bear, her actions were carefully watched by the Wall Street crowd. Then came news that Cisco's floormen were bidding for stocks. It seemed evident that Hetty Green had come down to pick up bargains. For the first time, a ray of confidence broke through.

By midday, buying pressure had grown to the point where the decline had been halted. This was particularly noticeable in the Vanderbilt stocks. Had the Commodore been able to raise funds to save his skin? A quick check showed that the Vanderbilt men had been inactive. Further investigation indicated that many of the orders had come from Jay Gould's brokers. Gould's intentions were immediately evident. Backed by Russell Sage, the only man in America with sufficient funds for such a drive, Gould was attempting to purchase Vanderbilt's empire from under him. This dramatic shift led some Wall Streeters to conclude that Jay Gould had caused the panic merely to gain another victory in his fight with the Commodore. Now he had won his victory and, by buying stocks, had indicated a halt to the panic. Despite this rumor, more failures were reported. Jacob Little & Co., A. M. Kidder, and several smaller houses announced their suspensions, and it seemed that more would follow shortly. That Friday night, in the bars on lower Broadway, brokers talked of Vanderbilt's ruin, the Gould-Sage coup, and the debris left in the train of their conflict. They drank to an end to the panic, now that the struggle was over.

This view of what had happened the preceding two days was inaccurate. Forgotten was the dramatic failure of Jay Cooke & Co. and the reasons for that firm's troubles. In its attempt to resolve the panic as a struggle between two men, the district ignored the basic economic problems faced by the entire nation that autumn. Railroads, agriculture, and banks, key industries which held the nation together in 1873, were all in trouble. Gould's conversion to the bull side of the market would not change this; toasts to higher prices could not restore the damage already done by years of overexpansion, corruption, and recklessness.

Nor was the belief that Vanderbilt was in serious trouble based on a realistic assessment of his position. To be sure, his stocks were depressed, and the Commodore had been unable to save many of his friends during the last two days. His holdings were still secure, however. Vanderbilt owned his stocks outright, and although unable to purchase as many additional shares as he wanted at bargain prices, he was not obliged to sell his holdings to meet obligations.

These facts were driven home Saturday morning, when Osgood, Kissam & Co., Davison & Freeman, and Scott, Strong & Co. released a joint statement that Vanderbilt had been purchasing stock through their offices, and in particular had acquired substantial blocks of Western Union. A careful check indicated that these claims were exaggerated but had a kernel of truth. The Union Trust suspended operations, but Vanderbilt told reporters he hoped to have it back on its feet by Monday. By the time the Exchange bell signaled the opening of trading, Wall Street knew the Commodore was still powerful, having weathered the most serious threat to his positions that could have been mounted.

Despite this, prices continued to fall. No amount of good news seemed capable of reversing the patterns set on Thursday and Friday, or save the many brokerages and banks in danger the previous evening. After the first hour, stocks were offered with no bids in sight. News of Wall Street bankruptcies came so quickly that it was difficult to keep count. It seemed that securities of the highest quality had lost their value, and that the public "had forgotten how to bid."

Western Union provided the day's most dramatic collapse, falling from 75 to 54¼ during the pre-call trading, before recovering to 59½. At first the stock fell irregularly, "backing and filling" along the way. Then price jumps became sizable; toward the end

SALES AT AUCTION OF WESTERN UNION COMMON STOCK, SEPTEMBER 20, 1873

Sales Before the First Call

Number of Shares	Price	Number of Shares	Price
1,200	75	200	71
1,500	75	500	75
500	74	400	70½
800	76	1,400	70
700	74	600	71
1,000	73	1,500	70
800	73	400	69
200	72⅞	200	68½
900	74½	400	70
600	75	1,200	69
3,000	73¾	300	68
200	74½	300	69½
500	74	500	67
1,000	73	400	69
200	73¾	2,200	66
500	74	500	68
1,000	73	200	67
200	72¾	500	65
500	72	400	68
100	71¾	200	64
900	74	200	63

First Call

Number of Shares	Price	Number of Shares	Price
300	62	100	64
100	67	300	63
200	63½	200	62½
300	63	200	62
100	67	100	63
1,100	68	100	63¾
1,800	62	200	65¾
200	65	500	63
500	61¼	100	62¼
100	60½	300	62⅛
1,000	60	200	63
1,500	60	100	62
700	60½	700	60
100	61½	100	59½
500	62	100	59
500	63	400	60

SALES AT AUCTION OF WESTERN UNION COMMON
STOCK, SEPTEMBER 20, 1873

First Call

200	68	100	57
100	64	200	59½
100	67	100	56
1,000	68	100	55¼
1,400	65	100	54¼
200	62	100	59½
100	65		

Source: *New York Herald*, September 21, 1873

of the first call, the stock sank rapidly as Jay Gould gleefully
beared down upon it.

Later on, reporters vied with each other to describe the scene
on Wall Street, as the very foundations of the nation's business
seemed to collapse. The *Nation* of September 25 outdid most in
its report:

Any one who stood on Wall Street, or in the gallery of the Stock
Exchange last Thursday, or Friday, and Saturday, and saw the mad
terror, we might almost say the brute terror (like that by which a
horse is devoured who has a pair of broken shafts hanging to his heels,
or a dog flying from a tin saucepan attached to his tail) with which
great crowds of men rushed to and fro trying to get rid of their
property, almost begging people to take it from them at any price,
could hardly avoid feeling that a new plague had been sent among
men, that there was an impalpable, invisible force in the air, robbing
them of their wits, of which philosophy had not as yet dreamt.

The newspapers wrote of banks refusing to accept certified
checks, or even greenbacks, insisting instead on payment in gold.
There were panics in Europe's capitals at the same time, and the
Herald believed the entire world was in the grip of a wave of
hysteria which could bring down empires; one broker called it
"the worst disaster since the Black Death." Not even news that
President Grant and Secretary Richardson were on their way to
New York to take charge of the situation could rally confidence.

In the face of all this, the Exchange Board of Governors was forced to act in an unprecedented manner. At 11 A.M. it announced that for the first time the New York Stock Exchange would close its doors "for an indefinite period." Thus ended the most hectic week Wall Street had seen up to that time. A dour George Templeton Strong recorded the events of the day in his diary:

To Wall Street. Nervous excitement seemed less, but bank officers and everybody said things were going from bad to worse, and the air was filled with prophesyings of woe. By twelve o'clock the Bank of the Commonwealth and the Union Trust Company had stopped, and the Stock Exchange had closed its doors. A wise measure and would they might never be reopened. The secretary of the Union Trust Company, Carleton, son of a Methodist divine, is said to have vanished into Faery Land, like King Arthur, with $250,000 of the company's assets. A run on the Fourth National Bank continues unabated and seems resolutely met. The tellers at most of the Wall Street banks seemed to be kept very busy. At the Bank of America were more depositors than drawers. At the Mechanic's Banking Association, an ominous preponderance of the latter. That concern, the Continental and the Bank of North America, are considered shaky. The central focus of excitement was, of course, at the corner of Broad and Wall Streets. People swarming on the Treasury steps looking down on the seething mob that filled Broad Street. There was a secondary focus at Cedar and Nassau streets, where folks were staring at the closed doors of the Bank of Commonwealth and at the steady current of depositors flowing into the Fourth National and then flowing out again with an expression of relief.

In Wall Street again after lunch and at the Fifth Avenue Hotel this evening. The National Trust Company . . . has stopped. Comparatively small failures are many. All this looks ill for my Minnesota Railroad bonds, wherein I was seduced to invest by ———, and very ill for the nascent Church Music Subscription list.

President Grant arrived within hours of the closing. Reverdy Johnson, Attorney General in the Taylor Cabinet more than a generation before, and still an important political and business influence, accompanied the President, as did Secretary of the Treasury Richardson, thought the strong man of the present Cabinet. The next morning they met with representatives of the

PRICES OF SELECTED ISSUES, SEPTEMBER 15–20, 1873

| | Closing Prices (fractions rounded off) | | | | | |
Issue	Sept. 15	Sept. 16	Sept. 17	Sept. 18	Sept. 19	Sept. 20
Erie R.R.	58	57	56	54	54	54
Harlem R.R.	129	129	127	125	106	103
New York Central R.R.	104	104	99	96	93	91
Pacific Mail S.S.	43	43	42	39	37	32
Rock Island R.R.	105	103	102	99	92	90
Union Pacific R.R.	24	24	24	22	20	18
Western Union	90	89	88	80	68	60

Source: *New York Times*, September 16–21, 1873

banking and brokerage community. Henry Clews was there, as was Augustus Schell of the Union Trust: both men were closely allied with Vanderbilt. A member of Grant's entourage later wrote that the suite was crowded with "bankers, brokers, capitalists, merchants, manufacturers and railroad men . . . beseeching the President to increase the currency by every means in his power, and declaring that unless the government came to the rescue nothing could save the country from bankruptcy and ruin." Banks were still able to settle obligations to other financial institutions through the use of clearinghouse certificates, but were unable to meet demands from depositors, certain to increase Monday morning. In 1857 some depositors had been willing to accept the certificates—which were based on frozen assets—in lieu of money. Hopefully, they would take them in 1873. But if they refused, then most of the city's banks would be forced to close.

Commodore Vanderbilt came to see the President, tell him of the difficulty, and aid in overcoming the financial stringency. On several occasions he told Grant and Richardson that the major cause of the crash was overexpansion, especially in railroads. Grant would have to curb speculators and recognize this fact if the economy were to be made healthy once more. For the moment, however, the banks needed the most help. Currency had gone into hiding; Europe could not be counted upon for assistance; and he and his group lacked the resources to save the situation by themselves. Government aid would have to be forthcoming. Vanderbilt suggested that federal deposits of from $20 to $40 million in legal tender in key New York banks would restore confidence and save the situation. If Grant would agree to such a plan, he and his associates would place $10 million in securities with the New York Subtreasury to guarantee the deposits.

Richardson turned down Vanderbilt's suggestion on several points, the most important of these being that he lacked legal authority to make such deposits. Instead, he proposed to purchase government bonds on the open market, thus injecting new money into the financial stream. This plan was accepted, and it was agreed that the purchases would begin Monday morning.

The Exchange Board had warned member firms that trading outside that institution would be considered a breach of regulations, punishable by expulsion. Few heeded this warning, however, and on Monday morning crowds gathered at New Street and elsewhere to buy and sell securities. The most talked about group was a team of Canadians who had come to New York to pick up bargains. Gould and Sage were also there, prepared to reap fortunes from the distress of others. Prices were not reported in the newspapers of that day, but afterward it was learned that they remained steady, and in many cases actually rose. This was not due to any good news or a return of confidence; indeed, the long lists of suspended banks and brokerages in the Monday-morning newspapers would have shattered the optimism of the most bullish speculator. Rather, it was a sign that Sage, Gould, and their group were continuing the buying program started the previous week.

Meanwhile, runs developed at several leading banks. The Union Trust remained closed, and Strong's rumors were confirmed: a teller had absconded with a small fortune the previous Saturday. Depositors screamed their anger at Vanderbilt, who, as all knew, was the power behind President Augustus Schell. If he could offer to deposit $10 million to help the entire community, could he not spare funds to save his own institution? What the mob didn't realize was that although Vanderbilt had amassed large blocks of stock, he had little cash; the $10 million he had offered the New York banks was not to be in currency, but rather in securities. Only Sage and Gould appeared to have sufficient money to save the banks that morning, and they were busily using their reserves to purchase depressed stocks. Gould was asked by the *New York World* to comment on the panic. He blamed it on poor railroad financing and "the bad financial managing of the government."

While Gould spoke, Secretary Richardson moved to correct this problem. More than $3.3 million worth of government bonds were purchased on the open market, with the promise of more to come. In this way Richardson injected new money into the market. At the same time, a committee of five bankers formed at the clearinghouse reported that some $5 million worth of its certificates had been accepted by depositors, saving at least a dozen institutions from certain closings. These certificates, which paid 7 percent interest, would be acceptable in lieu of cash by all members of the clearinghouse. Although useful, they could not be utilized outside of the city. Acting quickly, the committee suggested that all depositors who wished to withdraw funds from New York banks be required to come in person to present their certificates of deposit. Similar roadblocks were placed in the path of correspondent banks attempting to draw their funds from the city. The measures were adopted, and they worked; interbank transfers fell sharply after September 20.

Henry Clews & Co. failed on Tuesday, September 23, but his was the only major bankruptcy of the day, a fact given great prominence by all the city's newspapers. On Wednesday, however, several important brokerages closed, among them Howes & Macy, which had offices in most major cities. News reached Wall Street of economic distress throughout the nation, as business ground to a halt due to currency shortages. Chicago banks were paralyzed, and the city was forced to resort to barter. In Pittsburgh, most blast furnaces were banked, and several firms were reported near failure. Richardson continued his operations, and by week's end told Grant that over $14 million had been pumped into the economy by his office. But this was not enough, and the bankers demanded more purchases, along with federal bank deposits as suggested by Vanderbilt.

The President refused to do more than purchase bonds at first. To those who protested, Richardson said, "This, gentlemen, is not my funeral." But as the week wore on, demands for currency inflation of one sort or another grew. Grant wrote to a friend, stating that he was willing to take all *legal* actions possible, but would not do anything not authorized by the Constitution or Congress. Evidently he believed Wall Street was holding back, refusing to use its resources and asking Washington to pull its chestnuts out of the fire. "The banks are now strong enough to adopt a liberal policy on their part," he wrote, "and by a generous system of discounts to sustain the business interests of the country." The President clearly minimized the seriousness of the situation and overestimated the powers of the New York banks. In early October he wrote, "I do not believe that the present panic will work to individuals half the injury it will work general good to the country at large." Grant thought the panic would cause a hoarding of gold, which in turn would lead to greater use of silver. As silver entered the financial stream, the currency would become inflated, and so provide a larger amount of currency, the prerequisite for prosperity. This is what the inflationists—those who demanded he issue more greenbacks—had demanded. They would get their additional currency, said the President, but it would come in the form of silver, and not paper. What Grant forgot, however, was that silver had been demonitized by the Mint Bill of 1873—a measure he himself had signed a few months earlier!

Despite the inability of government to play a strong role on Wall Street, the initial frenzy had disappeared by the end of the week. Almost all the secondary institutions in the financial district were closed, as were a good number of major banks and insurance offices. Money remained scarce, and the insolvent firms were obliged to come to terms with the condition. Howes & Macy led the way with a plan for reopening its 115 offices.

We proposed to continue our business as usual by receiving special deposits in trust to new accounts, pledging ourselves to use these deposits only on payment of your respective checks, against the new account, and as fast as we can collect and realize from our loans and securities to pay your pro-rata installments on our present indebtedness until the whole shall be liquidated, the same drawing the usual amount of interest until paid.

Henry Clews intended to reopen on the same basis, hoping to segregate new accounts from the old and pay the latter at some future date. Although these plans were not wholly satisfactory to investors, there seemed no other alternative if normal business were to resume. By Saturday morning, September 27, there were clear signs that customers were ready to do business with the fallen firms. Then came news that Commodore Vanderbilt had succeeded in borrowing currency abroad, and so would be able to save all his enterprises as well as satisfy depositors at the Union Trust. These developments led the Board of Governors to believe the Exchange might be reopened. In the late afternoon, it announced that trading would resume on Tuesday, September 30.

Although the Board had banned all sales in outside institutions and on the curb during the ten-day closing, sales were made, prices quoted, and other transactions carried through. On Tuesday morning, then, all Wall Street knew how stock prices had fluctuated the previous week, and had good ideas of what the opening bids would be at the Exchange. Therefore, many were surprised when sales appeared well above the September 20 close. Indeed, brokers were encouraged by the fact that prices remained high

PRICES OF SELECTED ISSUES, SEPTEMBER 20 AND 30, 1873

| | Closing Prices *(fractions rounded off)* | |
Issue	Sept. 20	Sept. 30
Erie R.R.	54	52
Harlem R.R.	103	113
New York Central R. R.	91	92
Pacific Mail S.S.	32	33
Rock Island R.R.	90	91
Union Pacific R.R.	18	20
Western Union	60	66

Source: *New York Times*, October 1, 1873

throughout the day, and did not lose ground the rest of the week. The *Times* thought: "There is a much brighter look to Stock and transactions. This virtually marks the close of the panic. . . ."

The opinion of the *Tribune*: "The Stock Exchange was reopened yesterday, without any revival of the panic; before the session closed the official announcement was made that no one had failed, and there was not a single delinquent member on earlier transactions. This virtually marks the close of the panic. . . ."

As expected, the *Herald* wrote of the opening with gusto. "A crisis in our financial dealings has been met and passed without loss of confidence, without fear, largely without distrust. Here are growth, understanding, increased knowledge, firmer self-reliance. The experimentalists of '37 and '57 have become today the safe engineers in times of peril." And as if to reinforce beliefs that prosperity had returned, the Treasury released an additional $3 million in gold on October 1.

The newspapers were wrong in thinking that conditions would now return to normal. True, there were no failures the first day, but on the second Northrup & Chick closed down. George Grinnell & Co. was expelled from the Exchange for failure to meet obligations. Patterson & Co., a major drygoods concern, declared bankruptcy. The City Savings Bank, one of the oldest in New York, went under. Not a day passed without news of several failures. Business conditions remained poor, and President Grant's periodic statements on finance caused more gloom that would have existed had he remained silent. "The President's financial ideas are not as good as his intentions," remarked the *Tribune*. By month's end, stock prices had slumped badly, with some hitting new postwar lows.

PRICES OF SELECTED ISSUES, SEPTEMBER 30, OCTOBER 30, 1873

Issue	Closing Prices (fractions rounded off)	
	Sept. 30	Oct. 30
Erie R.R.	52	45
Harlem R.R.	113	101
New York Central R.R.	92	83
Pacific Mail S.S.	33	27
Rock Island R.R.	91	87
Union Pacific R.R.	20	16
Western Union	66	46

Source: *New York Times*, October 1 and 31, 1873

Bad news seemed the order of the day, with a special dividend from New York Central the only item to cheer the district. Charles Phelps, Deputy State Treasurer of New York, absconded with $300,000 in public funds. William Hogue & Co., W. M.

Whittemore & Co., E. W. & J. P. Converse, and dozens of other
brokers and businessmen were forced into bankruptcy. The great
cotton empire of A. & W. Sprague went under; William Sprague,
the junior partner, was one of the nation's leading business and
political figures, being married to Kate Chase, daughter of the
Chief Justice. No sooner had this news been digested than the
city learned that E. J. Blake, president of the Mercantile Bank of
New York, a major institution, was captured with bank funds in
his possession. And so it went for the rest of the year, and into
the next—more failures, thievery, and misery.

BANK SUSPENSIONS, 1870–1878

Year	Total Suspensions	National Banks	State Banks	Mutual Savings Banks
1870	3	1	1	1
1871	10	0	7	3
1872	19	6	10	3
1873	41	4	33	4
1874	57	10	40	7
1875	28	3	14	11
1876	59	8	37	14
1877	89	8	53	28
1878	140	10	70	60

Source: *Historical Statistics*, p. 636

By then, it was evident that the panic was over but the depression only in its early stages; not until 1879 would recovery take
place. In this six-year period the nation underwent its most severe
depression up to that time, one second only to that of 1929–32
in damage done the economy and social fabric of the nation.
Business declined 32 percent (in 1929–32 the fall was 55 percent). There were more than 5,100 bankruptcies in 1873, and in
the peak year of the depression, 1878, the figure reached 10,478
concerns with assets in excess of a quarter of a billion dollars. The
wholesale price index fell from 133 in 1873 to 91 in 1878; wheat
fell from $1.78 a bushel to $1.25 in the same period and continued
to decline steadily for the next decade. Farm indebtedness reached
new highs almost every year in this period, leading to renewed
demands for inflation. Silver production, on the rise prior to the

panic, shot upward as new finds were exploited. By the end of the first depression year, farmers and miners demanded additional currency so as to reverse the depression and enable farmers to pay their debts in cheaper money and miners to obtain a market for their silver. Free silver agitation began in earnest; the lines were drawn clearly for the first time as a result of the panic. The money question would dominate American politics for the next generation, and at times would seem the issue around which revolutionary forces could gather. The 1873 panic was not merely a severe jolt to the economy; it marked the end of the era dominated by problems of slavery and secession (despite the fact that Reconstruction would continue for another four years) and the beginning of one in which monetary and class issues would occupy center stage.

The 1873 panic left in its wake the wreckage of hundreds of careers—but it also marked a new step upward for Jay Gould. As a result of the panic, Gould was able to pick up bargains, among them control of Union Pacific Railroad. Forming a coalition with Russell Sage, he went on to acquire the Wabash and a huge empire in the West, along with important interests in New York elevated lines. Western Union, which he had beared before and during the panic, also fell under his control. Other people's disasters became Gould's opportunities, and he took full advantage of each situation that came his way.

Jay Cooke never recovered from his failure. Although he lived for another thirty-one years, he had only a small part of several medium-sized enterprises in this period. Writing of his failure after the shock had been dissipated, the *Tribune* said:

Nothing can wipe out the debt the country owes the patriotic and marvelously energetic bankers, who in the darkest hours of our Civil War popularized the great loans and furnished the money to pay our soldiers; nothing can obscure the fact that the very enterprise which has finally dragged them down was of national concern. Whatever may be the result of the crisis in Wall Street, we shall regard the disaster to Jay Cooke and Company as nothing less than a public calamity.

Cooke had overreached himself, attempting to run railroads instead of concentrating on those financial matters he knew best.

In addition, he was helped down by one whose abilities and outlook were more in tune with the new industrial America.

J. P. Morgan emerged from the panic unscathed. Although he was not yet the leading force in the financial community, the fall of Jay Cooke left a vacuum which he would fill. In this respect, at least, Morgan was to gain from the miseries of the decade.

By manipulating his holdings, borrowing heavily under threats of dire retribution, Commodore Vanderbilt emerged from the panic with his empire intact. Although active during the depression, he would not live to see the next bull market; his actions during the panic would be his last significant role on Wall Street.

The Commodore lived four years longer, spending this period in rounding out his railroad system and speculating about the afterlife. When ill he would summon "Dr." William Bennett, an electric healer, who would "magnetize" Vanderbilt to relieve the pain. The Commodore's favorite spiritualists were Tennessee and Victoria Claftin, who claimed to receive information from the Greek orator Demosthenes. Vanderbilt was convinced that they were genuine; he set them up in a Wall Street office, where investors could hear lectures on the next world, read pamphlets on female rights, and place orders for stocks and bonds.

The Claftin sisters were also healers. At their insistence, Vanderbilt placed saltcellars under the legs of his bed, where they acted as "health conductors" to his body. The Commodore's illnesses doubtless led to this interest in spiritualism. It should be noted, however, that even a sick Vanderbilt was healthier than most men. In 1869, at the age of seventy-five, he had married a southern gentlewoman with the unusual name of Frank A. Crawford. Prior to this, his second marriage, the Commodore had enjoyed chasing after women a third his age.

Vanderbilt fell ill in 1876 and was confined to bed. Reporters gathered outside his Washington Square mansion, awaiting news of his death. But they had a long vigil, for the Commodore outlasted one doctor and almost another before he expired. He died the following year at the age of eighty-eight. Vanderbilt's last words were, "I'll never give up my trust in Jesus." He died while Frankie Crawford was singing the hymn "Nearer My God, to Thee."

Drew survived the Commodore by two years. The old fraud

had lost everything in the 1873 panic, and he never recovered. Uncle Dan'l went bankrupt with liabilities of over $1 million. His assets included a watch and chain worth $150, a sealskin coat, and a few religious books. Their total value was less than $500. Drew returned to Putnam County and lived there a while in semiretirement. He could not stand being away from the Street for long, however, and he returned to the city, this time as an observer and not a participant. His death in 1879 went unnoticed by the newspapers of the day.

The next few years were not easy for President Grant. Although he never lost his hold over the people, he proved repeatedly his incompetence for his office. Grant did manage to push through Congress a bill providing for the resumption of specie payments, and there were fewer major scandals during his second administration than there had been during the first. The depression continued, and Grant did little to alleviate distress. In 1875 the House overwhelmingly passed an anti-third-term resolution, directed against what many felt were the President's ambitions to remain in Washington. Secretary of War Belknap was brought up on inpeachment charges the following year, and a new wave of scandals seemed in the offing. While such matters occupied Grant's attention, greenback and silver agitation grew, resulting in the formation of the Greenback Party and a bloc of silver Senators who demanded correction of "the crime of '73," in which silver had been stricken from the currency list. Nothing seemed to go right for Grant. Even in the field of Indian affairs, setbacks took place; in 1876, General George Custer and 265 of his men were slaughtered by Sitting Bull's Sioux Indians at the Battle of Little Big Horn.

The election of 1876—one of the most corrupt in American history—resulted in the elevation of Rutherford Hayes to the Presidency. On December 5, Grant delivered his last major speech to Congress, apologizing for his many errors and blaming them on inexperience. My mistakes, he said, were "errors of judgment, not of intent."

Grant left Washington in March, to receive new honors and a host of honorary posts. Not a wealthy man, he had to take many odd positions in order to support his family. Then, in 1880, it appeared that he might gain the GOP Presidential nomination again, but this attempt failed. In 1882 President Chester Arthur asked Grant to serve as American Commissioner to draw up a treaty with Mexico; the offer was accepted. The ex-President enjoyed Mexico and formed many friendships in that country, especially with Don Matias Romero, his Mexican counterpart. A refreshed and optimistic Grant returned to New York in 1883, seeking new ventures and with all thought of retirement forgotten. It was then that Ulysses S. Grant, whose postwar career was remarkable for a notorious inability to understand financial matters, embarked on a new career: he would become a stockbroker.

6.
GRANT'S LAST PANIC: 1884

Repercussions of the 1873 disaster were felt in the congressional elections of 1874, when large Democratic gains were made in most parts of the nation. Voters seemed to believe that financial manipulations and political deals made by the GOP had been instrumental in causing the panic and depression; now they indicated a wish for peace and an end to chicanery. Despite the evident lack of desire for new legislation, Grant and the hard-money faction pressed on in their drive to return the nation to gold. Having fought off attempts to expand the currency through the issuance of greenbacks, Republican moderates counterattacked by introducing the Resumption Bill late in the year. After much debate, the measure was passed and signed into law before the new, inflationist-minded Congress could meet. Under its terms, greenback circulation would be limited to $300 million (which meant that $82 million in paper would be withdrawn). Fractional paper money was to be replaced by coins. Most importantly, on and after January 1, 1879, greenbacks would be fully convertible to gold.

Passage of the Resumption Act led to cries of anger from inflationist elements in all interest groups, who were convinced that such a measure would lead to the disappearance of greenbacks, constrict the currency, and create a new wave of business failures. Crop prices would fall sharply, causing more agrarian misery; wages were certain to be cut in such a situation. Farmers, workers, and parts of the business community viewed resumption with grave forebodings. An inflationist coalition formed to support the coinage of silver as an alternative to greenbacks. This group gained a limited victory in 1878, when the compromise Bland-Allison Act was passed, which provided for the purchase and coinage of from $2 million to $4 million in silver a month. In addition, the greenback limit was raised from $300 million to $347 million. Other attempts to block resumption failed, however.

The premium at which gold sold in relation to greenbacks dropped steadily as January 1, 1879, approached. In 1875 the average price was 117; on January 3, 1878, it was quoted at 102. By December 1, the price was barely over 100, and the premium disappeared on December 17. On that date, for all intents and purposes, greenbacks sold on par with gold for the first time. Contracts specifying payment in gold were settled routinely in greenbacks during the Christmas season. Still, there was fear that once convertibility became law, the Treasury would face a rush of greenback holders demanding gold. The Treasury was prepared for such an eventuality, having accumulated a large gold reserve in New York and other important cities.

January 1 was a bank holiday, and so there could be no runs on financial institutions that day. The Gold Room was deserted, as were all the other exchanges. Someone wrote on a blackboard placed in the room, "PAR." That old exchange, the scene of some of the wildest moments in American history, was obsolete.

Wall Street was bedecked in finery on January 2, with bunting flying from the Customs House, the Sub-Treasury Building, and leading banks. Clerks piled large bags of coins at tellers' windows, preparing for the rush. The doors opened at 10 A.M. One person entered, demanding coin for his $210 in greenbacks. Others straggled in, and by noon some $3,000 had been redeemed. Before the Sub-Treasury closed, $132,000 in greenbacks had been turned in for gold, while approximately $400,000 in gold had been exchanged for paper money. Within hours Wall Street learned that there had been a general absence of enthusiasm for exchanging paper in other parts of the nation. Clearly, the American people had confidence in their government, a fact evinced by a lack of interest in gold hoarding. Wall Street celebrated the event, as America embarked on its career as a "hard-money nation." To some, the event marked the beginning of the end of the depression.

Farmers and workers disagreed. Wages remained low, and unemployment was as bad as before. The newly created Knights of Labor joined with other groups to demand higher wages and shorter hours. There had been increasing amounts of labor violence and strikes after the 1873 panic, culminating in 1877, the worst year for labor disorders the nation had known; 1879 seemed to promise a heightening of the class struggle that appeared brewing in America. Similarly, the farmers were plagued by overproduction, low grain prices, and a decline in exports due to bountiful harvests in Europe. To the broad mass of laboring people, the depression

PRICE TRENDS, 1873–1879

Year	Wheat Price (wholesale)	Steel Rails (100 lbs.)	Wholesale Price Index (1910–14 = 100)
1873	$1.78	$120.58	133
1874	1.52	94.28	126
1875	1.40	68.75	118
1876	1.32	59.25	110
1877	1.64	45.58	106
1878	1.25	42.21	91
1879	1.22	48.21	90

Source: *Historical Statistics*, pp. 115, 123

was real, with no end in sight. In January 1879, several iron foundries closed, some because there was no demand for their products, others because prices had fallen substantially below the costs of production. A round of wage reductions hit the New England textile firms. The *Nation* thought the best word to describe economic conditions was "stagnation." *The Commercial and Financial Chronicle*, which had supported the Resumption Act, now asked, "Where is the prosperity promised with that event? Wheat is no higher. Corn is no higher. There is no money in any of the earth's products. Where is the promised prosperity?" In London, where the impact of a record European wheat harvest in 1878 was still being felt, bankers thought that once the effects of resumption had passed off, "we may expect to find gold steadily drifting from that side to this." In early 1879, Britain's wheat reserves were as a five-year high. American farmers, aware that such reserves meant a lower price and smaller demand for their harvest, were gloomy. Throughout the Midwest, granger agitation grew, along with demands for currency expansion. And as the farmers met that March, the wheat price dropped to $1.17. By April, wheat was quoted at $1.10, and still falling. Some farmers prepared for revolution. It would come, thought the *Times,* when wheat fell below $1.00.

The farmers had still one more enemy to face that spring. The weather turned bad in April, with storms, cyclones, and cold weather beginning early in the month and continuing into May. In late June, Iowa and Kansas farmers reported rust disease on their crops. Even nature seemed to be conspiring against the American farmer!

The ravages of nature were not confined to America, however, or even to the Western Hemisphere. Europe also was undergoing an unusual spring and summer. For the first time in memory, snow fell heavily on France in May and early June. Britain suffered through rainstorms that lasted weeks. On July 3, the House of Commons set up a special committee to investigate the weather, and three days later the Archbishop of Canterbury led the nation in prayers for better weather. The *Tribune* wrote that the entire continent, from Russia to Britain, experienced frosts in June. James Gordon Bennett noted that Jay Gould had set out for the continent on July 5, and hinted that some connection existed between his trip and the calamities in Europe. By then it was evident that European farmers were having a more difficult time of it than their American counterparts. On July 7 *The New York Times* noted that the wheat harvests in Ohio and Indiana would be 15 percent higher than in 1878, despite the weather and rust. Meanwhile, the London *Times* wrote, "The firmness of French exchange is said to be due to the prospect of a demand for gold for the United States, in consequence of a deficient harvest." By the end of the month it was certain that Europe's harvest would be the worst in a decade; the continent would not produce enough grain to feed its own population. Four months later the London *Economist* wrote: "It is the American supply alone, which has saved Europe from a general famine." This supply, exported in huge quantities, provided a bonanza for the grain farmers of the Midwest. Although the price of wheat continued to decline, increased sales provided farmers with sufficient funds to end talk of rebellion. As the impact of the upturn on the farms overflowed into other sections of the nation and sectors of the economy, the movement toward recovery gained steam. By year's end, it seemed that the long depression had ended.

PRICE TRENDS, 1879–1883

Year	Wheat Price (wholesale)	Steel Rails (100 lbs.)	Wholesale Price Index (1910–14 = 100)
1879	$1.22	$48.21	90
1880	1.06	67.52	100
1881	1.15	61.08	103
1882	1.20	48.50	108
1883	1.04	37.75	101

Source: *Historical Statistics*, pp. 115, 123

Nature conspired in favor of America in 1880, as the cotton crop of India failed and Europe's wheat farmers had another poor year. During the last three months of 1879 Britain exported $20 million in gold to America to pay for agricultural imports, while France contributed $30 million and Germany $10 million. On January 1, 1880, the New York banks had $53 million in specie; a year earlier they had held less than $20 million. Secretary of the Treasury John Sherman told agents that "gold coin, beyond the needs of the Government, having accumulated in the Treasury," made it possible to pay out gold in place of paper whenever individual government representatives felt it wise. Throughout the year, Americans turned in their gold, since paper was more convenient and it was common knowledge that more than enough gold lay waiting in the banks. In 1881 a drought destroyed a portion of the Midwestern wheat crop, but Europe suffered more from the weather, and exports climbed. Not until Europe's farmers were once again favored by nature, in 1882, did the American prosperity grind to a halt. For three

years, from 1879 to 1881, it seemed that American farmers had led
the nation out of the depression which had begun in 1873.

PRICE TRENDS, 1873–1882

| | Balance of International Payments | | Exports of Wheat Flour | |
| | Exports | Imports | Bushels | Value (millions |
Year	(millions of dollars)		(millions)	of dollars)
1873	675	856	2.6	19.4
1874	707	767	4.1	29.3
1875	623	722	4.0	23.7
1876	654	634	3.9	24.4
1877	716	614	3.3	21.7
1878	813	595	3.9	25.1
1879	813	612	5.6	29.6
1880	963	848	6.0	35.3
1881	971	834	7.9	45.0
1882	859	915	5.9	36.4

Source: *Historical Statistics*, pp. 562–63; Clement Juglar, *A Brief History of Panics*, p. 15

It was not long before the agricultural and business boom was
felt on Wall Street. The financial district was generally quiet after
1873, as interest in speculation was replaced by a desperate desire
to survive. Many brokerages closed down, not due to financial
embarrassment, but to a lack of customers. Prices showed minor
fluctuations, and most of the bull and bear groups faded from the
scene, leaving Gould and a few others to cause excitement from
time to time. The trend was generally downward, however, with
the bottom being reached early in 1879. Then, as the meaning
of the agricultural situation dawned on investors, activity increased sharply, and prices began to rise. By 1880 the district was
once again lively, as the old speculators returned and a new
group appeared to take the place of those who were destroyed in
1873. The rise in volume was accompanied by a renewed interest
in brokerage, and dozens of retired bankers reopened their establishments to participate in the securities boom. The price of
membership on the Exchange rose, and the Board of Governors
was able to raise the initiation fee from $500 to $1,000, with no
dissenting voices.

NEW YORK STOCK EXCHANGE STATISTICS, 1875–1883

| Year | Sales at the Exchange | | Common Stock Indices | | |
	Shares	Value of Sales	Industrials	Rails	Total
		(millions)			
1875	53.8	$2,862	2.27	13.16	4.45
1876	39.9	2,132	2.27	12.00	4.06
1877	49.8	2,601	1.80	9.22	3.14
1878	29.9	2,157	1.78	10.00	3.38
1879	72.8	4,136	1.90	12.44	4.12
1880	97.9	6,819	2.10	16.08	5.21
1881	114.5	8,198	2.45	19.38	6.25
1882	116.3	7,689	2.41	18.18	5.90
1883	97.0	6,261	2.25	17.44	5.63

Source: *Historical Statistics*, p. 591; Francis Eames, *The New York Stock Exchange*, p. 95

Although the Exchange still dominated trading, other markets continued to exist and prosper. Knots of traders could be seen each day scattered along Nassau Street, Pine Street, William Street, and Broadway, buying and selling shares, entering into combinations, and in general transacting business away from the open markets. Such individuals would often be dressed in checked suits and other flamboyant garb, or, at the other extreme, in funeral black. The

PRICES OF AN EXCHANGE SEAT, 1872–1883

Year	High	Low
1872	$ 6,000	$ 4,300
1873	7,700	5,000
1874	5,000	4,250
1875	6,750	4,250
1876	5,600	4,000
1877	5,750	4,500
1879	16,000	5,100
1880	26,000	14,000
1881	30,000	22,000
1882	32,000	20,000
1883	30,000	23,000

Source: Frances Eames, *The New York Stock Exchange*, p. 85

former group wore derbies, while the latter preferred high silk hats. Heads of important banks and brokerages always wore frock coats and stiff collars. Matthew Hale Smith, a florid observer of the period, wrote:

At ten o'clock, Wall Street, at the corner of Broad, is an interesting spot. Men rush in from all directions. Knots and cliques gather for the contest. Muscular brokerage is at a premium. Young roughs are dressed like expressmen, with low-crowned hats, docky coats, stunning jewelry, and flaming rings. Old men are nowhere. At the Gold Board, youngsters and clerks, with powers of attorney, represent their firms. At the Stock Board, none but members are admitted. But each house has a young member who is trained for the monotonous call of the regular stocks. Members sit in elegant chairs, or are broken up into little knots, and quietly discuss matters. The cock-pit is empty. But when an exciting stock is called all is changed. Members rush for the centre of the room pell mell. The crowd, the rush, the jostle, the fierce pushing, the clang of conflict, is too much for old men. Young men and mere boys raise the din, buy, sell, loan, and borrow. Millions pass through their hands in a minute. Their tear up and down stairs, rush in and out, race down the street, and across, and pitch into quiet citizens as they turn corners.

Such men worked at a fever pitch in 1882. Prices had leveled off after the recovery, but volume was still high and business excellent. Toward year's end stocks began to dip on heavy volume, and several near-panics resulted. Bearish pressures appeared in January and continued throughout the winter and into the spring sessions. As usual, Wall Street was a quiet place in the summer of 1883, but toward the end of July the decline resumed. Several minor houses failed, bringing down others in early August. By then, many brokers had begun cutting short their three- and four-day weekends, and some went so far as to move back into the city in the hottest August in recent memory.

By the second week in the month, declines on heavy volume had become the rule. George William Ballou & Co., a noted bear establishment, declared its bankruptcy. "Our suspension was caused by the failure of certain customers to put up additional margin," was the explanation. "We could not reach them in

time. I think we will come out all right." Cyrus Field thought
the recent failures due to a currency shortage; "There is every
prospect that we shall import gold before January 1. The country
is in a very prosperous condition" was his comment. E. P. Fabbri
of Morgan & Co. told reporters, "I can see no reason for the great
depression and I hope for a better condition of affairs." Russell
Sage thought "All that we needed was confidence," while Jay
Gould told a *Times* reporter that he believed stocks were selling
too low. On August 14, recently elected president of the Exchange
A. H. Hatch asked his fellow Exchange members not to exaggerate the importance of recent declines. "The chief trouble with
the stock market is that liquidation has been carried too far.
Prices are very low indeed and people will soon begin to see
that securities are too cheap, and are likely to be scrambling
over each other's shoulders to buy." Hatch concluded on a cheery
note: "There is no more chance of a panic than there is of your
being struck by lightning, out in the sunshine. The situation
now is in no respect like that which preceded the panic of 1873."

Most brokers applauded Hatch's statement, with only a few
willing to state bearish fears. E. C. Stedman, one of the district's
most respected figures, was particularly strong in his support of
the Exchange president. His son and junior partner, Frederick,
who had recently joined the firm, was not present at the meeting,
and so his views were not recorded. At that moment the young
man was busily attempting to cover shortages in his accounts.

Young Stedman's problems began in December of 1882. When
stocks began to slide that month, many neophytes entered the
market on the bull side, hoping to make fortunes on what they
thought would be a January reaction. Stedman opened accounts
with Cecil, Ward & Co. and began trading. To prevent his father
from learning of his operations, Stedman had his accounts in
the names of George S. Stewart and "S. S.," among others.
Checks made out to Cecil, Ward were drawn on accounts opened
under other fictitious names. And as prices continued to fall, and
Stedman's losses grew, he constructed an elaborate tissue of
falsehoods on this foundation. By late June he was using securities "borrowed" from his firm as collateral for loans at Cecil,
Ward. Stedman arranged to regain these securities whenever he

felt members of Stedman & Co. might examine their holdings. All of this was highly irregular. Later on, a Cecil, Ward partner told reporters, "When he put up these securities we did not ask him where he got them. That was none of our business."

Frederick Stedman was unable to cover his losses on August 14, and told the management at Cecil, Ward of his difficulties. At that time the firm was in a tight financial situation, unable to meet short-term obligations. Attempts to borrow elsewhere were unsuccessful, and as a result, Cecil, Ward was obliged to suspend operations shortly after the Hatch speech was concluded.

News of the failure spread quickly throughout the district, and within a day all Wall Street had learned of Frederick Stedman's activities. Not unexpectedly, E. C. Stedman & Co. collapsed on August 16, followed by a group of associated firms. A panic such as that feared by some and believed impossible by Hatch now gripped the city. Matthew Smith took note of the crisis:

In Wall Street will be found the sharp, decisive, keen, daring intellect of the nation. Its influence is felt in every portion of the land. Men who "corner" stocks in Wall Street, corner wheat, flour, and pork, cotton, produce and coal. They can produce a panic in an instant, that will be felt like an earthquake, on the Pacific slope, sweep like a besom of destruction over the Great Lakes; be as irresistible on the seaboard as the long roll of the Atlantic beating with giant strength its rock-bound coast. A Wall Street panic comes suddenly like thunder from a clear sky. No shrewdness can foresee and no talent avert it.

As it developed, the 1883 panic was short-lived and relatively minor. A few brokerages suspended operations, and three small railroads went bankrupt. Stock prices fell, but no more rapidly than they had earlier in the year. Brokers did not blame the decline on the Stedman failure and subsequent events. Rather, they pointed to the fact that the government was paying off the public debt, and so further contracting the currency. Money was tight in all parts of the nation by early 1884, as it became clear that Europe's crop problems had ended. Gold shipments continued, and Cyrus Field's prediction that the flow would be reversed by January proved false. Silver coins minted under the terms of

the Bland-Allison Act began to replace gold in everyday transactions; a flight from the dollar had begun.

Then came news of poor American crops and a general slaking
of the export business. Many corporations issued glowing earnings
reports for 1883 and predicted better ones for 1884, but prices
continued to decline in January and February. The New York
and New England Railroad failed, and this was followed by
collapses of other lines, all for the same reason: shortages of
capital. The *Times* noted that similar conditions had preceded
the 1873 panic. In March and April gold exports to Europe
passed the $33 million mark, with no end in sight. Henry Vil-
lard's scheme to take control of the Northern Pacific ran aground,
and his bankruptcy—due to a capital shortage—shook Wall
Street. Prices declined as volume rose. Rumors of panic dominated
Wall Street gossip in early March. But then, as prices fell, new
bull groups were organized, and they began buying campaigns.
Prices leveled at mid-month; the much-feared panic had been
averted.

In March and April bulls and bears fought to a standoff at
the Exchange. The combat was not dramatic, and to some seemed
quite studied and sober. The bears noted that the gold drain was
continuing and stocks falling, while bulls replied that the nation
had more gold than a year earlier and the declines were not
severe. Both were correct, and there seemed no clear indication

FINANCIAL CONDITION OF NEW YORK BANKS, 1883 AND 1884

Week Ending	Loans	Specie	Legal Tenders	Deposits
March 17, 1883	$319,672,000	$48,551,900	$17,081,100	$289,615,500
March 8, 1884	348,279,900	71,898,100	29,693,900	355,085,500
March 15, 1884	351,087,200	65,746,900	28,786,800	351,275,500

Source: *New York Herald*, March 16, 1884

that either side would win the contest for market control. Accordingly, both withdrew in early April, and the market settled
down to routine trading with little activity, interest, or volume.
Indeed, Wall Street had become so quiet that Charles J. Osborne, head of his own house, announced his retirement. Osborne

said his health was not good, and he hoped to go yachting that summer. "Besides," he concluded, "business is so bad I might as well leave." The *Herald's* financial columnist agreed. "To write a line about today's stock market that would contain an atom of interest is about as hopeless a task as one could be forced to encounter. In fact, there was no market to speak of. . . ." Throughout the rest of April, the word "dull" appeared daily in all the columns describing Wall Street. Prices varied little from their late March prices in early May, the result of the bull-bear stand-off and the general lack of volume. James Keene, a master speculator, announced his suspension and bankruptcy on April 30. A few days later he told friends that his problems began when he started dealing in put options a month earlier. Had prices risen dramatically, Keene would have made a fortune; had they fallen, he would have emerged a millionaire. But they stood still, and so he went bankrupt. "After paying out millions of dollars in cash in the last few months in my efforts to protect my privileges in a falling market," said Keene, "I have finally determined today to call a halt in the interest of those with whom I have business."

PRICES OF SELECTED ISSUES, APRIL 28–MAY 3, 1884

| | Closing Prices (fractions rounded off) | | | | | |
Issue	April 28	April 29	April 30	May 1	May 2	May 3
Central Pacific	55	51	51	50	48	48
Philadelphia & Reading	42	43	42	43	43	43
Union Pacific	66	63	63	61	59	59
Western Union	65	61	62	61	61	60
Pacific Mail S.S.	46	44	45	45	44	45
Volume (1,000 shares)	448	562	562	520	518	418

Source: *New York Times*, April 29–May 4, 1884

Wall Street easily absorbed the news, and then turned to other, more pressing problems. President Chester Arthur, who had succeeded the slain Garfield, hoped for election in his own right that year. He was touring the nation in May, trying to win commitments from delegates to the GOP convention, many of whom were pledged to Secretary of the Treasury Sherman, James G. Blaine, and other Republican wheelhorses. At the same time, supporters of Grover Cleveland attempted to gain the Democratic nomination for their man, against a host of senators and governors who also met with delegates and laid plans. The political maneuvering was interesting—far more so than the dull stock market. Wall Streeters began to ignore trades, and talk at the clubs centered on Arthur, Blaine, and Sherman rather than on Keene and other market figures. The *Herald* and the *Times* reported that several leading bankers planned to leave New York shortly in order to participate at the conventions, while others hoped to depart a month early for their usual summer vacations. The city was hot and humid; junior partners could be entrusted to take care of whatever happened. In May, few expected the market to change until the crop reports came out in early autumn. Until then, the market would remain quiet and "dull." Jay Gould was busy with his railroads; there was no sign of a sudden raid from that quarter. Russell Sage's activities, always watched with care, were also normal. J. P. Morgan was preparing for a European trip, and William Vanderbilt was engaged in no new enterprise. All the leading figures of American finance and speculation seemed content with the markets and showed no desire to upset the quiet of the city. It was during those humid days of early spring that Ferdinand Ward set into motion a chain of events that would destroy a score of brokerages and shock the nation.

Ward was one of those bright young men who came to Wall Street soon after Black Friday. During this period the press often singled out a daring speculator who was dubbed "the Young Napoleon of Wall Street." Ward was one of these. For a while he dabbled in stocks, making several thousand dollars, which he lost while attempting to outguess Gould and the giants. Then he took a job at the Produce Exchange, where he worked as a clerk and in his spare time traded in flour and cotton futures. This time Ward was more successful, and, leaving the commodities markets, he began to speculate in railroad stocks and bonds. Ward was a natural showman, and his relatively small successes were blown into giant coups when he bragged to friends at the lower Man-

hattan saloons. Some—the more simpleminded and innocent—
believed his stories. One of these was Ulysses Grant, Jr., known
since his White House days as "Buck." Young Grant had a
friendly disposition, a pleasing personality, and little else. He had
trained for the law, with indifferent results. Then he went into
several business ventures, all of which turned out badly. Buck
was not yet thirty, but had already been used by several friends
as fronts for their enterprises. Were it not for his name, young
Grant would have made a passable clerk in one of the smaller
Wall Street houses. But as the son of the former President, he
was praised as a genius by New York's leaders, who were delighted
to be known as intimates of U. S. Grant's son. Ferdinand Ward
knew this, and he told Buck that together the two of them
could become millionaires. The young man—who had come to
believe in his abilities—liked Ward. Shortly thereafter, they
united to form the financial house of Grant & Ward.

When the former President returned to New York in 1881, his
son took Ward to the new brownstone at 66th Street where the
family lived and introduced his partner to his parents. Grant
had always been impressed by businessmen, especially those who
had power or confidence (qualities he often confused). Ward
told him of Buck's brilliance and their plans; the elder Grants
beamed at their son, whom they now called "the businessman
of the family."

Ward transacted a good deal of his business at the Marine
National Bank. The firm's president, James D. Fish, had seen
speculators like Ward before, but like many others, he was impressed by the Grant connection. When, in 1881, the former
President entered the firm as a limited partner, Ward began to
hint that lucrative government contracts would soon be forthcoming. Using such promises as collateral, he attempted to borrow
large sums from the Marine Bank and other institutions, while at
the same time attracting many customers to his brokerage—men
who hoped to gain from Grant's inside information. Fish thought
something was wrong with this arrangement, and not believing
the General would take advantage of his friends, he wrote to
ascertain his connections with Ward. Grant responded on July
6, 1882.

MY DEAR MR. FISH:

In relation to the matter of discounts kindly made by you for account of Grant & Ward, I would say that I think the investments are safe, and I am willing that Mr. Ward should derive what profit he can for the firm that the use of my name and influence may bring.

Yours very truly,

U. S. GRANT

The letter seemed to corroborate the many stories Ward had been telling Wall Street insiders for months. Convinced that money could be made through a connection with Grant & Ward, Fish entered into several deals with the firm. By 1883 he was using funds deposited at the Marine Bank for his speculations. They were safe enough, thought Fish. After all, Ward was speculating and investing on information provided by Grant. By then Ward was telling friends that Grant was about to gain several important contracts for Ward-controlled companies. If they deposited their funds with him, these funds would be returned with huge profits in a short time.

There was no basis for Ward's rumors. When the firm was formed, the Grants put up $200,000 in cash and Ward added what he said was the same amount in "gilt-edged securities," which later proved to be of dubious quality and worth far less than $200,000. Armed with the General's money, Ward then spoke of government contracts which would be theirs for the asking. Grant firmly refused to enter into such arrangements, saying:

I had been President of the United States, and I did not think it was suitable for me to have my name connected with government contracts, and I knew that there was no large profit in them except by dishonest measures. There are some men who get government contracts year in and year out, and whether they manage their affairs dishonestly to make a profit or not, they are supposed to, and I did not think it was any place for me.

Ward did not press the point, but in his own conversations with potential investors hinted broadly that Grant's influence was at work for the firm. The General heard these rumors and called on Ward to explain them. Grant was told that none of them were true; that Grant & Ward had little to do with government work; and that Ward's major interest at the moment was an advance granted a contracting group to construct several spurs on the Erie Railroad, for which all concerned would reap tremendous profits with little risk.

While the Erie contracts did exist, Ward's most important business was elsewhere. Together with Fish and others, he was speculating heavily on the Stock Exchange. Their choices were poor; Ward was a bull when he should have switched to the bear side, and he plunged heavily into several situations that went sour. By mid-1883 Ward was in serious financial trouble. Still, he managed to maintain his front. Ward sought out every friend of Grant's he could find, and through persuasion and retellings of old war stories, followed by extravagant tales of his prowess, managed to convince them that Grant & Ward would be the best place for their funds. And Ward seemed honest enough; the investors didn't complain when within a few months they received substantial profits from their investments. Almost all of them asked Ward to reinvest their funds, and some poured more capital into the company. On the surface it appeared that Ward had found the key to great fortune. Actually, he was paying dividends out of new capital. If and when the inward flow stopped, the firm would be ruined; unless Ward did better on the Exchange than he had in the past, the situation would fall of its own weight.

Not a word of this was leaked to the Grants. In late 1883, Buck told his friends that he was a millionaire. Another son, Frederick Grant, resigned his Army commission in order to enter the firm, and he invested all his money in Grant & Ward. Buck's father-in-law, former Senator Jerome Chaffee, was also convinced that Ward was a financial genius, and he gave the speculator a half million dollars, all of which were invested in Ward's secret speculations. Ward appeared regularly at Grant's brownstone, bringing checks which constituted profits on investments. When Buck or the General asked for details regarding the firm's business, Ward would smile cryptically, put his finger to his lips, and in other ways indicate that he was not free to talk of such matters—not even to his partners. The Grants were impressed; the questions ceased. Buck purchased a new livery and embarked on a career of being a man about town. The General's office was redone in red satin and wood paneling; he was given a large new desk, complete with sterling silver cigar humidor. He would come to the office regularly, sign a few documents, and meet people Ward would bring down for investments. Grant was impressed by the men who came to see him, and they with him. More investors, with larger amounts of money, came to Grant & Ward, and by late 1883 most of Grant's family had committed their fortunes to the firm. The General's fears of finding a place in business after leaving the White House finally disappeared. He thought himself a respected businessman, and his son a financial genius who, together with Ward, had helped him accumulate a fortune in excess of $2 million.

Ulysses S. Grant had few cares as he prepared to celebrate Christmas 1883. He was sixty-one years old, healthy and vigorous and successful. Despite the scandals of his administration, the people of the Union still loved him. There was talk of returning Grant to his old rank in the Army, and of a new trust fund to be established in his name. His family was well situated, and earlier fears for its future had proved groundless. A happy Grant went to a friend's house to celebrate the season on Christmas Eve. As he alighted from the cab Grant turned to pay the driver. He slipped on a patch of ice and fell on the pavement, where he writhed in pain. Grant was carried into the house and a doctor summoned. The injury was diagnosed as a ruptured muscle in the upper part of the thigh; although not serious, he would have to remain in bed for several weeks. A few days later, however, Grant suffered an attack of pleurisy. He was able to hobble from place to place in a few months, but he never fully recovered his health. Still, Ward assured him that all was well on Wall Street, and any business he might have to transact could be carried out from his home. Grant was also pleased to receive a letter from *Century Magazine* asking him to write a series of articles on the war. Grant refused, however; he was not a writer and he had no desire to raise new questions about his role in the fighting. Besides, according to his calculations, he was now worth almost two and a half million dollars.

By late April, Grant felt well enough to return to the financial district. Within a few months, he said, "I will be as good as ever." The General expected to be fit for action in time for the renewal of activity after the summer doldrums. Then, in early May, everything Grant had counted upon began to crumble.

The securities markets were quiet at this time. A glance at the list for the week ending May 3 indicates that most stocks closed at about the same prices at which they had opened the previous Monday. There were some exceptions, however. Union Pacific had declined from 67 to 59, while Western Union fell seven points from 67; Ferdinand Ward had been bullish on both issues, and now his purse was again empty. Nor was this his only problem. By this time, most of his speculations were being financed by funds on deposit at the Marine Bank. If he fell, then Fish would also be dragged down, and with him one of the largest banks of the city. His back to the wall, Ward went to see Grant on Sunday evening, May 4.

Obviously Ward could not tell the General and Buck what had happened at Grant & Ward. The Grants were basically honest, and if they learned of Ward's manipulations, they certainly would not cooperate to pull him out of the hole. The ingenious Ward, knowing his partners, told them a different story.

After assuring his partners that all was well at the brokerage, Ward began to speak of difficulties at the Marine Bank. It seemed that Fish's establishment held a good deal of the city's money —almost $1.5 million, to be exact. On Saturday morning, the city's chamberlain had withdrawn $300,000 in cash, leaving the bank dangerously short for the Monday opening. Should a handful of important depositors decide to make withdrawals, then Fish would be obliged to close the doors at Marine Bank. A run would then develop, which, given the tight financial situation of the time, could easily turn into a major panic. Grant had been through several panics; he knew what this would mean, and Ward's analysis of the situation seemed sensible.

Ward continued. Not knowing of this situation, he had deposited $600,000 of the firm's money at the Marine Bank. If Fish was forced into bankruptcy, then Grant & Ward would soon follow. Should Fish receive sufficient funds to take care of certain contingencies, however, then all would be well. What Marine needed, then, was a temporary loan of several hundred thousand dollars. Within a few days—certainly before the end of the week—the money would be returned. Could Grant help? If the General would obtain a loan of $150,000 from his friends, then Ward would attempt to raise an additional $150,000. This money would be added to the $240,000 Ward already had, and deposited at the Marine Bank, which had $660,000 on hand in addition to $1,300,000 in securities. It would save the Marine Bank, Grant & Ward, and the nation. Ward then suggested that Grant approach his old friend Victor Newcomb and ask him for the money. The General agreed, and he set out for the Newcomb house. Newcomb was not at home. Aware of the seriousness of the situation, Grant hobbled back to his cab and ordered the driver to take him to the Vanderbilt mansion.

William Vanderbilt was no fool. One of the most prestigious names on Wall Street, as well as a keen observer of the city's finances, he knew of the Ward-Fish activities and what was going on at the Marine Bank. Ordinarily he would have nothing to do with such a situation, and Ward knew this. But like most businessmen, Vanderbilt had affection for Grant, and he listened sympathetically to his request for a loan.

"I don't care anything about the Marine National Bank," he told the General. "It can fail without disturbing me; and as for Grant & Ward—what I've heard about that firm would not justify me in lending it a dime." Grant listened to these harsh words and must have felt that Vanderbilt, who was not known for his tact, would deny his request.

"But I'll lend you a hundred and fifty thousand dollars personally," said the rail tycoon. "To you—to General Grant—I'm making this loan, and not to the firm."

Grant rose to thank Vanderbilt, who, while writing the check, merely grunted his acknowledgment. Taking the money, the General walked slowly to the door and then to his carriage, which returned him to his home and Ferdinand Ward. There he learned that Ward had been unable to raise a cent. Grant gave the Vanderbilt check to Ward, expressing hope that it would be

enough. Ward promised to do his best and then left the house.
By then, Ward knew that nothing could save Fish and the
Grants. Now he would try to save himself.

The next morning Ward cashed the Vanderbilt check and
pocketed the proceeds. Then, in a last bid to make money from
his Grant connection, he penned a note to Buck. Ward told his
partner that the firm was still in sound shape but needed more
capital for current operations. He went on to list securities owned
by the company which were worth $1,323,700. Ward then con-
cluded:

We must get $500,000 on them, and have the check dated to-day.
Now go to Mr. Vanderbilt and tell him just how we stand, and that
if he will do this for us we will send him $800,000 or $900,000 of the
securities in the morning, whichever he may select of them. . . . Go
right at it, Buck, and remember that if it is not done it will be the end
of our business career.

Buck did not go to Vanderbilt, perhaps fearing a curt refusal
from the financier. Later on it was learned that the securities
mentioned were fictitious and that Ward meant to cash the
second check and flee the city.

General Grant left his home on Tuesday morning, May 6, and
arrived at his Wall Street office shortly after 10 A.M. There he
was met by a distraught Buck. "Father, you had better go home,"
he said. "The bank has failed."

Grant sank into his chair, dazed. He remained there for several
hours, attempting to unravel his affairs and trace Ward's manipulations for the past three years. At noon he saw Adam Badeau,
an old friend. "We are all ruined here," he said sorrowfully. "The
bank has failed. Mr. Ward cannot be found. The securities are
locked up in the safe, and he has the key. No one knows where
he is." With this, Grant rose and ordered his carriage. He left
the office and entered the street, where a crowd had gathered.
Alexander Noyes, then a young reporter, wrote of this moment a
half century later.

The outer door slammed open; it admitted General Grant, followed
by his negro servant. Moving rapidly across the room on crutches—

he had injured his hip by a fall the previous winter—the general looked neither to right or left. He made for his partners' private office, unaware that nobody was there. . . . As he moved across the room . . . he held tightly clutched between his lips a cigar that had gone out. Nobody followed him or spoke to him, but everyone in the cynical, "hard boiled" group took off his hat as General Grant went by. I have always liked to think that this was not so much a tribute of respect to a former Chief Magistrate as spontaneous recognition of the immense personal tragedy which was enacting itself before our eyes.

Grant never returned to Wall Street.

Meanwhile, depositors crowded outside the Marine Bank, attempting to learn what had happened; some screamed for Fish's head and others tried to organize a posse to capture Ward. W. C. Smith, a partner at Grant & Ward, told a *Herald* reporter that he hadn't seen Ward since Sunday. Like the Grants, Smith had been taken in completely by his partner. "We could have held on easily," he said soon after Grant & Ward closed its doors, "if we had only a day's warning, but the unexpected closing of the bank upset us." Smith thought the firm's liabilities were less than $5,000. When asked to verify rumors that Grant would lose everything he had if Grant & Ward remained shut down, Smith replied, "Well, if the firm loses, General Grant will lose also— that's all." The *Nation* summarized all that was known at the time on May 8.

At about 10:00 on Tuesday morning the Marine National Bank, Wall Street, suspended payment. Its capital stock is $400,000. Definite information as to the cause of the failure and the probable results was hard to gain on Tuesday. Soon after the announcement, came rumors of trouble with the firm of Ward & Grant [*sic*], brokers. The firm is composed of General U. S. Grant and U. S. Grant, Jr., Ferdinand Ward, James D. Fish, and W. C. Smith. It is asserted that this firm owed the Marine Bank about $600,000, loaned on certain securities. On Tuesday morning the bank asked for payment, which was refused. Mr. Ward, who is also a director of the bank, was said to have disappeared, and with him all the keys of the safe in which all the books and papers of the firm were deposited. Great sympathy is expressed for General Grant, who, it is said, knew nothing of the firm's speculations. The city has a deposit of $1,000,000 in the Marine Bank. It is not thought that the bank will be able to resume payments, and the exact condition of its affairs will not be known until the bank examiner completes his investigation.

Despite the shocking news, there was no panic at the Exchange. Prices held and volume rose only slightly. The examiners quickly

PRICES OF SELECTED ISSUES, MAY 5–MAY 10, 1884

| | Closing Prices (fractions rounded off) | | | | | |
Issue	May 5	May 6	May 7	May 8	May 9	May 10
Central Pacific	49	47	47	47	46	45
Philadelphia & Reading	42	41	36	36	35	36
Union Pacific	61	58	56	57	55	51
Western Union	62	60	60	60	61	60
Pacific Mail S.S.	46	45	43	44	44	44
Volume (1,000 shares)	420	666	437	561	371	609

Source: *New York Times*, May 6–11, 1884

learned of Fish's manipulations with bank money, and the former bank president was sent to the Ludlow Street Jail. A search was organized for Ward, who was found with the money in his possession, preparing to leave the country. Ward was eventually taken to the same jail, on May 24, and when Fish learned his former partner was only a few cells down from his, he shouted, "Don't let me get at him. I'll kill the scoundrel!"

Not even this news could shake prices at the Exchange. Still, an air of uneasiness began to hang over Wall Street. On May 10 the *Herald* wrote that the Marine Bank-Grant & Ward failures might "prove the worst ever on Wall Street." Rumors were spread that Ward was only one of the district's criminals, and not the worst. Market insiders, remembering the Stedman failure a year earlier, wondered which firm would fall next.

The answer came on Tuesday, May 13. John C. Eno, another of the Street's "Young Napoleons," fled the city with $4 million belonging to the Second National Bank. The twenty-six-year-old Eno had been named president of the Second National a few months earlier; it was learned that he had begun stealing from the institution as soon as he had taken office. The police began a search for Eno but gave up when reports of his arrival in Canada reached the city. The elder Eno was a wealthy and respected figure on Wall Street; he now stepped forward and offered to make up the loss. But it was too late; the Eno revelations, added to the failure of the Marine Bank and Grant & Ward, provided the spark for panic. Speculators now remembered that economic indicators had been bad all year, and they prepared to sell their stocks. Brokers and bankers rushed home from summer resorts to safeguard their positions.

Stocks fell sharply on May 14; the panic was on in earnest. During the day the Metropolitan Bank, headed by George Seney, closed its doors. A well-known patron of the arts who was on the board of a dozen charities, Seney was thought beyond suspicion. Now it was learned that he had used bank funds to speculate in railroad stocks. The market's sudden fall had led to his failure and the closing of the Metropolitan.

PRICES OF SELECTED ISSUES, MAY 12–17, 1884

| | Closing Prices (fractions rounded off) | | | | | |
Issue	May 12	May 13	May 14	May 15	May 16	May 17
Central Pacific	42	40	36	38	43	46
Philadelphia & Reading	35	34	33	33	34	33
Union Pacific	49	46	41	43	45	45
Western Union	60	55	50	53	56	57
Pacific Mail S.S.	44	43	36	34	37	40
Volume (1,000 shares)	513	505	621	483	441	462

Source: New York Times, May 13–18, 1884

Most of Seney's transactions had been carried on through Nelson Robinson & Co., which was headed by his two sons and his son-in-law; within less than an hour, the brokerage declared itself insolvent. Nelson Robinson controlled Goffe & Randle and worked in harmony with Donnell, Lawson & Simpson; these firms followed the same route. Hatch & Foote was next, and then J. C. Williams. Hotchkiss and Burnham failed. The Herald proclaimed these bankruptcies and stated its belief that "the panics of 1857 and 1873 bade fair to find their parallel on Wall Street yesterday. . . ." The *Tribune*, on the other hand, saw little to be worried about, especially since business remained undisturbed. "Probably never before was there so large a decline in the prices of securities within a day, with so little apparent excitement inside the Stock Exchange as has occurred to-day," it wrote. "The day's operations may well be characterized as the silent panic." The *Nation* was calm and realistic.

If anybody who never witnessed a panic before supposed that what he saw on Wednesday week was a repetition or renewal of the panics of 1857 or 1873, he was greatly mistaken. Those were commercial crises of the first order. The scenes of Wednesday were very exciting and very alarming to the ordinary investor, but they were not in any way indication that we were entering on such a period of disaster as followed the failure of the Ohio Life & Trust Company in 1857 or that of Jay Cooke in 1873. The history of commercial crises shows that although they vary in many particulars, they are uniformly alike in one most important particular. They always, to all but the very farsighted or pessimistic, come like thunderclaps out of a clear sky. The first note of danger is always heard on what seems to be a period of great prosperity, marked by high prices, large profits, great industrial activity, advancing wages, greatly extended credits, eager demand for money, and great mutual confidence. These have been the signs and forerunners of all the great financial convulsions.

It is needless to say that every one of them has been wanting in the crisis we are now witnessing.

Although the *Nation*'s analysis of panics was questionable, the fact remained that the atmosphere in May 1884 was not as gloomy as it had been after the first days of the 1837, 1857, and 1873 panics. The country was not fearful of a general collapse. Instead, interested observers seemed to sit back and wonder who would fall next. The *Tribune*, which remained calm throughout this period, editorialized that the situation appeared secure.

But the salient features of the situation remain plain and hopeful. The banks are strong and united; and there came out yesterday no further trace of trouble in any of them.

There is a general feeling that the worst is over.

There is universal caution.

And there is practically no evidence that this has been or can develop into, anything more than a stock-speculator's panic.

A. W. Dimock & Co. failed on May 16. Its head had speculated on several stocks, including Banker's & Merchant's Telegraph, of which he was president. Their declines left him without sufficient funds to cover his losses, and now he closed his doors. Fisk & Hatch, whose leading director was president of the Stock Exchange, followed, and several banks connected with the firm also folded. By midday it appeared that a full-scale panic might yet take place.

Whatever chance there might have been for a repetition of the 1873 disaster was averted by actions elsewhere on Wall Street. The clearing house scheduled an emergency meeting and afterward announced that $4 million in certificates would be released that day. Most of this money would be used to reorganize the Metropolitan Bank, which dismissed Seney and named the respected Henry L. Jacques its new president. With this, the Metropolitan announced it would reopen the following day, May 17.

There was no run on the Metropolitan, despite news that the Newark Savings Association, with connections at the bank and with Fisk & Hatch, had suspended. Other institutions failed the next week, among them L. Brownell & Co. and the Pennsylvania

PRICES OF SELECTED ISSUES, MAY 19–24, 1884

	Closing Prices (fractions rounded off)					
	May	May	May	May	May	May
Issue	19	20	21	22	23	24
Central Pacific	45	43	42	41	42	43
Philadelphia & Reading	32	31	30	26	25	25
Union Pacific	45	43	40	37	38	37
Western Union	57	54	55	54	53	53
Pacific Mail S.S.	39	38	39	36	36	35
Volume (1,000 shares)	338	395	433	401	439	425

Source: *New York Times*, May 20–25, 1884

Bank of Pittsburgh. And there were further examples of thievery. On May 21 Charles A. Hinckley, teller at the West Side Bank, could not be found. It was soon learned that he had stolen $95,000 of the bank's deposits and had fled to Canada. Still, none of these events caused more than a ripple on Wall Street.

By early June most of the debris had been cleared away, stock prices were well below what they had been two months earlier, but steady, and the nation was far more involved in political manipulations at the conventions than in what had happened on Wall Street. Grover Cleveland did receive the Democratic nomination, and neither he nor any other important Democrat thought the panic worthy of more than a mention. The GOP ignored Arthur's bid for renomination and instead chose James G. Blaine as its nominee. They, too, said little of what had happened on Wall Street. To most Americans, the 1884 panic was a passing diversion. Insiders had been hurt and the tribe of speculators taught a lesson. But business conditions were much the same as they had been a month earlier. "The explosion in Wall Street has had no answering echo anywhere," concluded the *Nation* on May 29. "It has fallen upon general business with no more rebound than a blow upon a mass of putty." The reasons for this were evident. The markets had still not recovered from the panic of 1873 and the brief flurry in 1883. Prices were so low they could scarcely decline further. In addition, business conditions had turned downward in 1883. Weak firms had already been liquidated, and those that remained were strong enough to sustain the failures of 1884. "General business has already gone through its crisis," wrote the *Nation*. "The slow shrinkage of three years has left little or nothing for a bank panic to work upon. The bank panic was for this reason short-lived."

Europeans were amazed at the sangfroid of their American cousins. Engels, writing from England, thought the panic would usher in a new revolution, one which would fulfill his predictions and those of Marx. "What the downbreak of Russian Czarism would be for the great monarchies of Europe—the snapping of their mainstay—that is for the bourgeois of the whole world the breaking out of class war in America. . . . I only wish Marx could have lived to see it." But the class war did not take place.

The London *Spectator* expressed amazement that the Americans did not gird themselves for a new period of crisis.

The millionaires of America make corners as if they had nothing to lose. Let some amuse themselves financing as if it were only an expensive game. The English, however speculative, fear poverty. The Frenchman shoots himself to avoid it. The American with a million speculates to win ten, and if he takes losses takes a clerkship with equanimity. This freedom from sordidness is commendable, but it makes a nation of the most degenerate gamesters in the world.

And the *Gil Blas* of Paris, writing on May 16, expressed similar thoughts.

The New York news still heavily depresses the bourse, but Americans have *l'habitude des fortunes rapides et des brusques ruines*. Without a sou in the morning, they are millionaires after lunch, and after supper perhaps have lost everything. Instead of blowing out their brains, however, as surely would be the result in Europe, they drink half a dozen glasses of whiskey and go to bed as if nothing unusual had happened. Two years after our *krach* we continued to feel the effects, but in a fortnight the Yankees will have forgotten all about their *krach* and perhaps be busy getting up another one.

Such statements indicate that the writers did not understand the generally depressed state of American business in 1884. As Horace White noted, "the decline in stocks has been gradual, and

PRICES OF SELECTED ISSUES, MAY–DECEMBER 1884

| Issue | *Closing Prices (fractions rounded off)* | | | | | | | |
	May 1	June 2	July 1	Aug. 1	Sept. 1	Oct. 1	Nov. 1	Dec. 1
Central Pacific	50	45	34	42	41	51	38	36
Philadelphia & Reading	42	23	25	28	27	27	21	24
Union Pacific	61	46	31	47	48	54	55	52
Western Union	61	62	56	62	64	65	61	63
Pacific Mail S.S.	45	42	41	47	49	52	52	55
Volume (1.000 shares)	562	312	298	384	210	204	115	313

Source: *New York Times*

there has been no collapse of credit, yet we are having all the other effects of a crisis in full measure." In 1884, just before the panic, manufacturing was "depressed to a degree hardly surpassed in our history. . . . It is a common remark among those who do not look below the surface of things that this is a 'rich man's panic.' "

Business activity during the next few years bore out White's analysis. By the end of September most stock-market indices were up from their summer lows, demonstrating that the panic had not caused any permanent damage on Wall Street.

During the rest of the decade, prices rose, reaching highs in 1888 before levelling off once more.

PRICES OF SELECTED ISSUES, 1885–1889

	Closing Prices on January 2 or 3 (fractions rounded off)				
Issue	*1885*	*1886*	*1887*	*1888*	*1889*
Central Pacific	35	44	43	62	36
Philadelphia & Reading	19	22	38	66	49
Union Pacific	47	55	61	58	64
Western Union	55	73	75	78	84
Pacific Mail S.S.	56	67	51	36	37

Source: *New York Times*

Volume rose in 1886 and then declined for the rest of the decade.

NEW YORK STOCK EXCHANGE STATISTICS, 1883–1889

Year	*Sales at the Exchange*		*Common Stock Indices*		
	Shares	*Value of Shares*	*Industrials*	*Rails*	*Total*
		(millions)			
1883	97.0	$6,261	2.25	17.44	5.63
1884	96.2	5,940	2.06	14.64	4.73
1885	92.6	5,480	2.19	14.14	4.60
1886	100.8	5,886	2.48	16.57	5.36
1887	84.9	4,509	2.60	17.11	5.53
1888	65.2	3,540	2.70	15.78	5.20
1889	72.0	4,059	3.24	15.80	5.27

Source: *Historical Statistics*, p. 591; Francis Eames, *The New York Stock Exchange*, p. 95

The economic indices, on the other hand, continued their downward drift, which had been in effect since the 1873 panic, and had been interrupted temporarily from 1879 to 1881. Thus, the generation of depression, which had begun in 1873 and would not end until 1897, continued.

PRICE TRENDS, 1883–1890

Year	Wheat Price (wholesale)	Steel Rails (100 lbs.)	Wholesale Price Index (1910–14 = 100)
1883	$1.04	$37.75	101
1884	.91	30.75	93
1885	.86	28.52	85
1886	.80	34.52	82
1887	.77	37.08	85
1888	.88	29.83	86
1889	.96	29.25	81
1890	.89	31.78	82

Source: *Historical Statistics*, pp. 115, 123

Both Horace White and the Europeans failed to notice still another aspect of the panic: the ability of Wall Street institutions to prevent serious dislocations. The clearing house's prompt action in issuing certificates and in aiding the Metropolitan Bank to reopen was an important step toward recovery. By the end of May, $24,915,000 in such notes had been issued, and they saved dozens of firms and banks from failure. Then too, what did *not* happen was as important as what did occur. In previous panics, Europeans had hastened to withdraw their funds from America. There were no such massive liquidations in 1884. The key man here was J. P. Morgan. In the midst of the panic, Cyrus Field cabled Junius Morgan in London, pleading for help. "Many of our businessmen seem to have lost their heads. What we want is some coolheaded strong man to lead." Junius turned the task over to his son. Young Morgan handled the situation well, purchasing stocks while American speculators sold, in this way helping to restore confidence on Wall Street. The scions of the Stedmans, Grants, and Enos had proven themselves to be men of clay; such was not the case with the son of old Junius Morgan. In him, Wall Street had finally found its leader.

Jay Cooke was finished as a force on Wall Street. Jay Gould, sick and worn out, no longer seemed interested in the games of finance; he had been caught napping by the panic and had almost lost everything as the bears attempted to squeeze him to death. Sick and depressed, he left the speculative arena for good a few months later. Russell Sage had been besieged by creditors during the panic, and in three days paid out some $7 million to meet his obligations. Sage was bruised, but he quickly recovered. He remained on Wall Street for the next twenty-two years, but his days of great power were in the past. William Vanderbilt would die in 1885, and Gould seven years after. Neither was to exert control in the future. Such a role was to fall to Morgan, who emerged from the panic with additional prestige and power.

What of the losers? The accountants examined the books of Grant & Ward and found the firm had assets of $67,174 and liabilities of $16,792,640. According to Ward's figures, the firm should have had over $27 million in assets. What happened to this money? Ward was unable to account for any of it. He admitted that Grant & Ward had been insolvent since 1882, and that he had speculated with other people's money and had "lost it." Ward was convicted of grand larceny and spent ten years in the state penitentiary. Fish was also tried and found guilty, and joined his partner in jail. Eno remained in Canada, entered the traction business, and died a millionaire. George Seney recovered his losses and never went to trial.

Ulysses S. Grant once again proved himself an incompetent in all but war. Still, the nation loved and respected the tired, sick old man. Speaking to his congregation the Sunday after the Grant & Ward failure, a New York minister said:

When a man has earned such a reputation as General Grant has for absolute simplicity, absolute truthfulness, straightforwardness and honesty, he is safe. General Grant has made mistakes; he has done things that I wish he had not done—possibly he wishes he hadn't done them; but when General Grant and his sons go into a large concern of which they knew nothing, any more than I do, and that concern plays the mischief with him and his boys, the whole nation rises up to say, "He is not to blame." If Jim Fisk were here and had gone under, do you suppose there would have been a man in the whole nation but would have said, "He is a rogue"? But General Grant has earned character and reputation and the whole nation says, "He was not to blame; simple, dear old fellow, he knew nothing of the wrong." (applause.) And just about this time the national Legislature is honoring itself by restoring him to the rank and pay of general. It is a noble thing for the country to do. I thank God for it.

The legislature did not vote Grant his pension, however, and an attempt to use money held in a trust fund was prevented due to technicalities. In early June, Grant had some $80 in cash, and Mrs. Grant an additional $130. All else was gone. Grant lay in his room and would not budge. Always a moody man, he now sank into one of his fits of depression. "I have made it the rule of my life to trust a man long after other people gave him up," he said, "but I don't see how I can trust any human being again."

Grant had always feared the pity of friends more than the scorn of his enemies. Now he underwent a series of new humiliations, resulting from the actions of those whose only wish was to express devotion and respect. Charles Wood of Lansingburgh, New York, who had never met the General, sent Grant a check for $1,000. It was a loan, he wrote, "on account of my share for services ending in April, 1865." Ambassador Matias Romero of Mexico, Grant's friend from his mission to that country, called on the family and asked Grant to accept some money as a loan. The General refused, and Romero fled the room, leaving his check for $1,000 on a desk. Others stepped forward with lesser sums. For almost a year, the Grants lived on what amounted to charity.

The General's major concern, after the well-being of his family, was to repay the Vanderbilt loan. Grant transferred his properties and medals to Vanderbilt in order to pay for part of the loan. Vanderbilt refused them. In a stiff, formal, and yet moving letter, he returned all of these to the family. A series of communications followed, in which Grant observed that unless Vanderbilt accepted the securities they would fall to creditors, since he was now a bankrupt. In the end, Vanderbilt reluctantly took the land and medals, which he turned over to the government.

Grant faced similar embarrassment at the hands of a group which started a public fund for him. Learning that Grant owed more than $160,000 to creditors, Cyrus Field and several New Yorkers put their prestige behind a fund drive that stopped only when Grant pleaded with them to end the effort. Although he appreciated what they were doing and had been tempted to say nothing for the sake of his family, Grant finally wrote Field and asked that the drive be stopped, and it was.

During the next year it seemed that Grant's fortunes might turn yet again. Remembering *Century Magazine*'s request for articles on the Civil War, and now needing the money, Grant began to write. At first the words came with difficulty, and *Century* offered suggestions that Grant write in the first person singular, telling his side of the war. Afterward, as he became used to writing, he began to enjoy the articles, reliving, as it were, the high points of his career. The articles were a success, and Grant was able to raise his fee. Then, finally, Congress acted to place Grant on the retired list, a move which carried with it a pension. This occurred while Grant conducted negotiations for his memoirs, and in the end signed a contract with the Charles L. Webster Company, Mark Twain's concern. Ironically, Twain became Grant's adviser in this period; the man who had satirized the Grant era as "The Gilded Age" now worked with the President whose administration had been the most corrupt in American history. Grant received an advance of $25,000 and a generous royalty arrangement. Together with Twain, he began to explore the war.

Grant's periods of happiness and enthusiasm were never long-lived. Shortly after beginning his memoirs, he fell ill with a sore throat. Doctors diagnosed the pains as cancer of an inoperable variety. In 1885, Grant knew he would soon die. Then followed a valiant attempt to finish the work before cancer made all activity impossible. The General pushed himself hard, and in the end succeeded. The *Memoirs* later proved a great success, selling over 300,000 copies and earning almost a half million dollars for Grant's heirs.

Even in death, Ulysses S. Grant's accomplishments were stained by his friends. Adam Badeau, his old comrade, asserted that he had written most of the *Memoirs* and so deserved a share of the royalties. The Grants offered Badeau $10,000 if he would withdraw his claims, but Grant's friend said it was now a matter of principle, and he brought the case to court. The nation was disgusted; Charles Dana of the *New York Sun* offered to pay Badeau off if he would withdraw his case. In the end, Badeau abandoned his attempts to gain money from the royalties, but not before further tarnishing Grant's honor and reputation.

Fortunately Grant did not live to see these last bickerings. In mid-July 1885, he fell into a swoon and rose from it only for moments. On July 23, Grant sank into a final coma and died. The man who had been ruined in the 1857 panic, whose accomplishments had led to wild speculation on Wall Street during the war, who was intimately tied to the panic of 1869 and that of 1873, and who had become the symbol of the 1884 panic, died with little money, but not before having provided for his family. Ulysses S. Grant, at once the most heroic and the most pitiful figure of the century, was a man whose entire life was bound in irony. No one had known more success than he, or more failure; more honor or more dishonor; more hate or more love. Even his last word was ironic. The shy, fumbling man who was considered a drunkard by many of his enemies called hoarsely for "water" just before expiring.

7.

GROVER CLEVELAND AND
THE ORDEAL OF 1893–95

The face of the nation was drastically altered in the two decades following the panic of 1873. The West had been taken; the frontier was no more. America seemed on the verge of playing a larger role than before in Latin America and the Pacific. In more mundane matters, public interest in rowing and riflery had been replaced by baseball, cycling, and football. Women had taken to the bustle and men were shaving their faces clean.

Most of the changes, however, were quantitative rather than qualitative. Between the death in 1874 of Millard Fillmore, a mediocre pre-Civil War President, and that of Rutherford Hayes in 1893, an equally mediocre post-bellum President, embryonic forces had matured and ripened; institutional flaws which had seemed worrisome now threatened to rend the fabric of society; what was once irritating had become pressing; the chickens of 1873 were coming home to roost in 1893. Problems which President Grant could ignore, hoping they would disappear, would destroy not only President Cleveland but also the surface stability that had existed since the end of the Civil War.

Small local meetings of the Farmers' Alliance had blossomed into Populism. The young railroad brotherhoods of the post-Civil War era were now strong unions, which could paralyze the nation with strikes. The high tariff of 1864 had been progressively raised, culminating with a protectionist victory in the McKinley Tariff of 1890. On February 12, 1873, a routine coinage act ended silver currency in the United States. Barely noted at the time, by 1893 it and subsequent problems revolving around the currency issue had become the central issues of the second Cleveland Administration.

When Grover Cleveland maneuvered for the Democratic Presidential nomination in the summer of 1884, Ulysses S. Grant, Chief Executive during the 1873 panic, was humiliated on Wall Street. Both literally and symbolically, Cleveland's public career from that year to the time he left the White House in 1897 was marked by panics, depressions, threats of revolution, foreign difficulties, and deep partisan strife. For more than twelve years Grover Cleveland would be the central political figure in America and a stanch advocate for a brand of economic orthodoxy under attack by several strong forces. Like Martin Van Buren before him and Herbert Hoover afterward, Cleveland would prove a capable man unable to prevail over his opponents, although his struggle was greater and more consistent than that of the others.

A cynic once said that every President must fight to overcome his principles if he is to succeed in office. Cleveland refused to enter such a struggle; his principles and philosophy were unshakable, a poor condition for the nation's first politician, an individual whose job it was to compromise when accommodation was called for, to maneuver and manipulate rather than confront enemies and define battle lines. Cleveland ran for the Presidency three times—in 1884, 1888, and 1892. On all three occasions he received a plurality of the popular vote, a record unsurpassed until Franklin Roosevelt's 1944 victory. Twice Cleveland received a majority of the electoral votes, losing the tight 1888 race to Benjamin Harrison. He is the only President whose terms did not run contiguously; Cleveland is one of eleven presidents to be inaugurated twice for that office. He is usually ranked among the better-than-average chief executives, and has been called the best man to occupy the White House after the death of Lincoln and before the coming of Theodore Roosevelt. Yet he left office despised by the leaders of his own Democratic party and shunned by most Republicans of the opposition. In the years between the panic of 1884 and that of 1893–95, the growing difficulties of national problems, coupled with Cleveland's inability or unwillingness to attack them in any way other than frontally, led to ultimate defeat and rejection.

Cleveland recognized his flaws and problems early but could do little about either. Even during his first Administration, from 1885–89, he clashed with Congress on such issues as the tariff, monetary policy, conservation, Indian affairs, and the role of the former Confederacy in national affairs. The President lost more often than not; by 1887 he was tired and discouraged. That winter he met a young boy, whose father he attempted to persuade— again unsuccessfully—to take a diplomatic post. "My little man," said Cleveland, "I am making a strange wish for you. It is that you may never be President of the United States." Soon after, James and Sara Delano Roosevelt, and their son, Franklin, returned to Hyde Park.

In 1892, eleven-year-old Franklin Roosevelt went on a tour of Europe, while fifty-five-year-old Grover Cleveland campaigned first for the Democratic Presidential nomination, and then for the Presidency itself. Considering Franklin Roosevelt's social position and age, the European trip was normal. The young man would make several voyages to England and Germany before entering prep school at the age of sixteen; this was expected of sons of the developing American aristocracy.

The nation was in economic disarray in 1892, resulting from a clash between two concepts of America's future and two programs. Any President who would serve from 1893 to 1897 was certain to face more vexing problems than any Chief Executive since Lincoln. But Cleveland was a stubborn man, convinced of the correctness of his course of action and philosophy. Furthermore, his narrow defeat in 1888 still rankled, and he was determined to win vindication at the polls. Leaving a comfortable and lucrative position at the Wall Street law firm of Bangs, Stetson, Tracy and MacVeigh, where he handled few cases and hobnobbed with the most powerful financiers in the nation, Cleveland campaigned for a "reasonable" tariff and "sound" money, against President Harrison, whose slogans and speeches were approximately the same. Both men feared the impact of Populist James Weaver, who wanted to punish the trusts, spoke of nationalization of some businesses, and demanded increases in the currency through greater silver coinages.

Wall Street backed Cleveland. William C. Whitney, Secretary of the Navy during Cleveland's first administration and now connected through marriage to Standard Oil and several Wall Street banks, managed the campaign. J. P. Morgan led the district in contributing to the Democratic war chest. American business had not abandoned the GOP. Rather, the community recognized in Cleveland a more forceful and able defender of its interests than the colorless Harrison. True, the Democrat had been in favor of a lower tariff, a position which eight years earlier had made him anathema to businessmen. But in 1892, the tariff seemed less important than the currency issue, and Cleveland was an unwavering defender of the gold standard. He would not be swayed on this point—not by reformers nor by defenders of the status quo. What if he would not bow, as Harrison had, to the wishes of Wall Street? Such compromises would not be necessary, since Cleveland substantially supported the Wall Street point of view to begin with. Later on, a cynical politician would say, "Everyone has his price but an honest man. You get him for nothing." Cleveland was Wall Street's honest man in 1892.

Given this support and the normal Democratic superiority throughout the nation, he won a decisive victory, the most decisive since 1864. Cleveland showed strength in such GOP strongholds as Ohio, Wisconsin, and Illinois, and received 277 electoral votes to Harrison's 145, representing a popular vote of 5.6 million to 5.2 million. Weaver did better than expected, gathering 22 electoral votes and more than one million popular votes. It was soon clear that the real contest in 1892 was not between Cleveland and Harrison, but between the kind of nation represented by both of these men and that of the Populists and James Weaver.

The inhabitants of Grover Cleveland's America thought they had great problems for which solutions had been found. Overproduction was a central issue. It could be seen in railroads, where five lines traveled through territories that produced enough business for two, and in which dozens of small companies and a few giants were capable of turning out three times as much steel as the nation could absorb. The national economy of post-Civil War America could best be described as surging—declining rapidly and rising quickly, usually as the result of grain prices and the export of foodstuffs. In prosperous times, manufacturers expanded their facilities in order to take advantage of the market; when business fell off, the same men continued to expand, hoping to gain a larger share of the market and so maintain profits. Competition forced prices down, cut into profit margins, and placed many otherwise solvent firms in precarious positions. Small movements in raw-materials prices, transportation or marketing costs, and consumer or foreign demand, could and did lead to waves of bankruptcies and foreclosures. To such businessmen, remedies were to be found in combinations such as holding companies, trusts, gentlemen's agreements, and the like, which would soften the impact of competition and enable each cooperating firm to maintain margins and profits. Another solution lay in reducing production costs. This meant low wages and complete opposition to unions. In order to maintain prices and assure the domestic markets, manufacturers supported high tariffs on finished products, but low ones on raw materials.

Cleveland's Americans were of two minds on the currency issue. On the one hand, it seemed that those who advocated the coinage of silver made good sense. An increase in the money supply would lead to higher prices and an economic upswing, easing pressures which had existed during much of the period since the 1873 panic. On the other hand, higher prices for finished goods would also mean larger bills for raw materials and labor; in the end, the manufacturer might be back where he started. Higher prices would turn many would-be purchasers against American goods in favor of European; not only would exports suffer, but the domestic market itself would be threatened unless tariffs were raised to new levels.

The coinage of silver would make the United States the only major trading nation using the metal; it could not be accepted for settlement of international obligations. Such distinctions might mean little to the average laborer or small farmer, but they were of vital importance to businessmen. Ten silver cartwheels could never be the same as a gold ten-dollar coin for reasons of international trade. Thus there would be a greater demand for gold currency than for silver. Gresham's law would result in the hoarding of gold and the devaluation of silver. Europeans would withdraw their funds from America, once they recognized the shakiness of the monetary system. In the end, America would become insolvent insofar as international trade was concerned. Such nightmares haunted businessmen and turned them against any compromise with the silverites. Grover Cleveland was squarely behind the gold standard. He was their man.

James Weaver's America was strikingly different. Silver miners found themselves without a market for their production. Small businessmen were being crushed by the ever growing trusts and combinations on the one hand and shrinking profit margins on the other. Farmers were in the midst of a generation-old depression, broken by short periods of prosperity, of which they received but a small share. They raised the crops, and the bankers took the profits. They harvested grain, and the railroads that brought it to the cities made more money by carrying wheat in one day than they did in a season. They threshed the wheat, which sometimes sold for fifty cents when they were ready to sell, against a dollar when the seed was planted. America was an agricultural nation, and exports of grain and other farm products were far greater than those of manufactured goods. In fact, since 1873, grains had been the backbone of American exports. Without these shipments, America's cities would die. Yet the cities reaped the profits; the farmers seemed to reap only the wheat.

Weaver's Americans thought they could remedy this situation easily enough. In the first place, they wanted low tariffs on manufactured goods, to reduce prices by forcing businessmen into competition with foreigners. Some farmers spoke of higher tariffs on agricultural goods, but to most this seemed unnecessary. Weaver's Americans wanted to break up the industrial complexes which dominated both worker and farmer. As for the banks and railroads, some would regulate them, while others spoke of nationalization. But the key to their program was the currency question. The laborers were told that an expansion in the money supply would mean higher wages; some, though by no means all, believed it. Silver interests knew that expansion meant an assured market for their product; they were inflationists to the man. As for most small farmers, they had been inflationists since the Civil War, at first backing greenbacks, and then, failing there, switching to silver in the 1870s.

The farmers' arguments seemed to make sense. Europe needed

America's foodstuffs more than its gold. What if the yellow metal
went into hiding at first? If the Europeans were made to understand that the nation's farms stood behind silver, they would learn
to accept the white metal. For, unless they did, the flow of wheat
would end, and the old continent would starve. Faced with the
alternatives of changing their monetary ideas or putting down
revolts by starving populations, Europe's businessmen would accept silver. Those farmers who made up the bulk of Weaver's
voters did not think of North vs. South, as did sloganeers attempting to capitalize on Civil War memories. Nor did they think of
rich vs. poor, as some Marxists then and now think they did;
battle cries notwithstanding, they lacked a true class consciousness. It was to them a struggle between urban and rural economies
and values, and they came to this conclusion not through abstract
reasoning, but by observing the world in which they lived and
functioned. In 1896 they would agree with William Jennings
Bryan, when he called the conflict one between "the idle holders
of idle capital" and "the struggling masses." But frenzied applause
greeted Bryan's next broadside.

You come to us and tell us that the great cities are in favor of the
gold standard; we reply that the great cities rest upon our broad and
fertile prairies. Burn down your cities and leave our farms, and your
cities will spring up again as if by magic; but destroy our farms and
the grass will grow in the streets of every city in the country.

For this reason, said the farmers, urban America would have to
accept silver. Expanding the thought, Weaver's supporters concluded that Europe would take silver for the same reason.

Cleveland's America and that of the Populists both had problems which evoked solutions. Each could present plausible cases
and persuade listeners of their validity and fairness; each could
write of the silver issue, making it appear reckless in one pamphlet
and sensible in another. These arguments had existed throughout
the post-1873 period, but little had been done by either side to
meet the problems. By the 1890s, the economy demanded a choice
between the two Americas, whose symbols had become gold and
silver.

Although the two interests had conflicted with each other for a generation, and in different forms the struggle could be traced as far back as Bacon's Rebellion in 1676, a new chapter had begun in 1890, at which time three events, two related and one not, combined to precipitate a crisis which could not be solved by the usual temporizing.

The year had opened with news of aggressive British expansion into American and other world markets, a move which frightened some domestic manufacturers and led them to demand higher tariffs. American farmers were in a better position. The 1889 European crops had been poor, and those of 1890 only slightly better. Farm prices rose in the former year, but remained stationary in 1890. Some farmers blamed the development of new grain areas in the Argentine and elsewhere for the lack of price increases, and they became concerned lest America's role as Europe's breadbasket be lost. Others thought the major threat came from American manufacturers. In 1880, the United States exported more than $685 million in foodstuffs, over 83 percent of all exports, while manufactured goods sent overseas were valued at $103 million, or 12.5 percent of the total. In 1890, agricultural exports were worth $630 million, less than three-quarters of the year's total of $845 million, while American businessmen sent $151 million worth of goods overseas, almost 18 percent of all trade. The message seemed clear enough: a combination of new food areas plus the great growth of American industry would transform America into an urban, industrial nation, to the detriment of the farmers. The fact that machinery exports had increased in spite of English competition only served to bolster this belief. The United States was already the world's leading producer of iron and steel, and a close second to Great Britain in coal. To the farmer, business seemed gigantic; to the businessman, the chronic overproduction and tight margins of the past had not been overcome, and many feared the slightest economic tremor might start an avalanche of liquidations.

The money problem complicated matters in 1890, and in a way which seemed strange to Americans of the next century. In the years following the 1884 panic, federal receipts rose regularly, primarily as a result of protective tariffs that obliged foreigners to pay a stiff price for entry into the American market, but were not high enough to keep goods out of the country. At the same time, government expenditures rose at a slower rate. In 1885, federal receipts were $323.7 million and expenditures $260.2 million, leaving a surplus of $63.5 million, most of which was used to reduce the interest-bearing debt to $1,196.2 million. More surpluses followed; by 1889 the debt was $829.9 million, and falling rapidly. At that rate the nation would be debt-free by 1900. The problem was that for each dollar of reduction, a dollar left the currency, bank reserves, and economic stream, contracting credit and causing prices to drop still lower than before. Clearly, since most bank notes were based in part on government bonds, the fewer the bonds, the fewer the notes. The surplus was intolerable; something had to be done about it.

Many proposals to reduce government income or increase expenditures flowed into Washington. Since the largest single income item was customs duties, Congress might have lowered the tariff to the point where it brought in almost no money at all, or raised it so high as to prevent foreign goods from entering the country. The former solution was opposed by business, while the agrarians found the latter unacceptable. Since income could not be reduced, both Democrats and Republicans concentrated on finding ways to disburse more money. The days of federal spending programs were forty years in the future, and despite several popular proposals for massive river and harbor improvements, and one to build a town hall for every hamlet in the nation, they all failed to gain passage. In addition, President Cleveland vetoed every bill that smacked of corruption while he was in office from 1885 to 1889. President Harrison was less fastidious, and under his direction spending rose sharply, but still not enough to offset the receipts.

The surplus and its effects on the economy were the main topics of discussion in Washington that session, and the field on which several bargains could be struck. The agrarians combined with some businessmen and miners to put forth a new silver purchase act, while big business offered a steep increase in tariff rates. As usual, each side made persuasive statements for its point of view. Silver coinage would lead to inflation, which in turn would bring the country out of its slump, said the first group, while the second observed that a high tariff would keep foreign goods from American shores, and as a result, increase employment in factories while at the same time cutting down on customs receipts and so eliminating the surplus. Neither, however, had the votes to put its bill through Congress. Accordingly, each side moderated its program and sought a deal with the other: business support for a limited silver purchase act in return for agrarian votes for a higher tariff. The agreement was struck in late June.

On July 14, Congress passed the Sherman Silver Purchase Act, which directed the Treasury to purchase 4.5 million ounces of the metal a month at the market price. Payment was to be made in Treasury notes, redeemable in gold or silver at the holder's option. The old Bland-Allison Act had created a silver currency that was not legal tender; the new silver certificates would be "as good as gold" in every sense. Agrarians viewed the Sherman Act as a notable victory, a significant step toward "free and unlimited coinage of silver at the ratio of 16–1."

The silverites paid the price on October 1 by voting for the McKinley Tariff, the second major event of the year. The new average rate of duties was 48 percent, the highest of any tariff in American history up to that point. Industrial goods were amply protected, and signs of cooperation with the agrarians could be seen in the repeal of the sugar duty and the substitution of a 2 cent per pound subsidy to domestic producers, as well as the first general impost on agricultural goods. The tariff did its work well; together with other developments, it led customs duties down from $299.7 million in 1890 to $219.5 million in 1891 and $177.5 million in 1892. In this same period, veterans' pensions rose from $106.9 million to $134.6 million, and the surplus declined from $85 million to $9.9 million.

The passage of these two important pieces of legislation led many investors to believe the economic crisis had passed. Although Congress also accepted the Sherman Anti-Trust Act, threatening reprisals against large-scale enterprises, it was assumed this law would not be enforced strictly. The Silver Purchase Act initiated a period of wild speculation in the white metal, whose price rose from 93½ cents an ounce in 1889 to $1.21 on September 3, 1890.

Expectations of currency inflation coupled with a lessening of competition from imports resulted in speculation on Wall Street and Chicago, as market operators formed pools to corner grains and push stocks and bonds upward. Sound-money advocates had warned of a flight from the dollar if the Silver Act was passed. For a brief period—September to October, 1890—these fears were forgotten. Then the nation was struck by repercussions from the year's third major occurrence.

In the 1880s, the Argentine seemed a most promising area for investment. Its soils were rich, the climate mild, and labor cheap and plentiful. Several prominent London banks, including Baring Brothers, began to promote the economic development of the country. An "Argentine craze" occupied Lombard Street, and for a while British investments in the United States were cut back so as to participate more fully in South American development.

For once, the Barings and their allies were wrong: the Argentine Republic had a weak and corrupt government, an unstable currency, and workers who proved to be as inefficient as they were inexpensive. Bad weather and poor farm locations added to the burdens. By early autumn of 1889, it seemed clear that the wheat crop would fail. This news was followed by a coup in Buenos Aires, which brought further difficulties, including a financial panic. Demand for Argentine securities abruptly ended in London, and selling began. Then came news of mining failures in South Africa, causing a new selling wave to hit Lombard Street. The bankers tried to maintain a steady market, but prices continued to plummet. Finally, on November 20, Baring Brothers was forced to default on several obligations. Later in the day the directors announced the firm was insolvent; Baring Brothers closed its door with liabilities of $75 million. Not since the Overend, Gurney collapse of 1866 had such a major firm fallen. Recognizing the importance of public confidence, the Bank of England intervened, supporting Baring Brothers through loans floated overseas. A major panic was averted, but British investors, their fingers burned, refused to touch foreign securities.

News of the Baring collapse led to anxiety and mixed feelings on Wall Street. On the one hand, the Argentine collapse meant a wider market for American wheat and the end of a major threat to that important export. On the other, American firms had become dependent upon British capital for a good deal of their expansion; from February to August, some £100 million worth of American stocks and bonds had been sold in London. The Baring collapse caused an immediate drop in flotations, and a subsequent loss of new capital for the borrowing firms. Railroads were particularly hard hit. In January, E. H. Harriman wrote the directors of the Northern Pacific that "It would be unwise at this time to pass any resolution adopting a policy for a large expenditure of money." Great Northern president James Hill said in May that "We are going to have a panic next September. It will take five years to get over it." Hill was thought to be exaggerating. As it happened, the panic began in November, and its results lasted for more than seven years.

"When London catches cold, New York sneezes." So it was with the Baring failure. The New York banks were hit with massive withdrawals and had to resort to clearing house certificates such as those used in 1873 and 1884; more than $15 million worth were issued and used effectively. Twenty-nine brokerages failed; several prominent trust companies suspended operations. Stocks declined sharply, especially those associated with the Barings. Atchison, Topeka, and Santa Fe, a favorite with the British firm, fell from a high of 50⅜ to 23½ in a matter of weeks.

The sharp 1890 panic ended when Wall Street learned that the Bank of England was supporting the London market. By November 25 Jacob Schiff was able to write to his friend, London banker Ernest Cassel, that he had become hopeful.

Things look brighter today, but it seems that the public has already forgotten the lesson of recent weeks. I myself am still pondering so intently the abyss which the financial world faced, and which has fortunately been bridged by the courageous intervention of London's *haute finance,* that I am unable to entertain the idea of another bull market for the present.

The bull market came nonetheless. The effects of the McKinley Tariff, a good wheat year, and promises of industrial expansion led prices upward. The Baring panic had frightened British bankers and investors, who sent gold to America late in 1890 and early in 1891. This gold, together with silver coinage under the Sherman Act, added some $100 million to the currency in the last half of 1890, causing a mild inflation, renewed economic growth, and talk of better things to come. Some financial leaders spoke of a new upward push in the economy and an end to the recurrent problems of the past twenty years.

Such individuals ignored other aspects of the McKinley Tariff and the Sherman Silver Purchase Act, and the scars left by the Baring collapse. The new customs charges discouraged foreign investment, although trade did not suffer unduly. At the same time, silver certificates and coins worried holders of American debts and stocks, who now felt they might not be redeemable in gold. The Baring panic precipitated these fears, causing dislocations early in 1891. At that time, foreigners began selling their American holdings, used the money to buy gold, and then shipped it back to Europe. Foreigners and Americans alike used silver certificates to pay debts and began hoarding gold. Signs of a flight from the dollar were clear. In 1890, the government had received 95 percent of its customs receipts in gold; by late 1892, the figure was down to 5 percent, the rest being paid in silver. In the first six months of the year, some $41.5 million in gold left America for overseas destinations. Despite record American harvests and grain exports in 1891—events which ordinarily would lead to an importation of gold to pay for the foodstuffs—the outward flow could not be stanched. By the end of May 1892, the Treasury gold supply was down to $114 million, a scant $14 million above legal reserve limit. Meanwhile, more than $420 million in silver certificates were in circulation, against $268 million two years earlier. Insofar as most domestic transactions were concerned, silver had replaced gold; the legal tender provision of the Sherman Silver Purchase Act was, in effect, putting America on a double monetary standard: little but silver was used within the nation's boundaries, while foreigners refused to take anything but gold. British, French, and other trading nations expected devaluation of the dollar at the least, with complete financial collapse predicted by some. Officials of the Harrison Administration admitted publicly that the government's financial solvency was in danger. Government leaders went to the New York banks and asked them to cooperate by selling gold to the Treasury. Most were reluctant to do so, since they expected gold to sell at a premium in a short time, and in any event they needed reserves to cover their own accounts.

The *Commercial and Financial Chronicle* of December 12 saw little hope for the currency. Ignoring exhortations of the outgoing administration, the gold shipments continued. The cause was evident to all: it was the "lack of confidence which our policy is causing Europe to feel in our financial stability. No more foreign capital comes to the United States and as fast as Europeans can dislodge their holdings in America they take the money away." And who could blame the Europeans? Even Americans had lost confidence in the dollar. A small but increasing trickle of American funds in the form of gold exports started to leave the country late in 1892, for investment in Canada, Europe, and some of the despised Latin-American countries, all of which seemed stronger than the United States. Well over $100 million—some say as much as $250 million—left the United States from 1892 to 1897, a sign that many affluent citizens doubted the financial future of their own country.

This, then, was the situation as Cleveland prepared to assume the Presidency, selecting a cabinet and conferring with his Wall Street supporters.

"There has never been a time in our history when work was so abundant, or when wages were as high, whether measured by the currency in which they are paid, or by the power to supply the necessaries and comforts of life." Thus, Benjamin Harrison reported on the nation's economy in his last message to Congress, in January 1893. While it was true that wages were higher than they had been a year before, prices had risen as well, the result of more dollars in circulation. Each increase in silver coinage caused more gold to leave America. In December 1892 and January 1893 more than $25 million had left for Europe by boat; at the end of January the Treasury's reserve was down to $108 million. The outgoing government made a last plea for aid to the New York banks, which responded by exchanging $6–$8 million in gold for notes. Harrison thought that would be enough to see him through to the end of his term. He was right; on March 4, when he left office to return to Ohio, the gold reserve was $100,982,410. Another day and the legal limit might have been broken.

This was not the only problem left the Cleveland Administration. The Philadelphia & Reading Railroad, a chronic invalid which nonetheless paid its usual bond interest in January, went into bankruptcy on February 25, declaring debts in excess of $125 million. Prices snapped that month and began to decline, as many merchants refused to accept silver in violation of the law. There was labor unrest and threats of new strikes. Not since 1861 had an American President surveyed so many major problems on assuming office.

Cleveland entered the White House with confidence, supported by the business community and aided by what was considered a strong and able Cabinet. The key man there was Secretary of the Treasury John G. Carlisle, who had formerly been a Senator from Kentucky and before that Speaker of the House of Representatives. After Cleveland himself, Carlisle was the leading Democrat spokesman for tariff reform and the gold standard. The new Secretary was not trusted by some of Cleveland's New York friends. In 1875 he had been considered a radical who opposed gold resumption. Then, in 1884, he had tried to win the Presidential nomination by opposing Cleveland at the convention. In the years that followed, however, the two rivals became friends. Cleveland thought Carlisle the ablest man in public life; iron tycoon Abram Hewitt considered him a financial genius. He was neither of these. At best, Carlisle was an astute and shrewd politician, who lacked the President's honesty, having instead a talent for compromise and making friends. A hedger by nature, he was uncomfortable as an all-out combatant for gold. The pressure proved too great for him, and in the end Carlisle took to the bottle. The Secretary of the Treasury at that moment had to be a strong man. Carlisle was a weak reed and an ineffectual statesman. Yet, Cleveland never lost confidence in him, at one time indicating that Carlisle was his choice for the presidency in 1896.

The new administration had begun its maneuvers for a sound currency two weeks before taking office. At that time, Cleveland approached the Wall Street bankers to find out if they would take a bond issue of some $50 million. The gold was to be "brought from abroad and put in our Treasury, and I want it done promptly and in such a manner that the par value of the bonds shall be forthcoming to us free from commission." The President-elect did not state that the issue would be floated, but merely that he wanted to know what support he could count on in order to deal more effectively with the crisis. Word leaked to Wall Street that Cleveland and the bankers had come to an agreement. Stock prices rallied; perhaps the expected crisis would be avoided.

The new administration did not float the issue, but Cleveland did order plates prepared, should such a loan become necessary. Instead, Carlisle was dispatched to New York to ask the bankers for further gold deposits. The President's advisers urged him to call a special session of Congress to repeal the Silver Purchase Act, but Cleveland decided to wait until he heard from Carlisle; calling the session would only convince the nation that he was a Wall Street tool and little else, and this was an impression Cleveland always tried to avoid. The gamble worked; the New York bankers agreed to take $25 million in notes, depositing a like amount of gold in the Treasury. For the moment, at least, the reserve had been saved. Then came news that the balance of trade had turned after a nine-month period in which imports had exceeded exports. Again, stock prices rose on Wall Street. On April 5, the *Times* reported on the ebullient atmosphere on the Street.

There was an entire change of sentiment in Stock Exchange orders today, and it was accomplished by what appeared to be a preconcerted movement to cover outstanding short contracts all along the line. It is too soon to say that a bull market is upon us, but the figures show that the tendency is toward higher prices. The professional element is still in control, but many orders were executed to-day which were for outsiders who have long been absent from the Street.

The Wall Street of 1893 was little changed from that of 1884. There were not many bulls—many of them had been crushed in 1873 and 1884, and few had appeared to take their place— and more speculators were eager to enter bear pools. Volume was

SALES AT THE NEW YORK STOCK EXCHANGE

Year	Shares Sold	Value of Shares	Railway Bonds	U.S. Bonds	State Bonds
1882	116,307,271	$7,689,453,436	$246,769,410	$18,555,850	$26,571,260
1883	97,049,909	6,260,809,961	284,768,100	17,046,150	6,986,500
1884	96,154,971	5,939,500,000	499,955,200	14,905,150	2,826,900
1885	92,538,947	5,479,859,840	660,659,400	15,261,200	14,678,053
1886	100,802,050	5,885,662,200	587,237,500	12,793,500	20,394,411
1887	84,914,616	4,508,778,899	347,127,330	7,110,400	15,306,800
1888	65,179,106	3,539,519,143	345,914,057	6,573,700	5,188,285
1889	72,014,600	4,059,231,891	398,825,425	3,698,850	5,932,350
1890	71,282,885	3,977,664,193	401,829,220	2,625,550	4,870,400
1891	69,031,689	3,812,247,419	383,715,000	1,460,800	3,475,100
1892	85,875,092	4,874,014,262	485,857,400	1,729,100	4,793,950
1893	80,977,839	4,550,260,916	351,854,450	2,143,250	3,792,800

Source: Francis Eames, *The New York Stock Exchange*, p. 95

seldom more than 200,000 shares, although a record 1,473,953 were traded on February 20, 1893, when bear pools shook the market. Despite churning activity that year, volume was far below what it had been a decade earlier—another indication that the securities market had not recovered from the panic of 1873, much less that of 1884. There was a steady erosion of activity, both in shares sold and value of shares, and then a partial recovery. Trading in government bonds dried up, the result of refunding operations and the non-issuance of new securities in the period when the debt was being paid off rapidly. The state bond market also declined in activity, another sign of stagnation after the 1884 panic. One more indication of the general torpor of the market could be found in the price of a seat on the Exchange. In 1880, one sold for $26,000. Then the price began to fall, until in 1893 membership could be had for $15,250 plus a $500 initiation fee. Since both commissions and volume were low, with no hope for a rise in either, brokers felt a seat was worth little more. Some left investment banking entirely to enter other areas of business or become speculators. To place their dilemma into focus, one need only observe that in March 1967 some 224,784,000 shares were traded on the New York Stock Exchange, more than two and a half times as many as were traded in all of 1893.

Railroad securities still dominated the market in 1893. At the beginning of the year, approximately $13 billion worth of rail issues were listed for trading, and $9.5 billion of this amount were bonds. At that time $3 billion in state issues were listed, and less than $700 million in federal obligations. The industrial section was quite small—less than $500 million worth of stocks and bonds were on the list. The Consolidated Stock Exchange functioned, as did several smaller markets, but the New York Exchange was still the leader on Wall Street.

In April 1892, the New York Exchange tried for the fourth time to institute central clearing operations, and on this occasion it succeeded. Twice a day small armies of runners would enter the Street, carrying securities to and from the clearing house. The post of runner was considered the lowest rung on the Wall Street ladder, but some were able to rise from it rapidly. E. H. Harriman

had once been a runner, and in 1892 Bernard Baruch was learning the ropes as a runner-clerk for A. A. Housman & Co.

Wall Street lacked strong leadership at this time. Jay Gould
had passed from the scene, and no one seemed able to replace
him. J. P. Morgan was making a name for himself, but as yet
had not impressed his fellows sufficiently with his skill. Jacob
Schiff of Kuhn, Loeb was a powerful force in the constellation
of German Jewish firms which also included Lehman Brothers.
Between this element and the Protestant brokers there was cor-
diality, but not much mixing. Since business had to go on, and
interests of the two groups were similar, they belonged to the
same clubs and organizations. When John Carlisle came to New
York to discuss gold deposits with the bankers, he lunched at
the Union League Club, which, though solidly Republican, welcomed the Secretary of the Treasury. There he spoke to the city's
leaders, including Cornelius Bliss, the club's president, and Jesse
Seligman, its vice-president. Together these two men led the
others in raising money to support the dollar. On the surface,
at least, harmony reigned in Washington and Wall Street.

Then, in early April, a thunderbolt hit the financial district. It
had nothing to do with gold or prices, although the exports continued and prices were in a slow decline. Rather, it concerned
the blackballing of Theodore Seligman at the Union League.
Despite the fact of his father's vice-presidency and his own social
position in New York and business connections on the Street,
Theodore was denied admission by the younger element of the
club because he was Jewish. Cornelius Bliss and Senator Chauncy
Depew had favored him, as did most of the old-timers. But the
younger group thought some segregation necessary, and so voted
against Seligman. One of those who opposed him spoke plainly
of his position.

To speak frankly such is the fact. I think that a majority of the men
who frequent the club habitually are opposed to the admission of
Hebrews. Their opposition is not based upon any dislike of particular
individuals, but upon the general belief that men of the Jewish race
and religion do not readily affiliate in the social way with persons not
of their own persuasion. We know that there are a great many

Hebrews in New York who are cultivated, public-spirited, and of high business standing. We respect them and do not dislike to meet them publicly; but practical experience seems to have proved that they are more contented and successful socially among themselves than when thrown individually among other associations.

Jesse Seligman resigned from the club, as did other Jewish members. Jacob Schiff was livid with rage. Morgan was silent, as was Elihu Root. The *Times* regretted the episode, noting that "this unfortunate incident would never have been allowed to happen in a year when a campaign fund was to be raised." It happened, instead, when the currency was in greater danger than at any time since the Civil War. By late April, many Wall Streeters were not talking to one another. Leadership was lacking; cooperation was difficult. And all the while, the gold situation worsened.

As early as April 11, the *Times* reported dangers to the $100 million reserve. "About $3,000,000 of gold goes abroad today. This cuts the Treasury 'free gold' about a half. There were $7,000,000 reported on Saturday. If the steamers at the end of this week carry away as much as is taken by the steamers at the beginning of the week, the entire 'free' surplus will be wiped out." Prices on Wall Street fell, and volume picked up. Rumors ap-

PRICES OF SELECTED ISSUES, APRIL 1893

	Closing Prices (fractions rounded off)						
Issue	April 1	April 17	April 18	April 19	April 20	April 21	April 22
American Tobacco	101	94	93	90	89	88	88
Chicago Gas	90	87	87	84	85	85	85
Delaware & Hudson	132	130	130	129	127	128	127
General Electric	108	104	104	100	100	98	99
Lake Shore	129	129	130	129	127	129	127
National Cordage	67	60	61	60	60	60	59
New York Central	107	107	106	106	105	106	106
Northern Pacific	17	16	17	17	16	16	17
Union Pacific	38	36	36	35	35	35	35
U.S. Rubber	54	57	59	56	57	56	56
Western Union	95	91	92	91	90	91	90

Source: *New York Times*, April 2–23, 1893

peared, as they always do at such moments. There was talk of bear pools in the sugar and whiskey trusts; lead and cordage were also being manipulated. Money was increasingly scarce, and several firms were unable to sell their bonds. On April 18, Thomas M. Barr & Co., a leading coffee dealer, declared bankruptcy with liabilities of $275,000. When asked the cause of his downfall, Barr replied that speculation in the commodities market was at its worst in his experience. Barr had been forced to deal heavily in futures, and when coffee prices fell, he was left insolvent. Other, smaller firms followed Barr into bankruptcy, and the loss of confidence continued. "The sentiment on Wall Street is growing very bearish, and if something doesn't happen of a hopeful character pretty soon the market will become so heavily oversold that it will not be difficult for a few daring speculators to bring about a very sharp upward turn." So thought the *Times* on April 19. Every selloff had been followed by a recovery; the newspaper expected one to come in a few days.

Gold reserves finally fell below the $100 million limit on April 21, sparking new activity in the metals markets and further shipments overseas. Prices declined on Wall Street that morning but recovered most of the loss in the afternoon, closing fractions lower. During the next week, stocks were uneasy, awaiting action from Washington. Secretary Carlisle did not help matters when he said that the Treasury would continue gold payments only "as long as it has gold lawfully available for the purpose." But, according to the law, payments should have stopped when the reserve hit $100 million. Did Carlisle mean to say that he might be forced to redeem gold obligations with silver? Some Wall Streeters began to remember the Secretary's past—the fact that he had voted for the Bland-Allison Silver Purchase Act. Was Carlisle a silver supporter in disguise? Toward the end of the week, prices began to decline once more.

At this moment of crisis, all eyes were riveted on Chicago, where the Columbian Exposition was to open on May 1. Grover Cleveland would be there to inspect the huge Krupp cannon given the city by the German arms manufacturer, a map of the United States constructed entirely of pickles, and the Chicago-New York long-distance telephone. With the country in a festive

PRICES OF SELECTED ISSUES, APRIL 1893

| | Closing Prices (fractions rounded off) | | | | | |
Issue	April 24	April 25	April 26	April 27	April 28	April 29
American Tobacco	80	82	81		80	79
Chicago Gas	86	86	86		86	84
Delaware & Hudson	128	129	129	H	129	128
General Electric	98	100	100	O	99	98
Lake Shore	129	130	129	L	129	128
National Cordage	60	61	61	I	60	58
New York Central	106	107	107	D	107	107
Northern Pacific	16	16	16	A	16	17
Union Pacific	36	37	36	Y	37	36
U.S. Rubber	59	59	59		59	58
Western Union	90	92	91		90	90

Source: *New York Times*, April 25–30, 1893

mood, the stock market opened lower on Monday, May 1. The decline continued into Tuesday, and on Wednesday the Street was hit by its worst selloff since 1884. During the afternoon many stocks fell on rumors of insolvency. On Thursday came news that the huge National Cordage Company—the Cordage Trust—was bankrupt. Few expected this to happen, although Cordage had declined more sharply than most issues the previous week. The board of directors had been optimistic since the beginning of the year, and days before the failure had paid a substantial dividend on the common stock. The directors sadly noted that only a few months earlier the company had been solvent, with $5 million worth of binder twine ready for market. Then came the gold crisis, contracting business and credit. Customers delayed orders; banks would not grant loan extensions. Later on, the firm's president would say "the failure was entirely due to the inability to get credit, which had never been curtailed before in our history, and the uneasiness due to the general distrust in regard to the silver question and the failure of the Reading Railroad Company." It was also true, however, that the firm had been overcapitalized, as were most trusts, and the tremors of April had led it to fall like a house of cards. Fall it did, with liabilities of over $10 million. The company's warehouses and offices were taken over by receivers, while National Cordage common fell seventeen points on May 4, to close the week with a loss of more than 60 percent.

PRICES OF SELECTED ISSUES, MAY 1893

Issue	Closing Prices (fractions rounded off)					
	May 1	May 2	May 3	May 4	May 5	May 6
American Tobacco	74	67	64	60	63	75
Chicago Gas	82	81	71	70	73	74
Delaware & Hudson	127	127	126	125	124	124
General Electric	95	92	89	80	78	81
Lake Shore	128	126	126	124	127	127
National Cordage	52	50	37	20	21	20
National Cordage pfd.	100	100	83	67	57	60
New York Central	105	106	105	103	105	105
Northern Pacific	16	16	15	15	15	15
Philadelphia & Reading	25	26	24	24	25	25
Union Pacific	36	36	34	32	35	34
U.S. Rubber	57	56	49	46	46	45
Western Union	87	87	84	83	85	85

Source: *New York Times*, May 2–7, 1893

Despite a recovery the following day and a broad advance on May 6, whatever confidence had remained after the breaking of the $100 million gold cover was gone. Prices started a slow but regular downward movement. Bullish rumors began to appear. On May 10 it was announced that "Russell Sage has been the biggest buyer in Wall Street. He has told his friends that he now has twice as many stocks as he had held at any time during the last eighteen months." The Rockefellers were said to have begun buying operations, and George Gould was supposedly accumulating rail issues. There was talk of pools in Western Union, Chicago Gas, and other market leaders, and of good news soon to come from the offices of the Northern Pacific. The rumors were either false or these powerful individuals were unable to control the market; the decline continued.

The Wall Street collapse was a reflection of the nation's monetary problems. In mid-May several bankers announced that the silver dollar was worth less than 55 cents in gold, and some New York banks refused to accept them. Notes drawn on Western and Southern banks, which had indicated an unwillingness to settle drafts in gold, were no longer honored in New York, and a wave of failures began in the West, soon to spread throughout the nation. Then came still another blow. On June 26, India announced it would no longer purchase silver for coinage purposes. The British colony had been the market for nearly one third of the world's newly mined silver. Now this metal, along with the American product, would flood the United States. On June 26, the price of silver in New York had been quoted at 78 cents; by July 1, it was 65 cents. On that date the gold reserve was $95,485,413, and melting rapidly. Cleveland was forced to act. He had hoped that by not calling a special session of Congress, he would still fears regarding the currency. Now it seemed nothing would save the dollar but prompt repeal of the Sherman Silver Purchase Act. Accordingly, he called a special session for August 7.

During July, as Congress prepared to convene, news of bank failures and business foreclosures were daily occurrences. The issuance of clearing house receipts once more helped save some institutions, but they could not prevent the fall of others. No one would accept the silver certificates; gold sold at a premium. Anxious Americans, in their flight from the dollar, began to purchase pounds sterling with silver, paying premiums, which the British insisted upon. By the end of the month only the Treasury would accept the silver certificates, and its offices were flooded with Americans eager to exchange them for gold.

Industrial conditions reflected the money disaster. Corporation earnings were poor for the first half of the year, and throughout June bad news hit Wall Street every day. On July 19, a Boston mortgage broker was forced to sell a $220,000 mortgage for $9,000 in gold, as a result of the sharp decline in real-estate values and the increase in the gold price.

Toward the end of the month—when speculators were wondering whether Congress would be able to repeal the Sherman Silver Purchase Act before the gold cover was gone—Wall Street suffered its second panic of the year. No single dramatic event signaled the new crash. Rather, the poor earnings reports, tales of tight money, gold shipments, and the like, deepened the general gloom which had existed since the National Cordage failure.

The New York, Lake Erie & Western Railroad went into receivership on July 25; for the fourth time in the past forty years, the road was bankrupt. That same day the Wisconsin Marine & Fire Insurance Company closed "temporarily," its officers claiming, however, that the firm was still solvent. Other banks and insurance companies shut down in Indianapolis, Louisville, and Chicago. New York bankers told the press that their institutions were solvent. Several went to the trouble of advertising their liquidity in the newspapers. This pattern was similar to what had happened several times during the past month, but now it led to declines of greater magnitude than before. Stock prices fell on Monday, July 24, with volume rising to 291,000 shares. There was another decline on Tuesday, followed by a crash and panic on July 26, when volume reached 462,000 shares.

PRICES OF SELECTED ISSUES, JULY 1893

	Closing Prices (fractions rounded off)					
Issue	July 24	July 25	July 26	July 27	July 28	July 29
American Tobacco	54	55	55	56	53	50
Chicago Gas	53	50	46	49	47	42
Delaware & Hudson	115	114	104	105	110	106
General Electric	49	48	42	45	35	38
Lake Shore	115	115	107	112	111	109
National Cordage	10	10	10	12	12	12
New York Central	99	96	92	98	97	97
Northern Pacific	9	8	8	8	9	8
Union Pacific	17	17	15	19	18	17
U.S. Rubber	30	26	25	29	30	25
Western Union	75	73	67	72	70	69

Source: *New York Times*, July 25–30, 1893

Activity let up a trifle after that, but prices did not recover their losses. Instead, they drifted downward, with the exception of those which were the victims of insolvency rumors, such as General Electric, which gyrated wildly later in the week and continued irregular thereafter, despite protests of solvency from its directors and officers. Most listed stocks hit their panic bottoms in late July.

RANGE OF LEADING STOCKS IN 1893

Railroads	Opening	Lowest		Closing
Baltimore & Ohio	94	54	July 27	67
New York Central	109	92	July 26	98
Pennsylvania	54	46	Dec. 18	48
Atchison, Topeka & Santa Fe	34	9	Dec. 30	10
Chicago, Milwaukee & St. Paul	77	46	July 26	56
Illinois Central	99	86	July 18	89
Northern Pacific preferred	47	15	Aug. 16	18
Union Pacific	39	15	July 26	18
Chesapeake & Ohio	22	12	July 26	16
Louisville & Nashville	72	39	Dec. 28	44
Miscellaneous				
American Sugar	111	61	July 26	81
American Tobacco	121	43	July 31	70
National Cordage	138	7	Aug. 25	20
Pacific Mail Steamship	27	8	July 27	14
U.S. Rubber	46	17	Aug. 17	42
Western Union	96	67	July 26	82

Source: William Lauk, *Causes of the Panic of 1893*, p. 99

Grover Cleveland was not unaware of what was going on in New York. Carlisle and others gave him running reports of happenings in the money market and the rumors along Wall Street. All agreed that repeal of the Silver Purchase Act would be the most bullish news the financial district could receive and in addition would be instrumental in restoring confidence to depositors at banks throughout the nation.

The President was never known for his subtlety of thought and action; he was blunt, direct, and tended to simplify matters. To him the major reasons for the panics and slump were the actions of 1890: the Sherman Silver Purchase Act, the McKinley Tariff, and the Baring disaster. If the effects of these three events could be counterbalanced, all might be well once more. Accordingly, Cleveland decided to ask Congress to act in August so as to

correct the problems created three years earlier. As he made
plans, his head was in bandages, and he could barely speak.
Friends and associates thought he had a toothache. Actually, the
President had been operated on for cancer of the palate in early
July. The operation had been kept secret in order to prevent
new panics and fears, but it obviously added to the problems of an
already beset man.

The nation's mood was grim as Congress met in special session
on August 7. The panic of the previous two months was over,
but convictions that the nation's very existence was in question
remained. Businessmen and political leaders alike acted purpose-
fully in an almost dispassionate manner. The silverites thought
they would win, whether or not the Sherman Act was repealed.
If Cleveland had his way, they would lose a round, but if gold
shipments continued, the nation would be forced back to silver,
and so the result would be a sweeping victory for the agrarian
coalition. If they defeated repeal, then the destiny of the nation
would once again be in the hands of the farmers. Cleveland's
supporters hoped that repeal, coupled with other strong actions,
would convince both foreigners and Americans of the soundness
of the dollar, and so end the gold exports.

Each group mobilized its forces before the opening of sessions.
On the one side was a coalition of Eastern Democrats and Republicans, combined with propertied elements in the South and
Midwest. On the other were the farmers, some Southern Democrats, and most of the West. Together they listened to the
President's message, in which he recommended "the prompt
repeal of the provisions of the Act passed July 14, 1890, authoriz-
ing the purchase of silver bullion, and that other legislative action
may put beyond all doubt or mistake the intention and the
ability of the government to fulfill its pecuniary obligations in
money universally recognized by all civilized countries."

A three-week debate followed, ending in votes on several proposals. Repeal won the day, carrying the House by a margin of
239-109 and the Senate by 43-32. The gold forces were jubilant.
"Praise is due first to the Administration of Grover Cleveland,
which has stood like a rock for unconditional repeal," wrote the
New York World. The *Times* also applauded the President. "At

that moment, as often before, between the lasting interests of that nation and the cowardice of some, the craft of others in his own party, the sole barrier was the enlightened conscience and iron firmness of Mr. Cleveland." The President had indeed been firm, rejecting compromise and in the process drawing the lines between silverites and gold supporters ever clearer. The Treasury would no longer purchase silver; the gold reserves would be saved, thought many Administration leaders. The price, however, was high. The silver forces were led by Democrats, who now opposed Cleveland as never before.

Although repeal ended the Treasury silver purchases, it did not have the desired effect of restoring foreign confidence in the dollar. Even as Congress acted, *Bankers Magazine* of London wrote that "The Americans are a people of magnificent achievements and of equally magnificent fiascos. At present they are in the throes of a fiasco unprecedented even in their broad experience," concluding that the nation was in the midst of a revolution; "the ruin and disaster run riot over the land." Henry Adams, ever gloomy about the nation's future, blamed everything on the Wall Streeters, who possessed the "dark, mysterious, crafty, wicked, rapacious, and tyrannical power . . . to rob and oppress and enslave the people." He believed, as did others, that the silverites would act at the first opportunity to gain revenge on Cleveland and the supporters of gold.

This opposition grew and rapidly manifested itself. Cleveland had now corrected the first of the "mistakes of 1890." The second was the McKinley Tariff. Representative Wilson introduced a low tariff bill in the House, one which would enable foreign goods to enter America, paying customs duties and at the same time providing competition for American producers. The bill passed the House by a vote of 204-140, but was amended to death in the Senate. The Wilson-Gorman Tariff, which finally passed the upper house in July 1894, was lower than its predecessor but by no means could be considered a reversal of the McKinley rates. Cleveland was angered; the man of principal again refused to compromise, and he did not sign it. As a result, the new tariff became law without his approval or signature. The Wilson-Gorman Tariff, which pleased neither agrarians or businessmen, further alienated Cleveland from his supporters. Nor did the President gain friends from business for his opposition to that part of the tariff which levied an income tax, the first since the Civil War, which would have netted the government some $75 million a year. The tax measure passed, though it was declared unconstitutional the next year. Its main importance was to show agrarians that Cleveland opposed taxing the rich, while prominent Eastern Republicans wondered about his effectiveness in getting what he wanted from Congress. As far as the President was concerned, his attempt to correct the second wrong of 1890 had not been a success.

The legislation of 1893–1894 did not halt the gold losses, nor did it help the economy to recover. The panic year had seen 642 bank failures (5 percent of all American banks) and more than 15,000 commercial bankruptcies. In 1893 the nation had 177,823 miles of railroads; 32,379 of these belonged to lines in receivership. The Northern Pacific fell in August, and in October the Union Pacific declared itself insolvent. The Atchison, Topeka & Santa Fe followed in December, along with the New York & New England. General Electric continued under pressure. Westinghouse, which had collapsed in 1890, was again in trouble. In fact, there was scarcely a large company, trust, or railroad

PRICES OF SELECTED ISSUES, JUNE–DECEMBER 1893

	Closing Prices (fractions rounded off)						
Issue	June 1	July 1	Aug. 1	Sept. 1	Oct. 1	Nov. 1	Dec. 1
American Tobacco	60	65	50	69	80	88	87
Chicago Gas	72	69	40	55	57	68	68
Delaware & Hudson	121	120	108	112	120	131	136
General Electric	71	72	41	40	42	48	37
Lake Shore	122	121	109	119	122	128	128
New York Central	102	102	98	102	101	104	103
Northern Pacific	14	13	7	6	7	8	7
Union Pacific	28	26	19	23	20	18	23
U.S. Rubber	45	38	25	30	32	43	42
Western Union	82	82	73	80	81	90	89

Source: *New York Times*

not reporting difficulty or actually failing, and few banks were spared periodic runs and forced closings. Some firms stood the strain. The Tobacco Trust remained strong; Western Union's business rose; the New York Central remained solvent. But only a handful found themselves in such happy circumstances.

Stock prices fell during the summer, rallied weakly in the autumn, and closed the year steady. By then it was clear that repeal of the Silver Purchase Act had not restored confidence. Business was still at a low ebb, farm prices were at their worst point in a generation, and the gold reserve stood at $80 million. By January 18, the gold cover had fallen an additional $11 million, as the shipments to Europe and withdrawals for domestic hoarding continued.

In most respects, 1894 was as bad as 1893, and in some, more frightening. Cleveland divided the nation by his handling of the Hawaiian question, although all factions applauded his strong stand in the Venezuela boundary dispute. Almost every month saw the growth of tensions within the country, however. In January, Carlisle floated a $50 million bond issue, which Cleveland hoped would replenish the Treasury gold supply. The issue was sold, but most of the money for it came from gold withdrawals, and so did little good. Meanwhile a fire broke out at the World's Fair, destroying almost all the buildings, with property damages of $2 million. In February Jacob Coxey and others began to form "armies" to march on Washington to demand legislative and administrative actions to relieve the depression; during the next few months newspapers implied that the armies might become the vanguard of revolution. In March Richard Bland attempted to push a bill through Congress to provide for new silver coinage. Cleveland vetoed the bill, and this led to renewed conflicts between the two forces. There was a mine strike and riot in April, as Coxey's Army entered Washington; the move fizzled in May, and Coxey was arrested for trespassing. Later in the month, the Pullman strike began in Chicago, causing violence and bloodshed, during which Cleveland lost the support of Governor John Peter Altgeld and organized labor. In June the Democratic Silver Convention in Omaha adopted the slogan "Free and unlimited coinage at the ratio of sixteen to one," and

the farmers and miners, too, broke with the President. The Pullman strike ended in early July, but new labor uprisings were reported elsewhere, and there was violence in Kensington, Illinois,
as union leader Eugene Debs was indicted on charges of criminal
conspiracy. That summer the two best-selling books in America
were W. H. Harvey's *Coin's Financial School,* a defense of silver,
and Henry Demarest Lloyd's *Wealth Against Commonwealth,* an
attack on the trusts. H. P. Robinson, editor of *Railroad Age,* later
wrote:

It is probably safe to say that in no civilized country in this century,
not actually in the throes of war or open insurrection, has society
been so disorganized as it was in the United States during the first
half of 1894; never was human life held so cheap; never did the
constituted authorities appear so incompetent to enforce respect for law.

The Commercial and Financial Chronicle looked about in midsummer and saw disaster in all parts of the country.

The month of August will long remain memorable . . . in our industrial history. Never before has there been such a sudden and shaking
cessation of industrial activity. Nor was any section of the country
exempt from the paralysis. Mills, factories, furnaces, mines nearly
everywhere shut down in large numbers, and commerce and enterprise
were arrested in an extraordinary degree . . . and hundreds of thousands of men thrown out of employment.

Some conservative writers saw in the silver agitation and the
Pullman strike the makings of a grand coalition—a farmer-labor
organization—which would attempt to bring down industrial
America. Others, such as J. W. Schuckers, former secretary to
Salmon Chase, thought the coming battle would be sectional.
"The South and West—the tributary sections—were being taught
that they have a master in Wall Street," he wrote in June 1894,
as the polarization of the nation proceeded.

The situation continued to boil through the rest of the year,
as the Administration seemed unable to cope with violence or
solve the money problems. A second bond issue in November
netted $55 million, but again most of this money came from gold

withdrawals, and although reserves rose above $100 million for a short time, they fell almost at once as a result of new demands at the Treasury.

Wall Street was one of the few areas of reasonable calm and stability. The district was quiet and listless. In 1892 some $100 million in bonds had been floated; in 1894 the figure was less than $37 million. Prices fluctuated sharply in the first half of the year, but ended on a firm note. Despite labor unrest, Coxey's Army,

PRICES OF SELECTED ISSUES, JANUARY–JUNE 1894

Issue	Closing Prices (fractions rounded off)					
	Jan. 1	Feb. 1	Mar. 1	Apr. 1	May 1	June 1
American Tobacco	70	81	76	84	86	84
Chicago Gas	60	64	64	63	63	74
Delaware & Hudson	129	136	135	138	138	132
General Electric	33	35	42	42	40	34
Lake Shore	120	128	128	130	130	131
New York Central	97	101	100	102	100	98
Northern Pacific	5	4	4	6	5	4
Union Pacific	18	20	22	21	18	17
U.S. Rubber	40	30	39	41	39	39
Western Union	82	84	86	84	85	84

Source: *New York Times*

declining gold balances, the inability of the Administration to hold together its coalition, and other signs of economic and political disintegration, prices were steady. The continuation of these problems, along with additional threats of revolution and economic disturbances, did not lead to new eruptions in the second half of the year. Not even Populist gains in the congressional elections of that year resulted in panic, nor did the relative failure of the bond offering.

Part of the reason for this lack of selloffs could be found in the generally low prices that already existed in 1894. Equally if not more important, however, was the role of the Wall Street establishment in salvaging the economy.

When the panic erupted, there were several powerful houses on Wall Street, but none were preeminent. The Seligman affair

PRICES OF SELECTED ISSUES, JULY–DECEMBER 1894

Issue	Closing Prices (fractions rounded off)					
	July 1	Aug. 1	Sept. 1	Oct. 1	Nov. 1	Dec. 1
American Tobacco	88	89	103	97	99	91
Chicago Gas	78	72	74	70	74	70
Delaware & Hudson	129	135	135	132	124	125
General Electric	36	35	40	38	35	35
Lake Shore	129	129	136	134	131	133
New York Central	96	97	102	100	98	98
Northern Pacific	4	3	6	4	4	4
Union Pacific	11	7	14	12	11	12
U.S. Rubber	36	35	37	39	41	41
Western Union	83	84	90	87	87	86

Source: *New York Times*

only served to intensify rivalries in the district, which was un-
prepared to act in concert to save the situation. Leadership was
needed, and it appeared in the form of J. P. Morgan.

Morgan was fifty-six years old in 1893, and at the prime of his
life. As the head of Drexel, Morgan & Co., he had helped in the
refinancings following the 1873 and 1884 panics, working then as
one of several bankers called upon for assistance. At the time of
the 1893 crash, Morgan was attempting to reorganize the defunct Richmond & West Point Terminal Company. Acting
quickly, he was able to save the firm and then absorb it into the
Southern Railway Company, which was capitalized at $370 mil-
lion; within a year, the new line was showing earnings of $3
million, and Morgan was hailed as a financial genius. Through
J. S. Morgan & Co. in London, and Drexel, Harjes & Co. in
Paris, he was able to market bonds overseas when most American
houses had little credit in Europe. A well-known figure before,
Morgan now emerged as a leading power on the Street. It was
Morgan who was called upon to rehabilitate the Philadelphia &
Reading later in the year, a task which he again accomplished with
skill. Drexel, Morgan & Co. was responsible for the Northern
Pacific reorganization in the fall, and in 1894 Morgan undertook
the refinancing and rehabilitation of the Erie. In September he
began to set the Union Pacific back on its feet, after seeing the

great Southern System through its problems at the height of the panic. Morgan would reorganize the Lehigh Valley and other small lines in this period, as well as save several more from disaster. By early 1895, he was able to command the respect of creditors and bankers alike. Wall Street again had leadership.

This is not to say that Morgan was the only person standing between solvency and disaster. Jacob Schiff was prominent in Chesapeake & Ohio and Louisville & Nashville reorganizations and was able to float bond issues for the Pennsylvania, Norfolk & Western, and the Denver & Rio Grande. Other investment bankers were active in railways and commercial houses, and they were able to maintain enough liquidity to prevent the entire economic structure from collapsing.

Early in 1894, Wall Street had looked to Washington and Grover Cleveland to save their kind of America. Cleveland's inability to gain passage of his tariff bill, along with other failures, led to a disillusionment with the President. By year's end, the Wall Street Community had started placing its confidence in men like Schiff and, most importantly, with J. P. Morgan. In 1892 Morgan and his group had supported Cleveland for the Presidency. Now, in early 1895, Cleveland's only hope to stop the gold flow rested with J. P. Morgan. Europe no longer trusted the dollar; but many influential Europeans trusted the word and power of Drexel, Morgan & Co.

Some $31 million in gold left America for Europe in December 1894, and an additional $45 million went in January. There was talk of a third bond issue, but few thought it would do much good. The first had saved the gold cover for a matter of a few months; the second was dried up in three weeks. Holders of silver certificates would bring their notes to the Treasury for redemption in gold, which they would then hoard. The Treasury would place the notes back into circulation, and within a short time they would return, again to be redeemed in gold. An "endless chain" of redemptions was in effect, and there seemed little the government could do about it. Carlisle talked of currency reforms to placate the silverites; bankers speculated as to what would happen when the gold ran out. The Assistant Treasurer in New York was rumored to have remarked that he would have no more gold for disbursement sometime in late February. At Sherry's and other restaurants, gamblers began to bet on the day of bankruptcy. Writing to the President on January 24, Isador Straus said:

I had occasion to visit Wall Street yesterday, and finding a very grave feeling of apprehension, and talk of extraordinary heavy shipments of gold, some putting the figures as high as five million dollars this week, I took it upon myself to ascertain from different sources the immediate cause for so acute a condition.

There is no doubt that Europe is thoroughly aroused as to our inability to continue on a gold basis, and they are consequently selling their holdings in American investments as rapidly as the market will take them without inordinately depressing quotations. That naturally calls for heavy gold shipments, which nothing but a restoration of confidence in the stability of our currency can arrest.

As Straus wrote, the Treasury reserve was nearing the $45 million mark.

With his back to the wall, Cleveland was forced to take drastic measures. First, he asked Congress to give him the authority to cancel greenbacks and Treasury notes when they came to the Treasury. This would stop the "endless chain" which was then in effect. Secondly, he asked Congress for power to sell 3 percent government bonds specifically payable in gold. Representative William Springer introduced the measure, which immediately brought praise from the business press and opposition from the silverites. The *Omaha World-Herald* denounced the Springer proposal as "bonds, bankruptcy, and disaster," while the *Atlanta Constitution* thought "the people of this country do not care how soon gold payments are suspended." The Springer bill was defeated on February 7.

Cleveland met with Carlisle, Secretary of War Lamont, and attorney General Olney to map out strategy. Congress had foreclosed on any possibility of gaining new funds through the usual channels. It seemed as though the silverites were to win their gamble: the nation would soon be forced off gold.

The financial crisis had been brought on—or so Cleveland believed—by three events in 1890. As we have seen, the President had led the repeal of the McKinley Tariff, substituting the milder

Wilson-Gorman Tariff, and had ended silver purchases as set forth in the Sherman Silver Purchase Act. The third event—the Baring panic—had caused foreigners to begin their liquidation of American securities. If the flow of gold overseas could be ended, if foreigners could once again have confidence in America's future, perhaps the situation could be saved. There had been some talk of foreign bond sales in January, but Europe's leading bankers showed little interest in a new American issue, no matter what the coupon; they had decided that the credit of the United States government was no longer good. On the other hand, J. P. Morgan and his circle retained the trust of the European bankers. London and Paris would not accept Cleveland's name on a guarantee, but they might cooperate with Morgan. In effect, J. P. Morgan was considered more solvent than the United States Treasury.

Negotiations with Morgan had begun in earnest in late January. Assistant Secretary of the Treasury William Curtis had spoken to him on January 31, at which time Morgan promised to aid the Administration in any way he could. If necessary, he would use his influence with August Belmont, who represented those European interests which might purchase a bond issue. Curtis remained closeted with Morgan for hours, during which time they drew up a plan whereby the Morgan-led banks would take a $100 million bond issue, to be paid for with gold imported from Europe for the purpose. The bonds would pay 3¾ percent, and the syndicate would assume responsibility for the issue's distribution.

Curtis brought this offer back to Washington, where it was debated by Cleveland's inner circle. Carlisle opposed the plan, as did several others who thought they could get better rates elsewhere. In addition, they still had some hope the Springer Bill would be passed. If not, then perhaps a public subscription would be made—one which would not leave Cleveland open to charges of being a Wall Street puppet. As a result, Morgan's offer was rejected.

The defeat of the Springer Bill and continued drains on the Treasury made action imperative. Realizing, perhaps more than Cleveland, the gravity of the situation, Morgan set off for Washington on February 7, accompanied by some of his aides, intent on talking to the President. He rushed to the White House through the worst blizzard of the year and confronted Cleveland, Carlisle, Olney, and other Administration leaders with the facts as he saw them. The key point was that the New York Sub-Treasury had less than $9 million in gold coin at that time; Morgan knew of a single check for $12 million then outstanding. "If that is presented today, all is over," he told Cleveland. The President had no other alternative; he accepted the Morgan proposal.

In the end, it was decided that the syndicate would take a $65.1 million issue of 4 percent bonds at 104½, which would be paid for with 3.5 million ounces of gold, half of which would come from Europe, in amounts not to exceed 300,000 ounces a month. The entire question would be kept from Congress; Cleveland would sell the bonds using an obscure 1862 statute as his authority.

Both Cleveland and Morgan assumed great risks in concluding this agreement. The President hoped it would give new support to the dollar and stop the panic. The price he paid for his action was the complete severance from his agrarian and labor critics; henceforth he would be a President without a party. As for Morgan, his syndicate stood to make a huge profit if the issue was a success, a reward Morgan considered justified, considering the chances he was taking. *If* the increase in the gold reserve did not bring new confidence in America; *if* agricultural exports were not large enough to bring additional gold to the country; *if* the sixty or so European banking houses with which the syndicate had connections refused to take all the bonds, or attempted to convert dollars into gold once more; *if* the international situation flared up again—then the bond sale would be a failure. In such an event, Morgan and his friends would suffer a tremendous blow to their authority and credibility.

Morgan was partially successful. News of the bond issue was greeted enthusiastically, and it was quickly oversubscribed. The syndicate realized a profit which some reckoned at $5 million, and others as high as $9 million. But crop exports were not up to expectations, and Cleveland's Venezuela policy alienated many

British investors. Finally, Morgan had arranged an international agreement not to convert dollars into pounds sterling or buy American gold for the period of the flotation. This agreement was broken by an unknown outsider, and the flight from the dollar resumed. By January 1896 the Treasury's gold holdings were again at the $50 million level.

PRICES OF SELECTED ISSUES, 1895

Issue	Closing Prices (fractions rounded off)					
	Jan. 2	Feb. 1	Mar. 1	Apr. 1	May 1	June 1
American Tobacco	98	96	91	91	103	115
Chicago Gas	73	76	71	72	74	74
Delaware & Hudson	127	130	126	128	129	130
General Electric	34	30	28	35	34	35
Lake Shore	135	139	136	137	143	146
New York Central	98	100	96	96	98	102
Northern Pacific	4	3	3	5	5	5
Union Pacific	11	10	9	11	13	14
U.S. Rubber	44	42	38	40	40	47
Western Union	87	88	87	88	89	92
	July 1	Aug. 1	Sept. 1	Oct. 1	Nov. 1	Dec. 1
American Tobacco	109	112	94	100	90	83
Chicago Gas	63	58	65	70	68	63
Delaware & Hudson	130	130	131	133	131	127
General Electric	36	36	38	39	32	32
Lake Shore	150	150	151	150	150	150
New York Central	101	102	104	102	100	100
Northern Pacific	4	5	6	5	5	5
Union Pacific	13	14	17	14	12	9
U.S. Rubber	40	41	41	41	39	36
Western Union	92	93	95	92	91	88

Source: New York Times

Morgan could rightfully claim to have saved the situation in early 1895, even though the gold crisis recurred a year later. Now he proposed a second bond issue, this one for from $100–$200 million, under the same terms as before. The situation was different in 1896, however. The first issue had restored public confidence and had demonstrated to Cleveland that a regular offering would find a ready market. Accordingly, he offered $100 million of 4 percent bonds to the public, and received bids for $688 million worth at prices ranging from 100.7 to 120. The Treasury took in some $111 million as a result of the sales, but as Morgan had predicted, much of this had come from gold withdrawals from the Treasury by Americans. By July 23, the gold cover was down to $90 million.

The situation seemed bleak that election year, as the Democrats denounced Cleveland and nominated a silverite, William Jennings Bryan, for the Presidency. Never before had an incumbent President been so rejected by his own party. The Republicans named William McKinley, author of the McKinley Tariff and a supporter of the gold standard (who at one time had flirted with silver). For the first time since the Civil War it appeared as though a national election might spark a new conflagration. McKinley received the wholehearted support of the Wall Street community, while Bryan was strong in the farm areas.

Prices on Wall Street moved irregularly in the first half of the year, as it was clear that Cleveland would be in no position to dictate a candidate at the Democratic convention. At the same time, business reorganizations appeared successful, and there were signs of a recovery in the industrial sector. Thus, for the first time since 1892, Wall Street experienced spotty rallies and short bull

PRICES OF SELECTED ISSUES, JANUARY–JUNE 1896

Issue	Closing Prices (fractions rounded off)					
	Jan. 1	Feb. 1	Mar. 1	Apr. 1	May 1	June 1
American Tobacco	79	78	78	89	95	65
Chicago Gas	66	65	78	67	69	67
Delaware & Hudson	125	129	126	127	127	125
General Electric	26	30	31	37	36	33
Lake Shore	143	146	150	147	150	151
New York Central	97	98	98	96	98	97
Northern Pacific	4	4	4	2	1	8*
Union Pacific	4	8	8	8	9	7
U.S. Rubber	28	26	27	27	27	22
Western Union	84	84	83	84	86	85

* After reorganization
Source: *New York Times*

periods. Not even the rise to power of John Peter Altgeld, who seemed to dominate the Democratic party at midyear and who was attempting to reform it into a farmer-labor coalition, could take stocks to low ground. By early summer, then, many astute Wall Streeters were saying the long decline was over. The key to the future, of course, lay with the election.

The GOP won, carrying every Eastern state and the entire Midwest east of North Dakota and Minnesota, as well as Oregon and California, while Bryan took the South, the mining states, and the western tier of states in the Midwest. The electoral vote was 271–176, but the popular vote was closer—7 million to 6.5 million.

The 1896 election resolved the currency issue in favor of gold, but it did not end the panic and depression. This was accomplished by a combination of factors, of which three are of major importance.

In the first place, the silverites were correct in stating that the shortage of currency was a major factor in the nation's economic stagnation, and that an injection of new money would lead to inflation, but also to a much-stimulated economy. Their problem lay in the fact that not all would accept silver as currency, as before many had refused to accept greenbacks. As always, gold was the key to the situation. In 1891 the nation had $10.10 per capita in gold; in 1896, the figure was $8.40. Then, as Bryan and McKinley contested for the Presidency, gold strikes were made in the Klondike, in South Africa, and in Australia. Simultaneously, the cyanamide process for gold extraction, which enabled miners

GOLD PRODUCTION, 1893–1898

Year	Value of gold mined	Increase over previous year
1893	$157,494,800	$10,843,300
1894	181,175,800	23,680,800
1895	198,763,600	17,588,000
1896	202,251,000	3,487,400
1897	236,073,700	33,822,700
1898	286,879,700	50,806,000

Source: Mark Sullivan, *Our Times*, Vol. I, pp. 298–99

to process low-grade ores, was perfected. As a result, gold production shot up in 1897 and then continued to rise.

This increase in gold production led to a price spiral and con-
tentment for both the "gold bugs" and the inflationists. The
former still had sound money, while the latter got what they
had wanted all along: higher prices.

The second factor ending the panic and depression had its
origins in Europe and India, where crops were poor in 1896 and
1897. As Bryan campaigned in August, the wheat price was 53
cents a bushel. By Election Day it was quoted at 95 cents.

On Wall Street, prices declined during the campaign, as it
appeared for a while that Bryan could conceivably win the election. By late October, however, the tide had turned toward
McKinley, and prices rallied, ending the year with a moderate
advance. Although the industrials did not reflect completely the
success on the farms, the rise in rails indicated that this sector
of the economy, too, was on the way to recovery.

PRICES OF SELECTED ISSUES, JULY–DECEMBER 1896

	Closing Prices (fractions rounded off)					
Issue	July 1	Aug. 1	Sept. 1	Oct. 1	Nov. 1	Dec. 1
American Tobacco	91	59	60	62	77	76
Chicago Gas	60	52	55	62	71	74
Delaware & Hudson	124	120	119	124	124	126
General Electric	25	24	24	28	30	31
Lake Shore	147	143	141	147	149	153
New York Central	95	92	91	92	95	94
Northern Pacific	8	6	10	14	15	15
Union Pacific	7	6	5	7	9	10
U.S. Rubber	17	16	16	16	20	25
Western Union	82	79	78	84	85	87

Source: *New York Times*

The combination of an American bumper crop in 1897 and
further European and Indian failures led to dollar wheat and
the greatest exports since 1891. As a result, large amounts of gold
began to flow to America from Europe—some $120 million in
1897 alone—for the first time since the panic, excluding gold

imports gained through bond sales. By the end of 1897 the Treasury had $137 million in gold. Six months later the figure stood at $245 million.

Concomitantly, American industry continued to recover, the result of reorganizations, new capital, and opportunities abroad. The GOP passed the Dingley Tariff, which was higher than the old McKinley rates. Thus, domestic markets were protected as American businessmen began to search for opportunities overseas. Two years earlier it had appeared that the American economy was on the verge of bankruptcy. Now, in December 1897, Count Goluchowski warned of "the American invasion," asserting that "the destructive competition with trans-oceanic countries requires prompt and thorough counteracting measures, if the vital interests of the European people are not to be gravely compromised." Goluchowski concluded that "European nations must close their ranks and fight, shoulder to shoulder, in order successfully to defend their existence" against the American businessman. Clearly, the panic was over, and a new period of prosperity well under way.

Grover Cleveland, who had labored to save the gold standard, and as a result was labeled the errand boy of Wall Street, retired to Princeton, New Jersey, where he became engaged in University politics and issued pronouncements on the national scene. The bitterness of his second administration was dissolved in the good times that followed, and as America became an imperial power, his period seemed quaint and somehow irrelevant. By the administration of Theodore Roosevelt, many Americans had forgotten the issues revolving around free silver, and few could explain economic questions that had seemed so vital in 1893–96. In this atmosphere Cleveland's stubbornness seemed a virtue, and his refusal to compromise a sign of morality. As political figures become old, they become revered; this is especially true of old Presidents. In 1907 Cleveland was seventy years old, and on his birthday he was applauded by Mark Twain as one whose character could be compared with that of Washington. He was greeted by President Roosevelt and Woodrow Wilson, and a bronze tablet was placed in the room where Cleveland was born in

Caldwell, New York. On June 23 he became ill, and he died the following day. His last words were: "I have tried so hard to do right."

Cleveland's Administration had been one of panic and depression for Wall Street, but as he prepared to leave Washington, things seemed brighter. Volume rose, as did prices. The optimism which pervaded the economy in 1897 also appeared on Wall Street. There were problems, to be sure. Clearances were still slow, scoundrels were present in great abundance, and pools and corners seemed everyday occurrences. Such had always been the case in boom periods. The Union League Club remained the citadel of respectability. Theodore Seligman never became a member; Jesse did not set foot in the club again. But the scandal of 1893 was almost healed by 1896. As the *Times* had implied, such a situation would never have developed in an election year. All Wall Street, Jew and Christian alike, contributed to the GOP war chest to defeat Bryan. Jacob Schiff remained at Kuhn, Loeb, and became head of the German-Jewish community and the second most powerful financier in the nation. J. P. Morgan, who had changed the name of his firm from Drexel, Morgan & Co. to J. P. Morgan & Co. in 1895, was the leader of the district, with no rivals. He worked well with others, however, and never insisted on the whole loaf for himself. Morgan had nothing to do with Schiff insofar as social intercourse was concerned, but each man respected the other, and they managed to cooperate on several ventures in the next few years. This would come to a temporary end in 1901, however, when the two found themselves on opposite sides in the first gigantic Wall Street struggle of the new century.

8.

THE STRUGGLE OF THE TITANS: THE NORTHERN PACIFIC CORNER OF 1901

The turn of the century witnessed the golden age of American railroads. The giant lines—the Northern Pacific, the Union Pacific, the Great Northern, the Southern Pacific, the Atchison, Topeka & Santa Fe, the Chicago, Burlington & Quincy— evoked the kind of magic which is today associated with electronics and space travel. Even the older lines—the Erie, the New York Central, and the Pennsylvania—shared in this glamour. Children dreamed of growing up to become railroad engineers, while their fathers considered railroad securities to be the best growth issues available. Then, as now, the nation had its share of heroes; all admired Teddy Roosevelt, Admiral Dewey, and John L. Sullivan. But a special kind of admiration—one tinged with respect for raw power—was afforded the men who controlled the nation's large railroads. James Hill, E. H. Harriman, William Vanderbilt, and J. P. Morgan were known to all. Never before or since has the businessman held such a prominent place in American mythology. Compared to them, men like Jay Gould and Jim Fisk seemed antiquated, and even Commodore Vanderbilt a man of limited vision. At the most, they hoped to control transcontinental lines; Hill and Harriman planned to girdle the globe with their holdings.

James Jerome Hill was known at "the Little Giant," "the Prince of the Great Northern," and "the Devil's Curse of the northern plains" to different people. He arrived in St. Paul, Minnesota, in 1856 with the hope of becoming a trapper. For a while he worked as a clerk, learning all he could about the

Northwest. Failing to be accepted into the Union Army as a
result of a lost eye, he nonetheless helped organize the First
Minnesota Volunteers during the Civil War. Afterward he became interested in railroads and got a job at the St. Paul and
Minnesota, which led him into the Northwest on several occasions. Hill was struck by the vast potential of the region; all
it needed was a railroad to open it up to settlers. Taking control
of the St. Paul and Minnesota in 1878, Hill began to expand
its operations, gaining most of his funds from the sale of land
grants and bonds. At the same time he developed the Great
Northern Railroad, which would compete with Henry Villard's
Northern Pacific. Hill proved a skillful operator; his lines survived
the panic of 1893, which saw the bankruptcy of the Union
Pacific, the Santa Fe, and the Northern Pacific as well. Taking
advantage of Villard's distress, Hill acquired the latter line, which
now worked in conjunction with the Great Northern and was
known as the "Hill Lines" to Wall Street.

The Hill Lines prospered in the years following 1893 and were
instrumental in opening the "inland empire" of the Northwest
to farmers, lumbermen, and traders. But even this was not enough
for the Little Giant. By 1900 Hill started to make plans for
shipping lines to the Orient, a possible rail line through Asia
and Europe, and finally a true transcontinental line running
from New York to Seattle.

While James Hill planned his Northwest empire, E. H. Harriman became a millionaire on Wall Street through shrewd speculations and manipulations. Many of these were in railroad
securities, and Harriman developed a desire to take charge of a
line. More cautious than Hill, he started slowly, purchasing a
Hudson River boat in 1878. That year Harriman met Miss Mary
Williamson Averell of Ogdensburg, New York, and shortly after
they were married. Visits to his father-in-law's home led to an
interest in the development of northern New York. In 1881, Harriman purchased the rundown Sodus Bay and Southern Railroad,
rebuilt it, and sold the line to the Pennsylvania. Throughout this
period he learned much from his father-in-law, William Averell,
who, among his other activities, was president of the small Ogdensburg & Lake Champlain line. Harriman was named to the board

of the Ogdensburg in 1880, and at the same time was elected director of the powerful Illinois Central. By then Harriman had decided to leave his brokerage business and most Wall Street activities to others. For the rest of his life he would concentrate on railroads.

For the next decade Harriman acquired other lines, most of them in the East; he became the dominant voice in the affairs of the Illinois Central and had several clashes with J. P. Morgan. And throughout this period, he waited for the right moment to gain control of a major transcontinental line.

The Union Pacific was one of these. It had a good route structure and owned vast tracts of valuable real estate as well. But the line was somewhat outdated and deeply in debt. Accordingly, it was one of the first to declare bankruptcy in the 1893 panic. For the next two years the line struggled to remain afloat, with little success. Then, in 1895, what was left of the road passed into the hands of a new group which had connections with Kuhn, Loeb & Co., the second most powerful investment house on Wall Street. Jacob Schiff, the head of the firm, was asked to enter into the situation, refinance the Union Pacific, and help in securing new management.

Kuhn, Loeb was well equipped for the task but had an understanding with J. P. Morgan which might have stood in the way: Morgan would not invade Schiff's interests, and vice versa. Schiff contacted Morgan. Would the Great Man object to Kuhn, Loeb's sponsorship of the Union Pacific? The answer was "No." Morgan considered the line beyond salvage and agreed to allow Schiff a free hand. With this, Kuhn, Loeb entered the Union Pacific picture.

For a while the reorganization seemed to proceed satisfactorily, but Schiff soon became aware of others interested in the Union Pacific. Opposition to his plans developed in Congress, and many stockholders seemed particularly troublesome. Fearing that Morgan had changed his mind, Schiff called upon him. Was the House of Morgan behind the opposition? Morgan assured Schiff that it was not he. "It's that little fellow Harriman," he said, "and you want to look out for him."

Schiff then went to Harriman and asked whether the report was correct; he was assured that it was. What did Harriman want? Nothing less than control of the Union Pacific. Unless Schiff agreed to cooperate, Harriman would have the Illinois Central attempt a raid on U.P. stock.

Schiff and his group might have withstood such a raid, but after some consideration came to the conclusion that it would be wiser to take Harriman into the management. After all, Harriman was powerful and had proved himself an able railroad man. Why not? By late 1897, the refinanced Union Pacific was under the Harriman umbrella, with Kuhn, Loeb as its banker.

Harriman realized that the Union Pacific needed large capital improvement programs to bring its rolling stock up to date and its lines into good repair. He was prepared to make these expenditures. In 1896, the U.P. spent some $150,000 on improvements and repairs; by 1901, as Harriman's modernization program went into full swing, the figure for such items was almost $14 million. By then, the Union Pacific was one of the most modern lines in the nation. Fortunately for Harriman, this period coincided with one of bumper crops in the area, and revenues rose sharply, thus enabling Harriman to pay for the improvements. By the turn of the century, the Union Pacific was again strong, and Harriman ready for new frontiers. He visited Alaska, rebuilt the Kansas City Southern, and acquired the Southern Pacific. By 1901 Harriman was considered a railroad genius, and, like Hill, was also given the nickname of "the Little Giant." Harriman and Hill were the nation's two leading railroad figures and, as such, had similar ambitions. Like Hill, Harriman looked to the Asian mainland and Europe, and planned a worldwide transportation network. He too wanted a true transcontinental running from New York to the West Coast. Clearly, the two "Little Giants" were on a collision course.

Before either Hill or Harriman could enter the world arena they would have to take care of their American properties. Hill's Great Northern and Northern Pacific and Harriman's Union Pacific suffered from a similar problem: neither had direct access to Chicago, and without it, they could not tie the American East to the West. On the other hand, the Chicago, Burlington & Quincy had an eastern terminus at Chicago and an excellent system of feeder lines throughout the Mississippi Valley, but did not go farther west than Denver. Hill and Harriman realized that control of the C. B. & Q. was a necessary first step toward a transcontinental network. Both men set out to get it.

Hill's associate in this venture was J. P. Morgan & Co., which had aided in the purchase of the Northern Pacific and other properties. Harriman approached the C. B. & Q. through Jacob Schiff, as usual. Morgan and Schiff began their purchases of C. B. & Q. common in the spring of 1900.

At first, it appeared that Harriman was successful in his quest for the 200,000 shares needed for control. By June 6 he and Schiff had accumulated 69,800 shares, in the process causing the stock to rise sharply. But then they encountered difficulty; the supply of stock ran dry, and on July 25 Harriman owned only 80,300 shares, with no more to be had. It was clear by then that Morgan had gained the support of the C. B. & Q. board of directors for the merger with the Hill interests, and the board members would vote their own shares and those they controlled for a combination with the Northern Pacific. Now the Northern Pacific would have a terminal in Chicago, where it could link with the Morgan-dominated New York Central. The transcontinental was about to become a reality!

Recognizing defeat, Harriman asked Hill for a participation in the C. B. & Q. so that the Union Pacific could enter Chicago. Hill saw no reason to grant such a request, and so Harriman was left in the cold. "Very well," he told Hill. "It is a hostile act and you must take the consequences." But what could Harriman do about it? The merger was well on its way; Morgan controlled a majority of C. B. & Q stock; Hill was adamant. It appeared as though Harriman had accepted the inevitable; he sold his shares of C. B. & Q., making a large profit on the transaction. As 1901 approached, Harriman had a lot of money—more than $8 million from the C. B. & Q. sales alone—and a desire for revenge.

All seemed in order in the Morgan empire the following spring. The organization of the gigantic U.S. Steel complex was proceeding well and the C. B. & Q. affair was apparently settled. Accordingly, Morgan prepared for his annual European trip. He departed in April, leaving one of his partners, Robert Bacon, in charge

278   *Panic on Wall Street*

during his absence. The rugged, athletic Bacon had been a general partner in J. P. Morgan & Co. since 1895. He was able, trusted, and intelligent. Nevertheless, his powers were to be limited; Bacon was to take no important step before contacting Morgan.

Europe held no attraction for Hill, unless as an investment area. Now that the merger was set, he had to go into the field to prepare for the many changes it would bring. Besides, Hill always preferred life in the open, along the rails, to that in the heated boardrooms on Wall Street. So, as Morgan prepared to leave for Europe, Hill set out for the Northwest and his beloved Northern Pacific.

While the travel preparations proceeded, Harriman paced his hotel room, searching for a means to gain revenge on Hill and Morgan and at the same time an entry into Chicago. Many plans for thwarting the merger were considered; none seemed feasible. It was clear that Northern Pacific would soon gain the C. B. & Q. lines. Harriman pondered the new power this would give Northern Pacific. True, the financing for the merger would be costly, and would leave both Northern Pacific and Hill with little cash, but this could be made up after operations on the merged lines commenced.

It was then that Harriman began considering an audacious plan —one which a man of lesser stature would never have dreamed. He had a large amount of liquid capital, but not the C. B. & Q. Hill had little money, but controlled the Northern Pacific, which in turn held the C. B. & Q. Morgan was on his way to Europe, and interference from that quarter would be difficult. The way was obvious; Harriman would attempt to gain control of the Northern Pacific itself, in this way acquiring not only the C. B. & Q., but the very seat of the Hill-Morgan empire! If carried through, it would be the greatest coup in the history of Wall Street. Harriman immediately contacted Schiff and told him of his plan. The Kuhn, Loeb banker agreed to cooperate, and in early April he began to purchase shares of Northern Pacific on the open market, taking care that none would realize who was buying the stock.

The Wall Street of April 1901 could scarcely have been more optimistic. Industrial production was double the figure of 1896, and the nation's foreign-trade picture was equally bright. President McKinley, whose election in 1896 had marked the beginning of the prosperity, had been returned to office four years later by a huge majority and was touring the nation spreading good tidings. Foreign affairs seemed in fine shape; Europe was reasonably quiet and, more important, the Philippine insurrection came to an end as Aguinaldo agreed to stop fighting the Americans. Mark Twain continued his lectures to women's groups, but Buffalo Bill's Wild West Show was more popular and better attended. Spring was early in 1901, and brokers wore flowers in their buttonholes, and seemed extra confident and self-assured as they handled their orders.

Wall Street was in the midst of change that April. New flotations appeared every day; this was the age of the giant consolidations, headed by the billion-dollar U.S. Steel Company, which dominated the capital markets and seemed proof of America's leadership. The new company—which alone would produce more steel than all of Great Britain—was only one of the major trusts. Other formations of the period were United Fruit, Borden's Condensed Milk, Eastman Kodak, Corn Products, United Gypsum, and National Distillers.

The giant trusts were organized by investment bankers such as Morgan and Schiff, who would purchase smaller firms through the issuance of new securities, which would then be floated on the open market. Capital demands were huge, but in 1901 it appeared as though they could be met. To ease the situation, much of the money paid for merged corporations returned to Wall Street in the form of investment or speculation capital. For example, U.S. Steel comprised some 170 formerly independent firms, whose owners often became millionaires through the mergers. Many of these— in particular the "Pittsburgh crowd"—came to Wall Street to double and triple their money by speculating on the market. This led to higher prices and greatly increased volume at the New York Stock Exchange. In 1900 the turnover rate of a share of common listed on the Exchange was 172 per cent (102,386,252 shares traded of a total of 59,579,694 listed). This was higher than the rate of 1928, the most turbulent year of the twenties (132 per cent) and far more than that of 1950 (23 per cent), the wildest year of the fifties. In terms of the turnover rate, 1901 would see days in

which more than three million shares were traded, or 5 per cent
of the stocks listed. This would be equivalent to a 200-million-
share day in 1968.

Despite the fact that most of the new trusts were industrial and
not transportation, the railroad industry continued to dominate
in both listings and trading. In addition, rail mergers and improvements were usually paid for by the issuance of securities. In 1899,
such new securities brought $67 million to the roads; by 1900 the
figure had risen to $199 million. In 1901, as Harriman and Hill
formed their lines, more than $434 million in new rail issues were
taken by American and foreign investors. In that flush year almost
all securities had glamour. The brokers could hail the crossing of
the 100 level on the rail index late in April; four years earlier it
was less than 50. Some predicted it would cross 200 before 1905.
Prices rose; the bears were routed time and again. Volume was so
high that brokers were forced to work after hours, and stay at
their records long after the market closed on Saturday noon.
There was little time to notice any unusual movement in one or
two individual stocks. Besides, in that hectic April, wild fluctuations on heavy volume had become common. By then many
brokers had convinced themselves that the situation was not
abnormal at all, but an indication of what would become the rule
on Wall Street in the twentieth century. Others objected; a fall
was imminent, they claimed. Writing to *The New York Times* on
April 9, "W. R." asked:

Should not the danger signals be hung out in Wall Street? Isn't it
become a place perilous beyond all its own history—and that perilous
enough? Prices are away above what hitherto we ever saw, and, indeed, had anybody a year ago presumed to predict such market values
as now prevail, he would have been scoffed at. "Record breaking" is
pleasant to talk about, but in Wall Street it threatens to become
public-breaking.

John H. Duane of Bartlett, Frazer & Co. took a different view of
the situation:

The existing financial situation is remarkable, but it is not more remarkable than the foundations upon which it rests. We date our
present era of prosperity and rising prices back to four years ago. All

the good factors which were to be noted in the situation then can be observed today, and what is of more importance they have been reinforced by many powerful influences that make for increased stability, thereby justifying the readjustment of values that has been in progress since the November election.

This, then, was the state of Wall Street at the time Harriman conceived his scheme to capture the Northern Pacific. He would buy into the issue and before anyone realized it, would have control of the line. Necessarily, Northern Pacific stock would rise on heavy volume. But would this be unusual in a market in which almost every issue seemed to rise on large blocks? Harriman thought not, and neither did Schiff. Morgan might notice the movement, but he was in Europe. Bacon was a good man but would not realize what had happened until it was too late. As for Hill, he knew little of Wall Street and, in any case, would be almost three thousand miles away when the operation began.

Harriman and Schiff estimated that it would take from $80 million to $100 million to gain control by open market purchases. Some of the money would come from the funds gained through the C. B. & Q. operation. More would be obtained through the use of Union Pacific surpluses. Several million came from a U.P. subsidiary, the Oregon Short Line. Harriman's connections with William Rockefeller and the "Standard Oil crowd" were to be used, as well as George Gould's millions. Most important, James Stillman, of the powerful National City Bank, had always had an interest in the Union Pacific and close connections with Kuhn, Loeb; he too would make his contribution. Harriman could well believe that he would have no difficulty in raising the funds for the operation.

It is not known when Kuhn, Loeb began its purchases of Northern Pacific, but the first shares were probably contracted for in late March or early April. The stock's range in 1900 had been 45¾–86½; the range from January 1, 1901, to April 1 of that year was 77½–96. Northern Pacific common closed at 96 the week ending April 1, for a gain of 7⅝ points. Volume was heavy— 437,000 shares. In all probability this was the week of the first purchases.

Schiff did his work well. Although volume was high, little notice was taken of the gradual rise in Northern Pacific's price. From time to time shares would be sold to quiet any suspicions that might have been aroused, and to place the price in a more favorable buying range. By April 15, Schiff had accumulated some 150,000 shares of Northern Pacific common and 100,000 shares of preferred, in the process causing the common to rise four points and the preferred, one. Financial reporters observed the activity, but none suspected Harriman's plan. Instead, they noted that both Northern Pacific and C. B. & Q. were rising together, and concluded the cause to be anticipation of higher earnings once the two were joined.

With victory in sight, the buying became more aggressive. Northern Pacific reached 103 on April 20, and 107 on the 25th. Volume started to decline as fewer shares became available. And still the price rose—slowly and steadily.

CLOSING PRICES AND VOLUME OF NORTHERN PACIFIC COMMON

Week Ending	Closing Price	Volume
April 8	97⅜	259,445
April 15	99½	424,885
April 22	103	261,920
April 29	108⅞	336,574

Source: *New York Times*, April 9–30, 1901

Even this went unnoticed. Other stocks were rising; the newspapers were more concerned with the U.S. Steel flotations; there seemed a good explanation for the price of Northern Pacific. In any case, another story had captured the interest of Wall Street in late April. The New York Stock Exchange was about to move from its old, cramped quarters to temporary rooms at the Produce Exchange Building in preparation for still another move into a new, larger New York Stock Exchange to be constructed at the old site. Friday, April 26, was the last day of trading at the old location, and the public celebrated by sending prices up to new highs on heavy volume; Northern Pacific closed at 108¾ with 118,400 shares traded. The move took place over the weekend, necessitating a suspension of trading that Saturday. The following Monday was one of the wildest in Exchange history. As though to mark the opening of trading at the new location, volume hit an all-time record of 2,600,000 shares—an increase of more than 300,000 shares over the old mark. That day Northern Pacific rose 10¼ points, but other issues showed equally impressive gains. The record was broken again on Tuesday—3,200,000 shares were traded, and on Wednesday the figure was 2,700,000. "The same exciting scenes as those on Monday and Tuesday were again witnessed yesterday on the floor," reported the *Times*. "Brokers, now more or less unnerved by the steady strain under which they have been laboring for some time, howled and shrieked in the execution of their orders with even more vigor and force than is their wont. . . ."

Still, the rise in Northern Pacific—which reached 115 on May 1 —did not arouse suspicions, in the face of still more impressive performances by other issues, especially the rails.

To understand what occurred next, one must view happenings at Seattle and New York simultaneously. Then in the former city, James Hill noticed the increased activity in Northern Pacific stocks. Somehow, he felt that all was not well with his holdings, and he decided to go to New York to investigate. Calling upon his men at the Great Northern, he obtained a special train to the East. The tracks were cleared for him in advance, and Hill made the cross-country sprint in record time. Without pausing, he rushed to Wall Street. Hill knew that Morgan & Co. was not behind the stock; if it were, he would have been told. There was only one other force that might attempt to purchase huge blocks of Northern Pacific: Jacob Schiff of Kuhn, Loeb. Hill was friendly with Schiff, whom he had placed as a director of the Great Northern several years before. Now he stormed into the Kuhn, Loeb offices, and demanded information.

There are conflicting stories of what happened next. According to one, Schiff told Hill that he had purchased control of Northern Pacific for Harriman. "But you can't get control," answered Hill. "The Great Northern, Morgan, and my friends were recently holding $35,000,000 or $40,000,000 of Northern Pacific stock, and so far as I know none of it has been sold." Schiff did not question

CLOSING PRICES OF LEADING STOCKS (fractions dropped)

Issue	May 1, 1900	Nov. 5, 1900	Jan. 2, 1901	May 1, 1901
American Car & Foundry	65	64	71	78
American Sugar Refining	112	125	147	147
American Tobacco	103	97	113	127
Atch. Topeka & Santa Fe	26	32	48	76
Baltimore & Ohio	84	75	84	109
Brooklyn Union Gas	153	172	178	220
Chesapeake & Ohio	30	30	42	48
Chi., Burl., & Quincy	125	129	143	199
Chi. & Northwestern	163	163	172	214
Erie	13	12	27	42
Illinois Central	114	119	132	147
N.Y. Air Brake	115	124	100	170
New York Central	118	135	147	159
Northern Pacific	57	57	85	115
Northern Pacific pfd.	75	73	88	90
Pullman	182	190	201	231
Reading	18	17	25	44
Southern Pacific	36	38	44	67
Texas Pacific	19	17	26	40
Western Union	82	81	83	96
Wisconsin Central	16	13	17	23

Source: *New York Times*

this, but did claim that "we've got a lot of it." He continued, "You secretly bought the Chicago, Burlington & Quincy and refused to give us a fair share; now we're going to see if we can't get a share by purchasing a controlling interest in the Northern Pacific."

A second version is that Hill's first question was about Schiff's motives, and that Schiff replied that he had no intention of taking control of Northern Pacific. Instead, he and Harriman only wanted a say in the management of the company—one which would give them the long-sought-after Chicago terminal. This would "bring about the harmony and community of interest which other means and appeals to him had failed to produce." This version has much to recommend it, especially when we consider that the two forces, though rivals for power, were not unfriendly in a personal sense. Schiff and Morgan had the highest esteem for each other, and although Hill and Harriman were not the closest of friends, they maintained cordial relations during the difficult weeks that followed. On the other hand, there is no reason to believe that if it were possible for Schiff and Harriman to take control of the Northern Pacific—or anything else they wanted—they would not have done so.

Whatever had happened, Hill left the Kuhn, Loeb offices after the interview and headed for the House of Morgan to see Robert Bacon and plan strategy.

What had Bacon been doing during the last few days? All accounts agree that Bacon had been caught unaware by the Schiff actions of April, and that he would not act until orders came from Morgan himself. Bacon is usually portrayed as well-meaning and efficient, but a person lacking in imagination. But can this be true of a person who had risen so high in New York banking circles at a time when the most talented men in America were clustered in the financial community? Bacon had been a long-time director of the National City Bank and had won the praise of the nation's most powerful and astute commercial banker, James Stillman. It was Bacon, and not George F. Baker or other well-respected Morgan partners whom the Great Man entrusted with his empire. Certainly such a man would not have acted in so unsophisticated a manner. Yet it was true that Bacon had sold many of Morgan's Northern Pacific holdings in late April, apparently believing the price was too high. At least 13,000 shares were disposed of in this way, as well as an additional 10,000 shares which came to Morgan & Co. in the ordinary course of business. These sales would seem to indicate that Bacon had been caught napping and had actually aided in Schiff's program to capture the Northern Pacific.

There is another possible explanation for Bacon's actions. It cannot be uncovered in either his papers or those of other leading figures involved in the events of April and May of 1901, since these papers have not been opened to scholars, and those which are available have been released selectively. This explanation may possibly be found, however, by examining the price and volume figures of the period. They indicate that the Morgan group may have tried to outflank Harriman while he attempted to outflank them: as Schiff was buying Northern Pacific with Union Pacific money so as to gain control of the C. B. & Q., Morgan's group may have been maneuvering to gain control of Union Pacific, and so take Harriman's empire from him at the same time he took theirs from them!

As has been noted, concentrated buying in Northern Pacific common had sent the price of that issue from 85 on January 2 to 115 by May 1. In the same period, Union Pacific showed a sharper rise, going from 82 to 120. This is all the more impressive when we consider that Union Pacific had a greater capitalization than Northern Pacific—959,993 shares against 800,000—and it would take an effort greater than that of Schiff's to send it up so high. Throughout April, volume rose more rapidly in Union Pacific common than in Northern Pacific—despite the fact that the public knew that Harriman had lost his bid to take the C. B. & Q., and notwithstanding the apparent lack of good news from the company. Who was responsible for these purchases? On days when 40,000 shares of Northern Pacific were traded, more than 150,000 shares of Union Pacific changed hands. On May 2, as Hill sped to New York—at a time when according to all reports no one save Schiff and his circle knew of the maneuvering—Northern Pacific traded 46,500 shares. On that day, trading in Union Pacific was 489,100 shares!

Such major rises in volume were bound to cause rumors, and many appeared at the time. Since large blocks were being traded, the small speculators were immediately discounted; the purchases would have had to come from a major figure on Wall Street. Stillman, Rockefeller, Gould—all could have been responsible, but since they were allied with Harriman, they were eliminated. If Morgan were *directly* involved in an undertaking of this magnitude, he certainly would not have left it to underlings, not even Baker or Bacon. This left but one man: William K. Vanderbilt.

Vanderbilt was a most familiar name on Wall Street. The Commodore, of course, had been one of the giants of the financial district during the Civil War era. But his son, William H., and his grandson, William K., were not on the same level as the founder. William K. preferred the life of ease to that of running his large and wealthy empire; he was content to allow his railroad holdings—centered around the New York Central—to be managed by his friend and fellow member of the exclusive Knickerbocker Club, J. P. Morgan. Vanderbilt's appearances in financial circles were few, his influence small, considering his great wealth. Still, by May 2, the Street believed that he was behind the strong activity in Union Pacific.

Could Vanderbilt be acting on his own—assuming that he was truly the one behind the purchases? He had never acted so forthrightly before, nor would he in later years. Yet he was the only person remaining who could have been behind the purchases of Union Pacific, and by May 4 the rumors were so strong that they appear to have had some foundation in fact. Vanderbilt never admitted to it; but he did not deny the activity either.

If Vanderbilt was behind the purchases, it must have been with the support and at the behest of J. P. Morgan. The Great Man had just completed organizing U.S. Steel, the largest industrial complex in the world. He had always dreamed of establishing a similar transportation network. Could he have hoped to form one from the Hill Lines and the Union Pacific? This would certainly fit in with Morgan's character. But if this were so, would he not have told Hill about the plan? And would he have left for Europe with such an important project pending? Obviously, Hill would have to accept the project, and Morgan would insist upon complete control throughout the operation. If we can speculate one step further, we might reason that Morgan had told Vanderbilt to begin purchases of Union Pacific in late April and May; Harriman would then be caught off guard, expecting nothing while Morgan was out of the country. Then, when the Great Man returned, he would inform Hill, take charge, and direct the final intricate maneuvers. But Vanderbilt was inexperienced; he bought too heavily too early, and did not sell at times so as to stabilize Union Pacific's price. And so the story leaked; Wall Street was virtually certain of a Vanderbilt move to take the Union Pacific when it had no suspicions of a Harriman-Schiff drive for Northern Pacific. Union Pacific news—and not that of Northern Pacific— dominated Wall Street talk on the day Hill arrived in New York.

As Hill rushed to the Kuhn, Loeb offices that Friday, May 3, stocks rose in early trading at the Exchange. But the strain, both financial and psychological, was beginning to tell. Prices broke sharply before noon, and by the close of trading Northern Pacific showed a loss of 5½ points and Union Pacific 6. The sharp break caught the bulls unaware. Several brokers closed early; James Keene, Morgan's top floor manager, denied that he had anything to do with the decline. "There is no cause for worry," he insisted. Still, the first break in the wall of confidence appeared, and John Kee, a small-time speculator, hearing of the decline, suffered a heart attack and died at his broker's office.

Saturday morning trading was quiet, but after the Exchange closed, rumors of the Vanderbilt takeover spread throughout the city. The Sunday *Times* reported that a merger between all the major lines of the West was about to take place. "Nothing but a panic, it is said, can avert this end, and as these transfers amount to little more than an exchange of stock, and as the security is reasonably safe, there appears to be no reason for anticipating a failure." The *Times* also expected stocks to rise on the news the following Monday. As for Harriman, he would lose his railroad holdings and be forced to bow before the superior might of William K. Vanderbilt—and those behind him.

Of course, the *Times* readers knew nothing of what was going on behind the scenes. In fact, Vanderbilt had no chance of capturing control of Union Pacific; Harriman had a large enough block of stock to prevent any takeover at that time. Far from being destroyed, Harriman had set into motion the last activities which would bring him control of the Northern Pacific.

After meeting with Hill, Schiff contacted Harriman, and the two men met to discuss the situation. The banker assured Harriman that they indeed controlled Northern Pacific. True, they lacked a clear majority of the common stock, having only 370,000 shares out of 800,000—but Schiff felt that this number was sufficient to carry the day for Harriman. In any case, he had purchased enough preferred stock—420,000 shares—to control that issue. Indeed 35,000 shares had come from a Morgan associate, who did not suspect what was happening. Schiff had a majority of the combined common and preferred in his control, and since the preferred stock could vote, he felt certain that Hill could do nothing to thwart their plans. Still, Harriman felt uneasy; Hill had been equally certain of his control and had been proved wrong. Could Schiff be wrong in his conclusions?

That night Harriman again paced the floor of his hotel room. The excitement was beginning to tell on him, and in addition he felt sharp pains in his abdomen (which would soon be diagnosed as appendicitis). He would rest more securely if he knew that Schiff had a majority of the common as well as of the combined stocks. Accordingly, Harriman called the Kuhn, Loeb offices Saturday morning and spoke to Heinsheimer, one of Schiff's partners. Heinsheimer was ordered to purchase an additional 40,000 shares that morning, so as to give Harriman a lock on Northern Pacific. With this, he rested.

However, the order was not carried out. Heinsheimer relayed it to Schiff, who was at services in his synagogue. Refusing to do business on the Sabbath, Schiff told Heinsheimer to ignore the order; he would take full responsibility.

That Saturday Northern Pacific closed at 110, showing a gain of ¾. Only 23,000 shares were traded. By Sunday, Harriman knew he lacked a majority of the common.

Hill had the same forebodings that Friday night of May 3. The next day he saw Bacon and learned that Morgan & Co. had only 260,000 shares of common. Hill suggested that Bacon cable Morgan—who was then in Italy—for permission to buy an additional 150,000 shares, so as to gain a majority of the common. Bacon sent the cable after trading ended on Saturday. On Sunday the reply came: Morgan gave his permission. According to one biographer, Morgan was then enjoying the baths at Aix-les-Bains, and the companionship of a titled Frenchwoman who resided there. As far as he was concerned, his home office could handle the dealings in Northern Pacific.

Bacon's next step was to call in James Keene, "the silver fox of Wall Street," who often directed floor operations in Morgan maneuvers. A former cowboy, mule skinner, miner, and newspaper editor, Keene looked more like an English country squire. It was Keene who handled the half-billion dollars of common stock and the additional half-billion of preferred in the U.S. Steel flotation, a situation which he had managed with consummate skill. Now he was given the task of accumulating 150,000 shares of Northern

Pacific in the face of a sparse float and the Kuhn, Loeb organization.

Keene arrived at Wall Street an hour or so before the Monday opening and established himself in the offices of broker Talbot Taylor, which became the headquarters for the operation. His go-between at Taylor's was Harry Content, "the prince of brokers," who had lived through and participated in the panics of 1873 and 1893, and would still be active in the 1929 crash. Content was closemouthed and could be trusted not to divulge the existence of a Morgan push. Leonard Hockstader, Content's telephone operator, would send instructions to Eddie Norton, the floor manager for the group, and for Taylor himself. By the time the bell signaled the beginning of trading, the Morgan machine was ready to roll.

Although Schiff did not think it necessary to do so, he too organized his forces for the Monday opening. Otto Kahn, a financial genius who had entered the firm by marrying one of the early Kuhn, Loeb partners, and who would eventually succeed Schiff as its head, commanded the operation, and was assisted by Al Stern and several others. Since all he needed was 40,000 shares, Schiff did not think any more would be necessary.

Trading opened on high volume with sizable gains for many popular issues. To the onlooker, it was still one more chapter in the greatest bull market in memory. Activity was unusually brisk in Northern Pacific, but this did not attract too much attention at first. The Morgan and the Schiff forces did their work professionally, buying 1,000 share blocks, then selling part of it so as to keep the price stable. During the course of the day, Norton alone handled transactions for 200,000 shares, more than enough for Morgan's purposes had he not been obliged to sell from time to time. Similarly, Kahn and Stern bought and sold more than 100,000 shares between them.

The supply of stock dwindled as the contest wore on, and inevitably Northern Pacific common showed large gains in the afternoon trading. Not suspecting what was happening, many small speculators began to look upon Northern Pacific as a perfect short sale—they would sell stock they did not yet own at 125, and then buy it back later when the price fell. By two o'clock, most of the trades seemed of this type.

The market closed much higher than Monday, on 2,300,000-share volume. Northern Pacific common closed at 127½, up 17½. The volume was 363,400 shares, a record for that issue and almost half the total stock outstanding.

The drama continued Tuesday morning, and by noon brokers and speculators began to suspect that "something was on" with Northern Pacific. Some of the shorts began to cover, adding their purchases to those of Morgan and Kuhn, Loeb, while others established new short positions in the stock. On balance, there was more shorting than covering. This caused Northern Pacific common to zigzag all over the tape, rising as high as 149¾ and finally closing at 143½, up 16 points for the day.

That night both Hill and Harriman believed they had control of Northern Pacific. The Keene group had accumulated its 150,000 shares, giving Hill a majority of the common stock. As for Schiff and Harriman, they definitely had a majority of the combined common and preferred, and possibly a majority of the common as well. By then Harriman had realized that Northern Pacific common owners had the right to retire the preferred if they so desired. He expected the Morgan group to do this, but nevertheless felt certain that he was in command.

How could both groups have more than 50 per cent of Northern Pacific common? There was only one answer: some of their stock —no one knew how much—had come from the short sellers who, in the next few days, would attempt to buy for delivery when and if Northern Pacific fell. But how could it fall? There was practically no supply, and a great demand that Tuesday night.

Keene and Kahn were not buying Northern Pacific Wednesday morning; they had completed their work Tuesday afternoon. Still, activity was brisk in that issue, as the frantic shorts attempted to cover their sales. In order to gain funds for their purchases, the shorts sold their other holdings, causing a severe slump in the entire list. Talk of a Vanderbilt takeover of Union Pacific was no longer heard; the stock fell 8½ points on heavy trading. U.S. Steel, the cornerstone of the Morgan empire, declined 7 points. Fearful of the effects of a major panic, Bacon authorized Keene to lend Northern Pacific common to the shorts, hoping that this would stabilize the market. The attempt failed; Northern Pacific showed a 23-point rise for the day, closing at 160 with 49,600 shares traded. That night all Wall Street knew the worst: Northern Pacific was cornered; Bacon would recall the loaned certificates; Harriman would not sell any of his stock; the shorts would be unable to cover.

The situation was most unusual. Wall Street was accustomed to corners in which shorts would be squeezed, but in the end allowed to cover at a high price. Former corners had been operated by speculators, who chose a stock as a medium for gaining a fortune on Wall Street. The Northern Pacific situation was different. The House of Morgan and the firm of Kuhn, Loeb were not interested in squeezing the shorts; they meant to hold their stock in order to control Northern Pacific, and would not part with a single share in any circumstances or at any price.

As a result, the Thursday opening witnessed panic conditions on the Exchange floor. Brokers were trampled in the rush to sell all stocks except Northern Pacific and bid for that issue. News arrived of several shares available in Buffalo; a short hired a special train to bring the stock to New York. Small lots of 100 or 200 shares turned up elsewhere, and the bidding for them reached fantastic heights. A sale was recorded at 320 early in the day, and a few hours later at 700. At twelve o'clock the price was 1,000 bid and no takers.

Every other issue fell startlingly, and thousands of bankruptcies were set off. News of suicides reached Wall Street, and the next day the city learned of the fate of Samuel Bolts, Jr., a Troy businessman who, faced with ruin, killed himself by jumping into a vat of hot beer.

News of the panic quickly reached the Morgan and the Kuhn, Loeb offices. Neither Bacon nor Schiff had expected this, and both were anxious to avoid a panic which would destroy their other interests and which, in the end, would bring them no closer to control of Northern Pacific. Accordingly, they announced that they would not demand immediate delivery of short-sold shares of Northern Pacific. Frederick T. Tappan, head of the clearing house, was named to chair a special committee which would relieve the money market by providing $20 million for loans. Finally Schiff contacted Stern, and Bacon called Content; the two men were authorized to lend Northern Pacific to the shorts.

Stern was the first to reach the Exchange floor with the news.

He strode to the Northern Pacific post, which was clogged with hysterical brokers. "Who wants to borrow Northern Pacific?" he asked. "I have a block to lend."

The offer was greeted with an ear-shattering roar, and then the brokers lunged at Stern, each attempting to get to him first. Stern tried to take care of all, but they refused to wait. The hapless broker was bitten, gouged, and pummeled; one customer took off his hat and repeatedly hit Stern over the head with it in order to gain his attention. The disheveled Stern, known as one of the most dapper men on Wall Street, barely managed to escape, and he staggered from the scene, his clothes in shreds.

But the work was done; Northern Pacific slid rapidly from its noon high, as the shorts withdrew their bids. By closing, the common sold at 325, a gain of 165 points for the day but 675 points below its highest bid. Only 11,170 shares were traded.

CLOSING PRICES FOR SELECTED ISSUES, THURSDAY, MAY 9, 1901

Issue	Closing Price	Change
Atchison, Topeka & Santa Fe	66¾	−10⅝
Baltimore & Ohio	94	− 9
Chi., Milwaukee & St. Paul	141	−23½
Consolidated Gas	204	−15
Int. Power Co.	70	−13½
Northern Pacific common	325	+165
Union Pacific	90	−24

Source: *New York Times*, May 10, 1901

Reporters rushed to the Kuhn, Loeb and the Morgan offices to find out what had happened. For the most part, the Wall Street professionals remained silent, seeing no value in releasing information. But Hill, stunned by what had occurred and not used to such affairs, permitted an interview. "All I can do is to liken it to a ghost dance," he said.

The Indians begin their dance and don't know why they are doing it. They whirl about until they are almost crazy. It is so when these Wall Street people get the speculative fever. Perhaps they imagine they have a motive in that they see two sets of powerful interests which may be said to be clashing. Then these outsiders, without rhyme or reason, rush in on one side or the other. They could not tell you why they make their choice, but in they go, and the result is such as has been seen here for the past few days.

Russell Sage, the wily old "Money King" of Wall Street was quoted as saying that the panic was "a result of hoggishness." But Sage was one of the few who did well in the panic; his put and call contracts were skillfully handled, and Sage was reported to have made millions that week.

Conditions returned to as close to normal as might be expected on Friday. Northern Pacific fell 175 points to 150, or approximately where it had been prior to the squeeze. The sharply depressed issues also returned to their previous levels. Union Pacific showed a 22-point advance, B. & O. was up 11 points, and others followed. The Exchange remained closed on Saturday in order to give all a breathing spell. By Monday, the situation seemed well in control; the panic was over.

But what of Northern Pacific? Hill and Bacon realized that Harriman would have to be given some representation in its control, and the two forces met to plan the peace. There was no problem here; as previously mentioned, the participants did not consider that business rivals need be mortal enemies. Shortly after his appendectomy, Harriman called Hill to tell him that his health was good. Hill dropped by the Kuhn, Loeb offices and asked to see Schiff. When told Schiff was out, Hill asked partner Felix Warburg, "How is he?" Warburg told him that the senior partner was "not very happy." "Oh, well," replied Hill, "Schiff takes these things too seriously."

Schiff was concerned—and fearful—that the Northern Pacific episode would harm his relations with Morgan. Writing to the Great Man, Schiff assured him that "nothing was further on the part of Union Pacific interests than to do aught meant to be antagonistic to you or your firm, and that, as far as my partners and I are concerned, we have at all times wished, as we continue to do, to be permitted to aid in maintaining your personal prestige, so well deserved." Morgan on his part did not hold a grudge, and had no difficulty in working with Schiff on future projects. As expressed by Hill at a later date, "On both sides there were big men. . . . Recent events had broadened and instructed their view. Things being as they were, they were ready for agreement."

While Morgan continued his European vacation, his partners met regularly with the men at Kuhn, Loeb. On May 31, the two forces announced their agreement. Harriman and some of his associates would gain representation on both the Northern Pacific and C. B. & Q. boards. The Union Pacific would gain trackage rights over the Northern Pacific lines between Portland and Seattle. In the future, the two forces would act in consultation with each other.

Morgan returned to America on June 28 to find a scene of harmony between Harriman and Hill. Indeed, Hill proposed uniting their interests into a single major holding company. Morgan agreed to the plan in principle, and negotiations were opened at once. Neither side saw any obstacle in the way of what would become the Northern Securities Company, which was incorporated in New Jersey on November 12, with a capital of $400 million.

But for once they were wrong. The Northern Pacific panic had not only caused grief and hardship among Wall Street speculators; it also provided grist for the mill of those who warned of the increasing power of big business. The trust movement was in full swing; U.S. Steel seemed stronger to some than the U.S. government. A struggle between two capitalists could threaten the fabric of American business. The businessman reigned supreme in America, and now he hoped to conquer the globe. Statesmen warned that New York was on the verge of replacing London as the center of world finance. The Spanish-American War, looked upon in 1900 as a fight for glory and empire, was now portrayed as one for American business profits. Morgan seemed more powerful than McKinley in the early autumn of 1901. What if he combined all his holdings into one giant trust? Such an organization would invade every aspect of American life, and could prove destructive to the democratic process.

But the government did nothing. McKinley noted the growth of Wall Street power, considered action, but in the end decided to wait for new developments before acting. Always a cautious man, he preferred persuasion to direct pressure. This was the situation on September 6 when the President was shot by an assassin. McKinley died on September 14. When told of his death, Morgan said, "It is the saddest news I ever heard. I can't talk about it."

The new President, Theodore Roosevelt, promised to continue the policies of his predecessor. Roosevelt was believed "sound" on business issues, but at the same time he had a reputation for wildness. What would happen if the erratic Roosevelt and the massive power of Morgan met? The final answer would come in 1907.

9.
THE KNICKERBOCKER
TRUST PANIC OF 1907

J. P. Morgan was the center of attraction on October 8, 1907. As a delegate to the Triennial Convention of the Episcopal Church in Richmond, he spoke for moderation and compromise whenever possible. A bitter theological dispute had erupted that morning, and Morgan, acting to end it, rose and sang "O Zion, Haste, Thy Mission High Fulfilling." The factions joined in the singing, and by the time the song ended with a solemn Amen, harmony had been restored. Again, Morgan saved the day.

Then in his seventieth year, the financier realized that he had not long to live; his great business and political contributions seemed to have ended. Morgan devoted more time than ever to his religious and artistic interests. That summer's trip to Europe had been particularly fruitful; Morgan had purchased several Rembrandts, Rubenses, Halses, Van Dycks, and a host of other paintings, along with bronzes, ceramics, hangings, furniture, carvings, etc. Applying the lessons learned on Wall Street to his activities in the art field, Morgan had become the greatest collector of his era. At the same time, his respectful yet firm approach toward the workings of the Episcopal Church made him a leading lay figure in convention matters.

The middle of October found President Theodore Roosevelt deep in the canebrakes of Louisiana. Friends had asked Teddy to join them in a hunt, indicating that bears had been seen in the area. The nation seemed fairly quiet, and so the President packed his rifles and headed south.

The hunt was refreshing, though not successful at first. Bears were sighted lumbering through the cypress, red gum, and white oak, frightening the woodpeckers and black fox squirrels that flitted through the musty leaves on the floor of the forest near Stamboul, Louisiana, the President's temporary White House. The bears escaped, but Roosevelt managed to bag a deer with his first shot. Later on the President shot a bear—the only one taken on the hunt—and reported that he felt "bully." This exuberance was sharpened by the trip back to the capital. Writing to his son on October 22, Roosevelt noted that wherever he went he was greeted by cheers and enthusiasm, most unusual for a Republican in the lower Mississippi region. Not even an anti-Roosevelt broad-side from the governor of the state could dampen public demon-strations for the dynamic Teddy. "I have been greatly interested by what I have seen in the papers," wrote the President. This was a reference to the fact that young Ted might play on the Harvard football team. "I don't suppose you have much chance to make the first eleven," he continued ruefully, "but I shall be awfully interested to see how you do. Is your knee much hurt? Do you think you will be able to play again this year?"

The President could well afford to take time perusing the sports pages in mid-October. After one of the most hectic years in a most hectic administration, all seemed reasonably calm. Recovery from the San Francisco earthquake and fire of the previous year proceeded rapidly, and some in the city spoke of having the Olym-pic games of 1910 in San Francisco (the United States had won the 1906 games at Athens with a score of 75 points). The news-papers of 1907 were filled with stories of the William Haywood trial in Boise, Idaho, where "Wild Bill" was charged with com-plicity in the murder of Governor Frank Steunenberg. Haywood, head of the International Workers of the World, was defended by world-famous attorney Clarence Darrow, who chose a local lawyer, William Borah, to aid in the trial work. Across the country, in New York, the Gould divorce hearings crowded Haywood off the front pages, especially when Mrs. Gould demanded $250,000 a year in alimony. Washington was still recovering from the sensa-tional attempt to unseat Reed Smoot of Utah on charges that he, as a member of the Mormon hierarchy, supported polygamy and therefore could not possibly be loyal to the Constitution. Smoot denied the allegations and insisted on his adherence to the basic laws. By October the Smoot affair seemed ended, and the citizens of Washington turned to other matters, including a demand that their city license taxicabs, a move which New York had just made after importing the idea from Paris.

Washington also reported the formation of a branch of Sinn Fein, an Irish organization ostensibly dedicated to the preservation of the Celtic tongue. Sinn Fein officials in New York wrote of other possibilities, however, including a demand for Irish independence. The New York Irish did not send a representative to the docks on September 12, when a British steamship arrived in the city after crossing the Atlantic from Queenstown, Ireland, in a record time of five days and fifty-four minutes. New York papers demanded that Roosevelt support the merchant marine and American passenger lines, so as to regain leadership for the United States. At the time, however, hopes of beating the record set by the British ship seemed scant; it was thought that the *Lusitania* would rule the waves for many years.

The attention of the public flitted from item to item in the first nine months of 1907. Stanford White, America's leading architect, had been murdered by millionaire Harry Thaw in the summer of 1906. Thaw, who believed, correctly, that his wife, Evelyn Nesbit, had once been White's mistress, went on trial on January 22, 1907, and the most famous district attorney in America, William Travers Jerome, was in charge of the prosecution. For the next four months disclosures titillated the public, until Thaw was released on a technicality.

But the hiatus was not long; Teddy Roosevelt issued a blast against "nature fakers" like Jack London who, in *White Fang*, wrote of a bulldog fighting with a great northern wolf. No dog would have a chance against such a wolf, said Teddy, and he went on to criticize other nature writers, including Dr. William Long, who in one of his stories had a wolf kill a bull caribou by biting his chest. Long and others responded to the attack, and the nation was treated to a dispute between the President and a group of writers on the strong points of the wolf and the caribou. "My story was accurate," wrote Long; in attempting to have the last word, he swore that he had heard the story from "a full-blooded Sioux Indian who is studying theology."

Such matters engaged the public's attention in 1907. It was a

good year for most who read the newspapers and brought home
pay checks that October. The great prosperity that seemed to be
ushered in by Teddy's arrival in the White House—but that
actually went back to the McKinley Administration—appeared
intact, at least on the surface, and the nation was confident in its
belief that progress was inevitable. Wars might occur overseas
—the Russo-Japanese and Boer conflicts, for example—and the
United States might once more have to fight such small but
glorious engagements as the war with Spain, but these were considered with the same amount of gravity as the Thaw-White
murder trial. When Roosevelt seemed to edge toward a conflict
with Japan, the newspapers reported it as though it was part of a
sporting schedule. One read the box score of the New York
Giants' last game with Pittsburgh (often with Christy Mathewson
on the mound) and then a box score comparing the American and
Japanese fleets (the Japanese had more cruisers but the U.S. Navy
was ahead in battleships). Whatever might come, Uncle Sam and
Teddy could handle it.

Business was viewed in the same light. McKinley had seemed
friendly toward the large corporations, which every year gained
in assets and power. Many writers attacked the trusts, and so did
Roosevelt, who said that large corporations were like "subjects
without a sovereign." In 1906, he indicated that the federal government would take charge of the trusts and assure their respectability. The Justice Department brought indictments against
trusts in sugar, oil, and tobacco, and hit hard against the Union
Pacific, the headquarters of the huge E. H. Harriman empire. But
Morgan's interests were, by and large, left alone. U.S. Steel and
International Harvester were allowed to dominate their fields,
even after Morgan's Northern Securities Company was attacked
by the President. Publicly Roosevelt castigated the trusts, but
privately he courted their favor. In the election of 1904, Morgan
and the Wall Street crowd had supported Roosevelt against Alton
Parker, and in October of 1907 they saw no reason to regret this
decision. "We still continue to enjoy a literally unprecedented
prosperity," reported Roosevelt in his message to Congress of
December 3, 1906. On the surface, at least, there seemed little to
dispute this claim.

True, the prosperity was unprecedented, and therein lay the source of difficulty. The United States had entered a period of rapid growth in 1897 which continued—with several sharp interruptions—into 1907. The nation's exports almost doubled in this period, as did imports. The volume of money in circulation rose from $1.5 billion in 1896 to $2.7 billion in 1907, and deposits in national banks from $1.6 billion to $4.3 billion. The total assets of American financial institutions, only $9.1 billion in 1897, were more than $21 billion at the time of Roosevelt's address to Congress. The production of almost every item, from steel and locomotives to textiles and hairpins, rose sharply. And the prosperity was not confined to America; Great Britain, Germany, France, Italy, Japan, Chile, Argentina—in fact, almost every nation showed great progress in all fields. Worldwide conditions appeared ideal; trade was never better, and international peace conferences seemed to assure that no major war would disturb the continued growth of production in all parts of the world. Every year saw the fall of old records and the celebration of new ones, which would fall to still higher production figures.

There was one figure, however, which gave industrialists some trouble. World gold production had stagnated during the 1880s and well into the next decade. Then came new ore finds and processes for extraction. Production, which had been $157 million in 1893, had risen to $287 million by 1898, and this rise in the gold supply had been instrumental in setting off the boom. For a while, gold sales enabled prices to rise, industry to expand, and prosperity to return after the long depression of the early 1890s. But then industrial output began to outpace gold. By 1903, over $327 million was mined, and production rose each year, reaching $400 million in 1906 and $404 million in 1907. This slowing of the growth rate of gold, as demands for investment funds increased, rapidly caused a capital shortage. By 1906, bankers in every nation were deeply concerned with the tight money situation.

The condition was complicated by demands for capital in all parts of the world. The Boer War had cost the British government nearly $800 million, and of this amount, $600 million was raised on the money markets. To ease money, London lowered the interest rate from 2¾ to 2½ percent in 1903, but the tightness continued. Similarly, the Russo-Japanese War led to severe strains. Russia spent some $840 million during the conflict, while the Japanese bill was almost $1 billion. In comparison, the American war costs for its small clash with Spain were only $165 million. And most of these funds were raised through the issuance of bonds. Demands for new capital, less than $2 billion in 1902, rose to more than $3 billion by 1905. By then it was clear that lowering the interest rates would not lead to new outpourings of funds into worthwhile projects: the wellsprings for such funds had dried out. Inevitably, interest rates rose, as governments bid against each other for whatever capital remained on the world markets.

At the same time, in America, the great consolidation movements sparked by the Morgan interests continued, and these too required large sums of money. The U.S. Steel flotation of 1901 alone represented nearly $1.4 billion worth of securities. Visions of profits led to sharp rises on the world stock exchanges, and the New York Exchange was no exception. The Dow-Jones Average, which hovered in the mid-30s during the first quarter of 1904, went over 75 in 1907. Anything Morgan touched rose sharply in this period. So did Harriman's many interests. Using the vast reserves of the Union Pacific, Harriman purchased more than $131 million worth of railroad stocks in the second half of 1906. One of the few capitalists who did not contribute to Roosevelt's 1904 campaign, he was criticized by Teddy for his methods and goals. Undaunted, Harriman raised the Union Pacific dividend from $6 to $10 that summer, sending the stock up forty points, with the rest of the board following.

Prices on the European stock exchanges rose shortly thereafter. Even the Tokyo and Santiago, Chile, exchanges witnessed the greatest bull markets up to that time. Prosperity was in the air; the bears were few on New Year's Day, 1907. But at the same time, the credit lines showed severe strains. Call money fluctuated wildly, going from 3 to 30 percent some weeks, as wild gyrations became the rule. New York banks admitted that their reserves were low, and they raised interest rates regularly, expecting borrowing to slacken. It did not; no price seemed too high for money in late 1906 and early 1907. In Britain, the bank rate went from 4 to 5 percent on October 11, 1906, and eight days later to 6 percent, the highest since 1899. The demand for funds continued. On New Year's Day, there was talk of a 7 percent rate, a height not reached in more than a century. Businessmen knew that such a high money price might lead to a break in the economy, but they could offer no suggestions for alternatives. On four continents money flowed from commerce and industry to stocks and bonds, and there was no end in sight.

The tension could not continue indefinitely; many bankers warned that balances and gold holdings were so low that a dip in demand, coupled with withdrawals from banks, could lead to wave upon wave of failures. As early as January 1906, Jacob Schiff told a group of bankers that "If the currency conditions of this country are not changed materially . . . you will have such a panic in this country as will make all previous panics look like child's play." Within six months came news that the Bank of England's gold reserves had hit a thirteen-year low. On June 13 railroad tycoon James J. Hill warned of "commercial paralysis," which could result if the rapidly expanding economy were not fueled by regular infusions of capital. At least $1 billion a year was the figure Hill offered as capital needs for the American economy.

Hill and others went to the money market during the first few months of 1907 to refinance their debts. They found that long-term bonds could not be sold, and that they could float notes for from 5 to 7 percent only if they were limited to one or, at the most, three years. The failure of the market to absorb new blue-chip issues led to fears in the boardrooms of the New York banks. Apprehension replaced confidence in early March. There was no "hard news" to cause this change, but something subtle happened on Wall Street. For the first time in a generation, fear of widespread collapse seemed to be in the air.

The market broke on March 13, in the absence of any dramatic event and while corporations reported record earnings. Rail and copper issues led the decline, with all other groups in the van. Margin calls became common; bankruptcies were reported in ever-increasing numbers; brokerages closed their doors; call money rose to astronomical heights. Sound stocks fell more than 30 percent in price, and blue chips declined by a quarter of their March 12 values. But the decline was short-lived. Prices recovered toward the end of the month, and by the first week in April it seemed that confidence had returned.

The facts gave lie to the appearance. Individuals and banks which extended loans beyond safe limits in early March were unwilling to commit their funds in April. San Francisco, which had drawn more than $225 million from insurance companies in payment for earthquake and fire damage, was unable to float a loan in New York. The reason given was the corrupt government of that city, but Wall Streeters knew better; the money simply wasn't there.

More bad news followed. In mid-April values plummeted and disappeared on the Alexandria Stock Exchange in Egypt. The situation was saved only after London sent a $3 million gold shipment to that city. But the gold drain placed the Bank of England in a perilous situation, and a flight from the pound began. All eyes turned toward Europe and New York to await the next crisis. The financial community was caught unaware when stocks declined sharply on the Tokyo Exchange in late April, followed by a wave of bank failures throughout Japan. Then, just as after the March declines in New York, conditions were stabilized, and it seemed as though the worst was over. Prices rose on world stock exchanges; the public seemed optimistic again. But at the same time, wise money men began to hoard gold. The yellow metal flowed from weak to strong hands, just as stocks went from strong to weak.

Paris began importing gold from America in May, accomplishing this by the sale of American securities and the presentation of dollars to American banks. More than $3.3 million in gold was taken in this way during the first week of June. For the next few weeks reports of French gold purchases appeared regularly on the financial pages. On June 6, $1 million was taken; $3.6 million on June 8; Paris took $2 million more on June 14, and stocks fell sharply on the news; $2.5 million was transferred to French accounts on June 19, and London took an additional $1.1 million. During the next three days Paris bought $4.625 million and London $1 million in New York. The news caused trepidation, but not panic. Russia was floating a $50 million gold issue in Paris, it was noted, and Paris was getting part of the gold by liquidating some of its American holdings. This explanation seemed shallow, and was discredited when the purchases continued after the bonds were taken.

Nor was this the only reason for concern on Wall Street. A confident Teddy Roosevelt seemed intent on bettering his 1906 antitrust record. On January 14, Standard Oil of New Jersey was indicted on 529 counts of illegal acceptance of rebates and was fined $29,250,000. On May 19, the commissioner of corporations charged that Standard Oil had a virtual monopoly of the petroleum business. An Austin, Texas, jury awarded the state $1,623,900 in damages after finding the Waters-Pierce Oil Company guilty of violating the anti-trust act. Waters-Pierce was an affiliate of Standard Oil of New Jersey. Government Prosecutor Frank B. Kellogg prepared an action to dissolve the firm and released it in early September.

The apparent anti-business actions of the Justice Department shook an already insecure banking community. Conservatism became the rule on Wall Street. On August 9, Boston attempted to float a $4 million bond issue in New York and received bids for only $200,000. Three days later an issue of New York City 4 percent bonds went unbought, with bids of less than $2.3 million for the $15 million flotation.

Corporations which had counted on securities sales were unable to raise money on Wall Street. A large iron-manufacturing house went bankrupt in June as its bonds went unsold. Westinghouse offered 100,000 shares of its common stock at $50 a share, and only 33,000 shares were taken. The firm declared that it was still solvent, but the $34 million company was forced to cancel expansion plans. Still, with all this, stock prices showed only a slight decline, while confidence was eroded from within. By mid-September as farmers began to withdraw funds from New York for fall planting, the money market was teetering on the edge of destruction. The once solid banking institutions were like fully blown balloons, solid to the sight but easily destroyed with a single pinprick.

To find the origins of this catalyst we must look not at the Wall Street scene in 1907, but instead at the raw, violent, and untamed copper industry of Montana during the last years of

the nineteenth century. Montana was rich in copper, and the
red metal was much in demand in the new age of electricity.
Inevitably, Eastern capital was attracted to the copper fields, led
by the "Standard Oil crowd," which included H. H. Rogers,
James Stillman, and John D.'s speculative brother, William
Rockefeller. In 1899 this group brought together several operating mines and smelters to form the Amalgamated Copper Company, sometimes known as the Copper Trust. Swiftly the Trust
took control of the region, squeezing out small producers and
manipulating wages and prices to its own ends. Most were forced
to accept Amalgamated's leadership, but one operator—Frederick
Augustus Heinze—stood ready to fight the giant firm. Born in
Brooklyn and a graduate of the Columbia University School of
Mines, Heinze had been in Montana ten years when Amalgamated
appeared. By then he controlled the Montana Ore Purchasing
Company, which operated a smelter for small producers. As the
major independent smelter in the region, Heinze had things
his way until Amalgamated appeared. Now he prepared to battle
the giant Rockefeller combine. Instituting hundreds of suits
against Amalgamated, controlling Judge William Clancy, and
playing upon the ignorance of the miners, Heinze managed to
disrupt activities in the copper fields, cause embarrassment to the
Rockefellers, and establish a name for himself in the business
community as a troublemaker. In the end Amalgamated was
obliged to settle its difficulties with Heinze by buying his Montana
interests for some $10.5 million. The small operator had bested
the wealthiest man in America. But the game was not over.
The Rockefeller interests had long memories; Heinze would over-
extend himself some day, and when he did, he would be crushed.

When Heinze arrived in New York in the spring of 1906, the
whole country was talking about him. Thomas William Lawson,
a stock-market speculator, had written a book about the copper
industry called *Frenzied Finance*. In it Lawson, who had been
hurt in the past by the Rockefellers, wrote of manipulations and
trickery in Amalgamated's activities and offered advice on speculations in copper shares. The book had been released originally
as a series of articles in *Everybody's Magazine*, which was followed enthusiastically by the Wall Street crowd. Needless to say,

Lawson's book only heightened the Rockefeller's desire for revenge.

Meanwhile Heinze set out to make a fortune on Wall Street. In order to gain a front for stock-market activities, he purchased a seat on the Exchange for two of his brothers, who formed Otto Heinze and Company. Then he looked for a speculative vehicle. In his search, Heinze came across Charles W. Morse.

Morse was cut from the same cloth as Heinze. A Bath, Maine, speculator, he had made a fortune by combining many small ice suppliers into the American Ice Company, the closest thing to a trust in that commodity. Morse had milked the company dry and now searched for new areas of activity. Copper seemed promising, and so did banking. Morse met with Heinze and decided to combine with the newly arrived speculator in copper dealings. Heinze had convinced him that with sufficient capital they could gain several corners in copper stocks; once again, Heinze would make a fortune by tweaking Amalgamated's nose. The problem lay in gaining funds for the venture. Although both men were millionaires, the project would require more than they had.

Accordingly, Morse and Heinze decided to win control of a banking complex and use deposits for speculative purposes. Morse already dominated the Bank of North America. Now he used that bank's funds to purchase control of the Mercantile National Bank, and followed by using Mercantile's assets to gain control of the Knickerbocker Trust Company. The process was repeated several more times, until the Heinze-Morse combine had control of a network of small-to-medium-size banks and trust companies, whose funds were at their disposal. Knickerbocker Trust's president, Charles Barney, joined the venture, and coordinated activities for the combine. Oakleigh Thorne, head of the Trust Company of America, cooperated with the group, as did the Lincoln Trust and other similar institutions.

The next problem was to find a proper vehicle for speculation. At Heinze's suggestion, the combine incorporated a new firm, United Copper Company, which was capitalized at $80 million. United had few assets, but this mattered little; its major function was not to produce copper, but rather to be a new financial empire for the Heinze-Morse group. The time was early in 1907. United Copper appeared at the proper moment. Speculation was at its height, Lawson's book indicated that huge profits could be made in copper stocks, and Heinze and Morse had every reason to hope for success.

The plan was both old and simple. The combine would purchase shares and call options of United Copper on the open market, in this way gaining a corner in the stock. Funds from the banks and trust companies would be used for this purpose. As the price of United rose, speculators would be tempted to sell short. When ready, the combine would demand the stock it had contracted for with the calls. The shorts would be squeezed, and forced to pay whatever the Morse-Heinze group demanded.

The project was begun in February. During March, when almost all other issues fell, United Copper rose—and short selling in the issue mounted. Then the price leveled off as the combine carefully timed its purchases. By mid-October Morse and Heinze felt that the moment had come for their move. They did not realize at the time that other forces were at work to foil their scheme.

H. H. Rogers and the Standard Oil crowd had not forgotten their vow to destroy Heinze, and they watched his maneuvers with growing interest. Standard Oil had great influence among many of the brokers used by the combine in its activities. It was a dominant force at the clearing house, which had the power to help banks and trust companies in distress. Standard was able to control newspaper reporters and to plant items on the financial pages that could aid or destroy an individual or company. Rogers meant to use all of these to bring Heinze and his friends to ruin.

The drama began on October 10, as the market dropped, led by copper shares. Only United held firm, and the combine reflected that the short sellers were beginning to cover. True, Heinze and Morse had not completed their corner, but according to their records, they had more than enough shares to make a killing. On Monday, October 14, short covering began in earnest. As almost all copper shares declined, United went from 37½ to 60. Morse was overjoyed, and Heinze sent word to the brokers to demand delivery of his calls. Tuesday was to make both men multimillionaires.

For a variety of reasons, this was not to be. In the first place, the brokers did not act quickly enough or in concert. Whether this was due to Standard Oil pressures or not will never be known, but it is strange, to say the least, that what should have been a fairly routine procedure was so badly bungled. As a result, not all the calls went out together as planned. Also the general market decline must have frightened many holders of United stock, and they sold to make a quick killing. Next, several New York newspapers printed articles containing hints of wrongdoing at United—stories which were rumored to have emanated from the Standard Oil crowd. Finally, several Rockefeller-influenced banks began to call in loans made by the Heinze-Morse group, demanding that it sell stock—preferably United—to meet the obligations. For all these reasons, United Copper fell sharply on Tuesday morning. Large blocks of stock were dumped to further depress the price. On the floor of the Exchange it was whispered that the blocks came from Rogers and others, who had purchased them for this purpose. That day United Copper fell from 60 to 36. On Wednesday the slide continued, and United closed at 10. Heinze and Morse had lost their corner, and with it millions of dollars. But at least they retained their banks and other interests, and they could hope for eventual recovery.

Wall Street knew that the combine had used bank and trust company funds in their operations, and that the Mercantile National Bank was the linchpin of their organization. Depositors rushed to the Mercantile to withdraw their funds, and in a few hours the bank was forced to close its doors. Heinze sent an appeal to the clearing house for aid; the directors replied that none would come until both he and Morse resigned their positions at Mercantile. The two men had no choice, and on Friday, October 18, they announced their resignations. Their other interests seemed intact that weekend, and since the clearing house announced an investigation and shoring-up operation to begin on Monday, many expected a return to normal in short order.

This was not to be, for the panic continued from the first bell. Morse's American Ice fell from 16 to 9⅞, and his Knickerbocker Ice of Chicago from 51½ to 20. Others followed the slide, although the bellwether blue chips lost no more than a few points. But Westinghouse, capital-short after its inability to sell stock earlier in the year, declined from 103 to 79⅞, and was suspended from trading. The stock opened at 35 in over-the-counter trading on Tuesday, causing the collapse of two brokerages and hundreds of speculators. Runs on banks continued—not only those controlled by Morse and Heinze, but almost every institution in the city. The Day and Night Bank, recently opened to serve the Wall Street community twenty-four hours a day, had long lines around the clock. Every hour messengers would leave the bank with satchels full of checks chained to their wrists, to be taken to other banks and trust companies for withdrawals. Many were drafts on the Knickerbocker Trust, the last vestige of the Morse-Heinze combine's power.

The Knickerbocker Trust witnessed scenes rivaling bedlam that Monday, as depositors fought to withdraw their funds. But this was true of other banks as well; although the combine was known to be in control, most thought the Knickerbocker was as sound as many of the dozens of other financial institutions caught in the panic. Like them, the Knickerbocker appealed to the clearing house for aid. Since it was the third-largest trust company in the city, it was thought that the banking community would have to offer assistance if only to save itself. The clearing house rejected the petition, and word leaked that the enterprise was heading toward insolvency.

Events moved swiftly and suddenly. When it was learned that President Charles Barney had been involved in Morse's investments, his resignation was demanded and received. Barney was replaced by A. Foster Higgins, who had a reputation for moderation and conservatism. Higgins hoped to calm the fears of the business community, promise changes, and then receive clearing house aid. Before he had a chance to do this, another blow struck. The National Bank of Commerce, which took care of Knickerbocker's clearings, refused to honor notes drawn by any officer of that company. Newspapers printed stories of Barney's resignation and the Bank of Commerce action, and hinted of further disclosures.

Knickerbocker's directors held a private meeting Monday evening to discuss their difficulties. As the directors gathered at Sherry's Restaurant, waiters and busboys whispered tales of what went on behind the closed doors. At the same time, a line began to form outside Knickerbocker's gates; by early Tuesday morning it stretched more than two blocks. Acting against the advice of some directors, President Higgins opened the doors at the usual time that Tuesday morning, hoping this would restore confidence. The move failed; within a few hours, more than $8 million had passed into the hands of worried depositors. A week before, the handsome new Fifth Avenue building had had $67 million in deposits. That afternoon it closed its doors, announcing bankruptcy. Morse and Heinze were now finished; as he had always known he would, H. H. Rogers won the last round.

What of the rest of the American financial community? Would it be dragged down with Morse and Heinze? The chain of events which began in the Montana copper fields might yet conclude in the utter destruction of a previously weakened banking structure. Rogers had meant to punish one man. Would the episode end with the worst crash in the history of American finance? That night many thought it would.

J. P. Morgan was busily occupied with church matters and tending to a severe cold on Thursday, October 17, when he learned of the United Copper crash. The matter seemed serious enough for his attention, but not serious enough to interfere with church-convention business. Morgan agreed to leave for New York a day earlier than his expected departure on Sunday. Then he went to bed.

Sleep did not come easily that night. Some instinct told Morgan that this was more than the crash of a handful of wild speculators. The tight money situation had occupied his attention for some time. Could the Morse-Heinze failure set off a series of collapses on Wall Street? Morgan must have believed it could. Accordingly, he informed his retinue the following morning that they would leave at once.

The trip home by private train was pleasant and cheerful. Morgan jested with several bishops who rode with him, played solitaire, and told stories of his European trips. To casual onlookers he showed no sign of concern over Wall Street happenings.

The train arrived in New York on Sunday morning, and Morgan bade his guests farewell after putting them in cabs. It was thought that he would go to St. George's Church for services, as was his custom while in the city. But Morgan had no time for church that morning. He entered his cab and ordered the driver to take him to his home on 36th Street. On the way he disclosed to members of his family his fears of what might happen on Wall Street the next morning.

Morgan was greeted at the door by several of his friends and partners, who had learned of his arrival in New York and guessed what would be on the old man's mind. For the next few hours they told him of difficulties in the money market, sketched the United Copper situation, and spoke of tightness at the banks and trust companies. Morgan was particularly interested in the last item. As head of the House of Morgan, he had investments in many financial institutions, both in New York and elsewhere. One of these was the Knickerbocker Trust, but there were others. Morgan needed time to think. He ordered his aides out of the room, called for his cards, and started to play solitaire, while he smoked cigars and considered the problem.

That evening Morgan met with James Keene, E. H. Harriman, James Stillman, George F. Baker, and other leading Wall Street figures. Some had been on opposite sides of battles with Morgan in the past, but now they indicated their willingness to cooperate with him in shoring up the markets. William Sherer, manager of the clearing house, called: he would put his full facilities at Morgan's disposal. Secretary of the Treasury George B. Cortelyou, who had rushed to New York as soon as the panic erupted, also offered his support, and backed it with a deposit of $6 million in New York banks. The Secretary told Morgan that more would be forthcoming if and when he thought it necessary. In effect, Teddy Roosevelt, the trust-buster, was placing the power of the federal government in Morgan's hands for the duration of the panic.

Morgan slept fitfully that night; his cold was getting worse, but, more important, the smell of the hunt had aroused his warrior blood. Early Monday morning he called George Perkins to his side, told him to get permission from the city's bankers to examine their books, and instructed Perkins to plant optimistic stories in the newspapers. By the end of the day Morgan had concluded that most of the city's banks were indeed in satisfactory condition, but that the trust companies were not. Nothing would be done to save Knickerbocker Trust, but there seemed little reason why most of the other institutions could not be salvaged. Thus, Morgan did not aid the Knickerbocker; he spent most of Tuesday planning assistance for key institutions.

On Wednesday morning the panic spread to other trust companies. The Lincoln Trust lost $14 million in deposits within a few hours, and some smaller institutions gave notice to insiders that they would shortly close down operations. But the most serious problem involved the Trust Company of America, which had loaned the Knickerbocker some $175,000 and was heavily involved in all manner of Morse-Heinze schemes. President Thorne saw his assets melt rapidly from $60 million to $34 million, with no end in sight. On Tuesday he thought he could weather the storm. On Wednesday he asked to see Morgan to gain assistance. Instead, Thorne was sent to George Perkins and Henry Davison of the First National Bank. Meanwhile, Morgan met with the heads of other trust companies and tried to whip them into line. In essence, he demanded that they assist the Trust Company of America and combine for joint action during the panic. All were adamant and unimpressed as bulletins regarding the Trust Company of America reached Morgan. At one o'clock the firm's cash assets were $1,200,000; at 1:20, $800,000; at 1:45, $500,000; at 2:15, $180,000. Morgan turned to his aides and asked whether they thought the Trust Company could be saved. They believed it could. "Then this is the place to stop the trouble," he said, and ordered money sent to Thorne's office.

Morgan returned to the trust company leaders and again demanded their cooperation. Once more they refused; Morgan had less power over this group than he had over the bankers. But Morgan would not be stopped; if the trust companies wouldn't aid Thorne, then the government might. Perkins was sent to Cortelyou to ask that the government make deposits at the Trust Company. The Secretary replied that he was authorized to make deposits at banks only, and could not violate his orders. Very well, said Morgan; the way is clear. Cortelyou was instructed to deposit $35 million in New York banks, which then reloaned the money to the Trust Company. By Wednesday evening, it appeared that Morgan had held the line.

But the next day, Thursday, October 24, brought new problems. The Trust Company was safe, to be sure, but now another run of massive proportions developed at the Lincoln Trust. In addition, the Stock Exchange reported panic conditions, as the loss of confidence in banks led to waves of selling, margin calls, dumping, and sharply lower prices. Exchange President R. H. Thomas ran to Morgan's office and told him that unless funds were made available to the brokers, there would be dozens of failures. Morgan knew that this would destroy whatever confidence was left in the financial community. He called a meeting of bank presidents and told them of the situation. The Exchange would need at least $25 million in the next fifteen minutes. The bankers fell in line; within five minutes, Morgan had $27 million to save the Exchange.

The huge loan did not suffice to restore credit, however, and money was still tight. Again, Morgan cut the knot, ordering the clearing house to print script, which would be used as emergency money, to be redeemed in full once the panic was over. Those who refused to accept script would be indicating their distrust of America's financial institutions—and of J. P. Morgan. Knowing Morgan's reputation for not forgetting a slight, all accepted the script, which acted to ease conditions somewhat. At the same time Morgan threw $13 million more into brokers' loans in his attempt to prevent wholesale failures on the Street. The amount caused him some worry. Morgan was not superstitious, but he had asked his bankers for $15 million—and the most powerful men in America could not meet his demand.

Morgan was still in command Friday morning, but the confidence his friends had shown Sunday was starting to disappear. Perkins saw little hope in the situation; new crises developed whenever old ones were solved, and there seemed no way to plug all the holes on Wall Street. And some of the old problems Morgan had thought solved recurred. Panic erupted at the Trust Company of America Friday morning, and again Morgan had to fill the breach. The trust-company presidents refused to pool their resources, so Morgan was obliged to call upon his banker allies once more.

Morgan knew he was scraping the bottom of the barrel. His reputation was still strong on the Street, but he realized that should the hundreds of men milling outside his office learn of his difficulties in stemming the panic, the nation's credit would be gone in a tremendous wave of failures. All he could do was to keep his façade of power and try to hold on until 3 P.M. on Friday. Perhaps something could be done over the weekend to save the situation. A new approach was needed; Morgan was running out of time. Later on, George Perkins told a group of investigators that if Morgan had been called on for any more money that Friday afternoon, he probably would not have been able to raise it. In that case the nation would have collapsed into paralysis.

But the money was not needed. The banks, trust companies, and Stock Exchange closed on time that Friday, without a single new failure. This in itself seemed a hopeful sign. Morgan encouraged his friends to release optimistic statements to the press. Then he called the city's leading religious figures to his office and asked them to give encouraging sermons. Religious leaders of all denominations agreed to paint cheerful pictures that weekend. They left the Morgan mansion well after midnight, ending the hectic day. The financier then went to his study, lit a cigar, and played a last game of solitaire before retiring.

Trading on Wall Street was quiet Saturday morning as speculators were cheered by news that Morgan had obtained $3 million in gold from his London affiliate. The situation seemed stable enough for Morgan to travel to Highland Falls for Sunday in the country. The morning and afternoon were devoted to church and rest, but in the late afternoon Morgan braved a severe rainstorm and left Highland Falls for his New York residence, where his aides awaited him. Together they began to map strategy for Monday morning. At this point, a new crisis arose.

The finances of New York City had been in bad shape for years. Indeed, during the past few months Morgan had taken several bond issues of the city in order to tide over Mayor George McClellan during his period of difficulty. Now McClellan ap-

peared at the Morgan mansion. The situation was critical, he
said. The city's failure to sell new bond issues had led it to the
brink of bankruptcy. Unless the bankers could float an issue of
some $30 million, McClellan would have to declare his inability
to meet New York's obligations. Coming during a panic, this
news could destroy all Morgan had attempted to do not only in
the past week, but during the past two decades.

Ordinarily Morgan would have taken the issue. But the banking community of the city had already stretched its resources
and could not raise an additional million dollars, much less $30
million. Nor could such securities be sold abroad considering the
tightness of money in Europe. There seemed no solution to the
problem. Then Morgan had an idea. The city's bonds would be
taken by the clearing house, which would pay for them in scrip.
Such an approach had been used in previous panics, and Morgan's
support had made scrip acceptable to banks during the past
week. But would the clearing house be willing to underwrite
such a large issue? And would the public take so much paper?
Answers to these questions could not be obtained. There was
nothing left to do but announce the offering and its acceptance,
and once more place Morgan's word and prestige on the line. This
was done, and again public trust in the financier saved the situation: the flotation took place with surprisingly few problems.

But McClellan had to pay a price. Morgan no longer trusted
the well-meaning but inept Mayor. The city's books were turned
over to Morgan men for examination, and for a while the financier
became the guardian of New York.

Morgan and his colleagues were at their posts Monday morning.
Unfortunately, shortly before the banks and trust companies
opened, news arrived that Europe could offer no more gold to
America, and that American securities were sliding rapidly in
London and Paris. A line appeared before the Trust Company
of America, and the run on that institution continued. Within
a few hours similar developments were reported at other trust
companies, with an especially bad situation at the Lincoln Trust.
Morgan dispatched messengers to these institutions several times
during that day, and the bags of money they carried seemed to
still fears somewhat. Clearing house scrip, forced bank loans, and

government deposits kept the trust companies in operation for the next two days. By Wednesday it appeared as though the situation were on the way to being saved. More important, from Morgan's viewpoint, was the fact that the public knew that his influence had been enough to keep the Heinze-Morse-Barney Trust Company of America on its feet. If he could do that, he could do anything! Not that Morgan cared personally whether the shaky firms survived or fell. Through it all, his major fear was that a loss of confidence in the trust companies might spill over to the banks, and then to other areas of American finance. Should this happen, he and all he stood for would be finished. There is no doubt that Morgan's sense of responsibility motivated him throughout this period, as it had in earlier panics. But Morgan the businessman was never separated from Morgan the patriot. Since the beginning of the panic he seemed to have considered how he and his interests might gain in a concrete fashion from recovery.

Morgan looked upon Roosevelt as a sometimes irresponsible child-man who could usually be trusted to act "correctly" in most situations. He realized that the antitrust campaign was more bombast and spectacular byplay than an actual attempt to revamp the structure of American business. Nonetheless, at times Teddy could get quite stubborn, and then no one on earth could make him change his mind. For years the Administration had seemed uneasy about the huge U.S. Steel complex—Morgan's major claim to fame and one of his proudest creations. The company had a few shaky years behind it, and was still in need of ore reserves and new properties. Such acquisitions were blocked by price considerations and Administration policies. For instance, Morgan had long wished to purchase the valuable properties of Tennessee Iron and Coal. These were worth more than $150 million at the time, and U.S. Steel could not afford the price. Even if it could, such a purchase would inevitably bring forth antitrust prosecutions. The crisis of 1907 seemed to afford U.S. Steel a never-to-be repeated opportunity to gain government promises of noninterference as well as a rock-bottom price for the company. The financier made it quite clear to his friends and associates that he meant to acquire T.C. & I. as his price for aiding the trust companies. "Why should I get into this?" he asked after the initial panic had ended. "My affairs are all in order. I've done enough. I won't take all this on *unless I get what I want out of it.*"

T.C. & I. was controlled by the investment banking house of Moore & Schley. Grant B. Schley was George F. Baker's brother-in-law, but the Morgan partner would not aid him, perhaps out of fear of Morgan's anger. John Moore, one of the most popular men on Wall Street, with many friends both there and in Washington, thought that in time of difficulty he could call upon any of several bankers for millions of dollars. Accordingly, he had taken many loans on their block of T.C. & I. during the panic. Now he was in trouble, and Moore applied to Morgan for aid. T.C. & I. stock had not declined much during the panic, but news of the difficulty would send it down at least fifty points from its price of around 130. Morgan turned Moore down, although he had previously aided other, less substantial investment bankers. Then Moore & Schley offered all its stock for $90 a share plus a $5 million loan; the Morgan-dominated U.S. Steel board refused the offer, arguing it lacked the capital. In fact, however, Morgan thought he could get the stock at a still lower price.

Morgan then summoned Henry Clay Frick and Elbert Gary, the leaders of U.S. Steel, and told them of his desire to merge the two firms. At first the steelmen indicated disapproval of the idea. Then Morgan pointed out that T.C. & I's Birmingham plant was the lowest-cost producer in America, and that the company had over 500 million tons of iron ore in reserve. Finally, he simply said that he wished it to be done. Frick and Gary quickly changed their minds and agreed to follow Morgan's lead. They also agreed to bring Morgan's price to the finance committee of U.S. Steel; it was $84 a share, to be paid in U.S. Steel bonds, not cash. (In actual market prices, the shares were to cost less than $74 a share. While it is difficult to estimate the value of T.C. & I's ore assets *alone*, they were at least in excess of $250 a share. When developed, the property would be worth more than ten times that figure.) Frick and Gary then rushed to Washington to obtain Roosevelt's approval for the merger.

It was Sunday, November 3. Morgan had a report that the Trust Company of America was finally solvent, and that the

Lincoln Trust was less than $1 million short; with that amount of money, it could pay off all of its depositors and still have some cash in the till. Morgan also had word that London was now prepared to ship more gold to America.

But this was not the story Frick and Gary told Roosevelt. According to them, unless the merger was accepted, Moore & Schley might fall, ushering in a new panic which would destroy the nation. The picture was painted in the grimmest terms possible. Faced with such pressure, Roosevelt had no choice but to accept the merger; the President of the United States capitulated to J. P. Morgan.

The next step was to gain funds for the acquisition and at the same time form a fund to aid the two trust companies. Morgan agreed to purchase the U.S. Steel bonds; this would require some $23 million. When the trust-company fund was added to this, Morgan could reflect that $25 million would do the job.

But where could he get the $25 million? At first he tried Rockefeller, asking his assistance in making up a fund of $40 million. The Standard Oil group was told that the money would be used to save the trust companies. George Perkins, Morgan's emissary, explained that the news of Rockefeller support would certainly make John D. a popular man with the public. More important, it might lead the government to view Standard Oil in a more kindly light. Since the company was then appealing its $29 million fine, the second point certainly made sense. But the Rockefellers rejected the proposal; they did not need Morgan as much as Roosevelt did, and they knew that Morgan was using the trust-company crisis to gain a windfall for U.S. Steel.

This left only one possible source for the money: the trust companies themselves. In the past they had refused to help. Now Morgan meant to use all his muscle to force them into line.

The presidents of the city's major trust companies met in Morgan's library on Tuesday evening. Businesses were closed that morning and afternoon, since it was Election Day. But there were rumors of new panics to come on Wednesday. Then Morgan came into the room and told the presidents of his plan.

The New York trust companies would raise a fund of $25 million for the Trust Company of America and the Lincoln

Trust. These two companies would deposit two thirds of their
stock in a voting trust, to be controlled by the Morgan interests.
If they agreed, they would have Morgan's good wishes and support. Should they refuse to contribute to the fund, Morgan would
order the U.S. Steel finance committee to reject the merger with
T.C. & I. This news, quickly followed by the inevitable failure
of Moore & Schley, would set off a new panic which would destroy
every trust company in the city. The presidents had no choice;
even had they desired to leave, they would have found that Morgan
had taken the precaution of locking the doors. One by one they
rose to look at the agreement that Morgan had flung on the
table. Old Edward King of the Union Trust, who knew Morgan
socially, shook as he approached the document. Morgan put his
arm around King's shoulders and led him to the table. He placed
a pen in the quavering hand. "There's the place, King, and
here's the pen." King signed. The others followed silently. Then
Morgan unlocked the door and let them out. Now he had the
money for the trust companies, with enough left over for the
T.C. & I. takeover.

It is almost impossible to keep secrets on Wall Street, but
this was one that Morgan wanted leaked to the public. News
of the conference led to fewer and shorter lines at the trust companies Wednesday morning. Shares rose sharply on the Exchange.
The morning papers carried stories of the establishment of the
trust-company committee to safeguard the Trust Company of
America and the Lincoln Trust. This committee was headed
by King but really directed by Morgan aides. Then came news
of an additional $7 million gold shipment from London, with
word that the *Lusitania* would arrive with $10 million more.
"Sunshine movements" and "Prosperity leagues" appeared in
many cities, and the stock market began a long upward rise.
Money was still tight, and there would be a bad industrial depression in 1908, but at least the panic was over.

And what of the leading figures of those crisis-filled October
and November days? Heinze was through as a Wall Street tycoon,
as was Morse. The former went West for a few years, while
Morse was indicted for malfeasance and later served a term in
the Atlanta Penitentiary. On October 6, 1914, Edwin Gould

brought an action against Heinze to recover some $1,250,000 owed him for sales of Mercantile National Bank stock. As Heinze protested his poverty and lack of responsibility, Morse sat quietly in the back of the courtroom. The jury awarded the money to Gould, but he never collected; Heinze died, poverty-stricken, on November 4. Morse left Wall Street soon after, and was never heard from again. As for Charles Barney, he was by then seven years in the grave. Faced with ruin in 1907, he went to Morgan's office to plead for help. The financier refused to see him. Distraught, Barney put a bullet through his head.

Morgan and Roosevelt had plans for the future. The aged banker continued to groom J.P., Jr., as his successor and to map strategy for art-buying expeditions and Episcopal Church matters. Roosevelt quietly ended the antitrust phase of his Presidency, withdrawing suits against International Harvester and others. But he could not avoid the spectacular; within weeks he set into motion plans to dispatch the American fleet around the world. Still, he clung to his reputation as a trust buster and enemy of the Wall Street "interests." Perhaps in deference to this reputation, Roosevelt waited a few weeks before inviting Morgan to dine with him at the White House.

10.

THE YEAR THE STOCK
MARKET CLOSED: 1914

Shortly after midnight on April 1, 1913, J. P. Morgan died in Rome. While on his annual European trip, which this time included Egypt, Morgan fell ill. Many doctors had examined the seventy-six-year-old tycoon in March, but none seemed able to treat him satisfactorily. His son-in-law, Herbert Satterlee, issued optimistic communiqués daily, but on March 30 he admitted that Morgan had fallen into a coma. Morgan recovered briefly and spoke deliriously of his triumphs and religion. At one point he turned to Satterlee and said, "You bet I will pull through." Then came a second coma. Shortly before midnight on March 30, Morgan stared at the ceiling in his Rome bedroom, pointed upward, and whispered, "I've got to go up the hill." Within minutes, he was dead.

Messages of condolence flooded Rome. Kaiser Wilhelm and King Victor Emmanuel sent telegrams. Pope Pius X said a mass for the financier. Stock exchanges throughout the world paused for a moment in respect to the memory of J. P. Morgan. Reporters rushed to leading political and business figures for statements. "Mr. Morgan's leading characteristic was to be helpful and to do right," said Jacob Schiff. "His worth as a good and great citizen will, now that he is no more, be ever more fully appreciated, and we shall not see his like again." "There will be no successor to Morgan," said *The Wall Street Journal*. "He was the last of his line. Never again will there be another J. Pierpont Morgan," wrote the *World*. President Wilson was silent, but Theodore Roosevelt spoke well of his former adversary and friend; he was "struck by his very power and truthfulness. Any kind of meanness and smallness were alien to his nature."

The body was returned to America and buried on April 14. The Exchange closed and many leading bankers went to the streets to witness the funeral procession, which included Thomas Edison, Andrew Carnegie, George Cortelyou, Elbert Gary, George Baker, Albert Wiggin—scarcely an important business figure save John Rockefeller, who was represented by others, failed to arrive. The Church Temperance Society sent a delegation, as did Trinity College, the New York Yacht Club, and the Equitable Life Assurance Society. It was the funeral procession of a prince or a king. The Southern Railroad group was there, along with U.S. Steel, the International Mercantile Marine, and the American Bankers' Association. As the body was interred, special memorial services were held in Westminster Abbey. *The New York Times,* which had devoted parts of twenty pages to the financier on the day of his death, reported the funeral on its front page.

Some blamed Morgan's death on overwork; others believed it was simply the effects of old age. A few thought it was brought on by personal attacks after the 1907 panic.

The unexpected collapse of 1907 had shocked the nation, and it led to postmortems by two different groups motivated by opposite philosophies. The first was by the banking community. Morgan had saved it in 1893 and again in 1907. In those years disaster had been averted through the use of Morgan's prestige, and little else. What would happen when Morgan was no longer on the scene? The bankers set about erecting a structure which, hopefully, would enable them to pool their resources to act in Morgan's place. The Exchange put through a series of internal reforms designed to curb irresponsible brokers, and a law committee was established to investigate cases of suspected wrongdoing. The clearing house was given more power, and prominent bankers were added to its membership.

The most important measure promoted by this group was the Aldrich-Vreeland Act, passed in 1908 by a conservative Republican Congress. The Act provided for the issuance of a temporary currency in periods of emergency, gave national banks the power to borrow up to 90 percent of their pooled assets from the federal government at such times, and looked forward to the establishment of a central bank on the European models. The Act was inspired and drafted by Morgan partner Henry Davison, Paul Warburg of Kuhn, Loeb, and Benjamin Strong of the Morgan-dominated Bankers Trust Company. In effect, they wanted to mobilize the power of the United States Treasury behind the banking community in times of stress. The Act was signed by President Roosevelt. Secretary of the Treasury Leslie Shaw, who said that "financial panics in this country have caused more mental and physical suffering than all the plagues known to man," enthusiastically supported the Wall Street group. It appeared that a central bank, controlled by Wall Street and backed by Washington, would become a satisfactory replacement for the aged Morgan.

The political climate changed drastically the following year, however. William Howard Taft, the new President, was unable to deal with the reform elements as effectively as Roosevelt had, and a new wave of anti-business sentiment swept the nation. Taft supported those who desired central banking, going so far as to label such measures as "more important than the tariff, more important than conservation, more important than the question of trusts and more important than any political legislation that has been presented." But he could do nothing, and the split in the Republican party, combined with the growing demand for stronger antitrust measures, led to the election of Woodrow Wilson and a reform-minded Democratic Congress in 1912.

Those who offered a different medicine to treat panics such as that of 1907 took control of the White House and Congress in 1913. Reform Democrats in powerful positions, most of them from the South and West, joined with similarly minded Western and Midwestern Republicans to attack the "Money Trust." Looking upon the Aldrich-Vreeland Act as an attempt to assure domination by a small clique of powerful bankers, the reformers agreed with Wilson, who on June 23 demanded public, not private, central banking, "so that the banks may be the instruments, not the masters, of business and of individual enterprise and initiative." Three days later, Carter Glass of Virginia, chairman of the House Committee on Banking and Currency, introduced a measure which bore his name and which would provide for the establishment of regional federal banks.

This bill was the result of a series of hearings led by Representative Arsene Pujo of Louisiana in 1912–13 and counseled by Samuel Untermyer, during which the great power of the banking community was investigated. The bankers attempted to convince the Committee of the soundness of their plans, but failed. When they spoke of the importance of trust and honor and showed how it operated on Wall Street, Untermyer expressed disbelief. The climax of the hearings occurred when Morgan himself took the stand. The contrast between the old financier and Untermyer was striking. Morgan believed that he and his group were equipped by training and heritage to run the nation's financial affairs, while Untermyer thought such power was used solely for the purpose of aggrandizement. During Morgan's days on the stand, the two continually spoke at cross purposes. Untermyer tried to get Morgan to admit that money controlled America, while Morgan insisted that trust was more important.

Untermyer: Is not commercial credit based primarily upon money or property?
Morgan: No sir: the first thing is character.
Untermyer: Before money or property?
Morgan: Before money or anything else. Money cannot buy it.

There was no reconciling two such disparate views of business. Pujo recommended measures to control bankers; Glass accepted the demands of reformers for a public banking system. The Glass Act (later known as the Glass-Owen Act) was passed by Congress and signed into law on December 23, 1913. Within days, plans were being formulated for the establishment of the Federal Reserve System, which was authorized by the Act. Naturally, an enterprise of this nature would take time. The most optimistic thought the system might be in operation within a year. Thus, in midsummer 1914, Morgan was dead, Wall Street had been unable to establish a mechanism to take his place, and the Federal Reserve System, which might have done the job, was still being formed.

On the surface, at least, it seemed that war was far away that summer. The biggest items of news involved the future of the Progressive party, which had supported Teddy Roosevelt for the Presidency in 1912. Would the "Bull Moosers," as they were known, return to the GOP, or would they put up a slate of candidates for the congressional and gubernatorial races? President Wilson faced similar problems in his own party, as factional disputes threatened to destroy many local and state organizations. In New York, for example, Tammany Hall backed James Gerard for the Senate, while Wilson's circle supported Assistant Secretary of the Navy Franklin Roosevelt.

Most Americans seemed to care little for questions of foreign policy. The Mexican situation was troublesome, as Wilson strove to prevent Mexican bandits from crossing the border and attacking American towns. On April 14, the President ordered American troops to Tampico Bay, as a result of an incident involving the arrest of several American soldiers. Further complications followed, but eleven days later both nations accepted arbitration by outside powers, and shortly thereafter anti-American President Huerta resigned his post.

Meanwhile the nation's intellectuals read and discussed works by George Bernard Shaw, James Bryce, and H. G. Wells. America and Britain seemed closer together than ever before, and discussions of an Anglo-Saxon union appeared from time to time in the pages of small-circulation elite magazines and the Sunday supplements. Anything seemed possible; all were optimistic. When H. G. Wells wrote that man would soon reach the stage where he could predict the future as easily as he had organized studies of the past, many nodded their heads wisely. "What will happen in centuries to come when men shall stand upon the Earth as on a footstool and laugh and reach out their hands amid the stars?" asked Wells. They would see progress, writ in large letters, was the answer. And as he wrote, Secretary of State William Jennings Bryan busily concluded many nonaggression pacts, looking forward to the time when war would be no more.

The economy was in the doldrums in the summer of 1914. The hangover from the 1907 panic, a disrupted political situation, and discussions of radical economic reforms caused uncertainties. The Balkan War of 1912 had led to an increase in exports, but by 1914 the situation was back to normal. The nation's 1913 grain exports had not been as high as had been expected, however, while imports from Europe rose steadily. As a result, each month saw increased gold shipments to Europe; financial analysts observed that not since 1895 had there been such a large excess of imports over exports; not since 1907 had gold shipments been so high.

Chains of gold linked the world economies in 1914, and tugs on the chain would eventually be felt in the capitals and business centers of all nations. Threats of war, economic panic, political experimentation—anything that would significantly disturb the status quo would quickly lead to a flight of capital and higher interest rates. This had been seen in 1912 when, hours after Bulgaria, Serbia and Montenegro declared war on Turkey, the Bank of England raised its discount rate from 4 to 5 percent. In quick succession German bank rates went from 4½ to 5 percent and Austrian from 5 to 5½ percent. Nations began to liquidate foreign holdings and repatriate their gold. British consol bonds, the blue chip of international investments, fell to their lowest point in history, and French government bonds to a twenty-two-year low. Europeans sold their American securities, causing a sharp drop in prices. In that last five months of 1912, American grain sales to Europe had led to an import of $37 million in gold; European dumping in the first half of 1913 caused an export of $63 million in gold. Later on, experts estimated that some $250 million in gold went into hiding, as people throughout the Western world expected the Balkan crisis to erupt into a general war.

What would such a war mean to the American economy? The same experts thought it would destroy the nation.

Great Britain had some $3.5 billion invested in America, while Germany accounted for another billion and France for half that amount. Altogether, Europeans owned approximately $6 billion in American securities. In time of war, all of these would be sold in order to obtain gold for weapons, and such massive sales would destroy the American economy. The war would be short, said Norman Angell, the noted British intellectual. No country could afford a long war, since within a few weeks it would run out of gold to buy supplies. Any large-scale war would inevitably lead to widespread bankruptcy throughout Europe, and America would be sucked into the greatest worldwide depression in history. National leaders knew this, said Angell, and so would act in concert to prevent a general war from taking place.

This, then, was the conventional wisdom of 1914. Accordingly, few noted the assassination of Archduke Franz Ferdinand of Austria by Serbian terrorists on June 28, 1914. Those who did could not believe it would lead to more than an exchange of notes. The assassination, wrote the *Commercial and Financial Chronicle* of that day, "has impressed the political and financial observer, not least of all because of the small degree of consternation with which the world at large received the news. . . . After a day or two of abundant news and comment, the matter seems almost forgotten." The *London Economist* of July 4 reported that "the tragedy in the House of Hapsburg has had no effect" on the London Stock Exchange. Five days later the *Economist* wrote that "the Norway visit of the Kaiser marks the beginning of the dead season in German politics." "Everyone spoke of the possibility of conflict involving practically all Europe," wrote the financial columnist of *The New York Times*, "but no one here really believed that such a thing was likely to come about."

Such statements were not meant to lull readers into a false sense of security; there is no evidence of secret machinations behind the scenes by those who expected war and meant to profit by it. European bank rates had fallen all year, a sure sign that war was not believed possible. Stock prices were rising, and this was another indication that war would be averted. Bank rates remained low and prices continued to rise throughout most of July. Bankers in Paris, Berlin, London, and New York went on their usual summer vacations; those who stayed in the hot cities took care of what little business remained.

Summer was traditionally a slow season; business was extremely sluggish that July. Sitting on the verandas of their summer homes after church services on Sunday, July 26, New York brokers might have talked about the domination of the Philadelphia Athletics over the American League and rumors that beer tycoon Jacob Ruppert might purchase the moribund New York Yankees. Younger businessmen might still be recovering from Saturday-night cotillions, or recounting scenes from the big movie of the year, *Tillie's Punctured Romance*, with Marie Dressler and Charlie Chaplin. The Panama Canal had opened for barge traffic in May, and this was a new sign of American power. More important to some, however, was the Cape Cod Canal, which would be in operation in a few days and would reduce the distance from Boston to New York by seventy miles.

Had they turned to the newspapers that Sunday, they would have seen few signs of an expectation of war. "No modern war has been conducted to which the business world as a whole was unalterably opposed," wrote a *Times* columnist, "for war must draw its sinews from the money chests of business." Businessmen in all major capitals showed no sign of wanting war late in July, and American bankers were no exceptions.

A turn to the financial pages would have caused any banker who had doubts of this to feel even more secure. The stock markets were steady, and volume was low. Throughout July the trading floor of the New York Stock Exchange was quiet, with

PRICES OF SELECTED ISSUES IN JULY 1914

Issue	Closing Prices (fractions rounded off)							
	July 17	July 18	July 20	July 21	July 22	July 23	July 24	July 25
American Can	27	26	26	26	26	26	25	26
American Telephone & Telegraph	119	119	119	120	120	120	120	119
Bethlehem Steel	40	40	40	41	41	40	39	39
General Electric	149	147	147	149	148	148	146	146
Miami Copper	22	22	22	22	22	22	22	22
Texas Company	139	139	135	136	137	135	135	134
U.S. Rubber	56	56	56	56	57	57	57	56
U.S. Steel	60	60	60	61	61	61	60	60

Source: *New York Times*, July 18–26, 1914

rarely more than 300,000 shares being traded. On Saturday's half-day trading, 204,000 shares were exchanged, and this was normal. Price deviations were minor, as they had been throughout the month.

Obviously, there was nothing of interest in such news. After reading it, the banker might have dropped off for a nap in a hammock or rested in his gazebo.

Even as he rested, whatever difficulties there were in Europe appeared on the way to solution. Notes and ultimatums had been delivered to several capitals, but cool heads seemed about to prevail. In a note of July 25, Austria assured Russia that it had no desire to annex Serbian territory, and while our banker rested and reflected, Sir Edward Grey proposed a conference to deal with whatever problems existed in the Balkans.

While reading his newspaper the following morning on the way back to Wall Street, the banker might have received his first warning of difficulty. France and Russia agreed to accept the Grey proposal, but there were signs that Austria and Germany were recalcitrant. Would this mean war? Many bankers, for the first time showing the same caution they had demonstrated in 1912, and following what was accepted as normal financial procedure during unusual periods under the international gold standard, began selling securities and buying gold. That Monday, July 27, the gold price rose slightly, while stocks declined sharply on heavy volume in New York—475,000 shares.

The Tuesday headlines increased existing fears. "War Scare Draws American Gold to Europe," read the *Times,* and the story accompanying the headline reported that $13 million in gold had already left the United States for Europe, as that continent prepared for war. There were reports that the Royal Navy had been placed on an emergency footing and that France and Russia had renewed their pledges to each other, while the Czar gave assurances of support to Serbia and the Kaiser gave equally strong support to Austria.

On that day—July 28—Austria declared war on Serbia. Stock markets throughout the world were immediately inundated with sellers, as the price of gold reached new highs. The Montreal, Toronto, and Madrid Exchanges were forced to close their doors.

In New York, prices declined sharply, and volume rose to 1,020,000 shares.

The New York Stock Exchange opened warily on Wednesday, July 29. During the night there had been many rumors of peace moves in Berlin and London. German leaders, resisting pressures from their generals, urged a resumption of talks with the Russians, and there was no clear sign that Britain would join in any continental war which did not threaten her vital interests. Prices seesawed throughout the day, closing with a slight advance after 785,000 shares were traded. Still the gold shipments continued, and exchanges in Vienna, Budapest, Brussels, Antwerp, and Rome closed down. Most important, trading on the Berlin Exchange was suspended toward the end of the day.

There was no break either way in the news from Europe after the Wednesday closing. Indeed, if anything, the news offered some hope that war might be averted. There was talk that Russia would soon announce an end to its mobilization, and that the general European conference called at the Hague might yet prevent a full-scale war. But the gold purchases continued, and this was thought a sure sign that even if war were avoided, economic collapse would take place. Accordingly, major panics struck all remaining exchanges from the opening on July 30. Stocks tumbled immediately after the morning bell in New York; volume rose to a post-1907 high of almost 1.3 million shares. General Motors lost

PRICES OF SELECTED ISSUES IN LATE JULY 1914

Issue	Closing Prices (fractions rounded off)				
	July 25	*July 27*	*July 28*	*July 29*	*July 30*
American Can	26	25	23	24	20
American Telephone & Telegraph	119	120	118	117	114
Bethlehem Steel	39	38	36	35	30
General Electric	146	145	143	143	139
Miami Copper	22	21	21	20	18
Texas Company	134	131	120	125	113
U.S. Rubber	56	56	53	53	45
U.S. Steel	60	59	56	56	52

Source: *New York Times*, July 26–31, 1914

twenty points, and International Harvester thirteen, and similar declines of from 20 to 30 percent dotted the list.

By closing time, July 30, most brokers and bankers, along with the rest of the world, felt that a full-scale war was at hand. Russia had announced a general mobilization—after repeated warnings from Berlin that such an action would be considered tantamount to aggression. As the German General Staff met to consider its next move, the officers of the New York Stock Exchange consulted with leading bankers as to the wisdom of keeping the Exchange open. The discussions continued throughout the night in both cities. While German generals debated the pros and cons of war at that time, New York's financial leaders considered the impact of an Exchange closing.

Those who favored a continuation of trading observed that although there had been massive selling and declines on Thursday, conditions were not as bad as they had been during the panics of 1893 and 1907. On those occasions, the Exchange was kept open in order to instill confidence in the public. If trading had not been suspended when banks were failing and the nation seemed doomed, why should the Exchange close when the economy was sound and the banks intact? Besides, war might not come, and even if it did, the fighting would be short and limited. In these circumstances a Wall Street closing might precipitate a panic when none was indicated.

These arguments were easily parried by financiers who wanted activities to stop. The Exchange had indeed not closed in 1893 or 1907, but only because Wall Street had a strong force—J. P. Morgan—whose prestige was such as to enable the panics to be contained. No such person or persons existed in 1914. In addition, no other major exchange had closed in those past years. While it was true that the Thursday decline was not of major proportions compared to earlier crashes, most men in the group believed trading the following day would lead to large losses on heavy volume. Then, too, what guarantee was there that any war which might erupt in the near future would be short? Those who favored a closing wanted to take into account any possibility that might arise.

Most of these were drawn from the economic thought of the

time. Several developments might be expected in a wartime panic on Wall Street. Obviously American securities would be dumped, not only by foreign and domestic holders, but also by those who would ordinarily trade on overseas exchanges. Much of the world's securities business would be channeled through New York, and the panics which ordinarily would have occurred overseas would instead be concentrated on Wall Street. The demand for cash would eclipse any that had gone before. This would lead to a run on the banks, and in short order paralyze the nation's financial arteries.

America was still an agricultural nation in 1914, and the ebb and flow of its banking structure were geared to conditions on the farms. Typically, the nation would lose gold in the first half of the year, as imports of manufactured goods were high and exports low. In this period farmers would borrow heavily at the banks in order to get through the winter. Then, with the harvests, farmers would sell their produce and pay their debts. The wheat crop of 1914 promised to be the largest in American history, and cotton production was also high. In early July it had been expected that much of this crop would be exported to Europe, enabling the nation to import gold and the farmers to pay their debts. Some of this money could be used to pay the principal on the $450 million in bonds held by London and Paris which would mature in January 1915, and the rest to prepare for the usual gold outflow expected in that month.

If the war lasted more than a few weeks, blockades established by European belligerents would destroy the nation's trade. Grain and cotton exports would dwindle; their prices would collapse. The gold imports expected in August through December would not take place; instead, more gold would leave America as a result of securities liquidations. A long war would hurt the belligerents and in the process bankrupt the United States.

In such circumstances, any steps that could be taken to prevent the loss of gold and a run on the already loaned-out banks had to be taken. One measure which would help in this regard would be to close down all securities trading in America. And as the financiers spoke, debating the issue, the clinching argument came from Britain. The London Exchange, which had remained open during the worst days of the Napoleonic period, announced it would close its doors for an indefinite period. If the New York markets opened, they would be the only ones in the world to do so.

Exchange President H. G. S. Noble called a special meeting of the governing committee for nine o'clock. Calls were sent to those members still on vacation, and several rushed to Wall Street by car and carriage to make the meeting. Those arriving before nine exchanged stories of large bear pools being formed in the streets. A majority of the forty-two-member committee had arrived by nine o'clock, one hour before the opening signal at the Exchange —the ringing of a gong. President Noble waited until 9:15 before gaveling the meeting to order. The roll was called and thirty-six answered "Present." Noble then announced what everyone knew: the special meeting had been necessary to determine whether or not to open trading at ten o'clock.

Ernest Groesbeck, whose father had been Daniel Drew's favorite broker, and who himself was one of the most respected members of the committee, rose and introduced a motion to close the Exchange until further notice. There was no debate; all knew the issues, and time was running out. The motion carried by a large margin.

Groesbeck then introduced a second motion: deliveries of securities were to be suspended until further notice. This would prevent the possible insolvencies which might result if buyers were obliged to pay for stock purchased earlier without recourse to the call money market. In addition, it would save many arbitrageurs— men who had purchased securities elsewhere and had to sell them quickly in New York, or vice versa. These men too needed the call money market for their operations. Now that this market was to be closed, they would have been ruined if this motion had been defeated. The committee realized this: the motion carried unanimously.

Groesbeck's third motion was for the establishment of a special committee to carry on Exchange business during the suspension, enforce rules and regulations, and present recommendations as to when trading should be resumed. The third motion was passed without dissent.

At this point Noble sent word to the Exchange floor of the

closing, and instructions that the news be placed on the ticker as well. George Ely, Secretary of the Exchange, took the message to his desk above the trading floor. Literally seconds before 10 A.M. he announced the suspension of trading. Those who were there that day remember that the news caused no demonstrations or hectic activity; it was hardly surprising after the London suspension. Most brokers knew the move was necessary. The only question was "How long would it last?" The 1873 suspension had been for little more than a week. Few ventured to guess how long the Exchange would remain closed this time. The answer was not in the hands of Americans; it would be decided in Paris, London, St. Petersburg, Vienna, and Berlin.

Within hours—at 7 P.M. Berlin time—Germany declared war on Russia. Within a week all the major European powers were engaged in the World War.

By this time, Noble, Groesbeck, and other leaders of the Exchange were in full command of the situation at that institution. In addition, their counterparts at the Consolidated Stock Exchange and the Curb Market agreed to cooperate; with the exception of the few mining shares traded on the Colorado Stock Exchange, every securities market in the nation was closed. Writing of the period a year later, Noble stated that all seemed to agree that trading could not be reopened until a greater degree of stability had been restored and the psychology of panic dissipated. This meant that the banks had to be secured from runs; the export trade had to readjust to meet the new international situation; steps to guarantee a stable currency had to be taken; and there had to be some assurance that prices on the exchanges would not plummet once trading was resumed. Each of these problems was interrelated with the others; each had to be dealt with at once, for the lack of progress on any one front would doom the entire financial and economic structure of the nation.

As seen from Wall Street, the most pressing problems were those of the banks and currency. As chances of war increased, runs occurred on several banks and spread throughout the nation. During the two weeks beginning July 27, some $80 million in cash had been withdrawn from the New York banks and trust companies alone, and of this amount, $73 million was in gold, which was either sent to Europe or hoarded domestically. Loans were difficult to obtain, and when they were granted, the rates were 8 percent for prime customers. On the other hand, there was little panic in banking circles. Most financiers remembered the lessons of 1907 and applied them to the conditions of 1914. Cooperation between institutions was the rule. Clearing house certificates, which had saved many in 1907, were issued immediately, and by the end of September more than $211 million of the scrip was circulating between financial institutions to settle debts.

For a while it appeared that a flight from the dollar would take place. In early August the demand for the pound sterling was such that its rate shot up from the usual $4.89 = £1 to $7.00 = £1. The rise was made possible by the fact that the Bank of England, which normally sold gold at far lower rates, had to suspend gold dealings temporarily in early August. The decline of the dollar indicated clearly that Americans and others considered the pound to be the least vulnerable of all currencies. But a run developed at the Bank of England which resulted in the loss of $52.5 million in gold from that institution. The run could not be stanched; not even a rise in the discount rate to an unprecedented 10 percent would help. The bank had a reserve of 40 percent when the war began; within a week it was down to an all-time low of 14⅝ percent. By August 6, it seemed that Britain would shortly be forced to leave the gold standard. The situation was bad in New York, to be sure, but it was far worse elsewhere. As a result, the dollar-pound ratio quickly returned to normal. A reading of the exchange-rates section of the financial page would have convinced many skeptical Americans that the dollar was the safest currency in the world by the end of August.

The dollar was further aided by the implementation of an almost forgotten section of what in July had been considered a superfluous law. With the passage of the Glass-Owen Act, the hopes of those who had framed the Aldrich-Vreeland Act seemed crushed. There would be no central bank along the lines proposed by the bankers. But the Act was still on the statute books, including that section which authorized the Secretary of the Treasury to issue currency based on securities and other bank assets. The Aldrich-Vreeland Act set a limit of $500 million on such notes and authorized their printing so as to have the currency ready in times of emergency. Such currency would, of course, be redundant when the Federal Reserve System was established. The Glass-Owen Act provided for the repeal of the Aldrich-Vreeland Act once the reserve banks were in full operation, which the legislators of 1913 thought would be two years at the most. Accordingly, the Glass-Owen Act contained a provision extending the emergency currency provision until June 30, 1915. This provision was an afterthought, and almost failed to be included in the final draft. Thus, accident and chance enabled the government to use a huge amount of paper under conditions Wall Street could not have imagined in 1908.

The emergency currency was released to the banks in early August, and by mid-month, almost $68 million was in circulation; two months later the figure was in excess of $363 million. The availability of this currency, coupled with the use of clearing house certificates, eased conditions considerably, and by the middle of September the banking crisis seemed over.

Emergency currency could not be used to pay international obligations, however, and as foreign loans began to mature, the banks had to face still another crisis. Most bankers assumed that European creditors would demand payment of the principal in gold because of hoarding and in order to finance the war. Secretary of the Treasury McAdoo called a bankers' meeting for August 7 to discuss the matter. Some bankers suggested that a moratorium on international gold shipments be declared, but this was rejected, since the Europeans would view it as a sign of weakness on the part of the dollar. After much discussion, it was decided to form a gold pool to pay such obligations when presented. Such demands could exceed $500 million, and the nation did not have that much gold in its banks. The best the New York financial community could do was to raise a pool of $108 million in gold for the purpose of repaying international obligations.

What followed surprised those who thought the nation would be drained of gold in time of war. Although Europe imported gold from America in August, the demand was slaked in September. By December it seemed that the war would be a long-drawn-out affair, which might result in sweeping changes in Europe. In such circumstances, American securities seemed safer than European. Accordingly, Europeans did not press American banks for repayment of bonds; instead the loans were extended under favorable terms. At the same time, gold began to return to America for another reason. Just as there had been a flight from the dollar in August, so there was a flight to the dollar in December, as Europeans sent their gold to American banks for safekeeping. The economic forecasters were wrong: the war would not destroy American business, but rather would prove to be its greatest opportunity for expansion since the turn of the century.

It took a while for this fact to become evident. As late as August 30, Irving Fisher wrote, "This general depreciation of investment securities will doubtless lead to many bankruptcies, if not to a general crisis." But there were no major bankruptcies, and the chances for a crisis faded each day. On September 6, Dean Joseph Johns of New York University's School of Commerce agreed that the war would cause a severe dislocation in America, primarily due to the loss of raw materials, the closure of Europe's markets to American securities, and a severe gold loss to the belligerent nations. On the other hand, crises in European banking circles were bound to increase the prestige of American banks. While the war was on, American manufacturers would have a fine opportunity to enter South American and Asian markets formerly dominated by Europeans. Johns concluded that "New York is today the financial capital of the world. . . . It is likely that the bankers of South America and Asia will increase their deposits in New York—the only safe haven for the moment— and the New York bill of exchange will temporarily take the place of the London bill." A week later Colonel George Pope, head of the National Association of Manufacturers, said that the war would end with industrial America the most powerful nation in the world, and with New York the financial capital of the globe. The war would not wreck American industry but rather enable the American businessman to become the major economic force in the world markets. Nor was this a temporary phenomenon, said Pope, for each day of European war made the old continent weaker, and America more powerful.

Pope's words were borne out by the facts, for the dollar grew stronger each week. By November 12, it was back to its normal parity of $4.86⅝ = £1, and a month later the ratio dropped to $4.84¾ as, for the first time, the dollar sold at a premium over the pound.

The money situation was closely tied to foreign trade. Britain, France, Belgium, and Germany had accounted for almost 90 percent of America's exports to Europe in the twelve months preceding the assassination at Sarajevo. Now that Europe was at war, the warships of both belligerent alliances began sinking merchantmen bound for the other's ports. Trade ground to a near-halt. Germany, which imported 2.6 million bushels of American wheat in July, took none in August. Europe imported 21,219 bales of American cotton in August, and none in September; in August 1913, the continent had purchased 257,172 bales. Steel companies reported difficulties in obtaining alloy metals. Although orders were up, Bethlehem found it impossible to deliver to the belligerents. In January 1915 the nation's steel mills were working at only 50 percent of capacity. U.S. Steel's earnings were down sharply, and there was some question of whether the company could meet the interest on its bonds. The price of wheat fell from 95½ cents a bushel on July 30 to 85¼ cents four days later. Cotton that fetched $62.50 a bale in July sold for $36.25 in December. Unemployment grew in mill towns, and profit reports were glum. Seth Low, President of the New York Chamber of Commerce, reported that "Europe has placed an embargo on the commerce of the world."

The Administration moved swiftly to restore commerce to its normal level. President Wilson told a special meeting of congressional leaders on July 31 that the sea lanes would not be freed until Britain established naval mastery of the North Atlantic and the American merchant marine was enlarged. The Senate responded by approving a measure to enable naval vessels to be used as cargo ships, but the bill was killed in the House. On August 18, however, Congress made changes in the ship registry law that facilitated the transfer of registry from foreign to American flags. At the same time the Treasury Department established the War Risk Insurance Bureau to provide low-cost insurance for American vessels traveling through war zones. Secretary McAdoo urged

Congress to pass legislation granting the Administration the power to purchase foreign vessels for merchant-marine duty, but this bill was defeated by isolationist elements in the Senate. In every way possible the Administration strove to replace European with American merchantmen, and so enable goods to flow once more to Europe.

More important, however, was the British-German struggle for the North Atlantic. By January 1915, the British had completed their blockade of Germany, while the Central Powers were unable as yet to retaliate. After the war, documents were released showing that America cooperated fully with the British at this time, in some cases seeking British aid in purchasing German vessels to be converted to carriers, which would then bring food and munitions to Britain and France!

While Wilson and McAdoo attempted to open the sea lanes, American business worked to expand the domestic market for their products. A "cotton congress" was convoked by Southern producers, who demanded the government purchase their crops at no less than 75 percent of the average price during the past five years. The money would be obtained through the issuance of Federal Reserve notes. Several cotton men, referring to the aid given the banks, said that if Wilson could help those who preyed on the farmers, he certainly could help the farmers themselves.

The Democratic party controlled the executive and legislative branches of government, and the South dominated the Democratic party of 1914. Inevitably, several Southern senators introduced a bill requiring the Treasury to issue $250 million in bonds, to be used as the basis of loans to cotton planters. The loans would be secured by bales of cotton, whose value would be placed at $50 a bale. Had this measure passed, and had the planters defaulted—as they certainly would have done—the government would have owned most of the bumper cotton crop of 1914. The measure was defeated.

Other plans were put forth. On August 24, several cotton growers suggested that the federal government allow state banks in the South to issue emergency currency based on cotton instead of commercial paper and the like, but McAdoo rejected this plan as unworkable. Instead, the Administration proposed to issue emergency currency based on cotton deposited in licensed ware-houses, on the basis of 75 percent of the existing price. Since the market price was deflated, and the red tape involved in obtaining loans could hold up funds for weeks, few cotton growers used the system. Almost half the 1914 crop was sold, and it never reached its usual consumers.

If the market would not absorb cotton, perhaps charity—albeit disguised—and patriotism would. "Buy a bale of cotton and save the country," became a nationwide slogan in October. Individuals were told that unless the crop was purchased, cotton growers would fail by the score, and their distress would affect every part of the economy and nation. This could be avoided, however, if a million or more Americans each purchased a bale of cotton. Potential buyers were assured that their bales could be stored anywhere, including the back yard, and since cotton was almost indestructible, it could be sold later on at a profit. President Wilson himself started the campaign by purchasing a bale, and others followed. But this drive, like the other relief measures, could not save the 1914 crop. The story was repeated in other agricultural products as American farmers suffered hardships in the first months of the war.

Relief for the farmers came by December, and not from artificial purchase programs or congressional actions. First of all, the European crops of 1914 were as bad as American harvests were good; Europe needed American grain and cotton as much as Americans needed foreign markets. This would not be a temporary phenomenon, for millions of European farmers entered the armed forces, assuring poor harvests for the duration of the war. By late October, Britain had cleared the sea lanes, and American grains were sent to Europe in larger quantities than ever. From December 1914 to April 1915 the United States exported 98 million bushels of wheat, compared with 18 million in the same period in 1913–14. The price of wheat rose steadily, reaching $1.31 by the end of 1914—37 cents more than it had been before the war. In September the wheat farmers had complained that while measures were being taken to aid cotton growers, they were left to collapse. Three months later they found themselves in the greatest period of prosperity they had ever experienced. Nor were they alone in this, for textiles were needed for uniforms, and the price of cotton also rose to beyond its prewar level. The steel companies had more orders than they could handle for merchant ships and munitions, and by January were able to ship their goods to Europe. In November, British artillerymen were rationed as to the number of shells they could fire at the enemy; a year later most of their shells came either from American armories or had American parts or gunpowder in them. Bethlehem Steel, which entered 1914 with a backlog of $25 million in orders, reported a $47 million backlog on January 1, 1915; by the end of the year, the figure was $175 million. In December 1914 the war boom was real and developing —contrary to all that had been expected in early August.

While these developments unfolded—the adjustments at the banks and the securing of the currency, the depression of the export industries and their rapid recovery—Noble, Groesbeck, and their group labored to assure a stable securities market, once trading was resumed. Their tasks were both difficult and delicate. The special committee could not prevent individuals and groups from dealing in securities outside of their exchanges, although it did have the power to punish Exchange members who acted in this fashion. None of the members had the authority of a Morgan, and they could not change the atmosphere of Wall Street overnight by a series of dramatic moves. For the next four months the committee tried to deal with problems as they arose, counteracting pressures from both within and without the Wall Street community rather than initiating programs of its own. Without realizing it at the time, the committee was waiting for the changes in the trade and financial situation to become evident to the public and transform the bleak picture of July 31 into the more hopeful one of mid-December.

From the first, the committee's major problems were to prevent nonmembers from dealing in securities and to win the cooperation of other markets in its program. For example, the New York Curb, the outdoor market which eventually became the American Stock Exchange, offered to buy and sell listed securities on a cash-only basis. John H. Crockett, an independent broker with no Exchange affiliation, advertised in the August 3 *Times* his willingness to deal in securities from his office in the Continental Hotel on 41st Street. S. H. P. Pell & Co., an old, established concern, was forced to suspend operations in early August and petitioned the committee for permission to sell those securities it held as collateral for loans. The committee was able to obtain the co-operation of the Curb market, and dealings stopped there. Pell & Co. was allowed to liquidate its position under the terms of the Exchange constitution, and Crockett stopped advertising after August 5.

The committee was not as successful in preventing auctioneers from dealing in stocks. Storefront establishments sprang up in Boston, Chicago, and Philadelphia, where securities were traded regularly. Although there is no way of knowing the volume of such transactions, it must have been sizable, for several of these auctioneers were obliged to expand their hours and locations in September. None of their dealings were reported in the press of the day, for the committee had secured the cooperation of the financial writers, who agreed to a blackout of news regarding the storefront auction rooms, which in many ways resembled the earliest exchanges in American history—the auctions under the buttonwood tree in the third quarter of the eighteenth century.

Regional stock-exchange leaders cooperated fully with the committee, reporting dealings of Exchange members who attempted to circumvent the trading ban. On August 1, for example, the Baltimore Exchange wrote that a prominent member of the New York Exchange was attempting to sell securities through a trust company in the city at a large discount. Groesbeck called the action "reprehensible," and requested the name of the individual. In the end, no action was taken, since August 1 was only one day after the closing, but the committee made certain the Wall Street community learned of the report, hoping it would dissuade others from taking similar actions.

The Exchange was less successful in preventing the growth of an informal stock market in New York. Reports reached the committee of small groups of men who loitered on New Street, behind the Exchange building, and seemed to be engaged in mysterious transactions. A committee member was dispatched to the scene, and he reported finding nothing but "four boys and a dog." But the group was there, and it grew in size with each day. By the end of August a fairly large number of traders would appear on New Street at ten o'clock and remain in the area until three, openly engaged in securities transactions. The committee investigated the so-called "gutter market" on several occasions, and warnings went out to member firms that those involved in trading would be suspended. By October more than a hundred brokers were engaged in this business, and some took offices in the Columbia Trust Company, hoping to draw customers from other parts of the country as well. The committee was able to stop this, however. By obtaining the cooperation of the Columbia Trust and the Telephone Company, all lines were withdrawn from the offices, and so the attempt to form a new, underground exchange collapsed.

In retrospect, it may be said that the outlaw market did more good than harm. It provided an outlet for those who had to sell their securities to meet other obligations and so prevented several business failures and restored financial confidence to many small investors. More important, perhaps, was the drift of securities prices. Although the newspapers refused to publish New Street quotations, and the outlaw market itself did not distribute them until October, they were not secret to anyone who wanted a quotation. Contrary to expectations, prices were, for the most part, only slightly lower than they had been at the closing. There was little evidence of dumping, despite dire predictions by economists and business analysts. If the bears could take solace in the fact that Europeans were bound to sell their shares to finance the war, the bulls could observe that the dollar was the firmest currency in the world and that there was no evidence of a flight of gold from America.

Finally, the New Street market forced the committee to act quickly to restore the Exchange. On August 12, it decided to open trading on a limited basis at the clearing house. Stocks and bonds could be traded at prices no lower than those of July 30, and all transactions had to be on a cash-only basis. This would prevent speculation and forestall any quick dip in quotations. The clearing-house market did a slow business, with only 5,000 to 7,000 shares traded daily. It did, however, serve to restore a measure of confidence.

By the end of the month the domestic scene seemed calm; the great panic predicted in July and early August had not taken place. American investors appeared certain the war would not destroy the nation; prices were firm on New Street. The only major problem which remained was that of European dumping of American securities. On September 1, the committee asked member firms to report on the amount of money owed Europeans for stocks sold before the closing. It was learned that while Europeans owed American banks almost $700,000, American institutions would have to pay some $18.2 million to Europeans. Not only would this amount be due on the day the Exchange reopened, but more European selling was expected at that time. Meeting in late August, the committee concluded that massive foreign selling could be forestalled by convincing foreign securities holders of the soundness of the American economy.

During the next few weeks the committee entertained many proposals designed to solve this problem. One correspondent suggested legislation making it a misdemeanor for any American to buy securities from foreigners for the duration of the war. Another thought the Exchange should open "strictly for the sale of American securities held by foreign stockholders. If they wish to throw their stocks over we can buy them at our own price." A Western banker suggested the Exchange promote the slogan "Buy a Share of Stock." This campaign, patterned after the one for cotton, might lead many Americans to purchase shares held by foreigners. "This could be not only for the great benefit of this country but for Europe as well, for the reason that if Europe knew that there was a good absorbing power here it necessarily would not dump its stocks at frightful sacrifices." Still another suggestion was for all sales to be made on option contracts, callable by the buyer within sixty days. Thus, no sale would be completed unless the price was higher than it had been at the contract date.

The Exchange considered all of these recommendations, and many more. Meanwhile, conditions continued to improve at the New Street market and demands for a quick opening grew, as hundreds of Wall Street employees who had been without salaries during the closing clamored for their jobs. Once again, the committee reacted rather than acted. On October 5, Benjamin Strong was elected governor of the New York Federal Reserve Bank, and he said that the New York branch of the System would open on November 16. The Curb Association, the executive branch of the Curb Exchange, followed this by declaring its intention to open for trading the same day, while the Chicago Exchange announced its opening for the 23rd. Reluctantly, the Committee agreed to operate a restricted bond market on November 28. Prices rose, encouraging the committee to set a date for trading in stocks.

In early December, conditions for a reopening seemed good. The economy was sound and booming; confidence was evident throughout much of the nation. Thus, December 12 was set as the first day for restricted trading in stocks. Not all issues would be traded, and sales were to be for cash. Short selling and futures contracts were forbidden.

Stocks opened on heavy volume at slightly above the last New Street quotations, and then continued to rise. On December 15, the entire list was opened to restricted trading, and more gains were registered. Prices leveled off by the end of the year, but most issues were above their December 12 openings, and well above the lows registered on New Street.

PRICES OF SELECTED ISSUES IN DECEMBER 1914

	Closing Prices (fractions rounded off)					
Issue	July 30	Dec. 12	Dec. 13	Dec. 15	Dec. 16	Dec. 31
American Can	20	25	26	28	26	25
American Telephone & Telegraph	114	117	117	118	118	116
Bethlehem Steel	30	42	43	42	41	46
General Electric	139	*	*	141	140	140
Miami Copper	18	*	*	19	18	17
Texas Company	113	122	124	138	134	130
U.S. Rubber	45	46	46	57	54	51
U.S. Steel	52	*	*	55	51	41

* No trade
Source: *New York Times*, July 31, December 13–31, 1914, January 1, 1915

FLUCTUATIONS IN SELECTED ISSUES, 1914

Issue	Prices (fractions rounded off) New Street low,		
	July 30	Oct. 23	Dec. 12
Amalgamated Copper	49	38	52
American Smelting & Refining	53	46	57
Atchison, Topeka & Santa Fe	90	83	94
New York Central	80	73	83
Southern Pacific	88	77	91
U.S. Steel	52	39	41

Source: *New York Times*, January 3, 1915

The committee dissolved shortly thereafter, but all restrictions were not removed until April 1, 1915. By that time the Exchange was in the midst of a major bull market, the result of the previously discussed situation. Notwithstanding a sharp correction in May, the market moved upward steadily, ending 1915 on a high note.

PRICES OF SELECTED ISSUES, 1915

Issue	Closing Prices (fractions rounded off)	
	January 1, 1915	December 31, 1915
American Can	25	62
American Telephone & Telegraph	116	127
Bethlehem Steel	46	460
General Electric	140	174
Miami Copper	17	36
Texas Company	130	233
U.S. Rubber	51	56
U.S. Steel	41	89

Source: *New York Times*, January 2, 1915, January 1, 1916

This rise was possible despite the dumping of nearly a half billion dollars of American securities by foreigners. Approximately $53 million of U.S. Steel common alone was sold by foreigners to Americans. Still, the price of the stock more than doubled. Similar figures were reported by other Big Board companies.

What had happened was the natural result of forces already evident in December. Europeans liquidated their holdings at bargain prices, using the money to purchase munitions and other materials from American firms. The increased business led to higher earnings, which were translated into higher prices on Wall Street. In the process, New York replaced London as the financial hub of the world. The expected panic never came, primarily as a result of the quick action taken by the Exchange in closing operations in July. Instead there was a brief flurry of activity, a period of reorganization, and then the beginnings of a major bull market.

The days of panic seemed gone. The Wall Street leadership, though lacking the authority of a J. P. Morgan, had proved itself competent if not brilliant. By the end of 1914 the Federal Reserve System was in operation, and this, too, promised a large measure of stability for the future.

Although Germany lost World War I, the European Allies did not emerge as victors. Czarist Russia was no more; France and Britain had lost an entire generation of their best young men. As the battlefield of the war, France was scarred and barren; Britain's huge overseas investments were depleted, having been used to pay for the victory. The United States, which fought as an associated power, suffered comparatively few casualties and emerged from the armistice the mightiest industrial power in the world. In 1914, America was the leading debtor nation in the international community; in 1919, it was the largest creditor. In 1914, the European powers owned large blocks of American securities; by 1919, these were largely liquidated, and in the next generation Europe would be forced to come to New York to market securities and to Washington to obtain loans.

Little wonder, then, that the United States faced the twenties with a degree of assurance rarely matched in the nation's history. As for Wall Street, this confidence was reinforced by a belief that panics were a thing of the past. Charles Hamilton, first governor of the Federal Reserve Board, gave a hint of this when, delivering his initial address as governor in December 1914, he said:

If in the future business expands unduly under the spirit of speculation, the day of reckoning will come in the future as in the past.

Undue expansion will correct itself just as the air bubble will ultimately burst. I believe, however, that the Federal Reserve System
will materially check undue expansion by making banks conservative
as to their loans, because of the knowledge that any departure from
strictly commercial transactions will take away their ability to liquidate such investments by rediscounting in the Federal Reserve
Banks. . . .

Hamilton concluded that the System would prevent many
panics and cut short any that might appear in the future. One
form of panic, he added, would be relegated to "the museum of
antiquities." This was "the panic generated by distrust of our
banking system."

With words like these, the nation set upon the road to 1929.

11.

1929: THE MAKING OF THE MYTH*

"Some years, like some poets and politicians and some lovely women, are singled out for fame far beyond the common lot, and 1929 was clearly such a year. Like 1066, 1776, and 1914, it is a year that everyone remembers." Thus John Kenneth Galbraith begins his study of the stock-market panic of 1929, *The Great Crash*. In *What a Year!*, an evocative history of the period, Joe Alex Morris tells us that 1929 "was a year of transition. It led out of the roaring, raucous, hell-raising, materialistic and individualistic post-war period and pointed toward an era of tremendous social change. People later would speak of 'before 1929' or 'after 1929' as Noah's children may have spoken of the days before and after The Flood."

That 1929 is thought of as a pivotal year is evident. Along with 1776 and 1861, it is considered the end of an era and the beginning of a new period in the nation's history. To the average American, the 1920s were a period of speakeasies, lawlessness, gaiety, jazz, and "the last fling before America settled down to the serious business of taking its rightful place among the great nations of the world." Soon the period noted for Warren Harding, Calvin Coolidge, Babe Ruth, Scott Fitzgerald, and Sinclair Lewis would give way to the decade of Franklin Roosevelt, Fiorello LaGuardia, Father Coughlin, James T. Farrell, and John Steinbeck.

* A myth, according to most sociologists, is a belief which is held by a group to be true, and is accepted on faith rather than on examination of relevant evidence.

Many Americans seems to think of their history in terms of decades, and 1929 separated the happy twenties from the depression thirties quite neatly. Historians, who are wary of such divisions, and who usually think in terms of continuities rather than discontinuities, have tended to accept 1929 as a major dividing point nonetheless, forgetting that the major literary figures of the thirties wrote in the twenties, and that the men of the twenties did not throw down their pens in October 1929. Roosevelt and LaGuardia were well-known figures in 1928; Herbert Hoover was an important political force throughout the next decade. Indeed, there was not a single major movement of the 1930s which could not be traced to the earlier period. A perusal of the documents of the period—newspapers, magazines, speeches, novels—indicate that contemporaries did not look upon 1929 as a pivotal point in their lives; nor did they view the stock-market crash of October as anything worse than that of 1907, 1893, or 1873. Its importance was seen in retrospect, not prospect.

There are many reasons for the mythology of the stock-market crash of 1929, but the most important of these was singled out by the author of *The Great Crash*, who himself is partly responsible for its perpetuation. "As a year, 1929 has always been peculiarly the property of the economists," he writes, and historians as a group have been content to accept their conclusions. But while the economists have written excellent analyses of the reasons for the Great Crash, they often grant slight importance to the psychological and social factors involved in this event. Further, they have never shown clearly and convincingly the ties between the stock-market crash of October and the depression of the 1930s. Scholars can argue with great force that the depression actually began in 1928, indicating perhaps that the October crash was an effect rather than a cause. Others observe that the miseries associated with the depression were evident in the midsummer of 1930, but do not show how this was caused by activities on Wall Street nine months earlier. Indeed, writers that summer considered the market crash as one reason for the economic slowdown, but thought others to be more important. The decline in auto sales, inventory problems, chronic difficulties on the farms and in the mines, European complications, Prohibition—these were the major culprits. Only later, when a nation deep in depression had to find a scapegoat, did the businessman go into eclipse, and did the Great Crash become the symbol of a nation's entrapment by the forces of Wall Street. The persistence of the myth was assured when, in 1938, Richard Whitney was found guilty of malfeasance in securities operations and was subsequently incarcerated. As Alistair Cooke has observed, Whitney became a symbol of business chicanery in the twenties just as Alger Hiss was to become a symbol of New Deal disloyalty in the thirties. Too much can be made of symbols, and to convict entire generations or groups is both unfair and simplistic. Furthermore, it obfuscates rather than clarifies, and leads to moralizing rather than understanding.

If comparisons are to be ventured and simplifications made— as they inevitably will be—perhaps 1929 could better be compared to 1775 and 1860 than to 1776 and 1861. The battles of Lexington and Concord in 1775 took place at a time when only a small minority of the population wanted a war with Britain; the Declaration of Independence came later. During the Presidential election of 1860 most Southerners did not want to secede from the Union; things were different by the time of Fort Sumter. The stock-market crash occurred at a moment when most Americans had great confidence in the political and business leadership of the nation; this would not be the situation during the last two years of the Hoover Administration. With this in mind—together with the knowledge that hindsight can deceive and that the historian must have an awareness of the period on its own terms and a sympathy for his subject—we may trace the steps leading to and the causes of the greatest stock-market event in American history.

As is customary, the New York Stock Exchange and other markets remained closed on New Year's Day, 1929. The newspapers of that January 1 carried stories of police raids on speakeasies; thousands of New Year's Eve parties were interrupted by heavy knocking, followed by the crash of axes against wooden doors. In Albany, Franklin D. Roosevelt took his oath of office and assumed the governorship of the state of New York. Al Smith said goodbye to the city amid the tearful farewells of those who had worked for him during the 1928 Presidential campaign. The newspapers carried few stories of President-elect Hoover, who would wait more than two months before taking office in Washington. President Coolidge sent New Year's greetings, but he too was not engaged in newsworthy activities.

The New York Times printed many stories of retrospective glances abroad. Chiang Kai-shek acclaimed China's progress, and President von Hindenburg saw nothing to mar Germany's prosperity. The Soviet Union reported that its economy was moving forward at a record pace. There were some troubles in Britain. Unemployment was high and growth low; throughout the year there had been talk of devaluation. But there had been some progress in solving these difficulties, and Prime Minister Ramsay MacDonald thought that 1929 would see Britain turning the corner.

The business pages carried a story which evoked feelings of nostalgia and solidity. J. P. Morgan & Co. announced that H. S. Morgan, T. S. Lamont, and H. P. Davison would enter the firm as partners. The old generation was still vigorous and powerful; now a new generation would be prepared to take control when the heads of the House retired.

Interviews with business leaders showed them to be optimistic about the new year. True, there had been a slowing down in some areas, and the farm situation remained a weak spot in the economy. Some economists warned that credit purchases were getting out of hand; that the Federal Reserve's increase in the rediscount rate had not curbed speculation; that the foreign trade and reparations situation was dangerous. True, the gross national product had reached a peak of $90.8 billion, but gross capital formation was down while consumer expenditures were up. This seemed to mean that industry was slowing down, but sales were on the rise. What would happen when the purchases stopped? Was a depression possible?

Charles Mitchell, president of the National City Bank and a member of the New York Federal Reserve Bank, a major spokesman for the business community, scoffed at such talk. "Business is entering the New Year upon a high level of activity and with confidence in the continuation of prosperity," he said. Certainly the use of credit had expanded, and stock prices had zoomed in the last few months of the year, but these were both normal and desirable. "No complaint regarding the level of stock prices, how-

ever, is justified except from the standpoint of credit strain."
Mitchell could see no signs of such strains. Nor could Thomas
Watson of International Business Machines, who said, "We may
look with confidence to the progress of business in 1929." "All
major indicators point to a prosperous coming year," was the
opinion of Lewis Pierson of the Irving Trust Company. *Time*
Magazine seemed to agree, naming Walter P. Chrysler as "Man
of the Year," citing as reasons his introduction of the Plymouth
and DeSoto autos, his purchase of Dodge Brothers for $160 mil-
lion, and the beginning of construction on the Chrysler Building,
to be "the world's tallest skyscraper, a 68-story colossus." At *Time*
headquarters, Henry Luce and his staff were preparing to bring
out a new magazine, *Fortune*, dedicated to the proposition and
the "generally accepted commonplace that America's great achievement has been Business."

The financial pages of *The New York Times* carried its customary summary of the year's trading, which offered proof of what
most Americans already knew: the price of common stocks had
risen sharply in 1928. For example, Allied Chemical & Dye went
from 154 to 250; Chrysler from 63 to 132; General Electric from
136 to 221. Most stock-market indicators showed a rise of more
than 70 percent for the year. In the upward push, volume expanded greatly, going from 576,999,875 shares to 920,550,032.
Many observers thought that 1929 would be even better.

Alexander Dana Noyes, the *Times*'s venerable financial editor,
disagreed. For months he had been arguing for a correction, and
on January 1, 1929, he thought the situation ahead unclear.

Conservative judgement has only past experience to guide it; but the
rather uniform teaching of that experience is that an era of violent
speculation for the rise begins, like that which began at the end of
1924, in abnormally easy money; that in due time, if continued, it
converts the comfortable credit situation into one of great stringency;
that speculation ignores the high money rates, willingly paying the
price demanded for credit procured from unusual sources; but that
these abnormal facilities suddenly fail it in the end . . . conservative
prophets seem as yet to be too puzzled over the events of 1928 to
make categorical predictions.

To be sure, Noyes was a respected figure, and others were saying the same things about the rapid rise on Wall Street. For the most part, these were "old-timers"; their opinions were discounted by most speculators as ideas of men who did not understand the new type of stock market. Noyes still argued that good common stocks should not sell for more than ten times earnings. But what of a rapidly growing company in a dynamic economy? Couldn't such an issue sell for twenty or even thirty times earnings? Thirty times 1928 earnings would be ten times 1931 earnings—and equivalent to one or two times 1937 earnings! Surely such a stock deserved a higher price—and it quickly reached that price. What of Noyes's prediction of a "decline," "correction," or "fall"? Wall Street observers might have noted that Noyes had spoken that way when the market was at 80 on the Dow-Jones index; now it was nearly 300, and he hadn't changed his tune. If one had accepted Noyes's analysis, he would have failed to take advantage of the greatest bull market in American history. And what if there were declines from time to time? The market had always recovered from them, and then gone on to post new highs. Thus, Noyes was read, but not taken seriously. Market volume increased in January, as more people bought stock than ever before.

Often the picture is presented of a nation gone wild over the stock market in 1929. Although the market was a dramatic place in that year, this portrayal is by no means accurate. In 1929 American corporations reported having some 20 million shareholders, but many of these were counted several times. More realistic is an estimate, based on tax returns, of 9 million shareholders, but this excludes those who did not declare earnings, file returns, or in other ways managed to elude the Treasury Department, while it does include holders of World War I Liberty Bonds. Joseph McCoy, chief actuary of the Treasury, wrote in 1928 of some 3 million shareholders, excluding in-and-out speculators. McCoy found that some individuals reported hundreds of stock transactions in 1927, and that many could be counted as often as 500 times as a result. According to his report, most shareholders lived in cities and could be considered "upper middle class." Stock ownership was broadening, he concluded. Only 7 percent of all outstanding stocks were owned by millionaires; increasingly, said McCoy, middle-class America was becoming securities-conscious.

This is not to say that 3 million Americans speculated on Wall Street. Most purchased stocks for cash and then put them away in safe-deposit boxes. In 1929 there were less than 1.6 million active accounts reported by brokerage firms, and here, too, duplications complicate the picture. An active speculator might have as many as five or six accounts, while the "big boys" could have dozens, often three or more with a single firm. And not all of these accounts were necessarily speculative; in the late twenties it was common for a young executive to invest regularly. Such a man would have an active account, but his purchases would often be of a conservative nature.

Perhaps the best gauge of speculative activity was the number of margin accounts: in 1929, there were some 600,000 of these—out of a population of 120 million. These were the people most responsible for the churning action on Wall Street, and the ones criticized for irresponsibility by conservative investment analysts like Alexander Noyes.

Margin buying was not a new phenomenon on Wall Street. During the last decades of the nineteenth century many conservative investors would buy on margin. In effect, they would borrow money from the investment banker to purchase a stock or bond, with the security becoming the collateral for the loan. If the bond paid 8 percent, and the loan interest was 6 percent, then the borrower was actually receiving the extra 2 percent in return for the risk of owning the bond. Since most investors were more concerned with interest and dividends than appreciation, margin buying seemed good sense.

The speculators of the 1920s used margin in a similar fashion, but for a different reason. The rationale could be summed up in one word—the magic word on Wall Street in the twenties—"leverage." Just at a lever may be used to raise a heavy weight which could not be lifted otherwise, so leverage was employed to purchase securities worth far more than the original investment in cash. The individual who went into debt when he bought a Model T on time understood leverage. He might have had only $100, while the auto cost $400. He would finance the car through the dealer, giving him a note for $300, and would enter into a contract to pay so much money every month. The car itself would be the collateral for the loan. If the buyer defaulted, then the tin lizzie would be repossessed. More than $7 billion worth of consumer durables were sold through such credit arrangements in 1929. The use of credit was hailed by many business leaders—and enjoyed by thousands of consumers. Why should a family spend years saving for an automobile while being denied its use, when it could have the auto while it saved? Everyone seemed to benefit from credit—the consumer, the manufacturer, the distributor, the banks—and none suffered. Indeed, *True Story* Magazine seemed to consider credit one of the most important discoveries since the wheel. In an advertisement of October 14, 1929, the editors said:

For thousands of years the matter of credit has existed almost entirely between capital and business. Capital the lender, business the borrower. And in practically every case *with some sort of material wealth* in the form of collateral as the borrower's guarantee.

Now, suddenly the whole credit fabric, built up over thousands of years, has been changed almost over night. Within the past four or five years an annual obligation of approximately *two billion dollars* of that stronghold of credit, in a comparatively new form, has been passed down *to the individual* as a matter of *personal credit*, the only form of collateral being the very thing he bought!

In 1921, real income per capita was $522; by 1928, the figure had risen to $676. More Americans had more disposable income than ever before, and given the nature of advertising and the use of credit, the ability to satisfy his needs without waiting to accumulate large sums of money. The unleashing of this purchasing power gave a great stimulus to business, which in turn spurred employment, leading to an increase in the number of wage earners, who themselves used credit, thus enabling the upward cycle to continue. Inexorably, the increase in corporation earnings led to a rise in securities prices, and in the twenties this led to the use of leverage—disguised as and often presented as credit—on Wall Street.

If a consumer could purchase a $1,000 automobile by putting

down $100 and taking a note for $900, why couldn't he purchase $1,000 worth of the automobile company's stock the same way? It seemed good sense and good business practice; indeed, it made more sense than buying the car itself, for while the auto would depreciate over time, the stock was sure to rise. Thus, a stock buyer might purchase a share of Chrysler Corporation in 1926 when it sold for $50 a share by putting down $5 and borrowing the additional $45 from his broker. Chrysler sold for $150 in 1928, for a rise of 200 percent. But the stock buyer, in this same period, would have seen his $5 investment rise to $105 ($150 minus $45), for an appreciation of 2,000 percent! The market rise attracted new investors to Wall Street; the power of leverage in a rising market encouraged many of them to buy on margin.

Early in the decade investment analysts observed that most corporations had used leverage for generations in the form of their financial structures. They noted that bonds could be viewed as borrowed money, while stocks were claims against earnings after bond interest was paid. In 1923, Noyes offered as an example a firm with 100,000 shares of common stock and $1 million in bonds which required $50,000 a year to service. If the corporation showed a profit of $100,000, then the common stocks would receive $50,000, or $.50 a share. A doubling of the profit to $200,000 would leave $150,000 for the common, or $1.50 a share—a tripling of earnings. Thus, the more leverage a firm could manage in its financing, the better off the holders of common stock. In the prewar period, investors preferred bonds to stock since they offered more security; in the 1920s, the positions were reversed, as investors realized that stocks brought more "action."

By 1927, the leverage concept in corporate structure led to the creation of highly leveraged investment trusts. The investment trust was not new; it existed to offer professional management to those who purchased its shares. Generally speaking, the pre-World War trusts sold common stocks, but no bonds, and so were unleveraged. The new trusts of the late 1920s were highly leveraged. United States & Foreign Securities, for example, had three classes of stock (one common and two preferred) as well as a bond issue. Founded in 1924, U.S. & Foreign became the prototype for many of the 265 trusts formed in 1929 alone. The new trust companies of that year sold some $3 billion in securities to the public, and this money was almost immediately reinvested through stock purchases, many of them on margin. In mid-1929, an investor might purchase shares in an investment trust on margin, while the trust itself was using margin. It was conceivable that a buyer would put down $10 for $100 worth of stock, which itself represented $10 in equity and $90 in debt! In the early autumn of 1929, leveraged trusts were purchasing other leveraged trusts, compounding the situation still further. In this way, a wall of credit was being erected on Wall Street. If stocks rose even slightly, clerks could become wealthy; a ten-point rise in the Dow-Jones average could turn members of the upper middle class into millionaires. But what would happen if stocks declined ten points? In that eventuality, the margin buyer would be wiped out, for as the value of his collateral declined, he would be called upon to present "more margin." Should he be unable to raise the money, the lender would be free to sell the securities for what they would bring. Such sales would further depress the market, leading to more margin calls. There was an upward spiral evident to all in the rising markets of 1928–29; the possibility of a declining spiral does not seem to have been taken into account. One might say this was a "bicycle market." Like the rider of a bicycle, as long as the vehicle moved forward, it was easy to make progress and keep one's balance. But should the forward motion be stopped, the bicycle would fall to one side, throwing the rider. This was the fear of men like Alexander Noyes and other "old-timers."

If credit, margin, and leverage were the key words of the 1929 market, then the key men were those who obtained the funds needed to complete the purchases. These were the brokers, often affiliated with an investment banking firm. Their stock in trade was "tips"; their vehicle was "call money." Without the tips, they could not attract and keep customers, and without call money, they could not provide the wherewithal for the purchases. There was a great demand for both in the Wall Street of 1929, and a great supply to fill the demand.

The abundance of call money was made possible by many factors, which involve such diverse individuals as Benjamin Strong (head of the New York Federal Reserve Bank), Winston Churchill,

Montague Norman (of the Bank of England), and Secretary of the Treasury Andrew Mellon. Call money availability was affected by the position of the pound sterling, World War I reparations, the Dawes Plan, corporate earnings, the Federal Reserve structure, and America's foreign trade position. Throughout the 1920s, these men and forces operated so as to assure easy money for Wall Street.

The United States had emerged from the World War as the greatest financial power in the world; New York had replaced London as the leading capital market. A major reason for this was the huge amount of money owed America by the Allies, who had purchased war materials here during the first three years of the war, while America was a neutral. The Allies were able to pay their debts only after obtaining a large reparations bill from Germany. And the Germans would have been unable to meet these obligations without American loans and investments in the Reich. Thus, the United States loaned money to Germany, which then went to Britain and France, which in turn came back to America. In this way, Europe and America were inextricably united during the postwar world. Problems in Berlin quickly affected New York.

Winston Churchill was Chancellor of the Exchequer in 1925. Eager for Britain to once again assume world leadership, and viewing the pound sterling as a symbol of Britain's greatness, he insisted on returning the pound to its prewar relationship to the dollar and gold. In that year, the pound was pegged at $4.86.

The rate was unreasonable, and had the effect of pricing many British goods out of the world market. A flight from the pound to the dollar began at once, as Britain had its first of several financial crises in 1925. Indeed, gold from all parts of Europe came to America in great quantities in the next two years.

Had the situation continued, most European nations would have had to leave the gold standard. Given the complexities of the reparations situation, the United States would be dragged down with them in a major financial crisis. Accordingly, Secretary of the Treasury Andrew Mellon and Benjamin Strong eagerly accepted invitations from European central bankers to a conference on the question. In 1927 Montague Norman of the Bank of England, Hjalmar Schacht of the Reichsbank, and Charles Rist of the Bank of France met with their American counterparts. The situation might yet be saved, they argued, if the Federal Reserve cut its rediscount rate. Such an action would lower American interest rates in relation to those in Europe, and therefore attract funds to European banks. At the same time, low rates would encourage borrowing in America and stoke the speculative furnaces. Strong was unhappy about the latter probability, but in the end proved willing to further stimulate an already active American economy in order to save international liquidity. In 1927, the Federal Reserve lowered its discount rate from 4 to 3½ percent.

Wall Street greeted the lowered rate. It meant businesses could borrow funds more easily, and so expand operations and profits. More important, it assured a continual flow of cheap credit for the call-money market. Member banks were able to borrow money from the Federal Reserve at 3½ percent and then lend it as call money at 5 percent, making an easy profit of 1½ percent. Thus, the international situation was resolved in such a way as to encourage speculation on Wall Street.

Secretary Mellon was to stimulate activity in still another fashion. Throughout his long tenure at the Treasury he worked for and often achieved lower taxes for corporations. Oftentimes this resulted in companies receiving windfalls, and they faced the rather pleasant prospect of huge cash surpluses—more than enough for operating expenses and expansion.

In 1928, the demand for call money reached new highs, and banks found that the cries would continue at more than 5 percent. Inexorably the rate rose—to 6, 7, 8, and finally to more than 20 percent! Customers appeared willing to pay any interest asked for loans. It seemed to make sense. If a stock rose 100 percent in a year, why quibble about the difference between an 8 percent loan and one for 20 percent?

The corporations, realizing that 20 percent could be had in the call-money market, began to look at their cash surpluses and expansion programs in a new light. Why buy bonds at 5 percent, or invest in a new plant which might return 10 percent, when it would be much easier to lend money to margin buyers at 20 percent? Such loans were easily liquidated and seemed safe. Accordingly, many large companies entered the market for margin money. Electric Bond & Share disposed of $156 million this way, and Bethlehem Steel a like amount. Chrysler Corporation had $60 million in the money market, and Anaconda Copper $33 million. By October 1929, some $6.6 billion had been loaned by corporations in this manner. Much of this could be lost in market declines; the managers knew this, but they, like most Americans, did not expect stock prices to fall severely.

Almost $2 billion worth of bank deposits were invested in brokers' loans by October. The investment bank of J. P. Morgan & Co. had close connections with the First National Bank, the Bankers Trust, and the National Bank of Commerce; the National City Bank had its own investment-banking affiliates. In 1929, investment banking and commercial banking were closely related, meaning that the depositor in many banks was, in effect, making it possible for that bank to use his money to invest in call-money loans. If the market collapsed, the investments would be worth little, and could conceivably result in the closing of many banks and trust companies. But the bankers, like the corporation presidents and treasurers, did not expect a decline on Wall Street.

The easy money situation would not have been so serious in itself had it not been for complicating factors. Had the public purchased high-grade bonds or blue-chip comon stocks on 90 percent margin, the possibility of calls would not have been eliminated, but at least they would have been less possible than was the case. The speculators of the late twenties, dazzled by dreams of wealth, searched for those among their number who had "inside information," or knew how to "move a stock." As a result, a race of tipsters and heroes appeared, who were avidly followed by a host of new investors. John Levinson, who managed several syndicates in the late twenties, worked in conjunction with Raleigh Curtis, who wrote a column called "The Trader" for the *New York Daily News*. Levinson would establish a position in a security and then tell Curtis to speak favorably of it. The readers would purchase the stock, sending its price upward. Levinson made large sums of money, which he shared with his partner. Both men felt guiltless; after all, those who had purchased the stock also shared in the benefits from the rise. It seemed perfect: there were no losers in such transactions. Market operator David Lion had a similar arrangement with William McMahon, president of the McMahon Institute of Economic Research. A. Newton Plummer, a newcomer to Wall Street, was often hired to plant stories in financial and entertainment pages; a Plummer "leak" could send the price of almost any stock rocketing.

Then there were the "mystery men" of Wall Street—fabled figures who somehow knew all, and used their knowledge to make millions. Jesse Livermore, credited with having discovered new methods of stock analysis, was one of these. Arthur Cutten, a former Chicago bookkeeper who arrived on Wall Street in 1925 after having made a fortune on the Chicago grain markets, was another. The Fisher brothers, who controlled a fortune after selling their business to General Motors, were rumored to be in possession of a pool of $500 million, which they could throw behind any stock they thought might move. William C. Durant, the founder of General Motors, was said to have used his inside information to double his money each month. And there were others, all well-known to regular readers of financial pages. Should it be rumored that Durant or Livermore had "taken an interest" in a security, it would rise a half-dozen points. By mid-1929, the stock market resembled a sporting arena. If the Yankees could win the pennant because Babe Ruth was on the team, then RCA could move ahead forty points because Cutten and the Fishers were behind it. To Wall Streeters the drama of the Dempsey-Tunney fight was overshadowed by a bull-bear struggle between Cutten and Livermore. "Mr. Cutten may be said to be the leader of the largest and most influential group operating in the market today," said *The Times* in early September 1928. The Fisher brothers, Durant, and broker Mike Meehan were said to be members of his team, and rumors of their purchases and sales could determine the fate of a security.

When John J. Raskob left for Europe in March, he told reporters that General Motors stock should sell for 225. At the time its price was 187. Within two days, GM was over 210; a week later it reached 225. Theodore Merseles of Montgomery Ward had a reputation as a management genius, and this led Montgomery Ward stock to rise 100 points in three months.

In mid-December, Merseles joined the board of directors of Celanese Corporation, a firm which had little to do with merchandising. Still, Merseles had become a magic name; Celanese stock rose 5½ points the next day, and more than 20 in the next two weeks. In late January Wall Street learned of the formation of the Petroleum Corporation of America, capitalized at $110.5 million. The securities sold out in a matter of hours; the Street heard rumors that "Cutten-Fisher" was behind it. Much of the money came from banks and brokers' loans. Several months later, an issue of Standard Brands common stock was floated, but not before insiders were permitted to buy the stock at reduced prices.

Among those on the preferential list were Bernard Baruch, William G. McAdoo, Marshall Field, Norman Davis, and many other business and political leaders. "Our whole business system would break down in a day if there was not a high sense of moral responsibility in our business world." So spoke Herbert Hoover in early 1929. In retrospect, it is clear that this responsibility was lacking on Wall Street.

Although the list of important investors and prominent figures involved in wheeling and dealing on Wall Street was large and impressive, there were several aspects of its composition that worried experienced stock-market followers. In the first place, many of them were from the West. While Wall Street is no more sectionally conscious than any other part of the nation, Western speculators had always had a reputation for wildness. Several times in the past, waves of new millionaires—usually self-made men—had descended on Wall Street. Optimistic, self-confident, and relatively unsophisticated in financial matters, they were inevitably on the bull side and would push stocks to record highs in attempts to double their money. Their presence had been noted during the great bull market of 1901 by several commentators. "The Westerners," said the financial editor of the *New York Tribune,* " are leading the Wall Street parade."

Now, a generation later, *The New York Times* wrote in a similar fashion of Cutten, Durant, Raskob, the Fishers, and others in their group. "It is easily established that the West controls the present market," wrote an observer on September 30, 1928, "and that the orthodox market players of the East, meaning mainly conservative bears on the Stock Exchange and plenty of plungers too, have dropped millions of dollars in an ineffectual attempt to stop the tidal wave of stock buying. The difference has been that the Eastern market players, including most of the Stock Exchange members, have been playing the market by rote, following customs, precedents, rules of order, and established theories. The Westerners have been playing by ear and they have gotten away with it. The cash profits that they have taken from the market have been tremendous. Their paper profits are even larger." Raskob, whose prominent position at General Motors excused his eccentricity in fighting for Al Smith in the 1928 election, wrote in the *Ladies' Home Journal* that "everyone should be rich." If a person saved fifteen dollars a month and invested it in good common stocks, within twenty years—given the rapid growth of stock prices—he would have $80,000. There was still a faster way to success. Raskob suggested that a group of public-minded citizens get together to form an investment organization for "the little fellow." The investor would give the group $200 and a note for $300. In return, he would receive $500 worth of carefully selected stocks. Then, the purchaser would pay off the note at $25 a month. Since stock prices would invariably rise more than that, the purchaser in effect would receive $500 in stock for his $200 in cash! From anyone else, at a different time, the scheme would have been ridiculed. But this was 1929, and the writer was John Raskob; by September, plans were afoot to put the program into operation.

No one thought to ask, "What does Raskob know of the stock market?" Or the Fishers? Or Durant? These were businessmen who, while aware of financial problems, were unsophisticated in the ways of Wall Street. The other great speculators—Livermore, Cutten, and their groups—were not affiliated with any major investment banker. They were plungers and gamblers, who would find more comfort today in Las Vegas than at a board meeting of Lehman Brothers. In past bull markets, such figures as J. P. Morgan and Jacob Schiff—and even Commodore Vanderbilt and Jay Gould—were at the center of things. These were men who knew both business and speculation, and were aware of the relationship between the two. Such men were generally absent from the arena in 1929. It was, then, a market led by amateurs and gamblers, and followed by the hopeful and simple.

Significantly, no figure important in the last major panic—that of 1907 was central to the Wall Street arena in 1929. The men of the late 1920s knew only bull markets and sharp, though temporary, dips, such as those of 1921 and 1924. Would they recognize a bear market when they saw it? Were they aware of the signs of overconfidence which often preceded the fall? The answer was "No" to both questions.

In March 1929, Paul Warburg, a respected banker, an ancient Wall Street figure, and the leader of Kuhn, Loeb, spoke of the market. Warburg had seen the 1907 panic, and had been a major figure on the Street for two generations. Now he observed danger signals, and he warned that prices were too high. The rise of 1928 and 1929, he said, was "quite unrelated to respective increases in plant, property, or earning power." The "colossal volume of loans" had reached "a saturation point." Unless "the orgy of unrestrained speculation" were ended, it would lead to a market crash and "also bring about a general depression involving the entire country." Warburg's thinking was branded "obsolete," and he was accused of "sandbagging American prosperity." The rise continued.

E. H. H. Simmons, president of the Exchange, was an experienced, cautious man, who chose his words carefully. Not desiring to cause a panic, but at the same time wishing to warn of recklessness, he spoke of the market in May. "Speculation in securities is not at all a bad thing in itself," he opined. "It is, however, necessary to recognize that we may have too much or too little security speculation. . . ." Simmons concluded that he could do nothing about such gambling. "The New York Stock Exchange is not itself concerned with the course of security prices, so long as these prices result from fair, free, and open markets."

How fair and free were the markets? By midsummer, manipulations were openly discussed in brokers' offices. Readers of market letters would learn that "Radio will be taken in hand at 1:30 tomorrow." Accordingly, Radio moved ahead. General Motors "will move sometime Thursday morning." And GM would indeed move—usually because of the purchases of the readers of the letters. Plummer, McMahon, and Curtis continued to tout stocks effectively. The "Old Counselor"—really a University of Chicago professor—appeared on radio to offer advice on stock purchases, and his words were listened to by millions. Even so great a market figure as Bernard Baruch urged the purchase of common stocks. In a June interview with Bruce Barton published in the *American*, Baruch stated that "the economic condition of the world seems on the verge of a great forward movement." The bears, he said, had no mansions on Fifth Avenue. Baruch continued to exude confidence during the next few months.

But how secure was this master speculator, who had millions while Cutten was in elementary school? In Scotland for grouse hunting in August, Baruch worried about the high prices of seemingly worthless issues. He began to sell stocks and, with the proceeds, to buy gold. Baruch was concerned because many of his friends were still buying, and at one point was almost convinced he was wrong, and that prosperity would continue. Then, while walking to his Wall Street office, Baruch was stopped by an old beggar to whom he had often given a coin. "I have a good tip for you," said the beggar to the shrewdest market figure of the time. "When beggars and shoeshine boys, barbers and beauticians can tell you how to get rich it is time to remind yourself that there is no more dangerous illusion than the belief that one can get something for nothing," wrote Baruch years later. Baruch sold out—but continued to issue optimistic statements to the press.

Another Wall Street figure, who had also survived the 1907 crash, thought prices were too high. When he told his friends, he was accused of instability, and told to see a psychiatrist. The advice was taken, and the doctor listened to the arguments. The patient was told he was not insane—he was right! Then the psychiatrist joined Charles Merrill on a trip to their brokers, and both men sold their holdings.

What was the public to think? Noyes and a few other analysts warned of dangers in high prices. Roger Babson told people a crash was coming, and that it "may be terrific." But Economics Professor Joseph Lawrence and Edwin Kemmerer of Princeton said the opposite; indeed, they predicted still greater highs for stock prices. Professor Charles Dice of Ohio State, in his *New Levels in the Stock Market,* claimed that prices were only "registering the tremendous changes that were in progress." Economists Joseph Davis of Stanford and Edmund Day of the University of Michigan became advisors for investment trusts; they too thought prices would rise. Irving Fisher, one of America's leading economists, traveled from Harvard weekly to give talks to business groups and issue statements which—couched in proper academic phraseology and at times accompanied by complicated formulas—denied all accusations of manipulation. Later on, just as the market slide began, Fisher was to make one of the most memorable predictions in Wall Street history. "Stock prices," he said "have reached what looks like a permanently high plateau." Fisher's Harvard colleagues disputed his cheerfulness; the Harvard Economic Society was markedly wary early in the year. But as prices continued to rise, they changed their tune, and the Society indicated a general belief—shared by most of their colleagues throughout the nation—that prices were not unreasonable. The professors were listened to by a public eager for such predictions. There were few bears on Wall Street, and fewer still on university campuses throughout the nation.

One who had doubts in mid-1928 was Benjamin Strong. Still convinced that the easy money program of the Federal Reserve had saved Europe's financial structure, Strong nonetheless was worried about speculative activities in New York. A rise in the interest rate would dampen the American boom, and might cause difficulties in Europe, but Strong, then in the last weeks of his life, thought such a move was necessary. Accordingly, the New York Federal Reserve Bank raised its rediscount rate from 3½ to 4 percent that summer. The tight money policy was further advanced when the Federal Reserve raised the rate to 4½ percent, and finally to 5 percent in December. Commercial banks were obliged to raise their rates in sympathy, and the price of call money rose sharply, hitting 10 percent by year's end. But still the volume of trading expanded, as did the amount of call money outstanding.

Now the central bank used another of its weapons. Through

open market operations, government bonds were sold heavily, in the hope of drawing funds from the economy and so "drying up" the sources of call money. But the demand continued; call rates rose to 12 percent, with no end in sight. Such levels had been reached before, but only during panic times. The Street was optimistic in January; was a panic to follow? The question went unanswered; the speculation continued.

In February, Chairman Roy Young of the Federal Reserve issued two warnings against excessive speculation. Unless private banks curbed the unwise use of call money, the Federal Reserve would be obliged to enter the picture directly. The market had fallen sharply the previous December, but then recovered to close the month at a gain. Now, in March 1929, the market again plunged downward.

Young's warnings were followed by indications from the new President, Herbert Hoover, that he considered Wall Street speculation worth an inquiry. Rumors were afloat of many things, the least of which would be a further rise in the rediscount rate, and possibly federal legislation to curb speculation. Wall Street had operated without interference during the Harding and Coolidge administrations. Hoover and Young spoke as though a new period of controls was about to dawn. The speculators demanded a response from their leaders to this threat.

It was not long in coming. Charles Mitchell, though still a director of the New York Federal Reserve Bank, was deeply involved in stock-market activities, had made $6 million during the boom, and meant to preserve those conditions which had made this fortune possible. As head of the powerful National City Bank, he spoke loudly to the financial community and Washington, announcing that if and when the Federal Reserve attempted to curb lending, he would advance $25 million to traders —meaning the call-money market. "We feel that we have an obligation which is paramount to any Federal Reserve warning," exclaimed Mitchell, "or anything else, to avert any dangerous crisis in the money market." Professor Lawrence applauded Mitchell's action and attacked Young for having "undertaken a punitive excursion against the stock market without adequate provocation and in contravention of every principle of justice."

Lawrence issued a battle cry against the central bank, calling for Wall Streeters to declare their independence of the outmoded institution, and patronize only those banks which either ignored or left the system. "Although the provinces dominate in politics there is no reason why that dominion should extend into the field of finance."

The provinces answered through Carter Glass, Senator from Virginia and a father of the Federal Reserve System. Glass called for strong federal actions against the New York banking community, an end to speculation, and Mitchell's resignation from the New York Federal Reserve Bank. But Hoover said nothing; his hands were tied, for the Exchange was a New York corporation, and came under the control of the Governor's office. Franklin D. Roosevelt, in Albany for less than four months, also refused to act. The Congress failed to introduce new legislation. Wall Street had clashed with Washington, and had won its battle. Prices rose in late March, as a powerful surge of buying took place.

The market advanced sharply that summer of 1929, though a few dips occurred in July and August. Each decline led to renewed warnings from the few Cassandras, but they decreased in number and strength as the market rallied to post new highs after each decline. Even the *Times* was finally obliged to admit that Noyes's warnings may have been unduly conservative, and the financial editor received many letters from devoted readers who complained of his caution, observing that it had cost them large profits. In an article of September 1, the *Times* said:

One of the most striking features of the present chapter in Stock Market history is the failure of the trading community to take serious alarm at portents which once threw Wall Street into a state of alarm bordering on demoralization. In particular, the recent disregard of the succession of "smashed high records" for brokers' loans astonishes the older school of market operators. Undoubtedly the heavy margins required of traders by the commission houses have done much to build up this assurance. Traders who would formerly have taken the precaution of reducing their commitments just in case a reaction should set in, now feel confident that they can ride out any storm which may develop. But more particularly, the repeated demonstrations which the market has given of its ability to "come back" with renewed strength after a sharp reaction has engendered a spirit of indifference to all the old time warnings. As to whether this attitude may not sometime itself become a danger-signal, Wall Street is not agreed.

The weather was unusually hot that summer, and theater managers reported ticket sales were down; not even the "talkies" could attract full houses. The Philadelphia Athletics, led by Mickey Cochrane and Jimmy Foxx, and managed by Connie Mack, met Joe McCarthy's Chicago Cubs, powered by Rogers Hornsby and Hack Wilson, in the World Series, and took the championship four games to one. Still, the boardrooms throughout the nation were crammed with speculators and interested observers, who ignored the heat, the Series, and all else, in their dreams of wealth. The *Saturday Evening Post* printed a poem to illustrate the times:

> Oh, hush thee, my babe, granny's bought some more shares
> Daddy's gone out to play with the bulls and the bears,
> Mother's buying on tips, and she simply can't lose,
> And baby shall have some expensive new shoes!

Early that September, while the nation followed the series, went to the beaches, and purchased fall clothing, the stock market ran out of steam.

There was no sharp decline in September; rather, the market failed to continue its successes of the summer. As measured by the *Time*'s index, stocks fluctuated between 295 and 304 the last week in August; the range was 298–312 the last week in September. By October 1, it was evident that another small dip in the market was occurring. This was reflected in the prices of most shares. There were increased margin calls during the second week of the month, and more in the weeks that followed. But most analysts called the decline a "technical correction"; Charles Mitchell gave further assurances of aid; Irving Fisher thought the general trend was still upward; *The Wall Street Journal* was certain of an autumn rally. It was the old story, said the respected newspaper; "Some stocks rise, some fall."

PRICES OF SELECTED ISSUES IN SEPTEMBER 1929

| | Closing Prices (fractions rounded off) | | | | |
Issue	Sept. 1	Sept. 8	Sept. 15	Sept. 22	Sept. 29
Adams Express	591	520	550	580	530
Air Reduction	214	213	198	213	201
American Smelting	124	129	120	118	112
American Tel. & Tel.	299	296	287	298	295
Bethlehem Steel	138	134	128	122	116
Case (J.I.)	345	392	450	428	399
Chrysler	72	74	70	66	59
Continental Can	92	86	83	88	88
DuPont	213	228	210	205	192
General Motors	72	78	74	73	66
Nash Motors	85	85	84	83	79
Paramount-Famous-Lasky	72	71	70	72	72
Radio Corp. of America	100	110	107	95	87
Standard Oil (N.J.)	72	72	81	73	74
U.S. Rubber	47	52	55	56	53
U.S. Steel	257	248	233	232	225
Westinghouse	288	275	254	253	233

Source: *New York Times*, September 2–30, 1929

There was no major item of bad news in September with the exception of the failure of Clarence Hatry in England on September 20. Involved with all sorts of new schemes, including automatic photograph and slot machines, Hatry was a speculator who went to the well once too often. Wall Street assured investors that such a situation could not happen in America; the Hatry incident did little to disturb the Street's demeanor.

What if stocks did fall? They had declined in December, to rise in January; March had seen major losses, but there had been new highs in April. September's declines would surely be followed by record highs in October. A conscientious stock-market devotee might have kept a table such as the one above and looked at it carefully the morning of October 3—he would not have been unduly alarmed.

That day, stocks broke sharply, in the year's worst loss to that date. The story was on the front pages of many newspapers. Margin calls went out, and there was a small and brief panic in New York. But conditions righted themselves the next morning, and stocks rose once more. The rally continued, and on October 7, *The Wall Street Journal* reported that "stocks turned sharply for the better in the weekend session. Confidence regarding the immediate position of the market was greatly strengthened by the recoveries which took place in Steel, American Can, Westinghouse, and other leaders in the last few minutes of Friday's session." There had been rumors that Arthur Cutten was about to switch to the bear side. This was vigorously denied. "Mr. Cutten said no relaxation of the national prosperity was in sight, and expressed the opinion that the market structure could support brokers' loans of $10 billion to $12 billion." The rally continued, and on October 12, the *Journal* wrote:

In the way of news developments, bulls have had much the best of it over the last week or so, and this, perhaps, is the main reason why the market has been able to score such a quick comeback. A week ago you heard all over the Street pessimistic forecasts as to the future of the market. You read in a number of newspapers . . . to the effect that we were in a major bear market. Stocks are now 10, 20, and 30 points above where they were a week ago, and optimism again prevails.

But the same edition reported that the Massachusetts Department of Public Utilities refused to allow Boston Edison to split its shares four to one, stating that the stock had reached so high a price "due to the actions of speculators," and was at a level where "no one, in our judgment . . . on the basis of its earnings, would find it to his advantage to buy it." Ignoring such statements, Charles Mitchell told reporters, "I see no reason for the end-of-the-year slump which some people are predicting," while Irving Fisher thought prices would be "a good deal higher than . . . today within a few months." Reflecting its belief that it was still the golden age of American business, *Time* Magazine ran a cover story of chewing-gum tycoon William Wrigley, Jr., that week, followed by one of Harry F. Guggenheim in the next issue. All seemed well—though a trifle skittish.

The market collapsed on Friday, October 18, as leading issues showed losses of five points or more, and the decline continued into the half-day trading on Saturday. There was talk of large bear pools headed by Livermore and opposed by a bull pool directed by Cutten and the Fishers. Prices would recover, predicted the *Journal*; the "big boys" wouldn't allow them to fall much further. Even then, the situation was far from grim, as could be seen by examining prices of leading issues:

PRICES OF SELECTED ISSUES IN OCTOBER 1929

Issue	Closing Prices (fractions rounded off)		
	Oct. 7	Oct. 14	Oct. 21
Adams Express	530	633	536
Air Reduction	193	216	208
American Smelting	111	115	106
American Tel. & Tel.	290	305	281
Bethlehem Steel	118	120	111
Case (J.I.)	350	290	250
Chrysler	58	54	55
Continental Can	83	84	78
DuPont	189	189	178
General Motors	69	64	60
Nash Motors	81	79	75
Paramount-Famous-Lasky	72	73	71
Radio Corp. of America	88	91	83
Standard Oil (N.J.)	78	79	77
U.S. Rubber	53	54	51
U.S. Steel	217	230	209
Westinghouse	219	239	205

Source: *New York Times*, October 8–22, 1929

Still, the public had become aware that prices could fall as well as rise. The decline was now more than a month old; the growing impatience could be felt in the boardrooms. Irving Fisher tried to calm the bulls; the decline was merely a "shaking out of the lunatic fringe," he claimed. The *Journal* expected an upturn on Monday, October 21, and even Alfred Noyes thought the correction was almost over.

But the slide continued, as 6 million shares were traded and stocks declined across the list. Readers of *The Wall Street Journal* on Tuesday morning, October 22, were told that "there is a vast amount of money awaiting investment. Thousands of traders and investors have been waiting for an opportunity to buy stocks on just such a break as has occurred over the last several weeks, and this buying, in time, will change the trend of the market." Indeed, prices did rise Tuesday, again on heavy volume. The worst seemed over.

Wednesday morning trading was slow at first, as speculators tried to discover which way the market would go. By then it was an article of faith that any rise would be spectacular, but the declines would be equally severe. Then, around 10:30 A.M. prices dipped, and they fell for the rest of the day. American Telephone & Telegraph lost 15 points; Case—a major speculative vehicle, which had fallen 50 on Monday and then rose 28 on Tuesday—dropped 46 points; some investment trusts showed losses of still more. The same leverage which had made fortunes for many only months before now wiped out hundreds of accounts. Even Adams Express, one of the best managed and most conservative of the funds, showed a 96-point decline for the day. That night the financial community was in despair. As is often the case, the darkest moments followed those of brightest hope.

Later on—more than thirty years after the event—old Wall Streeters, recalling the atmosphere in the district prior to the Exchange opening that Thursday, stated that no bulls could be found. The entire community was bearish. Most were calm and collected, but there were many frantic speculators who planned to sell out as soon as possible.

Stocks opened sharply lower on extraordinarily heavy volume, and fell all morning. Readers of that morning's *Times* learned that Charles Mitchell was "still of the opinion that the reaction has badly overrun itself," while Lewis Pearson of the Irving Trust Company tried to dismiss previous declines by noting that "severe disturbances in the stock market are nothing new in American experience." As they read, formerly high-flying issues showed losses of from five to fifty points. There seemed no support, no bottoming out, no organized buying as had been expected and promised on such occasions. On the floor of the Exchange, brokers were too busy filling orders to ponder the meaning of the crash, while a crowd gathered outside the Exchange Building, and stood there silently, not knowing what to do. Some rushed into the visitors' gallery overlooking the floor, and they screamed as they noted the large declines; others wept, or looked upon the tumult as though it were the end of the world. At 11 A.M. the gallery was closed, to keep the hysterical and the morbid from the scene. Later on, it was learned that more than $9.5 billion in paper values had been wiped out in the first two hours of trading.

News of the collapse soon reached the district's bankers. All were either directly involved in market activities, or would suffer should a major panic develop. Many remembered 1907, and the role played by J. P. Morgan at that time. The public would expect a similar reaction from them; the banking community would have to shore up the market. They quickly decided to act. Around noontime the city's leading bankers gathered at the offices of J. P. Morgan & Co. at 23 Wall Street. Jack Morgan— old J.P.'s son—was then in Europe, but Thomas Lamont was there to represent his interests. He was host to Albert Wiggin of the Chase National; Charles Mitchell; William Potter of the Guaranty Trust; and Seward Prosser of the Bankers Trust. Within a short time they were joined by George F. Baker, Jr., of the First National. Together these men controlled more than $6 billion in assets. All were determined to use these assets to reverse the course of securities prices and send them upward again.

Such a move would restore confidence; some thought it necessary to save American capitalism. To be sure, the men who met at 23 Wall Street had these considerations in mind. But there were other, more personal reasons for their actions. Albert Wiggin was involved in several pools, which speculated in dozens of stocks, including that of his own bank, the Chase. Unless the market slide was arrested, he could lose everything he had. Mitchell was also deep in speculation, counting on a rising market. Both Mitchell and Wiggin were in the investment-banking business as well as being commercial bankers, and as such were in the process of underwriting large issues. In many cases they had already paid for the securities, which they hoped to distribute to their customers and friends. If the market collapsed, these securities would lose their value; the banks would have to take huge losses and might be forced to declare bankruptcy. Similar situations existed for Baker, Prosser, and Potter, as well as for almost every other banker in the district. Thus, the community felt it imperative to arrest the decline—not only for the nation's sake, but to save themselves.

The details of that hurried meeting were never disclosed. We know its results, but no more. It seems the bankers pooled their resources to form a fund of some $20–$30 million. This would be used to bolster prices of key stocks. Once the public learned "the big boys" were behind the market, confidence would be restored, and normal buying would resume. In this way the market— and the banks—would be saved.

Richard Whitney, Exchange vice-president and an intimate of the House of Morgan, entered the mad arena of the Exchange a few minutes after the meeting concluded. Few noticed him at first; despite rumors of organized support, the brokers were too busy filling orders to do anything else. Whitney strode to the U. S. Steel post and asked its price. The last sale was at 205 (up two points since the opening), but the bid-ask prices were a few points lower. Whitney then shouted an order for 10,000 shares, at 205 a share. The meaning of this bid was clear to all who heard it, and within minutes to the entire floor. Whitney was supporting the price of Steel, and was speaking for the bankers in so acting. The giants of Wall Street had decided to stop the panic! A cheer rose from the floor as Whitney went to other posts and placed similar orders for a handful of key stocks.

A degree of confidence returned to the Street and echoed throughout the nation. Sell orders continued strong, but now buying support appeared. Prices turned around; many stocks which had fallen a score of points by noon ended the day with gains (U. S. Steel, for example, had opened at 205½, fallen to 193½ at one point, but closed at 206). The panic—"Black Thursday"—seemed over; it hadn't been too bad. Thirteen million shares had been traded. The ticker fell more than five hours behind at times, and finally stopped at 7:08 P.M.

That night the *New York World* called it a "gamblers'" and "not an investors' panic." From England economists John Maynard Keynes and Josiah Stamp argued that the decline and shake-out might have been for the best, since it would liquidate unsound

PRICES OF SELECTED ISSUES IN OCTOBER 1929

Issue	Closing Prices (fractions rounded off)				
	Sat. Oct. 19	Mon. Oct. 21	Tues. Oct. 22	Wed. Oct. 23	Thurs. Oct. 24
American Bosch Magnito	57	56	58	50	46
American & Foreign Power	131	133	135	112	98
Eastman Kodak	218	223	233	218	220
General Electric	339	331	334	314	308
International Business Machines	237	235	238	231	206
International Match, Pfd.	77	75	77	71	70
Safeway	164	157	160	156	153
U.S. & Foreign Securities	48	44	48	46	44
Zenith	36	32	35	31	29

Source: *New York Times*, October 20–25, 1929

speculation. Keynes added that money previously used to purchase stocks on time could now be diverted to more useful enterprises. In time, he implied, we might look back on this day as a beneficial, rather than an evil, event. The next morning, President Hoover told the country, "The fundamental business of the country—that is, the production and distribution of goods and services—is on a sound and prosperous basis." Stocks rose somewhat on Friday, then declined on Saturday. While the rest of the nation tried to enjoy its Sunday, brokers and clerks toiled around the clock struggling to catch up on business and prepare for trading Monday morning.

The *Times* of Sunday, October 27, was dotted with optimistic statements from all parts of the country and from people in many professions and occupations. "There is nothing in the business situation to justify any nervousness," said Eugene Stevens of the Continental Illinois Bank. Alexander Noyes observed that unlike the 1907 panic and previous ones, there was no indication of business or bank failures. An investment trust ran an advertisement urging the public to be "S-T-E-A-D-Y."

But the public was not steady. Whatever optimism remained on Wall Street seemed gone. Prices were lower at the opening on Monday, and plunged toward new lows all day. When it was learned that another meeting would take place at Morgan's, a brief rally occurred, but when nothing more happened, prices resumed their downward path. Then came more rumors. Several bankers had shot themselves; Mitchell himself had pleaded with Lamont for a private loan; Hoover was helpless to act; Cutten was in the middle of a bear pool, alongside Livermore. After a while, the rumors—all untrue—had no effect. Toward the close, hope seemed lost, as cries of "Sell! Sell!" reverberated off the Exchange walls.

The bankers met once again at 4:30 P.M. The market was closed to trading, but feverish clerks still ran across the floor attempting to balance accounts, and the ticker was still punching out the tale of lower prices. No report came out of this meeting, however; nor did Washington or Albany have any news. The only talk that night in the speakeasies of lower New York was of margin calls, of disastrous bear pools, and of famous individuals who were "caught short."

The Tuesday, October 29, issue of the *Times* stated "that the investor who purchases securities at this time with the discrimination that as always is a condition of prudent investing may do so with utmost confidence." *The Wall Street Journal* thought the shakeout to be over, and good values around for the picking. The newspaper editorialized in a tone which might have led readers to believe the panic was over.

It was a panic, a purely stock-market panic, of a new brand. Everyone seems to agree that it was due to the fact that prices of some stocks were selling beyond respective intrinsic values and a correction has taken place in a number of stocks that show declines ranging from 50 to more than 100 points. . . . The recent break was due to the position of the market itself. It came when money was 5 percent, with a plethora of funds available for lending purposes, normal inventories, corporations flush with surplus money, sound industrial conditions, and so on. It is because of the fact that the slump was due to the market itself that the storm has left no wreckage except marginal traders forced to sell at a loss. Mr. Baker, Mr. Morgan, Mr. Mellon, Mr. Rockefeller, and others who held stocks outright, stand just where they were before the break. Their income is the same. They have lost a few tail feathers but in time they will grow again, longer and more luxurious than the old ones that were lost in what financial writers like to call the debacle.

The debacle was not yet over, however. The woeful statistics of Black Thursday were bad enough; on Tuesday, the very bottom fell out.

Sixteen million shares were traded that day, and almost every tick on the screen showed lower prices. There were two bankers' meetings; reports of new bull pools were circulated; sellers were told that Jack Morgan was on his way home to take charge of recovery. None of these tales stopped, much less reversed, the decline. The *Times* industrial average fell forty-three points. Margin calls went out all day long, and when they could not be met, more stock was thrown into the maw. This caused new calls for margin, followed by new waves of dumping. It continued all day, and might have carried stocks more than a hundred points lower had not trading ended.

Years later Wall Streeters would tell stories of what happened that day—of millionaires who became bankrupts in a matter of hours; mass suicides; waves of hysteria on Wall Street; and fantastic chicanery in high places. The reports of the time do not bear this out. There were few suicides, no bank closings, and although many were hysterical, it was no worse than anything that had occurred the previous week, or during many earlier panics. The *Times* index did fall forty-three points—but the day before, it had declined more than forty-nine points.

What, then, was so different about that Tuesday which later became a symbol of the Great Crash?

In the first place, never before had there been so much outright dumping of securities. Liquidations took place in all parts of the country, and by every class of speculator. As a result, the overvalued stocks of midsummer became the undervalued issues of October 29, Some took advantage of this situation by not losing their heads and by buying selectively. Joseph Kennedy was one of these, and Floyd Odlum another. They were millionaires in 1929; by 1933, they were worth tens of millions.

The second factor could be seen only in retrospect. That night, more optimistic statements were issued. The President reiterated his belief that the "fundamental business of the country" was sound. U. S. Steel and American Can declared extra dividends. By early morning, October 30, came news that the Rockefellers were buying stock. "The sun is shining again," wrote *The Wall Street Journal*, "and we will go on record as saying some good stocks are cheap. We say good stocks are cheap because John D. Rockefeller said it first. Only the foolish will combat John D.'s judgement." Stocks rose sharply that Wednesday; the panic indeed seemed over, as the first rally since the previous week remained strong at the bell. There were cheers when Richard Whitney announced that the market would open at noon Thursday and then remain closed until the next Monday. The brokers had conducted an enormous amount of business, and now would have to straighten out accounts. The market rose in the abbreviated Thursday session, and then closed.

Many stories made the rounds during the next three days. Brokers told of how they slept in shifts on pool tables; of how their false teeth flew out of their mouths as they screamed orders; of forgotten orders, stuffed in wastepaper baskets, and not filled until hours later, when prices were dozens of points lower. Alexander Noyes told of a young telephone operator who learned of the crash in midday on October 29. "That was my broker," she

PRICES OF SELECTED ISSUES IN OCTOBER 1929

	Closing Prices (fractions rounded off)					
	Thurs.	Fri.	Sat.	Mon.	Tues.	Wed.
	Oct.	Oct .	Oct.	Oct.	Oct.	Oct.
Issue	24	25	26	28	29	30
American Bosch Magnito	46	44	42	35	30	29
American & Foreign Power	98	102	99	78	55	74
Eastman Kodak	220	227	223	181	170	192
General Electric	308	306	297	250	222	247
International Business Machines	206	220	220	198	N.T.	162
International Match Pfd.	70	73	71	61	55	64
Safeway	153	150	148	138	115	64
U.S. & Foreign Securities	44	41	43	35	29	22
Zenith	29	29	29	26	20	20

Source: *New York Times*, October 25–31, 1929

LOSSES OF SELECTED ISSUES, OCTOBER 29, 1929

Issue	Open	Close	Loss
Air Reduction	125	120	25
Allied Chemical	205	210	35
American Can	130	120	16
American Telephone & Telegraph	225	204	28
Auburn Automobile	130	130	60
Crosley Radio	25	28	12
Electric Auto-Light	75	50	45
Fox Films	50	48	20
General Electric	245	222	28

Source: *New York Times*, October 30, 1929

wailed. "I'm ruined. All I have left in the world is my sealskin coat." That Sunday Irving Fisher was quoted as saying prices were "absurdly low." The *Times* marveled at the transactions of the previous Thursday, writing as though it was some enormous dead beast. During the trading day, some 15,000 miles of tape were consumed by the Dow-Jones tickers. Never again would such a day be seen by Wall Street! Alfred Sloan of General Motors opined that "business is sound," and was echoed by a chorus of lesser industrialists. In all, it seemed again—as though the crash was ended.

Once more, such hopes were shattered. Stocks fell sharply on Monday, and the *Times* index showed a loss of twenty-two points. Tuesday was Election Day and so Wall Street was closed. But the decline picked up speed on heavy volume Wednesday. From then on, prices continued their downward movement. By the third week in November, the *Times* average stood at its lowest point since July 1927. Thus, the entire gain of the giant bull market was wiped out. At this point—in the last week of November—volume began to dry up and prices leveled off. The bear market had run its course and now was exhausted. All who would be ruined by margin calls and the like were already on the scrap heap; those who might have led large-scale bull rallies were equally destroyed. Now the market began to rise slowly, on light volume. The rise continued through December; Wall Street entered 1930 with a subdued bull market.

PRICES OF SELECTED ISSUES IN OCTOBER AND DECEMBER, 1929

Issue	Price, Oct. 28	Price, Dec. 31	Change for Year
Air Reduction	194	124	+26
American Smelting	97	73	−25
American Telephone & Telegraph	266	223	+30
Bethlehem Steel	108	95	+ 7
Case (J.I.)	226	199	+22
Chrysler Motors	45	36	−96
Continental Can	68	52	−11
General Motors	54	40	−40
Nash Motors	66	54	−55
Paramount-Famous-Lasky	60	51	− 4
Radio Corporation of America	59	44	−43
U.S. Rubber	46	24	−23
Westinghouse	179	144	+ 6

Source: *New York Times*, January 2, 1930

In its year-end report, *The Wall Street Journal* noted that despite the crash, several groups were strong in 1929. On the whole, stocks of airplane companies, office-equipment manufacturers, department stores, and steel companies did well, while those of automobile manufacturers, amusement-related companies, tobacco firms, and meat-packing concerns declined.

Stock-market news disappeared from the headlines of *The New York Times* by mid-November. The front pages on New Year's Day 1930 carried stories of the deaths of seventy-two children in a fire in Scotland; Senator Brookhart of Iowa calling for the removal of Secretary of the Treasury Mellon—for failure to enforce Prohibition effectively; and the New York Republicans pledging aid to Governor Roosevelt—in his pension program. The one bit of business news was a story of Mellon's prediction of business progress in 1930.

As was its custom, the *Times* asked prominent business leaders to look ahead to the coming year and tell the public what they saw. James Farrell of U. S. Steel was optimistic; "It is confidently expected that after the turn of the year operations in the steel industry will substantially improve." Frederick Ecker of Metropolitan Life recognized the scar left by the crash, but he too thought 1930 would be a good year. "Any slackness that may be apparent in the general business situation during the early months of 1930 can be attributed almost entirely to the hesitant state of mind in which business has been since the collapse of the stock market, rather than to any important change in fundamental conditions." Alexander Noyes thought the crash was a "reaction from an orgy of reckless speculation." But the crash hadn't affected business; "no such excesses had been practiced by trade and industry. . . ." Noyes hedged his prediction, however: "We do not yet know whether this present episode is or is not an old-time 'major crisis.'" Andrew Mellon thought that some businesses might be obliged to declare bankruptcy, and spoke of it freely:

Let the slump liquidate itself. Liquidate labor, liquidate stocks, liquidate the farmers, liquidate real estate. . . . It will purge the rottenness out of the system. High costs of living and high living will come down. People will work harder, live a more moral life. Values will be adjusted, and enterprising people will pick up the wrecks from less competent people.

These words sound harsh, uncalled for, and unpolitical—but only when read in retrospect. At the time they appeared reasonable, moderate, and prudent. To the reader of that day, it seemed as though the crash had come and gone and—most importantly —*was not to be followed by a depression.* This was an unusual crash. It had not been set off by a titanic struggle between giants, the manipulations of a small band, or the failure of a key firm or bank. In fact, the optimistic forecasts of business leaders that day seemed justified. As for the stock-market crash, it was considered purely financial. Plungers, gamblers, and other disreputable individuals had lost their money; others were still in good shape. If the crash was severe, then the rise had been gratifying. Those who had purchased stocks at their lows in 1923—when the first stage of the bull market had begun—and held them on January 1, 1930, still showed large profits. Employment had not declined appreciably; there were no breadlines; few demanded government intervention in the economy that January 1 when the crash seemed a bitter memory. To the reader of that day, the panic was an exciting event—like the World Series—which had ended, and would soon be replaced by other, equally exciting events: a new World Series and a new bull market. The *Times* indicated this in an oblique way. In an editorial entitled "The Year's Greatest Marvel," the paper wrote glowingly, not of the market crash, but of radio contact with Admiral Byrd at the South Pole.

Why did this severe panic fail to lead to a depression? Without an answer to this question, the significance of the 1929 crash cannot be understood.

The banking condition is a key factor in any Wall Street panic. If the banks can remain solvent, then recovery can take place. Morgan realized this, and before him Commodore Vanderbilt. Even U. S. Grant knew that liquidity had to be maintained if the nation was to survive economically. It could be said that on January 1, 1930, there had not been a single major bank failure as a result of the October panic. Indeed, the record shows that 1929 was a good year for finance insofar as the lack of failures was concerned.

COMMERCIAL BANK SUSPENSIONS FOR SELECTED YEARS

Year	Total Failures	Federal Reserve Banks	Non-member Banks
1921	505	71	434
1922	366	62	304
1923	646	122	304
1924	775	160	615
1925	618	146	472
1926	976	158	818
1927	669	122	547
1928	498	73	425
1929	659	81	578
1930	1,350	188	1,162
1931	2,293	516	1,777
1932	1,453	331	1,122

Source: Board of Governors of the Federal Reserve System, *Banking and Monetary Statistics, 1921–1933*

In most respects, 1926 was much worse for banking than 1929. Yet, we do not speak of the crash of '26. The reason for this is obvious; business and banking recovered in mid-1927, and went on to greater heights, while 1929 was followed by the disastrous years of 1930, 1931, and 1932.

What saved the banks in 1929? And why did they crash in the following year? As has been seen, the call-money situation alone tied hundreds of banks to the stock market. When owners of stocks were unable to raise more call money, their securities were dumped, and the lenders had to settle for whatever they could get—usually less than the face value of the note. Billions of dollars were wiped out in the crash, both in paper values and in losses of call money. Yet there were no major bank failures. The reason for this was simple: the New York banking community was unable to save the market from the crash, but it acted promptly and effectively to shore up the banks in November and December.

The New York banks alone had some $1 billion invested in call money in mid-October, 1929. During the next two weeks tens of thousands of calls went out, and the inability to meet them led to the closing of many accounts. Normally, one would expect the amount of call money outstanding to fall—and it did. Those nonbanking institutions which had entered the call-money market in the early twenties and then increased their loans greatly in the next years cut back on such loans by $1.4 billion in the last two weeks of October, and by another $2.2 billion during the next month and a half. Meanwhile, non-New York banks lightened their portfolios by recalling some $800 million from the market in the same period.

Had this massive cutback in call money not been offset by new funds for those who needed them, the panic would have been far more severe. The New York banks realized this, and in late October decided to pump more money into the call market. By the end of the month, the New York banks reported having made available an additional $1 billion in call money. This amount was raised through rediscounting operations at the Federal Reserve and in part by the sale of federal bonds. The money was rushed to fill the breach left by the out-of-state banks and the nonbanking institutions, and was used wisely. In early

November many brokerages announced that they would suspend margin requirements, and carry those accounts which under normal circumstances would have been dumped. It was this end of mass selling that aided in the recovery which took place shortly thereafter.

Where did the New York Federal Reserve Bank obtain the funds to throw into the market? At the time of the crash, the Open Market Investment Committee was operating under an agreement to purchase no more than $25 million worth of short-term government securities a week. Such a small amount would hardly be enough to aid those banks which provided call money for Wall Street. Thus, the Federal Reserve Bank of New York disregarded its rule and immediately contracted for an additional $160 million worth of short-term notes, followed by more purchases in the next few weeks. By the end of November, the Bank had accumulated some $370 million of such securities. These funds were used to maintain interest rates which, in previous panics, had risen sharply and then led to further difficulties. George Harrison, who had succeeded to the governorship of the New York Federal Reserve Bank on the death of Benjamin Strong, clashed with Chairman Young and others in Washington who claimed he had overstepped his powers. He defended his actions by stating, with some justification, "It is not at all unlikely that had we not bought governments so freely, thus supplementing the reserves built up by large additional discounts, the stock exchange might have had to yield to the tremendous pressure brought to bear upon it to close on some one of those very bad days the last part of October."

Money rates did not rise sharply in early November, as many expected they would. Instead, the New York Federal Reserve Bank lowered its discount rate so as to make for an easy money policy. The rate went to 4½ percent on November 14, and to 4 percent on January 20, 1930; by mid-March it reached 3½ percent. The easy money policy was instrumental in restoring a measure of confidence and helped lead to the correction of December 1929–April 1930.

The prompt and effective action of the New York Federal Reserve Bank preserved the banking structure during the year following the crash, and, had recovery followed, Harrison would be remembered today as one of the heroes of the period. But there was no full-scale recovery; instead, the market broke again in May, carrying prices to new lows once more. By New Year's Day 1931, there was no doubt that the nation was in a depression. As a result, Harrison is an all-but-forgotten figure. Those who succeed in stopping panics become celebrated, while those who fail are either forgotten or considered inept. Harrison deserved a better fate.

There were several reasons for the depression of the 1930s, and the market crash of October 1929 was only one of them, and an indirect one at that. Harrison's actions aided recovery; Washington's failure to introduce the reforms necessary to bolster public confidence negated his accomplishment.

As has been mentioned, the nation had entered 1929 in the midst of a mild slump. Housing starts and new car sales were below expectations, but were not serious enough to warrant more than passing notice. The stock-market crash led to further declines, as wary would-be purchasers decided to wait before buying hard goods. Still, by the end of the year, the economic indices showed little for serious concern. Accordingly, President Hoover decided to do nothing for the time being. New to his position and a firm believer in self-aid, he felt that assurances from Washington and a hands-off policy would be the best medicine for the decline. On March 7, 1930, he told the nation that for the most part the economic picture was bright. The little unemployment that existed was concentrated in twelve states, and even there the situation was improving. Construction contracts showed an increase; new car sales seemed better than a year earlier. "All the evidence," said Hoover, "indicates that the worst effects of the crash upon unemployment will have been passed during the next sixty days." But employment slipped that month, and other figures showed an equally bad picture. As the stock market rose in its early 1930 rally, the economy began to decline disturbingly fast. The rate seemed to have no direct bearing upon securities prices. In fact, it was more rapid during the December-April rise than it had been during the September-November decline.

It might be argued that the crash led to greater pessimism and fear, and so accelerated the coming of the depression. There is little evidence to support this contention; there was no sharp break in the leading economic indicators in either October or November. On the other hand, it is undoubtedly true that the market crash unnerved millions of people and exaggerated basic economic flaws which had existed throughout the twenties.

Speaking to the Bankers' Club on January 25, 1930, President Simmons admitted that the abnormally high prices of the previous summer had made the market vulnerable to a considerable decline. But to claim that wild trading and a large turnover of shares led to the crash would be wrong. "Every serious break in the stock market is always attributed to overspeculation, but if we are to ascertain its exact responsibility for the 1929 stock panic we must consider the actual facts. . . . If mere volume of dealings or proportionate velocity of dealings on the Exchange were a cause of the panic, we should have had a panic not last fall but a year ago." Simmons admitted that he did not know what had caused the panic to take place when and how it did; he could not offer a program for reform to make certain it would not happen again.

Five months later—on June 10, 1930—Richard Whitney addressed the Boston Association of Stock Exchange Firms. The title of his talk was: "The Work of the New York Stock Exchange in the Panic of 1929."

After retelling the by then familiar story of the crash, Whitney indicated that the Exchange had learned some valuable lessons from the decline. In the first place, it was evident that a more efficient means of reporting price changes and delivering securities was needed. Secondly, he believed that the Exchange should work more closely with the Federal Reserve in the future. Whitney observed that in two months some $4.5 million in brokers' loans were liquidated, without a loss to a single lender. The third lesson was that more flexible magins would be needed. Finally, Whitney stated his conviction that it was extremely important for the market to remain open through all crises. He closed on a happy note.

No one, I am sure, likes panics. No one certainly likes periods of excessive liquidation in the security markets, least of all those of us whose lives and fortunes have been devoted to the security business. But if we must face such periods of adversity, we must do so boldly and like men. And the events of last autumn have increased in us not only this realization, but also our faith in this marvelous country of ours, and our confidence that in its financial market places even the utmost periods of stress and the days of most bitter adversity cannot long check or withstand our inevitable onward economic progress.

Thus, Whitney believed the market mechanism to be basically sound, and capable of withstanding further pressures. As he spoke, however, the market was falling, continuing a decline which had begun two months earlier and which would not end until March 1933. For a period of thirty-six months the toboggan would continue, taking most market indicators down more than 70 percent. In retrospect, the great crash of 1929 was not as important as the long slide of 1930–1933. But it was more dramatic, and so is usually considered the key to understanding the depression.

From late November 1929 to mid-April 1930, a period of four and a half months, the market rallied, and it seemed as though it would again move into new high ground. In this period, the economy appeared to gain strength, and by the early spring of 1930, the "correction" was considered over. It was thought of as simply one more pause on the road to prosperity. There had been declines of greater magnitude in 1924 and 1926–1927, and most observers thought more would come in the future. Few believed the 1929 crash to be the beginning of the worst period of hardship in American history. As it happened, the short-lived recovery of the first quarter of 1930 soon gave way to the severe dislocations which would be known as the Great Depression.

The first three months of 1930 may be considered a period of lost opportunities. If the Federal Reserve System had continued its shoring-up operations, and had reformed itself so as to act with equal vigor in the future as it had in October and November, the bank failures of 1930–33 might have been prevented. But no such institutional changes were made. Had the new President taken stronger actions in the economic sphere, and had Governor Roosevelt joined with him in demanding stock-exchange reforms, the decline might have been avoided. But they failed to act. Had the Exchange itself formed committees and planned actions to meet future difficulties, the bear market of 1930–33 might have been shorter. But Simmons did not know what to do, and Whitney thought no changes were necessary, save a few minor reforms in the training of customers' men. Such actions might have restored confidence and provided the psychological impetus toward further growth and the economic and political underpinnings to sustain prosperity. But they did not come.

Writing of the depression in her impressionistic study, *The Invisible Scar*, Caroline Bird shows the misery and hardship of the thirties, but begins by contrasting that decade with the optimism of the twenties. Like Galbraith and Morris before her, she opens with an aside to what has become a major symbol in American history.

1929. That number always means a year, and that year means the crash of prices on the New York Stock Exchange in the last week of October. Like 1492, 1776, and 1914, the bare number 1929 has passed into the language as the term for a vivid event and the big changes it brought.

The big change of 1929 was the end of the rich.

It might be more proper to say that 1929 brought an end to the dreams of easy wealth held by thousands of small speculators, and for a while at least to the time when bigger ones could make millions in a single trading session. For better or worse, the rich are still with us, and in greater numbers than ever before.

One might say, instead, that 1929 was destined to become a symbol for the reality of 1930 and the decade that followed, and that one should take care not to confuse the symbol with the reality.

12.

THE KENNEDY SLIDE: 1962

By the early 1930s the finacial district and the nation had learned that not all speculators had been ruined by the 1929 crash and the depression. By then, many Wall Streeters had converted to the bear side of the market and formed large pools whose object it was to push down prices still further. Cutten, Raskob, and the Fisher brothers—leading bulls of the pre-1929 market—were forgotten or ignored; after the district recovered from the initial shock of the decline, it enthroned a new set of heroes.

Tom Bragg, a minor figure in the bull market, now became the manager of several bear pools in American Telephone & Telegraph, making millions each time the stock fell a few points. William Danforth, who lost most of his fortune when he went short prematurely in 1928, made up his losses in late 1929, and through continued short sales emerged a multimillionaire. "Sell 'em Ben" Smith, who was reputed to have rushed into his broker's office on Black Tuesday, screaming, "Sell 'em all! They're not worth anything!" made $10 million a month on short sales for a while. The most famous of the bear raiders, however, was Joseph P. Kennedy.

The market crash occurred a month after Joe Kennedy's forty-second birthday. At the time, he was the leading figure in Film Booking Office and Keith-Albee-Orpheum, having graduated from banking and construction positions. Kennedy was also a skillful market plunger, a man with a reputation for hitting hard and, when necessary, below the belt. No one knew how much money he had, but it was certain that Joe Kennedy was a millionaire.

He lived in a large mansion in Riverdale which cost more than
$250,000, where his wife and many children were somewhat in-
sulated from the hurly-burly of Wall Street and Hollywood.
Kennedy drew $6,000 a week from his film operations alone,
and his investments and speculations brought in much more.

Joe Kennedy had no difficulty riding out the panics, but, like
many others in his position, he feared the very fabric of American
life was coming apart. Later on he wrote, "I am not ashamed to
record that in those days I felt and said I would be willing to part
with half of what I had if I could be sure of keeping, under law
and order, the other half. Then it seemed that I should be able
to hold nothing for the protection of my family."

As much to assure his own financial survival as anything else,
Joe Kennedy's interests turned to politics. He was a strong
backer of Franklin D. Roosevelt's Presidential ambitions, and was
able to claim, after Election Day, that he had been the first
businessman to hop aboard the Roosevelt bandwagon.

Clearly, Kennedy had reason to hope for an Administration
position in 1933. This would require him to relinquish many of
his holdings, and in particular put an end to his Wall Street
speculations. He indicated willingness to comply with a new code
of behavior. But before FDR called him to the White House,
Joe Kennedy entered and led one last pool.

With the end of Prohibition, securities dealing in one way or
another with liquor became speculative vehicles. Kennedy and
his group lit upon Libby-Owens-Ford Glass Company, a firm
which did not make bottles—it specialized in plate glass—but
was often confused with container manufacturer Owens Illinois
Glass Company. Together with such individuals and firms as
Walter Chrysler, Lehman Brothers, and Kuhn, Loeb, Kennedy
bought and sold some million shares between June and October
of 1933. In the end, the pool's profits were almost $400,000, of
which Kennedy took $60,805. It was small pickings compared to
his earlier coups, but it earned Kennedy the distinction of leading the last legal pool in stock-market history.

After 1932, Wall Street came under the continual scrutiny of
Washington. The securities markets were blamed for the depression, and the New Deal meant to prevent any recurrence of

such disasters. To some, this meant that finance capitalism had to be crushed; to others, self-regulation seemed the best approach. Roosevelt himself tended to view the problem pragmatically, supporting legislation designed to correct specific abuses. He would discover what had caused the crash, how abuses had taken place, and then move to bring governmental pressures to bear upon the financial district.

The first important measure to control Wall Street was the so-called "Truth-in-Securities Act" of 1933, which gave the Federal Trade Commission powers to oblige underwriters to maintain certain forms and procedures in the writing and distribution of literature. This was followed by the Glass-Steagall Act, which established the Federal Deposit Insurance Corporation and obliged financial institutions to separate their investment and commercial banking operations. The Wall Street community did not like these acts, but most business leaders thought them necessary in light of what had happened in 1929. No longer could wild claims be made by underwriters; commercial banks would not be a source for call money in the future.

The business community spoke with one voice against Roosevelt's next piece of legislation, however. The Securities and Exchange Act, signed into law on June 6, 1934, was designed to "put a policeman at the corner of Wall and Broad." With certain exceptions, all securities had to be registered with the SEC, and could be investigated by staff members. Speculative operations such as wash sales and matched orders were prohibited; planted tips and false or misleading statements became penal offenses. Insiders were controlled; all books had to undergo public audits. The SEC was charged with making certain that men like Raskob and Cutten, Ben Smith and Kennedy, could no longer make fortunes by manipulating stocks at will. "The Securities and Exchange Commission will usher in a new day for Wall Street," wrote the *Nation*. In effect, the financial capital of America would be moved from New York to Washington. The public would learn what had happened in the past, and would be spared recurrences in the future.

The Federal Trade Commission would enforce the Securities and Exchange Act until September 1, when the new Securities and

Exchange Commission was to be established. Meanwhile, FDR attempted to staff the Commission.

Joe Kennedy took off for Europe in September 1933, expecting to return to Washington in a few months to find an important job with the Administration. For a while he thought he would replace William Woodin at the Treasury, but nothing came of this. As the months passed, Kennedy became bitter. Had Roosevelt dropped him after his usefulness was over? Then came a feeler: would Kennedy accept the post of New York director of the National Recovery Administration? Kennedy had set his sights higher; he rejected the idea. This was followed by one of the greatest surprises of the period: after suggesting Kennedy for a post on the SEC, Roosevelt named him chairman of that body!

To many it appeared bizarre that a major Wall Street speculator would be named to police the district. Just a few months earlier Kennedy had engaged in operations now illegal under the terms of the Act. Indeed, parts of the SEC legislation had been written with people like him in mind. Secretary of the Interior Harold Ickes was flabbergasted. Writing in his diary, he said, "The President has great confidence in him because he has made his pile, has invested all his money in government securities, and knows all the tricks of the trade."

Whatever the reasons for the selection, Kennedy did a thorough job with the Commission. He ended the so-called "strike of capital," recommended more than two hundred prosecutions, and gained several key indictments in his year and a half in office. Through the work of Kennedy and his staff, the SEC had become a dominant force on Wall Street. By 1936 the Stock Exchange was no longer a closed club.

And what did Kennedy want from all this? Why would a person of his background take such a position? Many asked this question in 1934 and 1935, and were answered with statements like "He wants a political career," or "Joe thinks he can make money from inside information." Neither, of course, was true. Joe Kennedy never entertained personal political ambitions, and his operations at the SEC were above suspicion. Perhaps, suggested Ickes, there is another explanation for Joe Kennedy's actions. Writing in his diary in 1934, Ickes jotted down his belief that FDR named him to the post because he was "going on the assumption that Kennedy would like to make a name for himself for the sake of his family." The Secretary concluded: "I have never known many of these cases to work out as expected."

Whether it "worked out" as Joe Kennedy thought it would cannot be known. If it is true that he planned, even then, to place his son in the Presidency, then Kennedy must be considered one of the great political managers of American history. On the other hand, accident, chance, good fortune—call it what you will—plus the astuteness of John F. Kennedy and his circle, were probably more important than Joe's advice and money in the election of 1960.

In that election, young Senator Kennedy criticized the lack of initiative and imagination of the Eisenhower Administration, and he tried to give the impression that the nation had somehow stagnated. While it may be true that the Eisenhower years were relatively quiet when compared to those of Roosevelt and Truman, they certainly saw a continuation of the economic and social progress of the previous administrations. Indeed, in the period between Joe Kennedy's forty-second birthday in 1929 and his son's forty-third in May 1960, the face of the nation had been transformed. In little more than thirty years it had survived the worst depression in its history and its worst war, and then entered a period of cold war which seemed to have no end. From a population of 120 million the United States had risen to 180 million, a 50 percent increase which alone consisted of more Americans than had existed during the Cleveland Administration. The gross national product of 1929 had been $104 billion, and had fallen to $56 billion the year Roosevelt took office. As Kennedy campaigned for the Presidency in 1960, the gross national product was well over $502 billion. Isolationist America of 1929 was one of a half-dozen "great" powers. In the summer of 1960, the United States was the most powerful nation in the world. Its nearest rival, the Soviet Union, had a standard of living similar to the one of depression America. Some economists noted that the USSR had a faster growth rate than that of the United States; others replied that the *increase* in American gross national product since the end of World War II was greater than the *total* Soviet GNP that year.

In thirty years America had gone from the world of Charles Lindbergh and the *Spirit of St. Louis* to that of John Glenn and space travel. It had risen from an era of economic fear to one of plenty. To be sure, most were concerned with the threat of atomic warfare, but somehow this seemed more remote than had the possibility of a Nazi attack in the late 1930s. Security was important to the American of 1960, but few would have been willing to settle for what they had and nothing more. Not since the late twenties did the nation exhibit as much confidence in itself and its system as it did that summer.

This is not to say there were no problems. Racial difficulties beset many parts of the country; Asian experts were concerned with the growth of Red China and the possibilities of war in Indo-China; Africa might flare up at any time; Israel and the Arab nations were no nearer accord than they had been a decade earlier. Any of these areas might erupt, bringing an end to the relative quiet of the Eisenhower years, and the nation was prepared for such crises. But there was one area in which solidity seemed permanent: few Americans thought the United States would again suffer through a depression, and stock-market panics seemed a phenomenon of the past. Since the end of the war, the GNP had moved irregularly, but always upward. There had been minor dips in the stock market, and a few crashes—such as when Eisenhower had a heart attack—but nothing to compare with the infamous panics of 1893, 1901, 1907, and 1929.

In 1960, John Kennedy tried to paint as black a picture as he dared of the Eisenhower years. He spoke of a missile gap, of inaction in important areas, and of a lack of imagination in Washington. But he never considered or tried to talk of possible depression. Kennedy wanted to "get America moving again." At worst, he indicated the nation had stalled in its forward drive; at best, he seemed to say that he could better the already impressive performance of most areas of the economy.

Although growth had been maintained from 1953 to 1960, Kennedy considered it sluggish at approximately 2½ percent. With proper incentives and guidance, he said, this rate could be doubled. The Democratic candidate spoke of the slightly more than 5 percent unemployment rate as unbearable, especially since it fell most heavily upon Negroes and other minority groups. A doubling of the growth rate would cut deeply into unemployment and raise the GNP by at least $35 million. Walter Heller and other economic advisers thought that under such conditions the tax structure could be modified so as to afford incentives for businesses to expand and continue a more vigorous growth. Kennedy was accused of "growthsmanship." He seemed to say that America's ills could be solved through a quantitative increase in production. Democratic economists retorted that a doubling of the growth rate would increase per capita consumption, lower taxes, balance the budget, go far toward ameliorating racial ills, enable the United States to score a major propaganda victory over the USSR, and in effect usher in a new era of plenty. In the heat of the campaign, both sides exaggerated the role of economic growth. But each did score major points against the other. The Democrats rightfully charged that the economy was not performing as well as it might; the figures were beyond dispute. The Republicans, on the other hand, received no satisfactory response to the question: "How can this be done without forcing the nation into a new inflationary spiral?"

Historically, full employment usually led to wage increases, and full production to higher prices for raw materials. Increased demand meant heavy spending for capital improvements. All were ultimately translated into higher prices for the consumer who, as a producer, then demanded higher salaries, forcing the spiral ever higher. For eight years the Eisenhower Administration had attempted, with little success, to halt inflation through cutbacks of government spending and the encouragement of high interest rates. Despite this, prices rose (especially in 1957–1960), leading to a gradual erosion of values at home and a weakening of the nation's trade position with Europe and the rest of the world. Now Kennedy proposed to do away with inflation while encouraging the very elements which many economists claimed would lead to still greater price increases!

Although this dilemma was not debated before the voters in 1960, it was the subject of discussions among economists and businessmen that summer. By early autumn it seemed clear that the Kennedy approach would be to use federal pressure to curb unions in their wage demands and discourage business from raising prices. Unions faced with labor shortages would be pursuaded to refrain from asking for inflationary packages in their negotiations with management; when confronted with a market crying for their goods, businessmen would be asked to hold down prices. It was not made clear just how this would be done, but unless it were accomplished, suggested the Republican economists, Kennedy's doubled growth rate would more than triple the rate of price increases.

The question was still unresolved on Election Day, when the voters put John Kennedy in the White House by the smallest margin of victory in the twentieth century. The business community, which by and large had supported Richard Nixon, now worried that Kennedy's circle of economic advisers would attempt to put their theories into practice, leading to the greatest anti-business crusade since the New Deal. Other observers noted that JFK was not FDR, that 1961 was completely unlike 1933—and that financial sophistication could be expected from Joe Kennedy's boy.

Wall Street seemed to agree. After posting new highs during the campaign—when it appeared that a Nixon victory was in the offing—the market began to slide, reaching the 560 level on the Dow-Jones Industrial Index shortly before Election Day. Prices rose on news of the Kennedy victory, as investors apparently thought the new Democratic Administration would spend more than the Republicans and fail to hold the line on inflation. The industrials reached 616 by the end of the year, and Wall Street continued to talk of the "soaring sixties."

The underlying tone of the financial community in 1960 was bullish. Despite perennial talks by pessimists, predictions of new dips in the averages, possible stagnation, tight money, and the like, no major analyst thought the American economy would ever undergo another prolonged depression, and this seemed to foreclose on the possibility of a major decline in the averages followed by a drawn-out bear market. The legislation of the New Deal and Fair Deal, the nation's preeminent position in the world, and the burst of technological energy seen during World War II and after seemed to guarantee economic progress. By 1960, it was an article of faith that IBM's earnings would increase by at least 10 percent a year; that A. T. & T.'s net sales would never decline; that per capita income would increase each year; and that each generation would leave larger estates than the one preceding it. All this, thought most Americans, came from the benefits of capitalism, and was a clear demonstration of that system's superiority over "foreign ideologies."

But the capitalism of 1960 was strikingly different from that of 1929. Historians and economists had long observed that the American economy had never been completely "free," and that the government had played a significant role in business since the founding of the nation. But until 1933, the role seemed indirect, taking the form of tariffs, grants to special-interest groups, tax rebates, and the like. With the coming of the New Deal and World War II, the government's role became more direct. Federal agencies seemed omnipresent and omnipotent, from the Bureau of Internal Revenue to the Federal Housing Administration, through the armed forces and the many construction and farm programs. As if to seal the outright union of government and the economy, Congress passed and President Truman signed the Employment Act of 1946, which stated that "it is the continuing policy and responsibility of the Federal Government to use all practicable means . . . to promote maximum employment, production, and purchasing power." By 1960, most Americans, even those resentful of the growth of government, realized that Washington would not allow another major depression to take place.

Nor was this the only guarantee of stability and growth. The postwar world saw the rapid growth of huge investment enterprises, such as mutual funds, trusts, and pension funds. In 1949, these organizations held $9.5 billion worth of securities listed on the New York Stock Exchange. By Election Day 1960, the figure was well over $70 billion—approximately 20 percent of all listed securities. The managers of these funds, who often controlled more capital than Morgan at his prime, were limited in their investments by federal and state laws, but nonetheless were able to exert great pressures on the market. As new money continued to flow into their treasuries, they sought investments on Wall Street and vied with each other for positions in "growth equities." And the flow seemed endless, insuring—so it seemed—higher and still higher prices for good holdings.

Individual investors competed with the funds for such stocks, and when inexperienced hands entered Wall Street, large-scale fluctuations were inevitable. On the surface, stock-market activities among the middle-class seemed strikingly similar to those of 1929. But there were major differences between the speculator of 1929 and his grandson in 1960. In the first place, the latter either remembered or was told quite often of what had happened a generation before, and this curbed his activities somewhat. Then, too, the economy of 1960 was far more secure and stable than it had been earlier. Finally, the Securities and Exchange Commission and other bodies were able to prevent large-scale thievery (although the petty operators were never completely done away with), while the Federal Reserve insisted that margin buying be severely limited. The small speculator of 1960 paid at least 70 percent of the price in cash for a security investigated by agencies which did not exist in 1929, and which was often listed on the Exchange which itself policed Wall Street with care and precision.

In the past, market crashes were often accompanied by tight money, followed by business collapses, and ended by the appearance of a strong force. This had been the case in 1873, 1893, and 1907—and to a degree in 1929. By 1960, the Federal Reserve seemed able to prevent the tight money situation from getting out of hand. Businesses were far more secure in 1960; banks could no longer fail en masse. Finally, the fund managers and the enormous purchasing power of individuals, when combined with and supported by an interested government, could wield more power and instill more confidence than a J. P. Morgan. This was the mythology of Wall Street in 1960, and, for a change, there was a great deal of correspondence between faith and reality.

It took time for these forces to develop, and more time for them to become obvious and gain acceptance by the general public. All were present in 1947, but that year was one of the dullest in stock-market history, as many investors believed a postwar recession would soon take shape. The Truman victory in 1948 nipped an incipient bull market in the bud, and not even the Korean War, with its promises of revived economic activity, could lead the market much higher. Prices rallied with the election of Eisenhower in 1952, then slumped. By early September 1953, a new rally seemed in the making, with the Dow at the 250 level. Then the market picked up steam; funds began to stream to Wall Street, as the Eisenhower bull market took hold. Prices began to soar, and, although there were corrections, they continued to rise. The Dow crossed the 400 level early in 1955, and 500 the next year. By mid-1959 the Dow was near 650, and in early 1960 approached 700 before declining to the 650 level. By then, all the forces previously described were well known and constantly repeated by market analysts, most of whom praised what had become the greatest bull market in American history.

That such a market rise would be irregular and erratic was inevitable. The steel, copper, and machine-tool equities did well in 1956, and then declined. Tobacco, food chain, and drug stocks rose in the recession year of 1957. In 1958 electronics and automobiles took fire; 1959 was the year of rubber, meat packing, and motion pictures, and during the election campaign of 1960, vending machine, soft drink, and television issues were popular. But even then the averages declined sharply in 1960, and they regained the 600 level only after a year-end rally.

Market analysts were cautious in January 1961. President-elect Kennedy's appointments were sound, and although he continued to speak of his New Frontier, it was becoming increasingly evident that he would do little to rock the boat. Accordingly, stocks rose toward the end of the month; Kennedy's inauguration took place in the midst of a new leg of the bull market. Some analysts, especially those who followed the "Elliott Wave Theory," wrote that stocks could be expected to behave erratically, but spectacularly, in the next few months. Hamilton Bolton told his subscribers that "we are well entranced in the fifth and final upward wave—the last in a bull market."

The Dow-Jones Industrials performed well in 1961, despite the shaky start of the Kennedy Administration. The new President urged Congress to enact legislation to revise tariffs downward, set up a medical-assistance program, offer federal aid to education, and establish a new Cabinet department for urban affairs. Had they passed, these programs would have had important repercussions on the economy. For the most part, however, they were killed, either through congressional pressures or the inability of the President to effectively manage the bills through the legislature. Kennedy was even less successful in the foreign area, taking responsibility for the Bay of Pigs fiasco in April, suffering a prestige reversal in July when the Soviet Union constructed the Berlin Wall, and failing to deal successfully with the Congo and Southeast Asia problems. Despite this, the investment community thought values were still good, and the rush to buy continued.

DOW-JONES INDUSTRIALS AT MONTH-END TRADING, 1961

Month	D-J Industrials
January	648.20
February	662.08
March	676.63
April	678.71
May	696.72
June	683.96
July	705.37
August	719.94
September	701.21
October	703.92
November	721.60
December	731.14

Source: *Wall Street Journal,*
January 3, 1962

The averages, based as they were on a list of high-grade issues, told only a small part of the story. To be sure, the stable issues participated in the Kennedy bull market, but they lagged far behind the glamour stocks, which skyrocketed in early 1961. Most of these were technology-based issues, such as IBM, Litton Industries, Texas Instruments, and Fairchild Camera, or companies with striking new products, like Polaroid or Xerox. These stocks rose rapidly, but at least were based on proved patent positions and excellent management. This was not the case with the so-called "hot issues" of 1961, many of which were listed on the American Stock Exchange or traded over-the-counter. Even these were outperformed by the mania for new groups. And when speculators found the lists exhausted, or the run-ups put many older securities out of reach, they initiated a boom in the new issues market. For a while Small Business Investment Companies were in vogue. These firms, which had special tax privileges and specialized in investing in unproved firms, captivated speculators in the spring of 1961.

SMALL BUSINESS INVESTMENT COMPANY STOCKS, 1961

Company	Issue Price	May 19 Price
Boston Capital	15	25¾
Electronics Capital	10	54
Electro-Science Investors	11	38
Growth Capital	20	35½
Techno-Fund	12½	22
Venture Capital	7½	21
Virginia Capital	10½	16½

Source: *Business Week*, May 20, 1961, p. 135

Most of the SBICs were organized and offered to the public in 1961. Still larger increases were shown by other new issues of that year.

NEW ISSUES, 1961

Company	Issue Price	Date	April 14 Price
Albee Homes	16	March 20	27¼
Alberto Culver	10	April 5	22
Bristol Dynamics	7	March 21	18
Greenfield R.E.	20	March 28	19
Marine Capital	15	April 4	17⅝
Morton Foods	12½	April 5	21
Mother's Cookie	15	March 8	24½
Nytronics	5	March 17	14
Packard Instrument	10	April 4	21¾
Polychrome	8½	March 7	19¾
Rego Wire	4½	April 5	7¾
Shinn Industries	6	April 3	8
Shoup Voting Machine	11	March 30	17¼
Whippany Paper	15	March 8	14
Wyle Laboratories	19½	March 7	30½

Source: *Business Week*, April 15, 1961, p. 129

Later on it was discovered that many of these securities were manipulated by underwriters or by syndicates formed even before the stocks were offered to the public. In early January 1962, the SEC investigated the cases of Arco Electronics, offered at 5, which then rose to 24¾. Endevco Corp., which went from 13 to 16¾, and Geophysics Corp., whose rise was from 14 to 24½, were other issues to be looked into, as were Rocket Jet Engineering, Associated Testing Laboratories, Bristol Dynamics, Cove Vitamin and Pharmaceutical, Custom Components, and Hydro-Space Technology Inc. Prominent among the underwriters of these and similar issues were Michael Kletz & Co.; Maltz, Greenwald & Co.; Michael A. Lomasney & Co., and other small houses on and along Wall Street. The new issues market, increasingly noted for its wildness and severe cases of "sure-thingitis," was the closest the Kennedy market would come to the speculative fever of 1929. New issues became standard cocktail-party chatter in the nation's big cities; women's clubs abandoned lectures on art for discussions of investments. Brokers reported record crowds in their offices at lunchtime, as tape watching became baseball's rival that summer. Trading volume soared, setting a post-Hoover high. In 1961 the turnover ratio was 15 percent with 6.8 billion shares traded, against 1960's 12 percent and 6.2 billion shares (in contrast, 1929's turnover ratio was 119 percent and 943 million shares). "We all know the ridiculous," said broker Sidney Lurie. "But the stock market reflects every human frailty, and the big one now is greed. Others are fear and stupidity. They'll come a little later."

With all this, there were signs of fear in the autumn of 1961. It took subtle forms, and did not cause a break on Wall Street. New York Attorney General Louis Lefkowitz announced a probe of Nicholas Darvas, a dancer whose stock-market book had led to increased speculation. Mutual-fund sales were down for the fourth quarter. As stock prices rose, yields fell, and as money was withdrawn from bonds, the return on debt securities increased. Thus, bonds became more attractive to the "value-minded" investor. At year's end it was learned that only $2.7 billion of new money went into the stock market, while $5 billion was invested in corporate bonds, $5.1 billion in state and local bonds, and $5.2 billion in Treasury securities. Early in the new year, the Bank of New York ordered a cutback of 10 percent in its pension trust-fund stock holdings. Congress ordered an SEC investigation of the runaway market, and it opened with a probe of the American Stock Exchange and the roles of specialists; evidence of chicanery was uncovered from the first meetings.

The New Frontier seemed to pale, along with the Soaring Sixties. A cartoon in *The New Yorker* portrayed several businessmen discussing the market while on a homeward bound commuter train. "I had the weirdest dream about my mother last night," said one. "She said I should sell all my A. T. & T. when it hits 132."

Despite these problems and uncertainties, most analysts were optimistic regarding market prospects for 1962. "The market will perform better," said Sidney Lurie. Edmund Tabell believed the Dow-Jones Industrials would rise to 825 before encountering weakness. "We are looking for common stocks to turn in quite a good performance in the coming year," was the conclusion of H. Hentz & Co. Pershing & Co. thought that "after end-of-the-year adjustments are out of the way, we would look for a tendency to give credence to the extremely favorable forecasts for the year ahead." Fahnestock & Co. noted the accumulation of time deposits and large investments in short-term bonds. These came from people and institutions awaiting the proper moment to enter the market, and that time, the company thought, would come in 1962. But Paine, Webber, Jackson & Curtis predicted a general decline in the second half of the year. Merrill Lynch refused to deal in stocks selling for less than 2, and other houses instructed their brokers to warn customers against wild speculating. Exchange President Keith Funston warned against excesses regularly, through all media, and even took out advertisements on the subject. A survey showed that 45 percent of mutual-fund managers expected the averages to hit new highs early in the year, with 10 percent expecting a fall. But although fund purchases picked up steam, so did redemptions. By March, there was much talk of the "stand-off market," which would be resolved through a gigantic struggle between bulls and bears.

As the economy continued to perform well, and while such men as Frederick Goodrich of the United States Trust Company were "cautiously optimistic" about Wall Street developments, economists and business writers began to discuss the "profit squeeze." *Business Week* noted that from 1958–61, federal spending had increased by 20.4 percent; GNP by 19.6 percent, corporation sales were up 18.7 percent, and payrolls by 18.9 percent. In this same span, corporation profits increased only 3.3 percent. Yet stock prices moved higher in this period, buoyed by fantastic and glamorous tales of the future. Repeating what had become a standard Wall Street joke, the journal noted that stocks were not only discounting the future, but the hereafter as well.

When one considers the profit picture over the longer range, the picture was even more striking. From January 1, 1942, to March 1, 1962, the price of common stocks rose 601 percent, while corporate profits increased only 169 percent. From the beginning of the Eisenhower Administration to March 1, 1962, profits increased a bit more than 80 percent; stock prices were up 173 percent. Burton Crane, who had succeeded to Alexander Noyes's post at the *New York Times*, warned that another 1929 *was* possible. The large trusts were constantly purchasing stocks, causing their prices to rise. This resulted in extremely low yields for common stocks, and high returns for bond owners. What would happen if "the little guy" decided he wanted a greater return on his investment? If the mutual funds had to sell stocks to pay for large-scale redemptions, who would take up the issues? Such a situation could easily lead to a panic, collapse, and finally depression.

This sorrowful chain of events could be triggered by poor earnings reports, which could transform growth equities into stagnant holdings. A stock might well sell for eighty times earnings if it were growing at a rate of twenty percent a year. But should its growth rate be cut in half, its price-earnings ratio would undoubtedly come down sharply, perhaps to thirty times earnings. Thus, XYZ Corporation, earning $5.00 a share and selling for 400, could decline to 75 in a short period of time. The key, then, was growth —and not only of stock prices, but earnings per share.

The President was committed to economic growth without inflation. Could earnings growth continue in such circumstances? It could, given an expanding economy plus constant labor and raw-materials prices. President Kennedy, then, became committed to holding prices down along the line, while encouraging growth through reinvestment of profits. Business would be provided with tax incentives, while labor would be asked to keep wage requests down, if possible tying them to increases in productivity.

Although Walter Heller was the chief architect of this philosophy, its implementation was charged to Secretary of Labor Arthur Goldberg. Well known as a labor lawyer before entering the Cabinet, and the former general counsel to the Steelworkers Union, Goldberg was widely portrayed as organized labor's representative to the Kennedy circle. During the first year of the new administration, however, Goldberg spent more time attempting to hold down labor demands than in consulting with businessmen for price reductions. By early 1962, labor viewed the Secretary of Labor as a turncoat, while business applauded him on many occasion. When Goldberg made a speech in early March, in which he asked compliance with the Kennedy guidelines, AFL-CIO President George Meany retorted, "He is infringing on the right of free people and free society." Goldberg answered that it was the government's responsibility to "provide guidelines . . . to insure that the settlements reached are the right settlements." The government, said the Labor Secretary, "must have the courage to assert the national interest."

Although Meany referred to many of Goldberg's actions in his statement, what particularly angered him was the Secretary's role in the steel contract negotiations of 1961–62. From the first, Kennedy and Goldberg had hoped a strike could be avoided (there had been a 116-day strike in 1959 when negotiations broke down) and that both sides would agree to noninflationary settlements. In practice, this would mean that Steelworkers Union President David McDonald would accept a small wage package, in return for which the steel companies would forego a price increase. Mc-Donald seemed willing to consider the proposal, while the company presidents resented Kennedy's interference, arguing that unless a price increase were allowed, the companies would be unable to gain sufficient profits to modernize their plants and compete in the world market.

On January 23, 1962, Kennedy met secretly with McDonald

and U.S. Steel President Roger Blough, and again urged both to accept a noninflationary pact. Both men were adamant at first, but in the end, McDonald agreed to accept a ten-cent wage package. The President and McDonald thought this would bind Blough and the other steel-company presidents to hold the line on prices; Blough later claimed to have made no such pledge. The contract was signed on March 31, and Kennedy congratulated all involved on their statesmanship.

Ten days later, on April 10, the U.S. Steel board of directors voted to raise the price of steel six dollars a ton on the average. Within hours Blough was in the White House, where he handed Kennedy notification of the increase. "I think you have made a terrible mistake," said the President. "Why did you bother to come, if the price increase is already decided on?" Minutes later Blough left the office. Then Kennedy began to press buttons on his desk; Goldberg, Robert Kennedy, Heller, and others entered the office. The President told them what had happened, his fury rising steadily. He was reported to have said, "My father always told me that all businessmen were sons of bitches, but I never believed it until now!"

The next few days were among the most exciting of the Kennedy years. The other major producers fell in behind U.S. Steel, and the President began to attack the company's actions. Inland and Kaiser Steel, which had not gone along with the increase, were praised; investigations were promised; pressures were exerted. Speaking to the nation, the President said, "The simultaneous and identical actions . . . constitute a wholly unjustifiable and irresponsible defiance of the public interest."

Such an onslaught could not be withstood. Bethlehem Steel rescinded the increase, and shortly thereafter all the other companies backed down.

Kennedy had won his battle with the steel companies, and his popularity remained strong, even with the business community, which thought Blough and his group had bungled matters terribly. Organized labor now knew the President meant to hold management to the same guidelines it imposed upon the unions. In time, several steel company leaders privately admitted that even had Kennedy not acted, the prices could not have been maintained in the light of foreign competition. The President moved swiftly to assure business that he was no opponent of free-enterprise capitalism; the wounds seemed to heal quickly.

But a residue of mistrust remained. *The Wall Street Journal,* never friendly to the Administration, wrote: "We never saw anything like it. One of the country's companies announced it was going to try to get more money for its product and promptly all hell busted loose." *The U.S. News and World Report* thought the episode would please only the "advocates of state socialism—often the forerunner of Communism." The Senate Republican Leadership Committee criticized the action, asking, "Should a President of the United States use the enormous powers of the Federal Government to blackjack any segment of our free society into line with his personal judgment without regard to law?" More commentators, however, echoed the *New York Herald Tribune* in its assessment. The newspaper noted that the President had acted forcefully during the steel crisis, and this was a welcome change from the vacillating leadership in the Bay of Pigs incident and the Berlin Wall crisis. "We do respect decisiveness in an executive and so do the people," the paper concluded. "We can only wish it had been displayed in a better cause." This was the crux of the issue: for the first time since entering office, Kennedy had shown himself to be a strong President. The man who could not take a stand elsewhere—especially in the field of foreign policy —meant to stand by his determination to prevent inflation. The lesson was obvious: prices would be carefully watched; inflation would be retarded; earnings growth on the part of large corporations might be held back.

The stock markets had reflected this belief months before. The averages fell from a high of 734.91 to 720.10 in late December 1961. Then followed a recovery to 726.01 in January, followed by a reaction to 689.92 later in that month. The average rose to 717.55 in mid-February, fell back to 706.22, and rallied to 723.54 in mid-March. At this point a long slide began. Early in April the Dow-Jones Industrials fell to 685.67—giving what D-J theorists marked as a "sell signal." In effect, they said, the averages now signaled the beginning of a bear market by falling through a major resistance level. Then came the steel controversy, depressing prices still further. By the third week in April, Wall Street opinion had shifted to the bear side of the market. This had not been *caused* by Kennedy's clash with Blough; rather, the conflict had crystallized bearish sentiment already present in the district and had provided justification for the view that large and dramatic increases in earnings would be more difficult in the future.

At the same time, the SEC prepared to open its Wall Street investigations, the Billie Sol Estes scandal dominated the front pages, and word arrived that DuPont would soon distribute its holdings of General Motors, a move which many thought would depress the price of these key issues. "For the moment, Wall Street does not like what it sees ahead for the economy," wrote *Business Week* on May 5. "It thinks that the dramatic recovery in business is over; in fact, some analysts look for a recession later this year or maybe next year. Investors expect the profit squeeze to intensify and corporate earnings to slide gently from now on." The article went on to note the general weakness of the previous week.

The market also reflects a wide-spread belief that the Kennedy Administration is anti-business, that business will be the scapegoat when it becomes inevitably necessary to shake out the economy in order to remedy the U.S. balance-of-payments deficit. In this view, the steel uproar typifies the anti-business attitude. The episode didn't cause the downfall in stock prices, but it accelerated the trend.

By then, bad business news and sharp dips on Wall Street had become common. IBM, the bellwether growth issue, lost 31½ points on April 30, and other glamour issues followed. The newspapers noted that many groups had not performed well for many months. Since January 1, IBM had lost 125 points; Superior Oil 105 points; Rohm and Haas 94 points; Litton Industries 48 points; Beckman Instruments 46 points; and Texas Instruments 41 points. On May 1, the Dow-Jones Industrials—blue chips all—sold at a price-earnings ratio of 19.6–1; five months earlier the figure had been 23–1. And as the high-quality glamour issues lost more than the Dow-Jones Industrials, so the lower-priced and inferior quality speculative issues had dropped more sharply in the first part of the year.

**PERCENTAGE DECLINES OF GLAMOUR ISSUES,
JANUARY 1–MAY 1, 1962**

Issue	Percentage Decline
Transitron	45
Sparton Industries	43
Hallicrafters	38
Bell & Howell	38
Nafi	37
Ward Industries	36
Haveg Industries	35
Bobbie Brooks	35
Automatic Canteen	35
Walter Heller	35
Great Western Financial Corp.	34
Vendo	30

Source: *New York Times,* May 13, 1962

In this same period, several glamour *groups* showed similar drops.

DECLINES OF LEADING GROUPS, JANUARY 1–MAY 1, 1962

Group	Percentage Decline
Vending Machines	54.1
Aluminum	47.8
Cement	38.6
Special Machinery	38.5
Steel	36.6
Air Transport	34.1

Source: *Business Week,* May 5, 1962

The poor market performance during the first five months of the year was well known and publicized, as was the reason. Burton Crane, who had long argued that prices were too high, thought that the market would soon adjust itself to more realistic ratios. Writing on May 2, he said: "This happens to coincide with a growing belief that the rates of earning growth for some of the glamour stocks were no longer justifying the high price-earnings multipliers conferred by the markets in the past." At the same time, the *Times* announced that steel production had hit an eight-month low, a sign that the economic recovery of the past year and a half was slowing down. That week Walter Gutman of Stearns & Company, one of the most respected analysts in the district, was charged with leaking information to friends regarding his coming selections. E. M. Gilbert of E. L. Bruce & Co. left the country after failing to gain control of Celotex Corporation; shortly thereafter, wrongdoing was discovered at Bruce. This was followed by news that Swiss investors, long reputed to be among the most astute in the world, were selling American securities. "We are skeptical but not pessimistic about the U.S. outlook," said one Zurich banker. "The United States is facing a psychological rather than an economic crisis."

All of these statements and occurrences combined to lead prices downward in the first part of the month.

PRICES OF SELECTED ISSUES ON SELECTED DATES IN 1962

Issue	Closing Prices (fractions rounded off)			
	April 27	May 4	May 11	May 18
American Telephone & Telegraph	124	125	116	120
Chrysler	52	51	49	50
General Dynamics	31	31	28	29
IBM	454	486	446	451
Korvette	52	50	45	46
Litton	104	111	114	117
Polaroid	186	185	146	141
Sperry-Rand	19	20	18	18
Texas Instruments	82	88	84	88
U.S. Steel	60	57	56	57
Xerox	142	147	138	128

Source: *New York Times*, April 28–May 19, 1962

By May 11, the bear market was in full swing. That Friday prices declined rapidly, in the worst selling wave of the year up to that time. Financial columnist Clyde E. Farnsworth wrote that "a full-scale reappraisal of market values is under way." Shields & Co. noted that earnings would probably level off in the second half as a result of corporation timidity after the steel crisis. Most of the services advertising in the Sunday *Times* of the May 13 were bearish.

Despite the partial recovery of the following week, the mood remained grim. The financial page of the May 20 *Times* observed that open-end investment companies had increased their liquid holdings from $980 million to $1,284 million in the first three months of the year, and were continuing to increase investments in government notes and deposits. The *Times* thought such massive purchasing power would enable the market to turn back any selloff. On the other hand, it indicated that the funds were becoming disenchanted with growth prospects for the short run. The article also noted that a stock-market seat had sold for $150,-000 on May 16, a drop from the twenty-eight-year peak of $225,000 on March 24, 1961, and this was another indication of bearish sentiment.

Stocks declined sharply on heavy volume at the New York Stock Exchange on Monday, May 21, and the falloff continued into Tuesday. By Wednesday morning market analysts were reporting that all indicators were pointing downward, and news services observed the increase of short selling and the renewed interest in put options. Prices fell from the opening bell on Wednesday, and never rallied. More than 5.4 million shares were traded in one of the worst sessions in postwar history. At the close, tape watchers learned that the NYSE had registered 460 new lows against five new highs for the year.

During the day, President Kennedy held his regular news conference and, when asked about the economy, said it remained strong. He refused to express concern over developments on Wall Street. "I believe that the stock market will move when—in accordance with the movement of the economy as a general rule," was his only reference to the crash. A broker noted, "People have been sitting around praying all day."

More prayers were offered for astronaut Scott Carpenter, who prepared for his space flight the next day. Carpenter went up successfully on Thursday, May 24. In the past, such feats would have had a bullish effect on science-related issues, but the market continued its plunge, recording 442 new lows against four new highs. Edwin Posner, head of the American Stock Exchange, told reporters that "this definitely is not panic selling. We have had a ten-year bull market, and this evidently is the time for an adjustment. Stocks are now getting down to a realistic level." Keith Funston added that there was no slump in sight. George M. Mitchell of the Federal Reserve thought the market fall reflected a sluggish economy, and little more. Burton Crane observed that conditions were usually bad when reporters ran around asking important people their opinions of the market and economy.

The market closed the week badly, as stocks continued to slide on Friday. After closing, market statisticians reported that the Dow-Jones Industrials had fallen 38.83 points to 611.88, lowering the index by 4.19 percent. The value of all listed stocks on the NYSE had declined $30 billion, more than the combined gross national products of Australia, Sweden, and Ireland.

PRICES OF SELECTED ISSUES IN MAY 1962

Issue	Closing Prices (fractions rounded off)				
	May 21	May 22	May 23	May 24	May 25
American Telephone & Telegraph	119	117	115	115	113
Chrysler	50	48	47	47	47
General Dynamics	29	28	27	27	27
IBM	450	435	415	398	399
Korvette	46	43	41	41	41
Litton	115	111	107	106	112
Polaroid	136	127	125	130	136
Sperry-Rand	18	17	17	17	16
Texas Instruments	86	83	79	78	78
U.S. Steel	57	55	54	54	52
Xerox	126	120	110	108	114

Source: *New York Times*

The market was thirty-two minutes late at the close on Friday, as more than 6.3 million shares changed hands. Even before the last trade was registered, analysts were talking about what had been the sharpest decline since 1929. That night and over the weekend the newspapers were dotted with stories about the crash and advice from the experts. *Times* financial writer John Forrest noted the relative absence of panic selling and thought this encouraging. Keith Funston thought there had been a "considerable diminution of confidence," but no panic. Burton Crane summarized the week: "Stocks went down for five days in a row last week, five days that carried the market averages back to the levels at the end of 1960, and 15,000,000 shareholders suffered from unusual demands to their minds." Crane would offer no advice but said, "the professional would say, get out." The papers published melancholy lists showing how badly stocks had fallen since the golden days of 1961.

The advisory services were divided as to what would follow the decline. On the one hand, stocks had already fallen sharply and on Friday there had been periods of recovery. Accordingly, one service thought that "many equities have declined to zones of good support," and another wrote that "the selling, largely emotional, has been overdone against the present business background." On the other hand, a respected advisor considered stocks "still grossly overvalued despite its recent decline." The Dow-Jones News Service, following the theories of its founder, added, "Should the industrial average be able to hold around the 610 level, brokers say the dramatic effect alone may prove of near-term

DECLINES OF KEY STOCKS, 1961–1962

Issue	(fractions rounded off) 1961–1962 Highs	May 25 Close
Addressograph-Multigraph	109	56
American Electric Power	78	60
American Telephone & Telegraph	140	112
Bethlehem Steel	49	36
Certain-Teed	80	30
Du Pont	255	215
Ford	118	87
General Electric	81	66
IBM	607	398
Minnesota Mining	88	58
Polaroid	239	136
Sears Roebuck	95	73
Union Carbide	144	96
United Aircraft	56	46

Source: *Wall Street Journal*, May 28, 1962

help to the market generally—if it should not, however, these sources say that the technicians would be groping for a clue as to where a solid bottom might be found."

For many Americans, the decline of May 20–25 was a new experience. When told that it was the sharpest drop since the Great Crash—one advisory service asked in its advertisement, "Another 1929 Stock Market?"—they had visions of breadlines, NRA, WPA, and the like. Given these comparisons, and the many parallels drawn between the twenties and the sixties (one writer called Kennedy "the thinking man's Coolidge"), a panic atmosphere might have been considered possible. But one of the most striking elements of the 1962 crash was the almost total lack of panic. To be sure, those who held stocks were unhappy at seeing values melt almost overnight, but they remained calm in the face of it.

The reasons for this calm were not hard to find. Unlike 1929, the banking system was sound; corporations were secure; the government's role as a guarantor of the economy was not in doubt. Stock declines might cause investors to lose money, but margin calls were unlikely, since stocks were usually purchased for cash in 1962 or, at most, on 80 percent margin. Thus, many investors watched the decline with as much fascination as fear, with more interest than panic.

There was little of the usual badinage among brokers who met before the opening on May 28. Nothing had occurred over the weekend to dispel the bearish sentiment of the previous Friday. Afterward they would exchange stories of huge stop-loss orders (orders to sell if and when a security fell to a specific point) phoned in before the opening. Yet the atmosphere of panic was still missing. Not even when stocks fell from the opening, or when the ticker began to run late after the first half-hour of trading, did the note of fear appear. The 610 level, thought a support point by many theorists, fell quickly; by noon the D-J Industrials were at 600.90, and still falling on unusually strong volume. Every group participated in the fall, with the glamours leading the way. The ticker was unable to keep up with the rush, and began sending out "flash prices" of thirty key stocks as early as 10:20 A.M.; at noon, even these had to be dispensed with by the frantic ticker operators. By then, the would-be seller had no idea of current buy-sell prices for his stock, since the ticker was almost an hour late. Floor brokers stuffed orders in their pockets, hoping to fill them whenever possible. In many cases these orders were simply forgotten. (On June 7, the Board of Governors ruled that member firms which did not fill orders during the week of May 28 would not be punished under the negligence rule.)

The stock-market crash was headline news by noon, and was reported on all the major networks. Radio and television station managers ordered special programs that evening, scouring Wall Street and the universities for "experts" who could tell the public what had happened, and what to expect next. Statisticians busied themselves trying to figure how many billions in values had been liquidated, and boardrooms were stuffed with customers and the curious, who watched the tape carefully, told each other what the symbols meant, and in general commiserated with each other. But even there, the signs of panic were not present. "It was though some great natural calamity had occurred to some far-distant people, and we watched with horror and fascination, but not fear," said one broker after the day was over.

The market closed at the usual time—3:30 P.M.—in a flurry of last-minute transactions, and the exhausted brokers let out with their usual cheer. But the ticker kept pounding out the story of the decline. As usual, the Pacific Coast Stock Exchange remained open an hour later, but the last quotation on the New York ticker did not appear until the West Coast market was closed. Finally, at 5:58, the ticker stopped. The Exchange reported that 9,350,000 shares were traded—the fifth most active day in stock-market history up to that time—and that the D-J Industrials had fallen by 34.95 points, closing at 576.93, for a 5.7 percent drop. As usual, volume was lower on the American Stock Exchange (2,980,000 shares), but the drop was more severe (6.3 percent). The huge over-the-counter market was in a shambles, and quotes on several issues were unavailable until the next morning.

The postmortem began after the market closed. Keith Funston blamed the crash on the government. "There has been a growing disquiet among investors because of Kennedy's steel action," he said, adding, "The Securities and Exchange Commission hearings hurt the market." "Something resembling an earthquake hit the stock market," editorialized the *Times*. "In the climate of fear that sent quotations tumbling little attention was being paid to the rather cheering picture presented by current economic indicators." The President was urged to go on nationwide television to reassure the troubled, but refused to do so, remembering

MOST ACTIVE STOCKS, NEW YORK STOCK EXCHANGE, MAY 28, 1962

Issue	Volume	Close	Change
American Telephone & Telegraph	282,000	100⅝	−11
Standard Oil of New Jersey	148,200	46	− 5
General Telephone & Electronics	108,800	19¼	− 1¼
Brunswick	103,000	23¼	− 4⅝
General Motors	99,500	48⅞	− 4⅝
U.S. Steel	87,500	50⅜	− 1⅞
Bethlehem Steel	86,300	33¼	− 2½
Avco	81,900	18⅜	− 2⅞
Studebaker-Packard	76,200	7	− ⅛
American Machine & Foundry	69,100	20	− 4¾
Radio Corporation of America	67,500	47⅞	− 5⅛
Reynolds Tobacco	64,600	49	− 3¼
Korvette	63,600	37½	− 2⅞
IBM	57,600	361	−37½
Royal Dutch	53,900	33⅞	− 3

Source: *New York Times*, May 29, 1962

Hoover's mistakes of 1929. Walter Heller called the crash a "disturbing correction." In an article headlined "Stunning Blow to Market," *Izvestia* opined, "President Kennedy and his advisors would like to arrest the crash, but do not know how to do this." The Soviet newspaper was certain the decline was part of a diabolical scheme. "Certain circles in the United States are trying to use the market situation as a pretext for a new onslaught on the rights of the working class." On Wall Street a broker was heard to say bitterly, "This is what we get for putting a rich man's son in the White House."

Although the crash lacked true panic aspects, Wall Street did expect the usual support from a strong influence to materialize. This would not come from an individual like J. P. Morgan or a group such as the Federal Reserve or a consortium of bankers. Instead, Wall Street looked to men like Dwight Robinson of Massachusetts Investment Trust, Joseph Fitzsimmons of Investors Diversified Services, Walter Morgan of Wellington Fund, and Cameron Reed of United Funds for support. None of these names were familiar to the general public, or for that matter to most Wall Streeters. But each man controlled more money than did Morgan at his prime. They were the presidents of the largest mutual funds in America. The Massachusetts Investment Trust alone reported more than a billion dollars in assets. Like the other funds, MIT was in a highly liquid position on May 28, with more than 10 percent of its assets in cash and government securities. Now it entered the market, looking for bargains. A. Moyer Kulp, senior vice-president of the Wellington Fund, announced that his company was also buying stocks. "While we're not jumping in with both feet, we are investing selectively," he told reporters. "We came into the market with a twenty percent cash position," said a spokesman for the Dreyfus Fund, "and we have been buying recently." And the cash reserves grew in the days that followed. Mutual-fund investors had purchased $4.4 million worth of shares in the fifty-four leading funds on Monday but turned in $6.8 million. Reading the report of the crash, these small investors apparently decided that it was time for bargain hunting on their own. In many cases they had no idea of the worth of their funds, for the late tape prevented many mutuals from reporting their losses. Still, on Tuesday morning, small investors poured their money into their holdings. Some $26.9 million worth of funds were purchased Tuesday, against $6.9 million in refunds.

Henry Ford and Thomas Watson were asked to comment on the decline; both refused. But one Ford executive indicated that it would be proper for the Administration to issue some kind of statement. This would be a second aspect of the crash: Washington, not New York, would take leadership in any crisis which developed.

Early Tuesday morning the President met with Secretary of the Treasury Douglas Dillon, Heller, Federal Reserve Chairman William McChesney Martin, Jr., and a group of economists to discuss possible actions in light of the crash. Kennedy was told that any comparison between 1962 and 1929 was grossly exaggerated. The economy was healthy and the banks sound; drastic actions were not necessary. Some advisers suggested a "fireside chat" might be in order; a second group favored an immediate reduction in the margin requirements; a third thought a tax cut of from $5 to $10 billion would be viewed as a bullish sign. Kennedy considered all, and in time supported each, but concluded that no action would be the best policy. Six weeks later margin requirements were lowered, and the Administration pressed for a tax cut. Kennedy did not go on television that day. Instead, Administration spokesmen were instructed to release optimistic statements to the press.

Secretary of Commerce Luther Hodges observed that since most large companies were self-financing, the market decline and any capital shortage that might develop would not affect their plans. Hodges thought a tax cut would be proper, along with a new schedule of depreciation allowances. Other Administration leaders issued similar statements. Walter Heller dared paraphrase, in a half-joking manner, what FDR had declared in 1933 by stating: "I think the market has nothing to fear but fear itself." The only important businessman to speak to the press was J. Paul Getty, and the oil tycoon was hardly a Wall Street figure. Getty said that he had bought stocks during the previous week and on Monday. "When some folks see others selling they automatically follow suit," he explained. "I do the reverse—and buy. I don't think the slide will go on. In fact, I think there will be a rather substantial rise and very shortly." Walter Benedict of Investors Planning Corporation, a one-billion-dollar concern, was one of the few fund managers who tried to become a public figure. Benedict announced that his funds were buying, and indeed had purchased some $20 million worth of stock during the past two trading sessions.

By early Tuesday morning, news of support by the funds was bandied about by brokers and analysts. Later on, many Wall Streeters said they expected a rally to develop sometime during the day. But this was not evident shortly after the opening bell. Prices picked up where they had left off Monday, and sank rapidly. By the end of the first hour, the D-J Industrials were down another eleven points, falling at a slightly more rapid rate than they had the previous day. But then the funds and bargain hunters entered the arena, and for the first time that week, solid support appeared. It was not clear at the time whether the averages had turned, for volume was high and the tape late. At one o'clock, for example, the D-J ticker showed a loss of 13.61 points, when in reality, based on floor trades at the time, the average was up 7.72 points. But the brokers knew the prices were rallying, and shortly thereafter the customers' men relayed this information to the public. Buying pressure mounted.

By 1:30 the market was in the midst of its greatest rally since the end of World War II. From a decline of more than eleven points, it ended the day with a gain of 27.03, or 4.7 percent. Again the tape was late, ending its run more than two hours after the 3:30 closing. Volume was 14,750,000 shares—the second highest in Exchange history. Not until the end of the week were statisticians able to reconstruct exactly what had happened, and its magnitude. By Friday they reported that prices had declined 48.64 points from the previous Friday's close to noon on Tuesday, and then rallied 40.72 points from noon to 3:30.

MOST ACTIVE STOCKS, NEW YORK STOCK EXCHANGE, MAY 29, 1962

Issue	Volume	Close	Change
American Telephone & Telegraph	341,900	108½	+ 7⅞
Brunswick	198,300	26¾	+ 3½
Avco	193,500	20¼	+ 1⅞
General Motors	190,600	51	+ 2⅛
General Telephone & Electronics	145,500	21¼	+ 2
Standard Oil of New Jersey	140,700	50⅞	+ 4⅞
U.S. Steel	129,700	53¼	+ 2⅞
Bethlehem Steel	120,800	35⅜	+ 2⅛
General Tire & Rubber	120,200	23	+ 4½
American Motors	115,500	14	+ ¾
American Machine & Foundry	115,000	24¼	+ 4¼
Magnavox	110,200	33½	+ 3
Sperry-Rand	109,100	16⅛	+ ⅝
Certain-Teed	102,600	23⅝	+ ⅝
Korvette	102,600	37¾	+ ¼

Source: *New York Times*, May 30, 1962

President Kennedy received the news of the market rally in Middlebury, Virginia, where he and his family had gathered to celebrate his forty-fifth birthday. It was a fine present. The crisis was over.

Wednesday was Memorial Day, and the markets were closed. Some firms asked their employees to come in, however, so as to clear away the piles of paper which had gathered during the hectic Monday and Tuesday sessions. The atmosphere was calm and assured; many Wall Streeters expected the Thursday trading to pick up where Tuesday had left off.

The combination of the off day and the optimism bred by the Tuesday rally led to a mood of confidence for the Thursday opening. Trading was hectic, and brokers poured accumulated buy orders into the hopper. Prices took off at once and continued to climb on heavy volume. For the third straight session the tape ran late, the last transaction being recorded at 5:25. More than 10,700,000 shares were traded, and the D-J Industrials showed a gain of 9.40 points, erasing the last vestige of the crash.

With conditions apparently back to normal, volume and prices eased on Friday. The dramatic week of May 28–June 1 ended with

MOST ACTIVE STOCKS, NEW YORK STOCK EXCHANGE, MAY 31, 1962

Issue	Volume	Close	Change
American Telephone & Telegraph	414,800	113¼	+ 4¾
Avco	190,300	21½	+ 1¼
General Motors	128,600	51	——
Brunswick	120,600	28½	+ 1¾
General Telephone & Electronics	119,100	22⅜	+ 1⅛
Magnavox	114,200	34⅛	+ ⅝
U.S. Steel	107,800	54⅛	+ ⅞
General Tire & Rubber	103,800	24½	+ 1½
Bethlehem Steel	102,500	37½	+ 2⅛
American Machine & Foundry	101,300	26⅝	+ 2⅜
Standard Oil of New Jersey	99,700	52	+ 1⅛
Korvette	85,900	39¼	+ 1½
Zenith	77,400	53¾	——
Sperry-Rand	71,000	17⅜	+ 1¼
American Motors	70,400	14¾	+ ¾

Source: *New York Times,* June 1, 1962

many key stocks at approximately the same price they had been on May 25.

On June 1, a reporter asked former President Eisenhower what he thought of the situation. Ike blamed "reckless spending programs of the Kennedy Administration," and called for the end of what he termed a "planned economy." But, by then, the crash was over, to remain alive in the tall stories of brokers and others who would exaggerate its impact more each time they told the story.

Although the immediate danger of a large-scale correction had ended, and despite the apparent soundness of securities, scars remained on Wall Street. The new issues market was hard hit, and for the next five years remained dormant. Many salesmen, especially those attracted to brokerage during the boom, left Wall Street as their customers showed disillusionment with the get-rich-quick psychology that preceded the December decline. Some of the smaller over-the-counter brokerages went under, and others merged in order to remain solvent. Ross, Lyon & Co. left the underwriting field. Reynolds & Co. announced a temporary halt to its trainee program. The New York Society of Security Analysts reported that fifty of its four hundred members were looking for jobs; subscriptions to advisory services fell sharply.

During the next few months, many attempts were made to explain the crash. Many said that prices were "too high," but these were the same people who before the rise in mid-1961 said that prices were "too low." Stocks are always undervalued or overvalued in retrospect, but never in prospect. The simple fact of the matter is that no one knows the proper price for a stock at any given time.

It is true, however, that the growth theories of the late 1950s seemed out of place in 1962, as earnings leveled off and a serious attempt to prevent inflation was being made. Had not the steel crisis developed, it is likely that prices would have declined steadily on Wall Street with few comments or spectacular trading sessions. According to *Fortune* (June, 1962), "Kennedy's double-barreled blast hit the expectations of the average investor and businessman alike. Stocks went off immediately, and not long afterwards thousands of panic-stricken investors were throwing their securities into the hopper without even asking how much the shares would fetch. In a short time the various stock markets proceeded to revalue the nation's industrial assets downward by more than $100 billion. This revaluation sounds worse than it is, but it is bad enough."

EXTENT OF LOSSES IN THE 1962 KENNEDY SLIDE

Category	Market Value of Holdings on Dec. 31, 1961	Market Value of Holdings on June 18, 1962	Loss
American Individuals	$461.4 billion	$364.4 billion	$97 billion
Individuals Abroad	11.9	9.4	2.5
Pension Funds	21.0	16.5	4.5
Life Insurance Companies	6.2	4.9	1.3
Banks	1.1	.9	.2
Government Trust Funds	.6	.5	.1
Other Institutions	9.5	7.5	2.0
	511.7	404.1	107.6

Source: *Wall Street Journal,* June 20, 1962

The SEC investigated the crash, suspecting wrongdoing and hoping to correct it through new legislation. But after a thorough investigation, its special committee concluded that there were signs of incompetence, but none of malfeasance. The causes of the crash? The SEC concluded that "the history of the May 28 market break reveals that a complex interaction of causes and effects—including rational and emotional motivations as well as a variety of mechanisms and pressures—may suddenly create a downward spiral of great velocity and force. This, in turn, may change the impact of various normal market mechanisms, and thus temporarily impair the market's fair and orderly character." The Commission could do nothing about this. The report concluded: "Neither the Study nor the NYSE has been able to ascertain the precipitating 'causes' of the May, 1962 market break." Throughout the report there runs an undercurrent of suspicion of wrongdoing, but no proof is offered. The committee, in the end, appeared to dismiss the crash as a unique, isolated event, of a nonrecurrent nature.

This is not to understate the importance or magnitude of the 1962 crash. Stocks would continue to slide, touching an interday low of 524.55 on June 25 before rallying. Not until the end of the Cuban missile confrontation in October did a true rally develop, one which carried on for the rest of the Kennedy Administration and into the early Johnson years.

When measured from the December 1961 peak to the June bottom, the 1962 crash showed a loss of 27 percent in paper values. In comparison, the 1929–32 bear market saw values melt by 89 percent. Bear markets in 1937 and 1940 were worse than that of 1962, and the declines of 1947, 1952, and 1958 were almost as bad. But none of these had the potential for panic which existed on May 28, 1962. All the ingredients were there: a runaway stock market, disillusioned investors, weak leadership, and a dramatic political blow—and the panic did not appear. Instead there was a sharp decline, a rapid recovery, followed by a resumption of the Kennedy slide, which was finally succeeded by a new bull market.

The failure of a panic psychology to develop was notable, especially since many economists and analysts had been warning of "another 1929" for years. Apparently the financial panic is a thing of the past. Seemingly the new mechanisms of a mature capitalist society have made them relics. The programs of the New Deal, combined with the strengthened economic structure of postwar America, have given the nation a security it never possessed before. One might say that the world of Joe Kennedy has become remote, and many of the ideas and possibilities of his period were no longer present during his son's administration. But the SEC and other New Deal agencies, organized by Joe Kennedy's generation, made it possible for his son to survive the 1962 crash with little more than a bad memory.

13.

ANOTHER 1929?: THE
CRASH OF 1987

On Tuesday, August 25, 1987, the Dow-Jones Industrials went as high as 2747 before closing at 2722, up 25 points on the day. It was a new record.*

It was the fifty-sixth time this had happened in 1987. Since mid-May, stocks had soared beyond the expectation of almost every analyst, rising some 500 points. The Dow was now selling for more than twenty-one times earnings. This was not a record, but was lofty as such things went. As measured by the Dow, the market had advanced 43 percent since December 31, 1986. It was a continuation of a four-year trend. On August 15, 1982, the Dow had closed at 788. Measured by that familiar index, stocks had more than tripled.

After August 25, stocks drifted, losing more than 83 points for the rest of the week, ending at 2663. The Dow was still more than 100 points above where it had been at the start of the month, and prices would rise 24 points the following Monday. On Tuesday stocks fell 52 points, however, followed by a 9-point decline the following day, 3 points on Thursday, and 38 on the last Friday before Labor Day.

The Dow was now at 2561, after its worst sell-off since the previous April. This action generated little nervousness. After the correction stocks were still 634 points above what they had been since the first trading session of the year.

That week Al Frank, a droll schoolteacher-turned-market-letter writer, termed the situation "dicey," but while predicting the large

* For the sake of simplicity, all fractions on the Dow and other indices will be rounded out.

capitalization stocks might move sideways for a while, said he would be buying the smaller issues. As was his wont, Frank was fully invested and used margin lavishly. "We do think there will be the fabled 10 percent to 15 percent correction before the final top," he concluded. That out of the way, it would be clear sailing to Dow 3000 and beyond.

The dark, somber Martin Zweig, who had one of the better records during the bull market, was less sanguine. He told reporters that his new mutual fund was 66 percent invested, down from 91 percent at the beginning of the week. Zweig dithered. He refused to fight his technical indicators, which had started to point downward. "I don't know what's happening," he somewhat embarrassedly confessed to *Barron's* writer Maggie Maher. "But if the Dow goes down 10 percent, you don't know if it's going to stop. It could be a killer. So it's easier for me to go with it, sell my stuff, and be flexible. I'm too nervous to do it any other way."

Not as much of a celebrity as Frank and Zweig, publisher Dan Sullivan, known as The Chartist, might have attributed this to his missing out on most of the great bull sweep of 1987. Confiding that he hadn't purchased a share of stock since early February, Sullivan awaited the correction he thought was on its way. The Dow was up by some thousand points during the past twelve months, he reluctantly observed, and a 50-percent retracement would take it down to the low 2200s, at which point he expected to come in and start buying. "That type of correction would be acceptable within a long-term bull market," said Sullivan, conceding that "it would scare a lot of people."

No forecaster's words were more carefully listened to than those of Robert Prechter, who based his predictions on the traceries of the Elliott Wave, a complex and convoluted theory. One writer once paraphrased Otto von Bismarck's remark about the Schleswig-Holstein problem by saying of the Elliott Wave that only three men understood it. Elliott was dead, the second went mad, and Prechter, the third, wasn't talking. In any event, the theory informed Prechter that the market was then in the fifth and final wave, and would peak somewhere between Dow 3600 and 3700. This level, he thought, would be reached before the end of 1988. Might it get there in 1987? Perhaps so, the analyst replied. His specific advice for September was that "long-term investors should hold. For traders, or anyone sitting on the sidelines who isn't comfortably invested, this is a buying opportunity."

So it went. There was an air of skittishness on the Street, but that was hardly news. "The market climbs a wall of worry" was one of the enduring clichés, repeated by the bulls whenever challenged, and considering the record, they had a point. A large number of respected analysts anticipated the kind of correction that Frank, Zweig, Sullivan, and Prechter discussed.

Almost all agreed that after it was over the Dow would resume its drive to the 3000 level and beyond. Among them were many corporate leaders who were buying shares in their own companies. *The Insiders,* an influential and carefully watched market letter, reported heavy purchases the previous month, with major accumulations in such firms as Equimark, Harcourt Brace Jovanovich, Lomas & Nettleton, and Reliance Group. George Soros, manager of the offshore Quantum Fund, which had a reputed $2.6 billion under management, and who had been selected as *Fortune* magazine's investor of the year, not only had plunged into stocks but also had purchased a large volume of stock index contracts, and so was heavily leveraged.

There are always naysayers. Economist John Kenneth Galbraith, author of *The Great Crash,* went on record as observing forbidding parallels between the current situation and what existed in 1929. Skeptics noted that Galbraith usually had such revelations when a Republican was in the White House. Tom Holt, who put out an investment advisory newsletter, sketched images of blood in the streets, but he had been doing so for as long as most could remember, and wasn't taken too seriously. Charles Allmon, a well-considered fund manager and editor of *The Growth Stock Outlook,* sold stocks that summer and by then was 78 percent in cash and equivalents. Financial consultant Ashby Bladen, author of *How to Cope with the Developing Financial Crisis,* continued to warn of dire consequences resulting from unwise economic policies. The dour analyst had been saying so for seven years, or since the bull market had begun. A columnist for *Forbes* magazine, Bladen had stepped down months before because editor Jim Michaels had decided he was merely repeating himself.

Then there was the flamboyant Joe Granville, who in the late 1970s and early 1980s had the kind of reputation Prechter enjoyed in 1987. Granville had predicted calamity in his book *The Warning*, in which he listed no fewer than 184 ways the market resembled that of 1929. The book was published in 1985. Since then the Dow had doubled.

At the time, Granville was something of a joke, but this wasn't always so. On January 6, 1981, he had flashed a sell signal, and Granville was then so authoritative that the market promptly declined almost 24 points, shaving $40 billion off market valuations on record volume of 93 million shares. Granville then embarked on a whirlwind lecture tour, in which he predicted an earthquake in California and claimed to be teaching a simian to drive his car. There was no earthquake, and Granville continued to drive his own car. He turned bullish once again in early 1987 and in October wrote, "I believe that a major bottom was in place in September. . . . I would expect a higher market in the weeks ahead." Granville's predictions were superb; it was just his timing that was off. For example, there was a California earthquake on October 1, 1987, less than three weeks before its financial counterpart struck Wall Street.

The bears looked for a correction, but virtually all of them thought that once it was over stocks would head into the 3000s. "At the end of the year the market will be higher than it is now," predicted Roger Ford, of Prudential Equity Management Associates, "but the market will be on the edge the whole time." Steven Goldstein of Knight-Ridder was certain upside pressures would continue because "there's a lot of money on the sidelines just waiting to come in"—presumably on corrections. Market-letter writer Steve Leeb offered what amounted to a consensus view that the correction, when it came, would be on the order of 15 percent, which would take the Dow down to the low 2300s. Leeb added, "I'm very, very bullish for the long term." *Business Week* echoed these sentiments. After taking a few blows, stocks would rise once again. The reasons were compelling. "The economy is strengthening, inflation is modest, corporate profits are exploding, the three-year binge of corporate takeovers is still in full force, and the U.S. stock market remains the cheapest in the world."

Such was the general situation in early October. Chart watchers saw a similarity between the traceries of September 1986 and those then being worked out by the Dow a year later. During that autumn stocks rose steadily and were at an all-time high in December. They suggested it would happen again.

Some were tense, most were confident, and almost all except the perennial bears thought the recent sell-off was a temporary hiatus in the continuing bull market.

As it happened, the Dow had reached its all-time high on August 25. For the next two months it would drift lower, and then collapse in the most dramatic sell-off in market history. The headline of the October 20 *New York Times* said it all: DOES 1987 EQUAL 1929? Other than questions relating to peace and war, this is still the most important question facing the nation today.

History does not repeat itself, said Mark Twain, but it rhymes. The true lessons of 1929 were not to guard against margin abuses and understand Keynesian prescriptions, but rather that panics feed upon themselves, and the best way to deal with crises is first to fathom the problem before setting out on a course of action. In so doing, experience may best be utilized as a compass, to indicate direction, and not as a roadmap, to provide a specific course of behavior. For example, Charles Kindleberger, one of the most astute students of panics and crashes, thought that the absence of blunders by a lender of last resort can be a major consideration. "As for timing, it is an art," Kindleberger wrote. "That says nothing— and everything."

What precisely had happened in 1929? Between October 10 and November 13, the Dow fell by more than 154 points, which came to 40 percent of its valuation. Stocks next rallied, making up half the loss, until spring. They then declined erratically until July 8, 1932, having fallen from 381 on September 3, 1929, to 41 in two years. This, in its entirety, is what the general public considered to have been the Crash.

The economic outlook surely was bleak by the time it was over. The nation's gross national product had fallen from $103 billion to $58 billion. There were 12 million unemployed, which translated to one out of every four workers. The steel operating rate, then deemed a key economic indicator, was 20 percent. The budget deficit that year was $2.7 billion, which as several writers pointed out was more than the Union costs in fighting the Civil War. That kind of statistic impressed people in those years. And this is what was considered the bottom of the Great Depression, which was to last for the rest of the decade.

The Crash and the Depression were inextricably united in the public mind, the general belief being that the former was the direct cause of the latter. It was useless to argue that breadlines did not appear in America's large cities during the winter of 1929–1930, that the unemployment rate in 1930, though admittedly high, was 8.7 percent, and so below the 1921 level of 11.7 percent, and that given different leadership and economic policies it needn't have gone much higher. The Crash *cum* Depression scenario was annealed in the public imagination; as far as most Americans were concerned, there was a direct link between brokers and customers flying out of Wall Street's skyscrapers and the rise of Hoovervilles—though neither yet existed in 1929–1930.

During the next half century memories and legends of that period haunted the nation. When the market sold off sharply in 1937, there were cries of "another 1929," and the same would be heard during every important correction thereafter. It echoed and reechoed in 1946, 1957, and 1962. There was talk of another 1929 in 1966, when inflationary fears coupled with disillusion over the Vietnam War prompted an 18-percent sell-off in less than four months. Strikingly, all of these episodes, and other important negative developments, climaxed during the month of October, as though ghostlike memories of autumn 1929 lingered at the exchanges and had some effect on investors' psychologies.

The major test of the conviction that significant crashes were the destiny awaiting those who enjoyed significant booms came in the autumn and early winter of 1968. This event, if any, could have shaken the old verities, and so merits some consideration.

At that time the Great Bull Market that many consider to have begun in the late 1940s came to an end, doing so in a fashion that convinced some who feared utter disaster that the 1929 scenario would never be repeated. The key factor was not a dramatic event, but rather the lack of same: this bull market did not end in panic, but rather tranquilly, and the culmination was so unexceptional it was perceivable only in retrospect.

As might have been expected, the mood was euphoric in 1968, though as always there were skeptics. "There are a lot of fringe underwriters in now," said Stanley Nabi of Schweickart & Co., reflecting on the mania for new issues. Walter Stern of Burnham & Co. added that "there seems to be a weakening of the technical underpinning of the market." That autumn many Americans were reading *The Money Game* by Adam Smith, the pen name for George Goodman of *The Institutional Investor* magazine. "The real object of the Game," wrote Goodman, mocking the public's attitude toward the market, "is the playing of the Game itself. For the true players, you could take all the trophies away and substitute plastic beads or whales' teeth; as long as there is a way to keep score, they will play."

The market was in a bullish mode in early October. There was a dazzling session on the 14th, when a mind-boggling 21 million shares were traded with the tape running late much of the day. The Dow reached 969 shortly after noon, but ended at 959, up 3 points for the session. It hit 974 in interday trading a week later, and then declined.

On October 29, the anniversary of Black Tuesday, Alan Corey III, a twenty-five-year-old securities firm trainee, purchased a NYSE seat for half a million dollars, a price that matched the high for the year. The Dow finished at 951 on a volume of 12 million shares as the market turned wary on concerns regarding inflation, which that year would come to a shade over 4 percent.

These apprehensions prompted the Fed to tighten up on the money supply, and there were rumors a hike in the discount rate would follow. With this, stocks sold off. On December 2 several banks, led by Chase Manhattan, raised their discount rates to 6½ percent. The Dow was at 994, up more than 9 points from the previous session, when the news reached Wall Street. Then followed a massive price break, the average collapsing 30 points in less than two hours. A recovery followed, however, and the market closed at 983, down by less than 2 points for the day. There would be further declines and recoveries, but months later it was realized

that stocks had peaked in early December. The bull market had
come to an end.

Several reasons for the bull's demise were argued. For one thing,
in both absolute and adjusted-for-inflation terms, stock prices were
very high, almost 50 percent more on an inflation-adjusted basis
than they had been at the 1929 top. The telling blow, however, was
that familiar bull market killer: higher interest rates.

A year later the Dow was under 800, and the mood on the Street
was decidedly bearish. Not until May 1970, when the average hit
627 in interday trading, would it find bottom.

While it was difficult to console those who saw the value of their
portfolios shrink, they might at least have reflected that the decline
had been calm, there was no depression, and it certainly was not
"another 1929." The most sustained and powerful bull market since
that of the 1920s terminating in so orderly a fashion was encouraging.

There was a recovery in 1970–1971, followed by another sell-off in
late 1971, a rise in 1972, with the Dow crossing the 1000 level in
early 1973, only to fall to 570 during the Christmas season in 1974.
The Dow was back over 1000 in 1976, and under 750 in 1978.

There seemed to be a pattern in all of this, which was vaguely
comforting. The markets of the 1970s were volatile, but they traded
within a fairly predictable range. Once prices got to around the 1000
level they would fall back, and when a bottom was found, they
started up once again. By the early 1980s there were expectations of
further sell-offs akin to those of 1966, 1970, 1973–1974, and 1977,
but nothing more than that. This is to suggest that while the market
might catch a cold, and even undergo a bout of influenza, trepida-
tions regarding pneumonia were fading.

And for good and sufficient reason. Throughout the nation, economics and history professors ticked off the argument as though by
rote. The primary reason offered was that the world of the 1920s
bore little resemblance to that of the 1970s and presumably that of
the 1980s as well. There were allusions to the Securities Exchange
Act, the separation of investment and commercial banking under
the terms of the Glass-Steagall Act, the invigoration of the Federal
Reserve System, but most of all, the development of keener eco-

nomic intelligence and an awareness that Washington and Wall Street now knew how to deal with crises such as that of 1929. All these would make a repetition of the Crash scenario impossible. Thus, the ghost of 1929 was exorcised by cold, geometric logic.

This approach was dangerously misleading, indicating the speakers had developed a Maginot Line mentality, one of the more dangerous misconceptions.* The story often is told of two historians visiting the site of the Battle of Waterloo. "This is an important place," intoned one. "Napoleon once stood here." "True enough," responded the other, "but even more important is that Napoleon can never stand here again." And a knowledge of the 1929 Crash, as will be seen, can offer only limited appreciation of what happened in 1987. How could it be otherwise? The 1987 Crash occurred fifty-eight years after the 1929 debacle and was as distant from the world of Herbert Hoover as his was from the era of President U. S. Grant. If panics in the world of gaslight and horses and buggies offered few guidelines for one of electricity and autos, what lessons might that latter world have to guide individuals in our era of electronics and space vehicles?

In 1979, when the nation "celebrated" the Crash's fiftieth anniversary, scores of articles were written pointing out why it couldn't happen again. The conclusion was that future bull markets might come to an end as did that of the 1960s, which is to say in an orderly fashion. Thus, the ghost of 1929 seemed to have been exorcised by time as well.

Stock prices were historically low in 1979, though one wouldn't have guessed from the raw figures. The market had peaked at 381 in 1929; the 1979 high, reached in early October, was 898. Measured in nominal terms, stocks had doubled in this span. But this did not take into account inflation. Gauged in terms of the consumer price index (CPI), prices of goods doubled from 1929 to 1968, and did so again from 1968 to 1979. This is to suggest that, adjusted for inflation, stocks were far lower at the market's peak in 1979 than they

---

* It will be recalled that the French learned the wrong lesson from World War I, which was marked by trench warfare. After the war they constructed the most massive defenses possible along their border to guard against a new German attack. Of course, in World War II the Germans paratrooped their army behind the Maginot Line and then had little difficulty overrunning France.

had been in 1929. Just to match that high, the Dow would have had to rise to approximately 1600, or close to another double.

Might not even a yet higher valuation be reasonable? In 1979 America was far stronger and the markets much different from what they had been half a century earlier. To use the most conventional measure, GNP had risen from $103 billion to $2.5 trillion, a better than twenty-four-fold increase. Even after adjusting for inflation, the 1979 GNP was four and a half times that of 1929. Other indicators told the same story. In 1929 the price-earnings ratio for the Dow averaged 15.6, while it came to 6.8 in 1979. In the same period the dividend yield rose from 4.1 percent to 6 percent.

Had an individual returned to Wall Street after that fifty-year hiatus he would have found obvious changes, but would have had little trouble finding his way around. Both the New York and American Stock exchanges were still in the same places, as were some of the banks and trust companies. The ghosts of Alexander Hamilton and Albert Gallatin continued to haunt Trinity Churchyard. But the business had altered tremendously. In 1929, for instance, 3-million-share days were quite common; in 1979, 30 million shares were deemed average. More important, however, were alterations in the very fabric of the securities industry and the investment process. This was to have been expected—after all, it had been a momentous half century, and the pace of change would if anything accelerate in the next eight years. The transformation of the district and its operations would assure that a future panic—always assuming there would be one—would be quite different from any that went before. But the collective memory of an industry fascinated with cycles and offering well-remunerated employment to thousands who seek meaning in those cycles also guaranteed that, given a major collapse, the ghost of 1929 would reemerge and attempts would then be made to compare the two events.

This is not to suggest that all the news in 1979 was cheery. There were some disturbing signs, many deriving from those alterations in the economic and market structures during the 1970s. Enormous aggregations of capital in the forms of pension and mutual funds, to name two of the most conspicuous ones, were playing an ever-larger role in the markets. They manifested their presence in several ways, most visibly in the rise of block trading (orders of 10,000 or more shares), these coming almost exclusively from these institutions, some of which were more powerful than almost any other market force. For example, through several funds Prudential Insurance managed more than $150 billion, and American Express and Aetna Life & Casualty were also in the $100 billion class, with Metropolitan Life, Equitable Investment, and Merrill Lynch Asset Management not far behind. They dominated the markets. As recently as 1965 institutions averaged 9 large blocks per session, accounting for 3 percent of NYSE volume. In 1979 the average was 385 per session, this being more than a quarter of all transactions. Let several institutions and mutual funds simultaneously decide to get in or out of a stock and it could leap ahead or crash. In other words, the market was more volatile than previously.

Alterations in international currency relations, combined with the "oil shock," provided another problem. In 1971 President Nixon had begun severing the last ties between the dollar and gold, a move that signaled the initiation of a period in which exchange rates floated. In order to hedge on their overseas financial commitments, corporations were encouraged to make forward purchases of currencies. This prompted the Chicago Mercantile Exchange to create a market in which currency futures could be traded. As always, the markets accommodated themselves to new circumstances. This was the first of several such adjustments in the decade, in the process of which the financial landscape would be altered sharply.

After a collapse of the dollar, which stimulated the American economy, the situation seemed to return to normal. The confident mood didn't last for long. During the 1973 Arab-Israeli War the Organization of Petroleum Exporting Countries (OPEC) embargoed shipments to the United States, and in December doubled the price of oil. This added to the economic turbulence and, when taken together with the Nixon impeachment crisis, made that year one of the most disquieting in American history.

Apart from all else, interest rates fluctuated more wildly than at any time in a century. Higher rates contributed toward the development of "stagflation," a combination of inflation and recession once thought impossible by most economists. Bond prices declined because of the former and stocks as a result of the latter, and this too wasn't supposed to be possible.

In such a climate investors were increasingly drawn to short-term instruments in which the underlying prices of their investments remained stable, but returns rose or fell along with interest rates. Certificates of deposit and Treasury bills were two of the ways to invest, but far simpler were money-market mutual funds, where funds could be deposited by mail and withdrawn by writing a check against the account.

Observing the success of money-market funds, several load mutuals decided to enter the field, and by the late 1970s this form of investment enjoyed a renaissance. For a nominal charge a purchaser of one fund was permitted to switch to another via a telephone call. Franklin Fund led the way in 1974, and others soon followed. This meant that investors could go swiftly and at low cost from stocks to bonds or money-market instruments and then back again. So they did. While from 1972 through 1979 redemptions of mutual funds were greater than sales (the figure came to a record 17.9 percent in 1979), purchases of load mutuals with switch and money-fund options rose. In time the no-loads would enter the field, and then came the large wire houses, developing families of funds to be offered by their account executives.

Adding to the impediments caused by rapidly moving interest rates were new pressures on currency rates. Given a rise or fall of the dollar against some foreign currency, that country's debts and equities might appear more attractive. The mutuals responded by creating international bond and stock funds. Thus, investors could not only switch domestically, but leave dollar denominated holdings and dispatch their holdings overseas via a telephone call.

By the early 1980s millions of investors, bewildered by the way the markets were acting, sold stocks and bonds and purchased shares in the mutuals, with many subscribing to market letters specializing in switch timing. There was potential danger in this situation. What might happen if for any reason thousands of subscribers opted to switch out of stocks or bonds into some other form of investment? There were some safeguards against this, but the thought was troublesome.

Another important change came under the rubric of "deregu-lation," a key concept that gained favor in Washington as the 1970s rolled on. On Wall Street, however, it really began in the 1960s when a group of brash outsiders traded NYSE-listed stocks over-the-counter, in this way creating what came to be known as the Third Market. Manning their computer terminals, these dealers often offered better bids and asks, operated at lower costs, and claimed to be more efficient than the NYSE. The existence of the Third Market, coupled with institutional demands for lower com-mission charges, resulted in a frontal attack on the fixed-commission structure, under which the buyer or seller of 10,000 shares paid 100 times the commission charged anyone who bought 100 shares, even though the transaction was hardly more difficult. After a bitter struggle, the SEC ruled that from 1971 through 1975 fixed commis-sions would be phased out.

From the start it was obvious commissions on block trading would be slashed, but how might this affect the small investor? The answer soon arrived: as the established houses moved cautiously toward lower rates a new breed of broker, offering "plain pipe-rack ser-vices," appeared. These discount brokers would take and execute orders, but do nothing else. Their charges often were more than 50 percent below those of the older full-service brokers, and that suf-ficed to lure customers to them.

The full-service operations responded in two ways. In the first place, they too reduced commissions but, more important, became what their name implied: *full*-service houses. In the early 1970s all that a broker had to know was stocks and bonds. A decade later brokers hoping to develop clienteles offered real estate participa-tions, Ginnie Maes (securitized home mortgages), and an array of other instruments and stood prepared to explain them to interested customers.

There was still more to come. What would have been familiar to those who were on the Street in 1929, but not to younger brokers and investors, was the growing importance of foreign markets. Dur-ing the 1920s London was still deemed a pivotal money center, and Wall Street was ever cognizant of developments there regarding interest rates and securities prices. Such was the situation in the 1980s. As an increasing portion of the national debt was held by foreigners, as their active and continued participation in Treasury auctions became more significant, and as markets in general became internationalized, all learned to monitor developments overseas.

Brokers and customers in the 1920s started their day by asking what had happened in London before that market closed down and then discussed the implications for New York. A similar situation developed in the early 1980s, only now it wasn't London alone but, increasingly, Tokyo as well. A triad of markets had evolved, with trading moving from New York to Tokyo to London, and then back to New York. As the decade and the bull market wore on, investors learned to explore events in other markets: Korea, Australia, Hong Kong, Taiwan, and Mexico, as well as those of all of the western European countries. For some it had become an article of faith that the next major sell-off or panic— always assuming there would be one—would begin in Tokyo, and from there spread to London and then New York, whose collapse would reinforce that in Tokyo.

The situation was complicated by a major alteration in the structure of the securities markets that involved the creation of new forms of options. In their simplest form there were two kinds of options. A "call" enabled the owner to purchase a fixed number of shares from the seller at a stated price on or before a specified date. A "put" gave its owner the right to sell a specified number of shares at an agreed-upon price on or before the expiration date. These were not new; options had been "written" on securities and commodities for at least a century in New York, Chicago, and other markets.

Something new was added in 1973 when the Chicago Board of Trade organized the Chicago Board Options Exchange (CBOE). The CBOE's innovation was that it was an aftermarket for stock options. Earlier the owner of shares might have sold an option on them, and a speculator or hedger might have purchased it. Both would maintain their positions until the option either expired or was exercised. The CBOE maintained a continuing market in options, which is to say owners could sell any time they wished, while buyers could purchase as well. Options proved a boon for speculators, who found them preferable to buying stocks on margin, and the CBOE flourished.

What once had been deemed a useful and legitimate means of hedging investments and limiting risk now was on its way to being transformed into little more than a means of placing a bet on the direction a stock would head. It wasn't much different from what went on at the bucket shops of the 1920s. At that time customers would place margined orders, which were never executed. Both customer and broker understood that if the stock fell, the margin would be wiped out, and that if the price rose, he would sell, and the broker would pay the difference between the buy and sell prices. The distinction was that in the 1920s this practice was illegal, while in the 1980s it was open and aboveboard. Even so, it was possible to defend options as a means to hedge positions in stocks, and such was the justification usually presented.

Imaginative financiers added more options, and then in 1982 developed options on stock indices and even options on options, which could be purchased on low margin. Later on there were options on special stock groups such as technology, drugs, and gold mining. Of course no one could "deliver" an index; all knew they were dealing in an abstraction. So the agreement was that all of the contracts would be settled on or before a specified date—meaning the owners would sell, and the sellers would buy to even out their accounts.

These options, derived from the basic stocks, came in a dazzling and confusing variety, and some were being utilized imaginatively by wheeler-dealers engaged in "programs," under which they would conduct arbitrage operations between the index options and the underlying stocks.

"Portfolio insurance" was also becoming quite popular. In order to hedge a portfolio, the manager would sell stock index futures contracts. The cash raised by this operation would offset declines in the holdings. But the impact of this large-scale selling would cause the price of that index to decline, perhaps below the value of the underlying stocks, at which point arbitrageurs would step in and buy indexes and sell the underlying stocks. Then the process would be repeated, with the insurance and arbitrage programs driving stocks and indexes with no references to the fundamental and technical situations. Let a bell go off at one or another computer and the order would go out to buy (or sell) the option and simultaneously sell (or buy) the underlying stocks.

Stock prices still rose and fell on good or bad news, but now the stocks in the popular Standard & Poor's (S & P) 500 index might go up or down as a result of programmed trading. With this, brokerage houses repositioned some of their astute young men and women, who were assigned the task of figuring out which stocks would replace those removed from the index. These stocks invariably would rise after being named because they would receive more attention, and also for a related reason: by then some institutions and funds had become discouraged with these bewildering developments and established portfolios that mirrored the S & P 500. Now they would have to plunge in and buy the stocks.

By the summer of 1987 several firms had come to specialize in portfolio insurance, among them Leland O'Brien Rubinstein, Wells Fargo Investment Advisors, and Aetna Life & Casualty, whose clients were large funds. Most investors not only didn't know what portfolio insurance was, but wouldn't have recognized the names of some of the players and were unaware that major firms were so involved. Just how much insurance was in force is unknown, but industry estimates were that they covered portfolios worth between $60 billion and $90 billion.

Few outside the investment community really understood the arcane uses of these instruments, but one matter was fairly clear. The financial district, which at one time could justify its existence as a place for raising funds for American business and an aftermarket where the securities might be bought and sold, had taken on aspects of a gambling parlor. More so than at any time since the days of Jim Fisk, Daniel Drew, and Jay Gould—more so even than in the 1920s—speculation with little or no direct economic purpose had taken command, jarring the markets.

This became more of a problem when options on stocks, indexes, and index futures expired on the same day. Known as the "triple witching hour" by the mid-1980s, options action during "frightening Fridays" often caused havoc at the exchanges and was another sign that a new kind of market had been born, one for which there really were no precedents. The district appreciated what this signified. In the spring of 1986 twenty-eight-year-old investment banker Steven

Gruber, one of the new breed of Wall Streeters, remarked that in graduate school he had studied options theory. "People who came here fifteen years ago studied balance sheets."

It was an enormous business. By early October 1987, the net value of all stock futures contracts traded in the United States came to $3 trillion—against $2 trillion for underlying stocks—and the dollar trading in the S & P 500 index contracts often approached that of the NYSE. There was a tremendous tug-of-war between stocks and options, which additionally was between two cultures. The equities markets of New York were being challenged by the options markets of Chicago, and it appeared the latter were pulling ahead.

Symbolizing the contest was the friction between NYSE Chairman John Phelan and Leo Melamed, who not only headed the Chicago Mercantile Exchange but was one of the godfathers of financial futures. Phelan was concerned about the role index futures played in the movements of securities prices and programmed trading in particular. During the late 1970s, while vice-chairman, he managed to persuade the Exchange to install a new automated trading system to handle the 100- and 200-million-share sessions he expected to come in the early 1980s. By then, too, he also was warning of what he called a "financial meltdown," which might occur because of the unwholesome nexus between stocks and options.

It was an issue that divided the investment community, but must have seemed rather arcane to others. Even so, taken together these changes drastically altered the viewpoints and horizons of individual investors. During the last bull market investors understood stocks and bonds, perhaps owned some of each, and could have had load or no-load mutual funds. There might have been a foray into government notes and bills, and that would have been the extent of their knowledge and participation. In the mid-1980s these same investors might have had an account at a discount or full-service broker (or both) and dabbled in gold, collectibles, and real estate. They might have utilized options and options on indices, appreciated the subtleties of the foreign-exchange market, and had shares in some foreign firms. Such investors bought and sold Ginnie Maes and were in one or more families of mutual funds. They were prepared to switch or go to the money markets at a flick of an interest rate or revolution anywhere in the world. Investors scanned the newspapers for reports from Japan, Korea, Hong Kong, and Europe as well as Wall Street. They understood that Latin American debts could severely affect their portfolios. In 1969 investors knew little of the Federal Reserve and could not have named its chairman (William McChesney Martin). Now they appreciated the significance of open-market operations and the discount rate, and Paul Volcker not only was generally recognized as a celebrity in every sense of the term, but also was deemed the second most powerful man in America.

Investors could not help but be aware of the damaging effect of the worst inflation the nation had experienced since the Civil War, caused by currency expansion, an economy overheated because of economic policies followed in the 1960s and early 1970s, and the oil shocks. All of this traumatized many of them, who increasingly sought the security of money-market instruments and certificates of deposit. At one time investors had been informed and guided by economic forecasts, reports of new technologies, earnings, foreign affairs, and the like; now there was one paramount indicator: interest rates. Unless and until investors were convinced rates really were heading lower, they would remain liquid, and stand prepared for further shocks.

One of these came on Saturday night, October 6, 1979 (once again, October), when Chairman Volcker announced that henceforth he would ignore interest rates and focus instead on the money supply, doing so in order to "curb speculative excesses in the financial, foreign exchange and commodity markets, and thereby . . . dampen inflationary forces." The Fed also raised the discount rate a full point, to 12 percent. To underline its determination to fight inflation, the central bank now required member banks to set aside new reserves, thus reducing the amount of credit available for loans. Soon after, it sold Treasury bills and notes, thus constricting the money supply. On Monday, many banks responded by hiking their prime rates to 14½ percent. Taking this as a sign that the Fed intended to permit rates to rise as a way of dealing a killing blow to inflation, the stock and bond markets entered into a free fall, bringing an end to a rally then in progress.

By any measure—volume, volatility, or prices—what followed

was a wild week of trading. Stocks had closed the previous Friday at
898, on a volume of 48 million shares. By Wednesday, when volume
came in at 82 million shares, the Dow had fallen to 849, and within
a month was below 800. Short-term interest rates gyrated while
bond prices fell sharply in anticipation of higher levels to come.

During the months that followed, Volcker received much hate
mail from those affected by the move. Money creation slowed.
Measured in terms of M-1 (currency plus checking accounts) the
supply rose by an annual rate of 6.8 percent from December 1980 to
June 1981, dropped to 5.9 percent for the next six months, and
then, in the six months ending June 1982, the rate was 4.6 percent.

Interest rates did rise spectacularly. The federal funds rate (the
rate banks charge one another for loans) had gone from an average
of 7.9 percent in 1978 to 11.2 percent in 1979, then on to 13.4
percent in 1980. It seemed further boosts were on the way. In late
1980 Salomon Brothers' chief economist, Henry Kaufman, who had
a remarkable string of accurate predictions, went on television to
offer his latest prognostications. He was grimmer than ever. "There
are no bench marks anymore by which we can judge how high
interest rates can go," he told an interviewer. "I'd have to say the
chances are, with a prime rate of 20½ percent, it could go to 22, 23,
24 percent before we top out."

Rates did rise over the 20-percent level soon after. Home mortgages cost over 22 percent, which all but killed the residential
market though providing alluring yields for purchasers of Ginnie
Maes. Little wonder, then, that investors fled the stock market and
increasingly took refuge in short-term debts, money-market instruments, and certificates of deposit while professionals expanded their
activities in the futures markets.

When Ronald Reagan took office in 1981, the federal funds rate
was over 20 percent, the prime rate 21 percent, and other rates
were historically high. That winter savings and loan associations
were offering long-term certificates of deposit paying 22 percent per
annum. Moreover, there was reason to believe the situation would
worsen. The massive Reagan tax cut—30 percent in three years—
combined with a large-scale increase in defense spending assured
major budget deficits that would have to be financed through bor-
rowings.

According to the conventional wisdom, this would result in a "crowding out" of private borrowers as interest rates rose even higher. The nation would undergo a repeat performance of the stagflation of the 1970s, so the analysis went, as higher rates would spin the nation into economic decline. In vain the supply-side economists in the Reagan Administration argued that the stimulation brought about by lower rates would expand the economy, bring in additional revenues, and so balance the budget—in time. More than ever, the inflation fighters looked to Volcker for assistance, believing he would utilize the weapons of monetary policy to counter Reagan's expansionary fiscal policies.

As it turned out both sides were right, at least to a degree. The higher rates proved bitter medicine, but they worked. Inflation subsided at the price of the worst recession since the end of World War II and an unemployment rate that went over 10 percent for the first time since the Great Depression. When Volcker began his campaign the CPI was rising at a rate of 14 percent a year; by the summer of 1982, the rate was 4 percent. The inflationary era that had begun in the late 1960s had come to an end.

This much can be seen in retrospect. But investors, economists, and politicians obviously couldn't have known this at the time. Had they been prescient, they would have rushed to purchase long-term bonds and stocks, both of which would have benefited from the altered environment. As it was, sophisticated investors were dealing in the financial futures contracts, attempting to hedge against a new outburst of inflation.

The stock market was dormant in the summer of 1982 while the nation wondered how George Shultz, the new secretary of state, would perform in office; read about problems at the Continental Illinois Bank & Trust; and discussed the "Reagan Recession." Kaufman continued to believe rates would rise for the rest of the year, as did First Boston's highly respected Albert Wojnilower, a long-term bear. At the time, Wall Street hung on the every twitch of these two economists, whose pronouncements were thought unerring. They were known as Drs. Doom and Gloom, since in this period most of their predictions were for higher rates ahead.

The Dow fluctuated around 800 and seemed as if it would continue at that level for the rest of the year. The economic picture appeared bleak. In 1981 the nation recorded its highest level of business failures in a half century. Farm indebtedness was at an all-time high, coming in at twelve times farm income, and for the first time in thirty years the value of farmland declined. Housing starts were lower than at any time in the post–World War II period, while auto sales were at a twenty-year low.

There was a decidedly bearish atmosphere on the Street because of the bad news and the persistence of high interest rates. At the time the prime was 15 percent, and cautious investors could purchase six-month federally insured certificates of deposit paying 12 percent. Traditionally Wall Street considers the situation normal when interest rates are three to four points higher than the inflation rate. By this measure, interest rates were out of line, an indication that the general public did not believe the inflationary genie had been returned to its bottle.

In early October the Arizona Health Facilities Authority floated a $55.2 million issue of A-rated tax-exempt bonds. The three-year maturities sold to yield 9 percent, and the thirty-year maturities carried a 13-percent coupon. At the same time Ginnie Maes were available with returns of more than 16 percent. Stock prices were historically low. Blue chip Standard Oil of California sold at a price-earnings ratio of 6 and yielded 9.3 percent. Chase, one of the nation's premier banks, had a price-earnings ratio of 4 and yielded 9.4 percent. Digital Equipment, which did not pay a dividend, sported a price-earnings ratio of 9. The electric utilities were depressed by almost any measure—Carolina Power & Light offered an 11-percent yield and a price-earnings ratio of 7. So it went throughout the list.

In late July 1982 the Dow traded over 830, but then sold off, closing the month at 809. This puzzled Robert Kirby, chairman of Capital Guardian Trust of Los Angeles. As he saw it, most of the pieces were in place for a substantial rally. Yet stocks had lost 21 points the previous week and were 15 percent below what they had been a year earlier. The nation was in a recession, he conceded, but there were signs of improvement. Business loans were strong, and corporate earnings on the upswing. True, the CPI had moved up slightly during the summer, but Kirby thought this temporary.

Moreover, stocks were cheaper than at any time since the Great Depression, selling for a lower ratio of price to book value than he could recall. "I'm usually suspicious of the consensus view, but I have to agree with the current consensus that stocks can't go anywhere until interest rates come down," he asserted.

As it happened, the pivotal moment was about to arrive. The United States was in the midst of its most serious recession since the 1930s. Mexico was on the edge of declaring bankruptcy, and other debtors might follow. Volcker now determined that the time had come to reverse fields. Instead of utilizing the money supply as a weapon, he would return to using interest rates.

On July 30 the Fed cut the discount rate from 11½ percent to 11 percent. Kirby took this to mean Volcker had decided to ease up on his punitive policies. Paul Greenwald, vice-president of the Austin National Bank, agreed; he expected favorable action in stocks for the next few weeks, "but we don't believe this is the beginning of a major bull market."

The omens were mixed. On August 2 bond prices improved, an indication the credit markets anticipated lower rates. That day, on a moderate volume of 53 million shares, stocks advanced more than 13 points to close at 822, with analysts generally crediting the move to the decline in interest rates. "The Fed at long last recognizes that the economy needs some help," contended Eldon Grimm, senior vice-president at Birr Wilson & Co. Yet Budget Director David Stockman confessed the 1983 deficit could be $20 billion more than the projected $115 billion. The following day this news, combined with fears about the forthcoming Treasury auction, led bonds and stocks down.

The auction went well, with the government selling $6 billion in three-year notes at 13.17 percent. With one eye to Wall Street, Treasury Secretary Donald Regan predicted that long-term rates would decline by two or three points in 1983. Indicators remained mixed. At the same time the price of gold rose and the dollar strengthened, indicating anticipated higher interest rates.

On August 4 the Dow plunged almost 13 points to 803, its sharpest sell-off in over five months, and two days later it once again was under 800. By August 12, in spite of continued evidence that interest rates were declining, the Dow stood at 777, a twenty-seven-month low, having lost 45 points in eight sessions. Then came reports that money-market funds rose by more than $3.5 billion the previous week, a sign that the public anticipated higher interest rates. There now was a record $216 billion in those liquid funds, money that individual investors might draw upon quickly if they anticipated or perceived a stock-market rally in the making.

Much later, analysts would realize that the foundation for a new bull market was in place during this period. Everything needed was there—historically low stock prices, financial liquidity, indications that the economy was bottoming out, the kind of unrelieved gloom and uncertainty that so often precedes major shifts in market climate, and weakening interest rates.

On Friday, August 13, as though to underline a switch in strategy and confirm the spreading view that it was prepared to stimulate the economy, the Fed once again cut the discount rate, this time to 10½ percent, the lowest it had been in two years. Moreover, Volcker sent signals that additional reductions might be in store. Several banks promptly lowered their prime rates to 14½ percent while bond prices soared. That same day a new tax package, geared at raising $98.3 billion to help bring down the deficit, cleared the House-Senate conference, and this too was considered bullish news.

Stocks responded with an 11-point advance Monday morning, with prices higher down the line. The rally carried over into Tuesday, when 10 points were added in the first hour before stocks fell back, and the market ended the day up 4 points. Volume was 55 million shares, not particularly impressive, and the overall action discouraged the bulls. "If after the latest reductions in the discount and prime rates we don't get a rally that lasts at least one and a half or two days, we're probably in greater trouble than has been thought," said Robert Stovall, of Dean Witter Reynolds, while Alfred Harris, of Stifel Nicolaus, added, somewhat plaintively, that "it . . . appears that from this point the market will be anticipating a turning in the economy."

Significantly, Wojnilower switched his stance. Now he thought "both long-term and short-term interest rates on top-quality obligations will be noticeably lower next year" and saw the possibility of "lasting decline" in rates. His forecast was encouraging and prompted some defections from the bearish cadre. Still, investors had heard that refrain before, though admittedly not from so prestigious a source, only to see rates rise and the market fall back. Why should it be different this time?

But it was. On Tuesday morning, August 16, there came reports that Kaufman too had reversed his position, now going on record as believing rates had peaked for the cycle, and that short-term rates would decline as much as two or three points. At the time, long-term Treasuries sold to yield 12½ percent; Kaufman thought yields could fall to as low as 9 percent. On the heels of this came news that Goldman Sachs was recommending clients increase stock holdings from 35 percent of portfolios to 55 percent, cutting back on cash and bonds. "Keeping money in cash reserves has become a less viable alternative," explained Lee Cooperman, in charge of investment policy at the bank, adding that "bonds have lost some of their attractiveness."

Even so, predictions of lower rates fueled a rally on the bond markets. The Treasury market took off, as prices rose sharply, this meaning that, as Kaufman suggested, yields on old bonds were indeed declining. That afternoon Citicorp auctioned $150 million in ninety-one-day commercial paper, this affair monitored as an indicator of the direction of short-term rates. The previous week's rate had been 11.717 percent; the rate on August 17 was a sharply lower 10.04 percent.

Shortly after the opening it became apparent that a buyers' panic had been set into motion on the NYSE. Those who had sold borrowed shares, thus placing themselves in major short positions, saw prices rise powerfully. Panicked, they plunged into the market to repurchase the borrowed shares and close out their accounts. This caused prices to advance, triggering another episode of short covering. Meanwhile the nexus between the options and stock markets became more apparent than ever. Later on C. Derek Anderson, president of a San Francisco discount brokerage with a large options clientele, noted that "most of the stocks which were strong performers [that day] were stocks which have large underlying options." Large numbers of investors and speculators experienced the familiar emotional switch. During sharp sell-offs they would go from greed to fear in a matter of minutes, even seconds. Now it went the other way. Bears, seeing prices rise sharply, promised themselves they would buy when the expected reversal arrived. It didn't, and so they plunged in, fearful of being left behind in a new bull sweep. William Hummer, a Chicago-based broker, saw it happening at his desk. "I was talking to a customer who said he was considering buying stock, and when I told him the market was up 25 points, he told me to go ahead and buy."

Of course, there were still many who distrusted the rally, and they too were needed—after all, the new bulls had to buy stocks from someone. Alfred Goldman of A.G. Edwards observed that bear markets customarily end with heavy institutional liquidations— "a high level of disgust and lack of confidence" was the way he put it. Goldman looked for a subsequent decline. "I don't think we have the technical preconditions needed for a big move up from here."

So the rally continued, with every positive news item prompting additional buying while the negatives were increasingly overlooked or heavily discounted. Housing-start figures were released showing a sharp increase in July, and this led the construction, lumber, and coppers stocks to multi-point leaps, attributed to institutional participation. Several consumer loan companies lowered their borrowing rates, which triggered purchases of shares of companies producing consumer durables. The bad news increasingly was discounted or ignored. Complaints from restaurateurs that the new tax bill would harm their business were brushed aside, as Wall Street observed their establishments would be crowded with celebrants. General Motors said it was laying off 9,100 workers because of forecasts of lower 1983 cars sales; all of the auto stocks participated in the advance.

The Dow added 39 points on August 16 to close at 831. Volume was 93 million shares, barely under the record established during the previous year's Granville panic. Block sales were 1,596, surpassing the record established that session and demonstrating once again the power of the large institutions. On the CBOE 449,100 contracts changed hands, and this too was a record. Of no small significance was the fact that trading accelerated on advances and fell off when prices corrected. Finally, stocks ended the day close to their highs, indicating traders might expect a follow-through on Wednesday.

And so there was. Prices opened higher, with several issues delayed because of an imbalance of buy orders. From the first it was evident that the institutions were there en masse; when it was all over there were 2,456 block trades, breaking the previous session's record. "Big moves like the one that occurred Tuesday catch many institutions by surprise," explained Salomon Brothers' Lazlo Berinyi, "and it takes a day or two for them to catch up." There were reports of massive liquidations at the money-market funds, and while several conceded this was so, none thought there would be liquidity problems. The following day the funds reported an increase of $3.43 billion in assets for the week, indicating that switches were yet to come, and when they did, stocks would rise even higher.

When it was all over the public learned that volume came to a record 133 million shares; it had been the NYSE's first 100-million-share session. At one point the Dow was up by 18 points, but later on there was the expected round of profit taking, so the average closed at 829, higher by less than two points for the session. After the close several banks indicated that they would reduce their prime lending rate to 14 percent, a certain signal that stocks would continue to go higher the following day.

With all of this, the markets were orderly. There was a sufficient number of skeptics on the sidelines to indicate that there would be backing and filling for at least a few weeks. Robert Farrell, chief analyst for Merrill Lynch, looked for "a full or partial retracement." The Dow could go to anywhere between 850 and 870, he thought, but cautioned "we still could see new lows in the fall or at least have a significant test." Moreover, many large institutional buyers remained unconvinced that the rally could be sustained. The Maryland State Retirement System pension fund was 30 percent in cash, for example, and its managers told reporters they intended to remain liquid.

Prices continued to advance. On Monday, August 23, the Dow rose 22 points to close at 891, a new high for the year on volume of 110 million shares. There was more good news. Additional banks lowered their prime to 14 percent, and some leapfrogged the others, going to 13½ percent. Naturally the bond market soared, and now money-market funds indicated for the first time since early summer that liquidations far outpaced deposits. The Dow closed the week at 892, inching above 900 for a few minutes before falling back.

Stocks went over 900 decisively in early September, and by mid-October were again at what on four previous occasions had proved a major barrier: Dow 1000. Of course there was nothing magical about the number, but earlier failures to hold above that level had given it significant psychological and symbolic importance. The Street was divided on whether it would happen again. A fallback in mid-month encouraged the bears. Prices then rallied, and while there was some profit taking in December, the Dow was at 1045 on Christmas Eve.

When was there a consensus on the Street that this truly was a bull market and not just a rally? Such moments cannot be pinpointed, but it certainly was the case in late February 1983, when the Dow crossed 1100. It went on to the 1200 level in April, and to 1296 in November, after which there was the anticipated correction—for seven months, with the average flirting with 1000 again in the spring of 1984 before rising again, passing 1200 in the summer and 1300 by early 1985.

All of this was quite stunning. Old-timers and market historians observed that although the advance was spectacular, it was not as great as that of the 1920s. That the two markets were being compared was in itself significant.

Of course, there were important differences. The bull market of the 1980s began when many investors were vaguely troubled about the economy. There were huge budget deficits, and individuals who lacked even the rudiments of economic knowledge sensed there was something unhealthy about this. The trade deficit was even more troublesome. While economists debated whether this was a positive or negative factor, average Americans could not help but note that an increasing amount of their consumer goods bore foreign nameplates. In every year of the new bull market America imported more merchandise than it exported. Yet through it all American stocks continued to rise.

Why?

Part of the answer, especially in the first few years, might be the classic "catch-up." Stocks of companies whose profits had grown substantially during the 1970s finally rose to reflect this reality. In other instances the value of corporate assets had expanded because of inflationary forces, and shareowners of such firms saw the prices of their stocks advance. How far could this go? What might happen once this phase ended?

Another troublesome aspect to this new bull market was that it followed no discernible pattern. To better understand this point, one might begin by considering the differences between a market in which stocks are rising, which might be termed a bull move or interlude, and a major, secular bull market. The former happens for a wide variety of economic and political reasons, whereas the latter is sustained, reflecting important and permanent changes in the nation's economic underpinnings.

Traditionally bull markets of any great magnitude occur at times when society is being recast by some weighty new industry and a range of products that not only alters the economy and the lives of many Americans, but also captures the imagination of all whom they touch. This was so for all the powerful bull markets the nation has experienced. From 1829 through 1837 the catalysts had been canals, regional banks, and land speculation. Eastern railroads and gold mining provided stimulus from 1849 through 1853. Providers of all forms of military supplies and gold were the key ingredients during the Civil War, and the transcontinental railroads were major speculative vehicles in every bull market for the rest of the century and into the next. The Great Bull Market of the 1920s saw interest turn to automobiles, radio, and motion picture stocks. Television, computers, electronics, and space exploration gave the impetus in the 1950s and 1960s.

This is not to suggest that stocks in these industries provided the underpinnings for the advance, but rather that they added the glamour and spice without which the illusions of ever-upward movement and the euphoria found in all bull markets could not have developed.

There is an anatomy of such bull markets. Most begin when there is little interest in securities, often several years after the collapse of an earlier bull market. Disillusionment with investment is still strong, and individuals are concerned with yield and safety, not growth. Interest rates are stable; inflation may be recalled, but isn't a particularly pressing problem, and fears of recession are evident. Monetary expansion is taking place, stimulating the economy. The return on fixed-income securities and savings accounts seems unattractive. A portion of the public seeks investments that provide higher yields and is willing to accept some of the risk that may accompany them.

It is then they purchase paper that provides them with somewhat less safety but higher yields. By so doing they cause the securities to rise in price. When this happens, they sell and buy other high-yielding paper. The experience is repeated: their prices also rise.

This leads to the second stage, when investors come to realize that they are making more money in the form of capital gains than in dividends and interest, and this perception triggers purchases of securities that seem destined to rise in price. At this point the investors concentrate on the blue chips of the last bull market.

The old blue chips rise and vague euphoric stirrings are revived. Talk switches from "total return" to "growth," and investors seek out companies that were formed or came into prominence since the last bull market collapsed. These usually have short records of achievement but the potential to outperform the economy.

In both the first and second stages, investors display a backward-looking proclivity. Experience, not innovation, informs their decisions.

These two stages are typical of both bull markets and moves, and is a critical point. Bull moves never progress beyond this level, which is where bull markets are born. This is the time when those new glamour industries are the talk of the investment community and fascinate many Americans.

In the third stage investors purchase shares in these newer companies, indicating that their time reference has shifted from the past to the present. A new-issues boomlet begins as young companies sell stock for the first time. Prices rise more sharply, attracting a new generation to the market and prompting those who were burned the last time around to return.

The penultimate stage is the search for embryonic glamour companies and industries—a concerted effort to discover what is coming next. The time reference now has changed again, from the present to the future. Speculation grows, and all hail what in the nineteenth century were called "the new Young Napoleons," traditionally outsiders who have little respect for conventions, believe the world has been remade, and that the bull market is destined to continue indefinitely. The old professionals either adjust or consider retiring to the sidelines; amateurs and the newcomers take command. And for a while they do very well. Now stocks move up in defiance of the underlying companies' records. There is a divorce of reality and symbol. Fantasy becomes more of a force than ever.

The fifth and concluding stage takes place when investors purchase shares in "concept" companies, often with no record at all. Hype is the rule now as stocks soar into the stratosphere. Some of the professionals, who have missed the most recent move, return to the market. Volume is high and hopes higher still. Now the future seems far brighter than the past. This sets the stage for the final event: a crash or some other end to the bull market.

By 1984 or thereabouts, when the catch-up seemed over, some on the Street wondered vaguely where the glamour would come from and when it would appear. Would it be home computers? Biotechnology? Electronic toys? New forms of real estate syndication? These and other industries were discussed, and none seemed as significant as, say, the transcontinentals in the 1870s or electronics in the 1960s. Nor were there many exciting new issues, no sign that there would be a fourth or fifth stage in the bull market. Yet prices continued to rise in spite of basic and fundamental economic problems.

Bulls pointed to improving profit margins, and they indeed were widening. Bears referred to the "de-industrialization" of America. During the 1984 presidential election, Democratic candidate Walter Mondale suggested that as a result of the export of American manufacturing jobs, the nation would be forced to depend on others for a wide variety of goods, and the work force would be reduced to lower-paid service jobs. Americans would borrow, spend, borrow more, and keep on spending, getting deeper in debt both as individuals and as a nation. The voters responded by re-electing Reagan, and the market rolled on. By November 1985, the Dow rolled through 1400.

Why? As the Dow topped 1500 in December, 1600 in February

1986, and 1700 a month later, and as skepticism had all but faded, there was bewilderment about what it all meant. The Dow simply piled on advances and records—1800 in March, 1900 in July, and after another correction, 2000 in the first week of 1987.

By then it had dawned upon many who considered such matters that there was a glamour industry after all. It was transforming the economy as much as canals, radio, and electronics had in their times. The reason analysts had had trouble locating that industry was that it was more subtle, less tangible, than those earlier ones. Moreover, it was right under their noses and thus couldn't be readily perceived.

The new glamour industry was Wall Street and investments themselves. It wasn't solely traditional investment banking, but also included new forms and instruments that the bankers of 1929 and 1962 could have understood, but would have thought bizarre and improbable. In addition, the globalization of markets added another dimension while the deregulatory mood in Washington assured all involved that Wall Street need not fear any intervention from that quarter.

Just as earlier bull markets had been spearheaded or symbolized by such new men as William Duer, Jacob Little, Addison Jerome, Jim Fisk, Charles Morse, and Jesse Livermore, so this one was exemplified by a new group of Young Napoleons, outsiders like their predecessors. Through mergers and takeovers these men realized enormous profits. On other occasions they would pocket millions by wagering for or against a merger, in a recondite practice known as "risk arbitrage." Their names soon became quite well known—Asher Edelman, T. Boone Pickens, Irwin Jacobs, Sam Belzberg, Paul Bilzerian, and Carl Icahn were among the more prominent, while Ivan Boesky for several years was deemed the most representative and later on, the most notorious. While they often were lumped together, each man had his own style and interests. Pickens and Icahn were most concerned with acquiring companies and the arts of restructuring, though they occasionally made a fortune or two from failed efforts. Boesky had little interest in the byways of corporate America, concentrating instead on risk arbitrage. In Boesky the comparison to the plungers of the 1920s appeared most apt. "All in all, he was to the stock market of the eighties roughly what Jesse Livermore had been to that of the twenties," thought financial historian John Brooks, adding that Boesky was "an in-and-out investor so celebrated for his success that hordes of others, on learning of positions he had taken, blindly followed him."

Typically, one of the group would discover a company whose assets might be "redeployed" or in some other way have its value enhanced, make a tender offer bankrolled with borrowed money, and then take over the firm. Afterward some of its assets might be sold for cash, the money used to redeem some of the debt, or the promoters would refinance the company with new highly leveraged debt (usually known as junk bonds). Under the best of circumstances, the tycoon would be able to pay off most of the borrowed funds and be left with a sizable property, which then might be managed, sold off, or brought public once again. Even failure could be rewarded, since shares accumulated at low prices might be purchased by the besieged company (in the form of "greenmail") or tendered to another acquirer at a substantially higher price.

On other occasions the mogul would learn that a merger was about to be announced or take place and would amass a substantial position in the stocks, acquiring his rewards when the stock rose. There might be occasions when a planned merger would collapse, and if the risk arbitrageur guessed or knew this would happen, and shorted the stock, he would rake in the profits.

There were quite a few of these situations "in play" even before the market took off in 1982. The most spectacular was initiated by William Agee of Bendix, who made an unsuccessful bid to acquire RCA that spring. Agee next targeted Martin Marietta, which in response started buying shares in Bendix and then enlisted the aid of United Technologies, which made a tender of its own for Bendix. The next move was by Allied Corporation. Acting as a Bendix ally, Allied offered to purchase not only Bendix but also all of the Martin Marietta stock still in the public's hands, much of this done with borrowed money. The total outlay by all parties was on the order of $4 billion. As the companies parried thrusts that autumn, the public might have wondered just who would profit from all of this action. The most obvious beneficiaries were shareholders of the pursued companies, who were able to tender their holdings at much higher prices than when the fandango began. How might the economy, and the companies involved, profit or lose from the activities? Few except the shareholders, lawyers, and investment bankers seemed to think anything productive had been accomplished. When it was all over Martin Marietta was still independent, but Allied now owned 39 percent of its shares while Bendix was an Allied subsidiary. All had much-elevated levels of debt.

What did it mean? On September 27, 1983, *The Wall Street Journal* reflected: "There is obviously something amiss in an economy where corporate assets look more attractive to the investment strategists of other corporations than to ordinary investors." At the heart of the problem, the newspaper suggested, was the understated value of the assets of many large companies, which because of this were literally worth more dead than alive. "Corporate assets have been on the bargain counter for anyone who might be able to put them to more profitable use."

It was a refrain to be heard often in the coming years. There would be a good deal more of this activity in the future, especially as declining interest rates and a public awareness of the higher yields available from the bonds issued to finance some of these takeovers made the paper more acceptable and interesting.

Takeovers became all the rage in the years that followed, and in the process many large companies were engulfed. At the same time scores of frightened CEOs ordered their financial officers to initiate stock-buyback programs to shrink the equity base and give greater weight to shares in their hands or those of friendly interests. Some, with lavish treasuries, did so to make the company seem less desirable to a would-be raider. Others, with smaller cash positions, loaded up on debt and used funds generated in this fashion to initiate their own buybacks.

Whatever the method, the investment arena was flooded with debt, much of it low quality, while there was a generalized shrinkage of equities. Several analysts thought this helped account for the sharp rise in stock prices, as though stock certificates were a form of collectible that was becoming scarce. There might have been a sufficient number of investors who believed so, since news of buybacks and recapitalizations was invariably followed by higher prices for the shares of companies involved.

There were several methods of avoiding unfriendly takeovers. One increasingly popular way was the leveraged buyout, in which a group, usually but not always composed of insiders, would obtain the assistance of an investment banker to arrange the purchase of all outstanding stock, in this way taking the firm private. Led by Drexel Burnham Lambert along with Kohlberg Kravis Roberts, such leveraged buyouts became fairly common by mid-decade. In 1986 there had been 3,300 buybacks, mergers, and acquisitions worth $173 billion. These included Beatrice, R. H. Macy, and Safeway. The tempo of takeovers and buybacks was slowing somewhat; the prizes were getting larger. There were 1,500 of them during the first nine months of 1987, but these were worth $161 billion. Among the 1987 crop were Borg-Warner, Burlington Industries, Owens-Illinois, and Jim Walter.

By then some of the more sophisticated analysts might have realized that this was one of the novel twists of this bull market. There would be no traditional new-issues phase, but instead interest would turn to those old, sluggish, bloated, asset-rich companies that the raiders went after. This is to suggest that the new issues of the 1980s were the old issues of previous generations. The bull market had its glamour. Individuals who in the 1960s had looked for "another IBM" might have wondered whether IBM itself might become a vehicle for restructuring.

The prowl for possible takeovers had assumed bizarre proportions. That autumn Asher Edelman, who also taught a course titled "Corporate Raiding: The Art of War" at the Columbia University Graduate School of Business, proposed to reward with a $100,000 finder's fee any student who located a possible takeover he could go after. The school requested Edelman to withdraw the proposition; Dean John Burton declared that "the essence of academic study is the examination of ideas and concepts," and presumably not the way American finance capitalism was operating in 1987. Edelman complied and canceled the offer, but not before provoking a lively debate on the ethics of the action. A poll of his students disclosed that only one of them agreed with the dean. What it revealed about the others, Edelman, and Burton is a matter for some consideration.

By then too the public had become aware, through magazine and newspaper articles and television specials, of those enterprising individuals at investment banks whose major tasks were to devise new financial instruments and strategies. Salomon's Robert Dall and Lewis Ranieri, for example, created Ginnie Maes, one of the most important new "products" of the period. Such individuals, seated in their offices at the tip of Manhattan Island, were to the markets of the 1970s and 1980s what electronics engineers were to that of the 1960s and movie moguls had been in the 1920s. They were fabricating wealth and dreams.

There was something troublesome about all of this. Was anything of intrinsic value being created, any worthwhile service being performed? Earlier bull markets had been propelled by tangibles such as railroads and automobiles, and even the intangibles had worth; after all, an individual could enjoy a motion-picture show or watch a television program. The same could not be said of a money-market fund, index options, or a takeover. "When the capital development of a country becomes the by-product of the activities of a casino," said Lord Keynes more than a half century ago, "the job is likely to be ill-done."

There was a casinolike atmosphere in the currency markets, which a generation earlier had been dull and uninteresting but now attracted some of the Street's most brilliant and imaginative traders. As fluctuations in currencies became more pronounced, creating dangers, they also generated opportunities for speculation. Earlier that year a veteran bond trader told a reporter that "I used to watch interest rates. Now I watch currency rates." What he meant was that under this new international discipline it was more important to be able to predict successfully the dollar-yen exchange ratio than the direction of long- and short-term domestic interest rates.

This was an increasingly important matter. During the early 1980s the dollar was overvalued, especially against the yen and mark. Among the more important reasons for this were the American interest rates, which were substantially higher than those in Tokyo and Frankfurt, and so attracted foreign investment. This papered over problems of the trade deficit; the Japanese and Germans would use dollars earned from exports to purchase American securities and other assets. At the same time, the overvalued dollar made it difficult for Americans to compete for foreign sales. To correct this, Treasury Secretary James Baker labored assiduously to bring down the value of the dollar while encouraging his foreign counterparts to lower their interest rates as a way to stimulate their economies (which might encourage imports of American goods). He had some success in the former during 1986, as the dollar declined substantially, especially against the yen and the mark. Baker signaled his overseas counterparts to expect more of the same unless and until they took action to lower their interest rates.

This sharp and steady decline in the value of the dollar prompted a meeting of the West's leading finance ministers, which took place at the Louvre during February 1987. At that time two important decisions were made. First, the ministers agreed to attempt to maintain the parities of their currencies within a fairly narrow band. Second, the Americans would do what they could to bring down their budget deficit while the Europeans and Japanese would stimulate their economies, in part through lower interest rates that would help alleviate the trade deficit. All of this would stabilize the dollar, which was in the interests of everyone. It mattered little to a Japanese investor, for example, that the yield on thirty-year U.S. Treasury bonds was far more attractive than that available for their Japanese counterparts when he realized that the yen had appreciated vis-à-vis the dollar by almost 100 percent in two and a half years. When purchasing bonds in February 1985, he might have paid 262 yen for a dollar. The dollar kept falling after the Louvre meetings, and by October, had he sold the bonds for the same dollar price and used the proceeds to purchase his native currency, he would have received approximately 135 yen. Thus, close to half his investment stated in yen terms had been wiped out. Little wonder that Wall Street feared the Japanese would abandon the Treasury auctions, forcing American interest rates higher and bringing an end to the bull market.

There were additional complications. Budget balancing could cause some unpleasant side effects. In the unlikely event the United States succeeded in these efforts—through a combination of tax increases and spending cuts—the economy might spin into a sharp recession, which among other things would quickly be transmitted to the very countries that insisted these steps be taken. The Japanese, Germans, and other important trading partners wanted to maintain both their export surplus to the United States and the value of the American dollar, at the same time insisting that the United States undertake the very policies that would result in the opposite outcome.

To little avail, Baker continued to prod foreigners to stimulate their economies. When they failed to do so to his satisfaction he spoke of the need to have a cheaper dollar. The Europeans and Japanese frowned upon this apparent violation of the spirit of the Louvre Accords, the Americans refused to accept their prescriptions, and each eyed the others with growing suspicions and animosity.

That summer, as the presidential candidacies of Gary Hart and Joseph Biden sputtered and failed, and none of the other Democrats ignited much interest, it was observed that some of the most intelligent and attractive Democrats rejected the notion of making a presidential bid—Bill Bradley, Mario Cuomo, Sam Nunn, and Charles Robb were on the sidelines and not likely to move from there. Columnist David Broder suggested that the reason for this might be their superior intelligence. Perhaps they suspected that the policies instituted during the Reagan years would create difficulties in the early 1990s, and that anyone occupying the White House then would have unpleasant tasks to perform.

There was no shortage of frightful warnings during this period about such possible difficulties; on the Street, Phelan's admonitions about programmed trading had become somewhat routine. But there were new voices and other themes. Few offered analyses with as much clarity and force as Peter G. Peterson, whose experience in Washington as secretary of commerce and on Wall Street as head of Lehman Brothers prepared him for the task. Throughout the winter and spring of 1986 and into 1987 Peterson wrote and talked of America's economic ailments, receiving an attentive hearing, not only out of respect for his eminence but also because the ideas and interpretations he set forth were quite in vogue. Then, in a detailed and lengthy article in the October issue of the *Atlantic* titled "The Morning After," Peterson offered a sweeping analysis of the problems facing the nation, which crystallized the conventional wisdom of many Administration critics. In the nature of things the magazine was released in September, so Peterson must have signed off on it in August at the latest. It is entirely possible that the piece was delivered to the magazine's offices at around the time the market was recording its all-time high.

In Peterson's view, America entered the 1980s in a weakened condition largely because of a diminution of capabilities to compete economically. While some of the problems seemed resolved during the Reagan presidency, more often than not supposed solutions masked continuing underlying weaknesses and exacerbated old difficulties. For example, productivity growth declined from 1980 to 1986, as did investment in plant and equipment. The budget was out of control; contrary to popular belief, federal spending as a percentage of GNP actually increased under Reagan; and interest payments as a percentage of the national income and the budget had soared. From posting a fairly strong trade surplus the nation went to record the largest deficits in its history, and demands for economic protectionism were more strident than at any time since 1930.

Starting out from this base, Peterson commenced a critique of optimistic forecasts by government and some private economists and ended by offering his own prediction and prescription. From 1988 to 1992, he wrote, the United States would have to concentrate on extricating itself from its growing foreign indebtedness. The next fifteen years should be devoted to investment in infrastructure and industries; Americans should be prepared to pay for this with a lower standard of living. If such were done by 2007 or thereabouts, the country would find itself in fairly decent shape. To start things off, he favored a $100 billion sales tax, which would cut into consumption while helping to balance the budget.

Peterson was not overly sanguine that the American people were prepared to make these generational sacrifices. Moreover, the Reagan Administration, he complained, didn't perceive the problems. So Peterson made a somewhat jocular prediction: "On January 20, 1989, after the inauguration, President Reagan flies off to Santa Barbara. While he is in the air, the stock and bond markets crash, and interest rates soar. When Reagan lands in Santa Barbara, he announces to a swarm of reporters, 'See, I told you the Democrats would screw up the economy!' "

Peterson's broadside echoed the message contained in *The Great Depression of 1990* by Ravi Batra, which then was on the best-seller list in many cities. Unable to locate a publisher willing to take a chance on so idiosyncratic a work, Batra, a Southern Methodist University economist, had printed it privately several years before. Utilizing concepts provided by an Indian philosopher, Prabhat Ranjan Sarkar, Batra began by launching into a survey of world history, speaking of epochs of Laborers, Warriors, Intellectuals, and Acquisitors, then going on to an analysis of American economic and financial history, and following this with a discussion of panics and depressions. All in 125 pages.

Batra then set forth his major hypothesis: depressions occur every thirty years or so, but when one doesn't happen on cue the next one is even more severe. There was a depression in the 1930s, none in the 1960s, so the one due in the 1990s will be horrendous—unless steps are taken to prevent this from happening. Batra's solution must have appealed to Peterson, since it involved massive redistribution of wealth from the upper classes to the lower, in the form of a $133 billion tax.

Academics gave Batra's ideas little credence, which didn't phase him. "It surprises me that despite overwhelming obstacles I am finally getting recognition." He announced that the royalties from his book would be used to organize a movement he called Stop Another Depression (SAD) and seemed to bask in his celebrity.

The Peterson and Batra approaches were consistent with a strong streak of puritanism always present in the American character. Calls for sacrifice, when offered clearly and convincingly at critical junctures by charismatic and forceful leaders, often are well received. Peterson appealed to a small group of intellectuals, Batra to a much larger one composed of the economically unsophisticated, and if their messages were plausible to some, their remedies were not. Peterson's in particular were strikingly similar to Democratic rhetoric in the 1984 presidential election, in which Reagan had won every state but one.

Many Americans who read and heard about matters such as the budget and trade deficits considered them abstractions. When told they spent too much and saved too little, they may have felt vaguely guilty, but at the same time might have been comforted by the certain knowledge that they were wealthier than ever before.

While often portrayed as a nation of spendthrifts run amok with credit cards ever at the ready, plunging into debt with gleeful abandon, living from one paycheck to another, there was another side to the story. True, Americans were spenders, but they also accumulated capital for what they deemed worthwhile purposes, and in the 1980s much capital was amassed by tens of millions of Americans. Not only were trillions of dollars of net worth created by the movements of securities, but the inflation of real estate values, while frustrating would-be homeowners, enriched those who owned their own homes before the price increases struck. The individual who in 1975 owned a $30,000 house with a $20,000 mortgage and had $30,000 in securities, might have found himself in 1985 with a house now worth $250,000 carrying a $15,000 mortgage, and possessing $100,000 or so in savings and other assets.

That such a person saved little and piled on consumer debt didn't seem altogether unreasonable when viewed in this light. Nor was the governmental debt as distressing as might appear. That autumn it was some $2.1 trillion, give or take a few billion. The GNP was humming along at a $4.3 trillion clip. So the debt-to-GNP rate was approximately 50 percent. It had been 35 percent in 1973, so the advance was startling. On the other hand, the ratio had been 74 percent in 1943, due of course to military spending attendant upon World War II. But in 1953, the ratio was 72 percent, and few at the time, outside of conservative Republicans, considered this outrageous. Moreover, the 1987 debt wasn't monstrous when compared to the situations in some other countries that didn't seem particularly concerned about the matter. The Canadian debt was roughly 68 percent of its GNP, Great Britain's 54 percent, the Netherlands, generally viewed as a model of financial probity, 77 percent. The much-admired Japanese had a higher ratio of debt to GNP (68 percent) than did the United States.

The budget deficit, which added to the debt, might also be considered as a fraction of the GNP. That autumn it appeared the 1987 shortfall would come to some $150 billion. Given a $4.3 trillion GNP, this meant that the deficit would be on the order of 3.4 percent of GNP. This was lower than in any year since 1982, when it was heading upward, and in 1987 it was declining. Neither figure was unusually high; in 1976 the deficit as a fraction of GNP came to 4.1 percent and didn't cause much of a stir or become a crucial element in that year's presidential race.

Finally, Peterson observed that the national debt had doubled during the seven Reagan years. Stated another way, Reagan had increased the debt as much as all of his predecessors combined, a comparison that by then had become a cliché. But the same had been true for the seven previous years; under Presidents Gerald Ford and Jimmy Carter, the debt had risen from $456 billion to $906 billion. Those individuals who were so vocal on this point in 1987 were conspicuously silent on the subject during the 1980 presidential campaign.

Nor was this the only critique that might be offered of the Peterson viewpoint. While sounding like prudent and in fact traditional conservative Republican dogma (and Peterson was of that breed), it might also be viewed as a harmful exercise in fiscal and monetary sadism. Increases in savings and declines in spending might easily lead to a deep depression. The last President to speak of the need to both balance budgets and cut into purchases of foreign goods, and acted on these beliefs, had been Herbert Hoover. In 1930 he supported a tax increase and spending cuts to balance the budget and signed into law the Smoot-Hawley Tariff, two actions most economists and other students of the period and afterward consider to have helped cause and then deepen the Great Depression.

These were serious concerns. In the summer and early autumn of 1987, Americans debated many subjects, among them the wisdom of an American presence in the Persian Gulf, the Supreme Court nomination of Robert Bork, the Iran-Contra affair, arms control, the proper approach to fighting AIDS, and the presidential race. By the third week in October, all of these were relegated to secondary positions, as interest focused on the kinds of issues raised by Peterson.

Somewhat lost in all of this was the announcement of Paul Volcker's departure from the Fed and his being replaced by Alan Greenspan. Some bulls felt a trifle queasy at the switch, for by then Volcker had taken on heroic stature. But Greenspan knew his way around Washington, having served as chairman of the Council of Economic Advisors during the Nixon and Ford Administrations, where he had been instrumental in slowing down the growth of inflation.

Based upon his speeches, interviews, and writings, Greenspan appeared more willing to stimulate the economy and risk inflation than Volcker had been. Still, he was no supply-sider and had the support of conservative Republicans. Indeed, Volcker had some kind words to say about his successor, so that the transition went as smoothly as might have been hoped. A period of uncertainty, however, was clearly to be expected. No one thought Greenspan would wield power for quite a while as authoritatively as had Volcker, or inspire confidence until he was successfully tested.

From the first Greenspan was faced with a dilemma. If he opted for lower interest rates he would stimulate the economy, but also prompt additional imports, cause distress at the Treasury auctions, and perhaps invite a new round of inflation later on. Higher interest rates might attract foreign funds and fight inflation but could result in an economic slowdown. Either way, he would be criticized and second-guessed. Greenspan was in a no-win position that September. And to complicate matters further, there seemed to be no coordination at all between Greenspan and Baker.

Little of consequence was heard from the Fed during Greenspan's first weeks in office. During this period he concentrated on learning more about operations, making himself known around the circuit, and establishing the proper atmospherics. But the stage for action had been set. Interest rates started to inch up, but this was not deemed consequential. Then, on Friday morning, September 4, Greenspan committed a most Volckerian act: he announced the discount rate would be increased from 5½ to 6 percent.

When did the Crash of 1987 begin? Doubtless the history books will focus on Black Monday, October 19, a date difficult to quarrel with. But some attention should be given to September 4, which was when the crack in the dike appeared. The Fed gave off a clear signal that higher rates were on the way, that Greenspan would devote more attention in the future to inflationary problems. All of this is apparent in retrospect, of course. At the time it was only one move out of many, one story that was worth a few paragraphs on the business page. For the next month and a half other developments would build upon that rate increase. Alan Greenspan's action did not cause the Crash, but it did precipitate matters.

THE NYSE IN SEPTEMBER, 1987

	Dow Closing	Change	Volume (millions of shares)
September 1	2639		193
2	2662	+23	189
3	2599	−37	165
4	2561	−38	129
8	2545	−16	243
9	2549	+4	165
10	2576	+27	180
11	2609	+23	178
14	2613	+4	154
15	2567	−46	136
16	2530	−37	196
17	2528	−2	151
18	2525	−3	188
21	2493	−32	170
22	2568	+75	210
23	2586	+18	220
24	2566	−30	162
25	2570	+4	138
28	2601	+31	188
29	2590	−11	174
30	2596	+6	183

Source: *Wall Street Journal,* September 2–October 2, 1987

The September 4 action was the first boost since August 1986, and took the Street somewhat by surprise. To the money men, it seemed to signal the Fed's belief that the economy had picked up to the point where inflation once again might become troublesome. Most banks responded as expected, boosting their prime lending rate to 8¾ percent. The Veterans Administration chimed in with an increase in its ceiling rate on insured mortgages from 10 percent to 10½ percent. Other rates started to rise down the line.

Did it make sense? Those who supported Greenspan's action noted that the decline of the dollar could eventually be translated into inflationary pressures, and so was necessary. His critics argued that monetary policy had been tight, that whatever inflationary pressures existed were minor, and most important, given the parlous situation in the international arena, this was no time to increase interest rates.

The markets reacted as expected. Bonds collapsed while the Dow, which had been weak on Thursday, September 3, lost 38 points to wind up at 2561, off 79 points for the week. The NYSE was closed on Labor Day, and on Tuesday stocks opened lower and slid throughout the session, winding up with a 16-point loss at 2545 on volume of 243 million shares. There followed a rally to over 2600, and another sell-off. Stocks traded between 2524 and 2613 for the rest of the month, winding up at 2596 on the last trading day in September. The bulls commented on the market's resilience while the bears continued to expect the worst. But on the whole, as October arrived the bulls seemed to have won that round.

Nothing of consequence to disturb the bulls happened during the first few trading days in October. The Dow gained 43 points on Thursday, October 1, to close at 2639 and added 3 more points on Friday. After an uneventful weekend, it gave up less than a point on a quiet Monday.

The calm was broken on the morning of Tuesday, October 6. Stocks opened lower and dropped throughout most of the day, the Dow losing a record 92 points on 176 million shares, stunning a jaded brokerage community and its clients. The reason for the massive sell-off? Many thought it was programmed trading. Some blamed it on Germany's decision to raise interest rates and signs the Japanese would do the same. If this occurred, so the reasoning went, Greenspan might be obliged to follow suit, and this would result in tight money and a possible recession. Others spoke of the budget and trade deficits. There was a cadre convinced that pending legislation to discourage mergers and acquisitions was at the root of the problems. If ways were found to discourage some varieties of takeovers, it might mean an end to those tender offers stockholders dreamed about and eliminate the glamour portion of the fifth phase of the bull market.

By themselves none of these reasons were plausible. Programs had been around for years, and there had been nothing of the magnitude of this sell-off before. The budget deficit had been higher in 1986, and the market had performed spectacularly that year and in the first half of 1987. The falling dollar would do its part in helping exports and discouraging imports and in this way compensate for German and Japanese failures to act on their interest rates. There had been no news on the merger-and-acquisitions fronts to account for pessimism. A year earlier Ivan Boesky and others had been caught in bribes and influence peddling, and the markets responded with a major move to the upside. In other words, the Street's wise men had no trouble stringing together a list of reasons for a sell-off, but none could say, with any degree of plausibility, why it had happened just then.

Mario Gabelli, a well-known portfolio manager with a reputation for sniffing out takeover candidates, observed that investors had better get used to the wide swings of 100 or more points he saw coming. Many others spoke in the same tones. The most important of them was Robert Prechter, who, as will be recalled, was rather cheerful in early September. Now he backtracked somewhat, but not wholly. On October 7 Prechter wrote that further declines lay ahead. How far would it go? The Street's most prominent analyst that season thought stocks would look attractive at Dow 2300, which he called "an ideal buy spot." For the time being, however, Prechter was "just sitting still."

Even so, if the sell-off was impressive, so had been some of the pre-August advances. The bull market had astounded the bears by its recuperative powers before, and it could happen again. Besides, it was a worldwide phenomenon. Hong Kong's Hang Send index was up by more than 300 percent since the bull market began, in Tokyo the Nikkei index was 287 percent higher, and German shares in Frankfurt were up 241 percent. These markets had corrected and then gone on to post new record highs. Somehow, the thought that they were not alone comforted Wall Street's bulls. Perhaps this was the beginning of that long-anticipated correction which, when over, would form the base for a climb to Dow 3000. And if this were so, prudence would dictate entering the market on the buy side when it seemed the rectification had run its course. If Dow 2300 seemed about right to Prechter, it did to hosts of others as well.

Stocks fell steadily on the seventh, with the Dow down 30 points at 3:00 P.M. This was interpreted as a continuation of the Tuesday action and also attributed to the decision of several banks to boost their prime rate to 9¼ percent. But there was a rally in the last hour, enabling the Dow to close up more than 2 points, at 2551.

Bearish talk increased. The more pessimistic commentators observed that a widespread collapse might leave "air pockets" in the market so that individuals who had placed stop-loss orders might not get their prices. What if many mutual-fund owners panicked and tried to get out or switch at the same time? Could they get through to brokers over jammed telephone lines? And would the funds be sufficiently liquid to make the switches without dumping stocks on an already saturated market? "In a serious bear market, it's conceivable that mutual funds would hold off on cash redemptions and redeem in kind," San Diego–based investment advisor Michael Stolper told a reporter from *The Wall Street Journal*.

Whatever the reason—momentum, gathering fears, Prechter's dire prediction—stocks continued their decline during the rest of the week. There was a 34-point sell-off on Thursday and another 35-point loss on Friday. For the week as a whole, the descent was 159 points. To say that confidence was shattered would be an exaggeration. As always, there were bulls on the Street to talk of rallies and Dow 3000 by Christmas. But the overall mood was turning sour.

Monday, October 12, was another down day, but only by 11 points, and when stocks rallied 37 points on Tuesday, it seemed the decline might have run its course.

The major investment banks seemed quite hopeful about market prospects. Drexel Burnham Lambert judged that "the fundamental underpinnings of the market remain solid, as does our forecast of still-higher prices ahead." Byron Wein of Morgan Stanley predicted "a new high before this cycle is over." The Magellan Fund, which consistently outperformed the popular averages, was fully invested, indicating that manager Peter Lynch, a genuine Wall Street superstar, agreed with the Drexel and Morgan assessments. Salomon

Brothers' *Global Equity Market Outlook* told readers to expect "the global bull market to reassert itself and to continue into 1988."

All was not well within the investment banking community, however. That same day, Salomon announced it would eliminate its entire municipal finance department, meaning that some 200 professionals and 600 support personnel would depart. The next day Kidder Peabody eliminated a third of its municipal-bond jobs and fired approximately 135 people. Others followed: L.F. Rothschild, Continental Illinois, E.F. Hutton, and Citicorp.

The reason had nothing to do with stock-market conditions or the economy, but rather the narrowing profit possibilities in this field. Suddenly, however, the fever on the brows of overworked and (perhaps) overpaid Wall Street Yuppies was replaced by cold sweat. Had anyone mentioned panic to them that week, they would have taken it to mean job security rather than the markets themselves.

Stocks opened lower on heavy volume the morning after the Salomon announcement and never recovered. That session the Dow declined a record 95 points, 3.8 percent of its total value, on a volume of 207 million shares. It was the worst point loss in NYSE history.

What was happening? Concern regarding deficits had become paramount on the Street, and for the next few sessions at least it seemed these would move the markets one way or the other. On Wednesday, October 14, the Commerce Department reported that the trade deficit for August came to $15.7 billion, a decline from the record July figure of $16.5 billion, but a poorer showing than had been expected. Even so, the deficit with Japan had fallen to its lowest level in six months, and due to their higher prices the volume of imports was down more than the figures would suggest.

As was to have been expected in the highly charged political climate of the time, prominent Democrats rushed to lay blame for the perceived economic malaise on the White House. Campaigning in Iowa, Representative Richard Gephardt told an audience that "until we have an administration that fights for open markets overseas, American exports of manufactured goods and farm products will continue to fall and the heartland of this country will continue to be left behind." Speaking from Washington, Senate Majority

Leader Robert Byrd added: "As the United States plunged from the world's largest creditor to the world's largest debtor, there has been no sense of Administration concern, no sense of urgency."

Iran-Contra. Bork. The Persian Gulf. The Nicaragua imbroglio. The deficits. Now Wall Street. The Democrats were erecting a platform and approach they expected would enable them to retake the White House the following year.

The market lost 58 points on Thursday, October 15, closing at 2355. Volume rose to 263 million shares. Cries for some presidential statement came from brokers and commentators as well as from prominent Democrats, though all must have known that if Reagan had said anything to assuage fears, his critics would recall that Herbert Hoover had done as much in 1929. Taking time out from a European tour, Secretary Baker told reporters he thought the markets "will eventually adjust." The secretary played down fears of inflation, implying the recent discount-rate increase was not needed and would soon be rolled back.

At the time, Baker was in Germany and prepared to have it out with that country's political leaders. Once again he reiterated his dissatisfaction with West Germany's failure to lower interest rates, hinting that unless there was some action on that front, the dollar would go lower. This was correctly viewed as a confrontation with the Germans that might bring an end to the Louvre Accords.

The Dow opened at 2364 on Friday, October 16, up 8 points from the Thursday close. Prices drifted for the first two hours. Volume was high, though somewhat below that of the previous session. Then stocks started their familiar slide, though in an orderly fashion. There was a short-lived rally around noon, after which there was more heavy selling. By 2:00 P.M. it turned into a rout, and panic developed in the last hour, when 72 million shares were traded.

When it was all over the NYSE had recorded its first 100-point loss—108 to be exact—to close at 2247, on a volume of 338 million shares. This too was a record. Portfolio insurers accounted for more than 10 percent of the $5.1 billion worth of shares traded, and the figure for index arbitrage was $1.6 billion. For the week the market lost 235 points, another record.

The usual reasons for the decline were offered, along with a new one: the declining dollar would discourage foreigners from making purchases at the next Treasury auction, forcing rates higher, and this would trigger a recession. Treasury bond yields already were over 10 percent, and any further increase could lead to panic on that market, which could reinforce what was happening at the NYSE. Nor was this all.

One of the more closely watched technical indicators was the 200-day moving average. The conventional wisdom was that one should buy and hold as long as the market is over the average, and sell when it dips below. The Friday sell-off nudged the indices below the average, and with this, several mutual fund switch services gave the sell signal to their "hot line" subscribers. More significantly, Prechter did the same, although for different reasons. Taken together, these actions seemed to indicate Monday would be a rough session.

The mood worsened over the weekend. Seemingly oblivious to the impact his words might have on the financial markets, Baker told a television interviewer on Saturday that the Germans "should not expect us to sit back here and accept" that country's high interest rates. Thus, as Greenspan gave the signal for higher American rates to smother inflation before it became a problem, Baker was asking the Germans to stimulate their economy and played down Chancellor Helmut Kohl's protests that to do so would cause inflation there.

Everything was in place for a continuation of the selling on Wall Street. The economic and financial statistics were interpreted as being negative. There seemed a chance of protectionist trade legislation. The United States was at odds with the Germans and Japanese. The President appeared weak, politically wounded, and indecisive. Greenspan seemed confused, and whatever prestige Baker had garnered had been dissipated. Peterson's ideas regarding the need for puritanism were being discussed seriously, and sales of Batra's book had picked up. For at least two years analysts had warned of a correction in stock prices, and now it was happening. The critical question was not whether the sell-off would continue, but how long and far it would go.

During the previous week the conventional wisdom asserted there was support in the 2200 to 2300 range, but now this had to be rethought. Those analysts who earlier had seemed so certain of their

predictive tools hedged. How far might prices fall? Several spoke of
the 1600 level, and at the time this seemed rather drastic.

That Sunday a preoccupied President Reagan hosted a musicale
at the White House. The following week the Senate would deal with
the Bork nomination, and the outlook for confirmation was poor.
The report on the Iran-Contra investigations would soon be released. The Arias plan for a suspension of hostilities in Nicaragua
had divided Reagan's supporters. Within less than two months he
would meet with Soviet leader Mikhail Gorbachov in Washington,
perhaps to sign a wide-ranging arms accord that would create dis-
cord among his conservative supporters. Listening to a tribute to
Jerome Kern, Reagan knew that his wife, Nancy, was recovering
from a mastectomy. The problems on Wall Street could not have
been very high on his agenda that evening.

Even before the markets opened on Monday, October 19, it was
apparent that the session would be tumultuous. That morning portfolio managers at the major fund families geared up for anticipated
switching, knowing they would have to raise cash by selling equities. Fidelity Investment, the industry's leader with $75 billion
under management and 123 funds, placed orders to sell $500 million
worth of stocks and, before the day ended, dumped another $300
million on the market. The pension funds were sellers. The General
Motors fund, which had $35 billion in American stocks, started
selling immediately and continued on through the day, disposing of
$1.1 billion worth of stocks in thirteen clusters.

The index arbitrageurs were also active. While Fidelity was drawing up its sell lists, the large bank and trust company investment-
advisory units were preparing to institute more of the previously
described portfolio-insurance schemes. Money managers at Wells
Fargo, Bankers Trust, Aetna Insurance, and several large pension
funds—including Exxon and General Motors—placed significant
sell orders on S & P 500 index options; a record 85,000 of them
with a face value of over $11 billion were traded that day. Later it
would be learned that, prior to the opening, these five by themselves had placed sell orders on 30,000 contracts worth some $4
billion.

Look ahead for a moment. As the orders were executed the
purchasers would sell the underlying stocks, thus hedging their

risks and forcing prices down. In this way the programs were adding to downward pressures at the NYSE.

While these plans were being made the NYSE floor buzzed with news of collapses on the Tokyo and other Far Eastern exchanges, which had carried over to London. Now the tidal wave, reinforced by the sell programs triggered by options activities and the dumping by mutual funds, would hit New York.

From the bell, orders poured onto the floor and were backed up on NASDAQ. Dozens of stocks, among them leading blue chips, didn't open for an hour and longer. Such stalwarts as Sears Roebuck, DuPont, Eastman Kodak, Merck, and Westinghouse weren't traded that first hour, as specialists wondered how far down they should peg their quotes. Only 17 of the 30 Dow stocks had traded before 10:30 A.M. Exxon posted its first trade—a 6.48 million share block—close to two hours after the opening.

Because of this, market statistics meant little. Officially, however, the Dow opened at 2047, down 200 points from the Friday close. Then it rebounded, and after half an hour was at 2178, up more than one hundred points from the bell. While not altogether meaningless, these figures were hardly valid measurements of what was happening, since the tape was late and quotations for many stocks were still unavailable. Volume for the first half hour came to 51 million shares; twice that amount might have been recorded had humans and technologies been able to fill all orders and conduct all transactions. Significantly, most of the selling came from professional fund managers, with Fidelity accounting for 25 percent of the volume, and it was later learned that index arbitrageurs were responsible for 12 percent of total volume.

As the sell orders flooded to their posts, specialists seemed stunned. Small trades were transacted automatically, and these were backed up, but the larger ones had to be handled individually. The specialists were in a quandary. They were charged with maintaining an orderly market, but under the circumstances this was impossible. Later investigations differed about whether the specialists performed well under the kind of stress none had anticipated, but this mattered little to investors who put in sell orders when their stocks were at 50 only to learn later on that the order had been executed at 36.

There was now a new rush from the professionals to the options markets, where they were in for rude shocks. Traders formerly certain they could arbitrage stocks and options found that all the supposed rules had been suspended. First of all, it was impossible to calculate the S & P average, since so many stocks hadn't opened. Previous to October 19, dealers in the contract had known it was artificial. On that date it not only was artificial, but illusory. Then too, in the rush to sell S & P contracts, the spreads between the contracts and the stocks widened enormously. At one point the discount between the contract and the cash market was a gaping 20 percent. That session $7.6 billion worth of NYSE stock was traded, with the portfolio insurance portion coming to $1.7 billion. In the last hour and a half of trading 6,000 contracts were sold, worth in excess of $660 million. Afterward a *Fortune* writer calculated the market fell at a rate of one point every seventeen seconds in this period. Despite this rush, the insurers could not dispose of sufficient contracts to protect their clients. Those who used options for portfolio insurance also discovered there was no such certainty on Wall Street that day. It wasn't that the old verities were demonstrated to have failed; rather, the new ones were found wanting.

The session following the Crash, Phelan asked for a suspension of programmed trading, an indication he felt reasonably certain this would help restore order to the markets. It appeared his opinions regarding the use of options had been vindicated.

Margin calls went out on a wholesale basis. This wasn't new; they had been triggered on Friday as well. But once again, it was the volume of such calls that was astounding. Individuals who the previous week were worth several millions of dollars on paper were almost wiped out, and some found themselves with debts on stocks that couldn't be sold at sufficiently high prices to cover the loans. After it was over it was learned that a number of brokers had sold out clients without notifying them, and this prompted a series of lawsuits. There were wild tales of brokers and customers refusing to honor orders; the essential ethical base of Wall Street had started to buckle.

Short figures are compiled on a monthly basis. On October 14 the number stood at 510 million shares, continuing to decline from the record 546 million established in August. So there were signs that prior to then speculators were cutting back on their positions, fearful perhaps of a broad-based advance. When the figures for October through November were released, it was learned the short position had declined to 466 million shares by November 13, which was interpreted as having resulted from forced covering of positions.

One might have thought that some adventuresome souls would have shorted stocks during the sell-off, anticipating it would go further. Apparently this did not occur, perhaps due to uncertainties, fears, and a simple desire to get to the sidelines and await the next development from the markets.

Stocks continued their wild gyrations, powered by that panic selling and the margin calls as prices cascaded in a horrifying yet fascinating fashion. If there was pandemonium on the NYSE and American Stock Exchange floors, NASDAQ was in shambles. Dealers refused to buy some stocks at almost any price, and a number of market makers didn't answer their telephones. Small investors who had purchased shares in mutual funds with switch privileges tried to go from stocks to bonds or money-market instruments, and discovered a flaw in the strategy—the funds lacked sufficient telephone lines to handle the enormous number of calls, so the would-be switchers couldn't get through. This news was broadcast on radio and television, prompting others to make calls, thus exacerbating the already horrible situation. Fidelity had 200,000 telephone calls that day, and there would be 280,000 on Tuesday. Fearing a liquidity crisis, the organization asserted its right to delay payments for seven days in order to raise the needed cash.

Despite all of this activity, the vast majority of shareholders held fast. Several months later a study of 282 funds indicated that only 2 percent of total assets were redeemed during the session, and of that amount, 80 percent went from stock to bond and money-market funds. That week money-market assets rose by a record $9.7 billion.

Activities at the switch funds were the closest analogue 1987 had to offer to the 1929 runs on banks, and as the banks held in their time, so did the funds. There was no need to oblige investors to wait for redemptions or to redeem in shares of underlying securities rather than cash. Fidelity was never in trouble; the cash from its massive liquidation would take care of all switches and redemptions.

By the close that one fund family accounted for 4.5 percent of NYSE volume. But this action also contributed to the decline.

No one seemed to notice an event that *didn't* transpire. There were no reports of larger than normal bank withdrawals that day or in the weeks and months that followed. Nor is there reason to expect a change in the future. Deposit insurance, a legacy from the New Deal, was one of those reforms that prevented additional panic from developing. The pundits missed this one when considering all the parallels to 1929. The actions at the funds and the calmness at the banks assured many there would be no major crack in the financial facade.

THE DOW-JONES INDUSTRIALS, OCTOBER 19, 1987

Time	Average
Open	2047
10:00	2179
10:30	2154
11:00	2041
11:30	2124
12:00	2104
12:30	2070
1:00	2062
1:30	2053
2:00	1975
2:30	1961
3:00	1959
3:30	1867
Close	1739

Source: *Barron's*, October 26, 1987, p. 191

So it went throughout the session. There were occasional rallies, but for the most part it was straight down. At noon the Dow had lost 143 points, but two hours later was off by 273 points, and if anything the mood had worsened. By 3:30 P.M. the Dow had given up 380 points, and in the last half hour, on a record-breaking volume of 60 million shares, it fell another 128 points. The tape was running late, but when the final numbers were in, investors learned that the Dow had closed at 1678, down 508 points on the day, on a volume of 604 million shares. As measured by the Dow, stocks were off by 22.6

percent, which dwarfed the 11.7 percent given up on Black Tuesday in 1929. Recall that in 1929 it had taken more than a month for the Dow to decline 40 percent; in 1987 the market fell half that amount in a single session.

It didn't help to have an inexperienced new chairman at the Securities & Exchange Commission. David Ruder, who had taken over from John Shad, mused that it would be best to close down the exchanges for a few days, perhaps not realizing that this kind of signal, more than any other, would lead to heightened tensions.

Stocks were 36 percent below their August highs, but still above where they had been on New Year's Day. The high and low for the session were 2164 and 1678, a spread of 486 points, another record. Recall that on August 25 the price-earnings ratio for the Dow had been over 21. Now it was under 14, more reasonable perhaps but still above the 1970–1979 average of 12.

Brokers, bankers, investors, speculators, Washington, and interested foreigners had expected a decline, perhaps one on the magnitude of Friday's collapse. They were psychologically prepared for a bad day. What they got was an unprecedented disaster.

In one day more than half a trillion dollars' worth of values in American stocks had been wiped out. Another $600 billion had been lost in other world markets. The part of the public unversed in economic jargon learned a new term from the news media that night: "the wealth effect." Those Americans who held stock worth $100,000 before the crash had seen their holdings shrink to around $80,000. No matter that some called this a "paper loss"; it was felt nonetheless.

How might this influence the economy? If the newly fearful public delayed consumer purchases or put them off entirely, and if businesses cut back on expansion, there might be a severe economic decline. Ironically, critics who for years had called for a diminution of imports and a higher savings rate would get both in 1988. Americans wouldn't purchase Sony VCRs and Nissans and would save their money for what their grandparents, who recalled the 1930s, used to call "a rainy day." This might result in the loss of sales, production, jobs—a depression. Franklin D. Roosevelt had sensed this in 1933 when he told the American people the only thing they had to fear was fear itself. Perhaps that was an exaggeration, but the sentiment had a point. The greatest problem the American public had at that juncture was psychological, not economic. Panic was in the air, and what was needed was some kind of calming influence.

The media behaved quite differently in 1987 than it had in 1929, which also was to have been expected, given the different circumstances and roles. The 1929 Crash had been well tracked by newspapers, magazines, and radio, and afterward, by newsreels and even motion pictures. Anyone who wanted to find out what was happening at the markets could have done so easily. Yet almost all the reports in the leading newspapers were just that—reports. In those days reporters reported, editors edited, while commentators and columnists offered their opinions to a public generally aware of the differences. As they do today, the journalists of 1929 had sought precedents, and found them in earlier panics—1920, 1907, 1901, and 1893. Writing of the 1920 decline in October 1929, a reporter for *The New York Times* thought it had been caused by "the tying up of capital in company promotions and in speculation in all markets" and sought contemporary parallels. He and others rarely pontificated and didn't seem panicky themselves. They had seen it happen before, or at least so they seemed to believe. Almost all were looking to the banks. If they held, the situation would correct itself. There might be an economic slump, which probably would be painful to some but short, after which recovery would follow. Wasn't that the way it was supposed to happen?

It was quite different in 1987 in the aftermath of what from the start the newspapers and television analysts called Black Monday, thus immediately evoking memories of the Black Thursday and Black Tuesday of 1929. *The Wall Street Journal* ran one of its rare banner headlines the following day, and on the first page and elsewhere talked of disaster. Later on, *The New York Times* would pronounce "the end of business as usual" and conclude that "the economy will never be the same."

How could *The New York Times* (or anyone else, for that matter) know? In 1929 it was months before the most prescient observers understood just how serious the condition had become. This cannot be overly stressed, for the Great Depression was not inevitable, but rather was caused by decisions made in the Crash's aftermath. The same would be true for the 1987 collapse. On October 20 there still was no reason to believe that the market's decline, startling though it was, need usher in a new era in the economy or any other area. Yet each Sunday for two months *The New York Times* published charts tracking the market in 1987 against that 1929 performance, as though the latter would be some kind of lead indicator for the former.

Always 1929. Why not 1907 or some other panic year? In October there was no clear clue to just which previous Wall Street calamity the present one would most resemble. To say the least, the newspapers were being premature. Nor was this a one-day affair; on Wednesday stories appeared about home buyers "putting [their] dreams on hold" and the like. Again, how did the reporter know?

Even so, the leading newspapers and magazines were more responsible than most of the television reports that evening. The print media covered the story in detail, and if in places they sensationalized and seemed to search for the dramatic parallel, there were others taking a calmer view. Sensationalism was about all one found on the evening news programs. The newspapers did report on the strengths of the economy and discussed whether or not this might be the anticipated correction, which occurred during one day rather than a week or month.

As might have been predicted, news of the market crash dominated the television news programs that evening, with all of the networks preparing specials on the subject. Also predictable was the inability of the experts to agree on reasons the break occurred when and how it did. Later Chairman Phelan would estimate that some 20 percent of the trades came from programs; this activity clearly exacerbated the problems, he said. In response, the Commodities Futures Trading Commission put the figure at 9 percent. Even so, that would be a substantial and significant amount.

Perhaps the sanest statement of the evening came from George Goodman, who now was host of "Adam Smith's Money World." After a half-hour presentation of analyses and interviews, Goodman looked into the camera, smiled, and observed that while the market had put on a spectacular display, America was still there—the factories, the offices, the farms, and the mines—and that not much had changed since the sell-off began. The network and local television news programs, on the other hand, took the kinds of approaches found in the tabloid press. They concentrated on the weaknesses of Wall Street, the parlous nature of investments, and ominous observations that this was, truly, the beginning of a major calamity. Images of harried brokers, worried analysts, and most of all, stunned customers watching the tape, filled the screens. That night the most common term to describe what had happened was "meltdown." Cablenews Network's "Moneyline" show, perhaps the most carefully watched evening wrap of business news, was usually watched by 650,000 people; many more tuned in that Monday evening and heard a discussion between regulars Mike Kandel and Dan Dorfman. Arguing that it was too early to interpret the meaning of the day's events, Kandel urged caution, suggesting investors "stay put for now. The damage has been done." The fiery Dorfman took a different tack. "People will never look at the stock market again. . . . You're going to see dead money in the stock market."

It remained for *Barron's* to put the matter in some reasonable kind of perspective the following weekend with an article asking "1962 All Over Again?" In this piece market analyst Steve Leuthold attempted to demonstrate that while there certainly were similarities between what was happening on Wall Street now and the situation in 1929, there were more compelling reasons to believe that closer comparisons could be drawn to the 1962 collapse.

There was little in the way of comforting statements from Washington, and none at all from the President. Later on Secretary Baker and other Administration leaders would observe the economy was still strong, and the President would also say as much. But there was no symbolic action or gesture from the White House. What might have been done? The assignment of Paul Volcker to a post as special presidential advisor might have helped, and announcement of an economic summit could have calmed jittery markets in America and abroad. Nothing of the sort happened. But actions may have been taken behind the scene. Afterward there were rumors that Baker had telephoned Greenspan from the plane carrying him across the Atlantic to plead for statements and actions to calm the market.

If so, Greenspan must have agreed, for the Fed flooded the markets with money through open-market purchases of Treasury paper, this to assure liquidity and halt the panic. Interest rates clearly would be headed downward. This meant that bonds would rise in price. There had been a bond rally on Monday, barely noted by the media whose gaze was affixed to the more spectacular story in equities. Now bonds and debts of all kinds would advance again. This was no small matter. The government market alone was ten times larger than the stock market, and government paper rose in price during this period. Indeed, the gains in debts largely offset the losses in stocks. The media had little to say about this aspect of the wealth effect, and the lack of coverage, or even interest, is one of the more puzzling aspects of the period.

Tuesday trading began against a backdrop of news of some recoveries in overseas markets, attributed to the customary bounce back after so serious a decline. Even before the opening it appeared certain that the bond rally resulting from Fed activities would continue. Perhaps it would carry over to the stock market as well.

Perhaps not. After all, the panicky sentiment still ran high. It was evident that international harmony symbolized by the Louvre Accords had been dealt a blow, and that the dollar was headed lower. The markets were on uncertain footing. No one had a clear concept of just how much damage had been caused. But one thing was certain: by attempting to maintain some semblance of order, many of the NYSE's specialists had seriously depleted their cash positions, having committed over $2 billion of their $3 billion in capital. Toward the end of the Monday session several seemed to have abandoned their obligations and sold from their own accounts, draining reserves of shares, which meant they had only a bare inventory to offer potential buyers. The situation was dangerous, which indicated at the very least subsequent investigations would focus on the NYSE's specialist system along with the broker-dealer operations on the over-the-counter market.

As was the case on Monday, Tuesday's actions and reactions would be exaggerated. Once again NYSE specialists had difficulties with their shares, but this time because of massive bargain hunting—the typical reaction to major sell-offs. Orders came in a wave; thirteen of the Dow stocks opened later than they did on Monday, and DuPont didn't trade until a few minutes short of 1:00 P.M.

The market opened up 211 points, only to give up 87 of them in the first half hour. Again, these figures are not particularly meaningful. By noon the Dow was in the minus column, but there was a recovery soon after when Reagan ordered cuts of $23 billion in the federal budget deficit to conform with the mandate of the Gramm-Rudman Act. The Chicago Mercantile Exchange suspended trading in stock index futures, a move interpreted as bullish, since it would dampen speculative activities. On a volume of 608 million shares (the Monday record lasted one day), the Dow gained 103 points to close at 1841. After its first three-digit day on the downside, the NYSE had posted its first triple-digit gain, after having traversed 451 points in the course of the session.

THE DOW-JONES INDUSTRIALS, OCTOBER 20, 1987

Time	Average
Open	1950
10:00	1863
10:30	1930
11:00	1859
11:30	1761
12:00	1726
12:30	1712
1:00	1825
1:30	1812
2:00	1760
2:30	1827
3:00	1879
3:30	1853
Close	1841

Source: *Barron's*, October 26, 1987, p. 191

Then, in whiplash fashion, came a reversal overseas. After rallying, most of the foreign markets sold off sharply. Tokyo's Nikkei index fell 15 percent, and the slump continued in London, which posted a 22-percent decline for the two days. The same story held for the secondary markets—Singapore down 21 percent, Australia off 25 percent, and Hong Kong and New Zealand simply closed down. If there was need for proof that there now was a twenty-four-hour-a-day global market, in which information and money travel instantaneously from one continent to another, it was demonstrated during this period. The experience altered the ways Americans thought about investment and their abilities to outguess and outperform the full-time professionals. The brokers had their lessons too. NYSE specialists were still shell-shocked. Whether they would be there to perform their functions if and when there was another crash was problematical.

The rally continued; the Dow opened 175 points higher on Wednesday, but once more thirteen stocks opened one hour later than they had on Tuesday, and the laggards included IBM, Goodyear, Eastman Kodak, and DuPont. At the final bell the Dow was up by 183 points (a record) to go over the 2000 level once again, ending at 2028. John Phelan now seized the opportunity to announce that the market would close at 2:00 P.M. starting Friday, to enable brokers to clear up their paperwork. Stocks moved lower on Thursday by "only" 78 points. Movement was barely perceptible by recent standards on Friday. Although the fluctuations covered a range of close to 100 points, the Dow closed at 1951, up by less than a fraction of a point.

Even before the week had ended, there were indications reason was returning. A number of major concerns announced important stock-buyback programs—IBM, United Technologies, Citicorp, Ford, General Motors, Pacific Telesis, Honeywell, and McGraw-Hill, among others. The total came to more than $6.2 billion. When insider transactions information was released, it was learned that corporate executives had purchased shares in their own companies in record quantities since the decline, this generally considered a bullish sign. (Recall, however, that insiders had been heavy net buyers prior to the later summer decline.) There were rumors of meetings among Administration representatives and Congressional leaders to work out some means of cutting the budget deficit. Secretary of Defense Caspar Weinberger announced his resignation, and while he retained Reagan's confidence, this was taken as an indication the defense budget would be hit fairly hard.

THE NYSE IN OCTOBER, 1987

	Dow Closing	Change	Volume (millions of shares)
October 1	2639		193
2	2641	+ 3	189
5	2640	− 1	160
6	2549	− 92	176
7	2551	+ 2	186
8	2517	− 34	199
9	2482	− 35	158
12	2471	− 11	142
13	2508	+ 37	173
14	2413	− 95	207
15	2355	− 58	263
16	2247	− 108	338
19	1738	− 508	604
20	1841	+ 103	608
21	2028	+ 187	449
22	1950	− 78	392
23	1951	+ 1	246
26	1794	− 157	309
27	1846	+ 52	260
28	1847	+ 1	279
29	1938	+ 91	258
30	1994	+ 56	303

Source: *Wall Street Journal*, October 2–November 2, 1987

Not all the news was good. On the eve of the Crash, Salomon and Goldman Sachs each had lent $300 million to Southland, which planned to use the funds to go private in a leveraged buyout and then issue junk bonds and repay the loans. After the Crash it seemed that placements of such bonds might prove difficult, and it was evident that the $600 million was at risk. Nor was this all; Salomon had provided Bond, the Australian brewer attempting to find a niche in the United States, with $400 million to purchase Heileman Brewing, and that transaction looked increasingly shaky. There was some talk that Drexel Burnham Lambert might salvage either or both deals, garnering both prestige and profits, but that firm was also in trouble, since it maintained a large inventory of junk bonds that had been marked down in value.

Drexel, Bear Stearns, Goldman Sachs, First Boston, and almost all the other major investment banks reported problems resulting from the Crash. The best performers turned in sharply lower earnings, the worst had major losses. Yet none of the big players was in danger of being shuttered. Far better capitalized than they had been during the 1962 collapse, and infinitely stronger than their 1929 counterparts, each seemed capable of not only surviving, but prospering as the markets worked their ways out of the morass. Bank failures had been the cause of most nineteenth-century panics and crashes; this wouldn't be the case in 1987.

But there would be a price. Thousands of bright young MBA's had streamed into Wall Street during the bull market. By November the exodus had begun, and in December it had turned into a rout. First Shearson Lehman acquired E.F. Hutton, and the elimination of positions might result in the firing of some 7,000 people. Then Kidder Peabody announced it would eliminate 1,000 jobs in addition to those in the bond department already "severed." Rothschild would release another 700 employees, and there were smaller cutbacks at Drexel and Shearson Lehman. The Street faced a troubled Christmas. Weekly employee newsletters published by most investment banks usually carried one or two advertisements for used cars; that December there were scores of such notices. In January corporate recruiters reported that more MBA's from prestigious institutions were showing interest in management posts and fewer in investment banking.

That the shock waves from Black Monday would continue reverberating through the district and on to the nation and world was taken as axiomatic. Was *The New York Times* correct? Would the economy never be the same? One plausible answer was that change is the norm, not the exception. Something indeed had changed the previous month, but the difference might well have been quantitative rather than qualitative. This is to suggest that the Crash on October 19 had been awesome in its magnitude, but other than that was not very much different from the other major sell-offs in previous years, with 1962 being the prime example.

There were those who thought otherwise. In mid-November Cornell professors Avner Arbel and Steven Carvell released a report stating that while the Dow had risen more than 12 percent since the Crash, thousands of other stocks were selling at prices far below those of the blue chips. The post-Crash rally had involved the blue chips, as investors rushed to quality. The rest of the market was still in shambles, they appeared to be saying. "Our study shows some market similarity of price behavior with the 1929 crash and is not as optimistic as the Dow," said Arbel. The 1929 recollection persisted. Just as stocks recovered substantially from November 1929 to April 1930, so it might be that the same would happen in the winter and early spring of 1987–1988.

If this scenario was not to be replicated, the turning point might have come on Tuesday, November 24, when a series of sunny, unrelated reports hit Wall Street one after the other, climaxing several days during which the news was generally optimistic. For example, if anything, the economy was strengthening, with no sign of inflation. It turned out that payrolls swelled by 549,000 in October, the best showing since September 1983. During the first ten months of 1987 factory employment expanded by 26,700 jobs per month versus losses of 30,000 on the average in 1985 and 13,500 in 1986. Department stores recorded a 1.4-percent increase in sales for October, and furniture sales advanced by 1.6 percent. Auto sales were down by 2.6 percent, but this might be attributed more to a lack of incentive programs than to other factors. Later it would be learned that the events of October did little to halt America's spending spree; in November, in the face of a 0.4-percent drop in personal income, consumer expenditures rose by 0.5 percent.

These encouraging signs were followed by Secretary of State George Shultz's announcement that the United States and the Soviet Union had reached a substantial accord on a treaty banning medium and shorter-range missiles, and that there was a prospect that other agreements would follow. While not directly related to Wall Street and the economy, the news had beneficial psychological effects, and in addition might make budget-cutting easier in the future.

Despite grumbling, the House and Senate seemed as if they would agree on a bundle of minor tax increases and spending cuts, which would please those who insisted these were prerequisites for a return of confidence while not serious enough to spin the economy into a recession. Some progress on talks to find some resolution to the fighting in Nicaragua was also reported. Then the Commerce Department announced revisions on the third-quarter GNP, which had advanced at a 4.1-percent rate instead of the 3.8-percent preliminary figure reported earlier. This was followed by an announcement that the Chicago Board of Trade was considering drastic revisions in operations in order to limit declines and advances for stock index futures and so reduce volatility.

Finally, one after the other, several European countries disclosed reductions in key interest rates. The Bundesbank reduced its short-term repurchase rate from 3.5 percent to 3.25 percent. "The United States did something on the budget," said Hermann Rempsberger, chief economist for the Berliner Handels-und-Frankfurter Bank. "This is a signal to show that the Bundesbank is willing to cooperate." Then the Bank of France reduced its money-market intervention rate to 8 percent from 8.25 percent. Other cuts took place in the Netherlands and Italy. The concurrent shifts were not happenstance. Clearly the nations had moved in concert. There was talk of a new international monetary conference; perhaps the Louvre Accords were still in force after all. Stocks responded with a strong rally, the Dow ending the day up 40 points on volume of 200 million shares, ending at 1964. Wall Street had digested these news items, and as each was made known, buying pressures increased.

Still, fears remained. A month to the day after the Crash, the National Committee for Monetary Reform held its fourteenth annual conference in New Orleans. Despite its appellation, the organization is actually composed of financial newsletter writers and editors bankrolled by James Ulysses Blanchard III, a local businessman, one of whose interests was a precious-metals firm. There were some 3,000 in attendance, each of whom paid $595 for the privilege of hearing Louis Rukeyser, William F. Buckley, and others discuss the economy and the markets. Those who had predicted bad times crowed over their successes while the fallen bulls showed emotions running from apologetic to defensive.

Robert Prechter was one of the speakers. Forgotten or ignored were his earlier predictions regarding Dow 3600 sometime in the next year or so. Now Prechter informed his fellows that there would be two rallies in late 1987 and early 1988, which would be followed by a "monolithic" collapse. As bad as the 1930s? Worse, said Prechter; it would be the most severe shakeout since well before the Industrial Revolution, and the Dow would go to around 400. Prechter's advice to those seeking specific advice was not the purchase of gold, that conventional haven for doomsayers, but rather cash. At this at least some of the gold bugs nodded agreement. The new line was that gold would have to be sold to raise cash to service the heavy loans then outstanding. "A bear market is a bull market in cash," Prechter intoned, and rumor had it that he was trying to sell his newsletter and then put the proceeds into Treasury bills.

As usual Martin Zweig was cautious. He told subscribers that the Dow was now 36.1 percent below its high. "Since the Dow Averages began in 1885, there have been only eleven other cases when the Industrials fell by 30 percent or more in economic environments unrelated to world wars," he remarked. "In every single case the economy entered a recession or depression."

A few days earlier most of Wall Street's fears had revolved around deflation. Now the talk was of possible inflation. Yet with all of this, the panic phase appeared over, and other than small bands of diehards such as had convened in New Orleans, even those most devoted to the disaster scenario seemed to realize the situation was quite different from that of 1929–1931.

There was some good news amid all of the carnage. The banking system was sound; despite the highest rate of failures since World War II, there were no concerns of runs on financial institutions. The Federal Reserve understood its duties in providing liquidity. Before the Crash there had been anxiety that many junk-bond issues would go into default given a major sell-off. It didn't happen. Due to the sales of their securities, credit balances in brokerage accounts in October rose a record $6.7 billion to $26.9 billion, another all-time high. There was plenty of liquidity, then, to power a new move to the upside if and when confidence returned. The economy appeared strong and resilient, and with a cheaper dollar, poised for better things. Third-quarter pretax corporate profits rose $13.4 billion on an annualized rate. In November, as the Street echoed with tales of more firings and diminished bonuses, nonagricultural payrolls expanded by 274,000. By December there were stirrings from abroad, indicating foreign investors would take advantage of the combination of a weak dollar and low stock and bond prices to go bargain hunting. But the overseas buying was cautious.

By then a presidential fact-finding committee, directed by Dillon Read Chairman and former New Jersey Senator Nicholas Brady, was investigating the Crash, and a second group, sponsored by the NYSE and chaired by former Attorney General Nicholas Katzenbach, was conducting its own study. Investigations were being made by the SEC, the Commodities Futures Trading Commission, the Chicago Mercantile Exchange, the Chicago Board of Trade, the General Accounting Office, and other nongovernmental or exchange bodies. As might have been expected, the CBT report exonerated the options market from blame, and the NYSE group did the same for that market's specialists. The Brady group, the most impartial of the lot and the one with the most complete and convincing report, laid most of the blame for the severity of the Crash on the program traders and portfolio insurance.

Doubtless there will be more to come. The Crash of 1987 bids to be the most investigated market phenomenon in history, in this aspect too eclipsing that of 1929. But even before the reports came, it seemed obvious that weaknesses had been exposed and changes would be made. If it were to remain in operation, the specialist system would have to be revamped and certainly refinanced. Phelan spoke out for larger capital requirements and convinced the SEC to permit major investment banks to purchase some of the weaker ones. By late November Merrill Lynch, Drexel Burnham, and Bear Stearns had acquired specialist firms, and so placed their solid resources behind them.

Who was at fault? The program traders? Portfolio insurance? The institutions? The Fed? The budget deficit? The trade deficit? The gyrating dollar? Consider the list, add others of your own, and then reflect that most of these factors either didn't exist in 1929 or did so in a radically different fashion.

The Crash of 1987 was like a huge whale washed up on the shore for no readily apparent reason. Why did it leave the deeps? How did it get there? What caused its demise? The dissection has begun. Not only do we lack plausible answers to questions being asked on the Street, in Washington, and at gatherings throughout the world, but we aren't certain we are asking the right questions. In other words, some perspective is required, and that comes with effort and time.

And what of the markets? In early 1988 a major struggle had been triggered, which might be summed up in a question: Would fears and wounds caused by the market decline lead to weaknesses in the economy, or would the strong economy be translated into stronger stock prices and a recovery on Wall Street? It was a classic conflict between irrationality and corporeality, perceptions and realities. Fear had been victorious in 1929–1933. It remained to be seen if a similar scenario would be played out in 1988. The individual investor had made up his and her mind, however. According to a Sindlinger & Co. survey, at the end of August there were some 50.7 million Americans in the market on their own. By late December the number had been sliced almost in half, to 26 million.

Paul Volcker put it succinctly when he said that "we can control events if we do the right things." He might have added that the crucial consideration is knowing what the correct behavior might be, and one of the major snares is a forced analogy, specifically trying to see 1987 as a replay of 1929—or, for that matter, of any other year. As the nation finds its way to a postpanic environment, this remains one of its most crucial problems.

The other danger lies in believing that whatever the future will bring has already been determined by past decisions and actions. If the 1929 experience has a lesson to provide those who are concerned with such matters, it is that it need not have been a prelude to the Great Depression. The economic damage in the first few post–Great Crash months was small compared to that felt in 1893–1895 or 1857, for example. The psychological injury was more important, as were the fallacious programs of the Hoover Administration in 1930. The danger of a new depression or severe inflation rests in policies and programs entered into in 1988, more than the great bloodletting of October 19, 1987.

CONCLUSION

Attempts to find logical explanations for financial panics have always been made and doubtless will continue to be made for the indefinite future. In his *History of Business Depressions* (1922), Otto Lightner tried to list the many causes he uncovered in the literature, and among them he found:

Underconsumption
Large exports of gold
Large imports of gold
Effects of fear of the tariff
Weak banking systems
Presidential elections
Unpopular taxation
Lack of foreign markets
Unemployment
Want of confidence
Inflation of values
Variation in the cost of production
Unpopular legislation
Unreasonably high prices
Centralization of capital
Manipulation of money power
Depreciation of currency
Inflation of currency
Contraction of currency
Withdrawal of money from circulation

Suspension of specie payment
Disturbed value of gold and silver
Lack of fixed policy in governmental affairs
Extravagance, public and private
Inefficiency of labor
Large immigration of pauper labor
Speculation
Depressed value of farm products
Exorbitant transportation costs
Artificial stimulation
Timidity on the part of money lenders
Bank failures
Conflicts between labor and capital
Buyers' strikes
Enforced economy, public and private
Starting needless enterprises
Political distrust
Withholding franchise from women
Want of training of girls for future duties
Faulty laws relative to the guardianship of children
The custom of issuing free railroad passes
High telegraph rates
The use of tobacco

To these Lightner has also added: sunspots, overpopulation, overproduction, excessive savings, foreign investments, falling prices, and several more. Obviously, some of these are frivolous, oversimplified, or overdrawn, and still others vague and not very meaningful. A few are worthy of examination, and this has been the burden of the present work.

Financial panics have been endemic to America, as to all Western countries. They seem to happen at special moments. After studying their histories and developments, we may come to several tentative conclusions, not to be confused with a "law of panics."

In the first place, most panics occur during periods of optimism. In 1791 speculators saw great possibilities for investment; the West beckoned in 1836; railroads were magic in 1857, and again in 1873, 1901 and 1907. Everything seemed headed upward in

1929, and new industries provided the glamour for 1962. On the other hand, the panic of 1893 was widely predicted in advance, and danger signals were flashed in 1884 and 1962.

Most panics were made possible, though not necessarily caused, by weaknesses in the financial structure. American banking was notoriously slipshod and inadequate after the disestablishment of the second Bank of the United States and before the formation of the Federal Reserve System. Even then, the Federal Reserve was manned during its early years by unskilled individuals unwilling to use their powers to prevent abuses. Faulty banking practices appear as important contributing factors in 1836, 1857, 1873, 1893, 1907, and 1929.

Most panics occur as "moments of truth" after periods of self-deception. Financial difficulties, known or unknown, appear and are not corrected. Then, when speculators and investors recognize their problems and inability to cope with them, panic may ensue. Such was the case in 1869, when gold speculators panicked as they realized a corner had been gained in the metal, and a similar situation developed with the conclusion of the Northern Pacific corner in 1901. The condition appeared again in 1962, when the bubble of speculation was finally burst. But this was not the case in 1837 and 1893, when the panics came more slowly or did not involve such a moment of truth.

One can discern a sense of futility at the height of a panic. The disillusioned of Wall Street, now having faced their problems, seem to have no hope of resolving them. Bull markets feed on an illusion of endless expansion, unstoppable by any human agency; panics are marked by fears of bottomless decline, which none seem able to arrest.

Just as weak banking helps intensify panics, so the presence of strong financial leaders may prove a mitigating factor. As British economist and editor Walter Bagehot said during the panic of 1873, "The best palliative to a panic is a confidence in the adequate amount of the bank reserve, and in the efficient use of that reserve." Alexander Hamilton's influence helped shorten the 1792 panic. Nicholas Biddle proved a "paper tiger" in 1837, and inability or unwillingness to use his influence made the panic of that year worse than it need have been, while Albert Gallatin's efforts enabled the banks get back on their feet again in 1838. Strong banking figures such as Vanderbilt in 1873 and J. P. Morgan in 1893, 1901, and 1907 were significant in the postbellum era. Morgan was a key figure, and his death was one reason for the establishment of the Federal Reserve System. The System's failure in 1929, despite heroic efforts by several members, was important in causing the depression which took place after the panic of that year. Similarly, the wise exercise of power on most occasions since then has saved the nation from suffering through needless periods of distress, and has been one of several factors in keeping the nation panic-free since 1929.

Prosperity, like victory, has many fathers, while panics and depressions share with defeats the problems of orphanhood. This is not to say that all society loses through panics. Undeniably, panics and depressions are to be feared and safeguarded against, but most of our panics had some salutary effects on the economy. The most important of these was the liquidation of foreign investment in the nineteenth century. Although Americans were harmed by panics in New York, foreign investors lost millions of dollars in the sharply declining markets. This was the case in 1792, 1837, 1857, 1873, 1893, and 1907. Before each of these crises foreigners, wary of American securities as a result of having had their fingers burned earlier, lost their doubts and were heavy investors just before the next crash came around. During the post-crash period foreigners would avoid the American markets, while native speculators and investors made fortunes by purchasing securities at depressed prices. Then, when the next boom was at a mature stage, these securities would be resold to foreigners, who once again would lose their fortunes in the crash which came shortly thereafter. There is no indication that this pattern was purposeful or that American and foreign investors knew it was happening, but it was the case nonetheless. It shows, among other things, that Americans were better judges of their own economy than the most sophisticated Europeans of the age. And it raises an interesting question. Now the conditions are reversed—with Americans exporting capital to Europe and undeveloped areas—what would the reactions of this nation's investors be to a major panic on foreign securities markets? Americans lost huge amounts of money when foreigners defaulted in 1929–32, but this was a pittance compared with the domestic decline, and so was generally overlooked. Notwithstanding the gold crisis of 1968, the nation has not undergone a foreign panic of major consequence since that time. Should one occur, the American reaction would be interesting to observe. In all likelihood, it would be similar to that of Europeans in the nineteenth century.

There is one final point to be made: panics are not necessarily followed by depressions. Depression did not immediately follow panics in 1869, 1901, 1914, 1962,—and, in a way, in 1929. Nor have there been connections between periods of economic stagnation since World War II and market irregularities in the same period.

Writing in 1929, Joseph Stagg Lawrence of Princeton, one of the most famous economists of his time, said that there was no possibility of a panic in the foreseeable future. *Wall Street and Washington* appeared only a few months before the Great Crash of October; Lawrence receded into the background soon after. His example should serve as a warning to all those who think that we have insured against future panics. Yet the fact remains that since 1929—and particularly since World War II—we have been free from those moments of fear and disillusionment.

Can it be that the conditions which once made for panics are no longer with us? For example, it now seems clear that many nineteenth-century panics occurred in late summer and early autumn due to currency shortages resulting from withdrawals by farmers prior to harvests. The seasonal outflow of funds would be matched by a return after the crops were paid for by importers. Accordingly, intelligent Wall Streeters were usually more cautious in late summer and through harvest time. Needless to say, these problems, of vital importance a century ago, are no longer of great moment. Changes in the economy, then, have brought with them a certain immunity from crises caused by seasonal crop movements.

Several panics were caused by stringencies in foreign capitals. This was the case in 1837, 1857, 1869, 1873, and 1893. As long as Wall Street was the tail to London's dog, we were vulnerable to repercussions from overseas. Although such problems still exist, they are not as vital today as they were prior to World War I. The British devaluation of the pound in 1968 stirred the financial community and caused great interest and concern, but it did not result in a panic as it might have three quarters of a century ago. The world's currencies and economies are more intertwined today than they were then, but most of the strings are pulled from Wall Street and Washington, and not from Paris, London and Zurich. If anything, American problems will lead to damaging panics overseas; now Wall Street is the dog and London the tail.

Gold has been a key factor in many panics. This was true of the 1837 crash, precipitated in part by the Specie Circular, and Black Friday, caused by the gold corner. It was a significant factor in 1873, 1893, 1907, and 1914. The 1929 collapse was caused in part by monetary theories involving gold which led to unwise decisions at the Federal Reserve in the twenties. Gold is still an important force in world finance, but it does not occupy the same central position in men's thoughts it did a century ago. No economist of stature believes, as did Jackson, Grant, and Cleveland, that gold has intrinsic value. Even Jacques Rueff, Charles de Gaulle's leading financial adviser, does not claim the nineteenth century gold standard, with its automatic mechanisms for trade correction, could work at the present time.

An economic collapse or some other cataclysm could lead to a rush to gold and a major financial panic. Such has been the fear of some bankers for the past four decades. In 1968 the world underwent its most severe gold crisis since the early 1930s. For a few days in March, speculators bought and sold billions of dollars worth of the yellow metal, betting that the American gold price of $35 an ounce would be altered in some way. At one point the London gold market was obliged to close, and the Paris quotation skyrocketed to well over $44 an ounce. In the end, the leading central bankers of the world met and agreed on a "two-price system" for gold, in which the central banks would retain the $35 price for transactions among themselves, while "free gold" would fluctuate according to supply and demand.

The American economy was the key to the gold crisis of 1968. Those who purchased gold in the late 1960s did so because they believed the United States had a chronic deficit and was unwilling to take steps to correct it. In effect, there was an oversupply of dollars in Europe. But as the Johnson Administration began belt-tightening measures, the price of free gold began to settle down. Significantly, no collapse developed on Wall Street in this period. Instead, the markets continued their steady decline which had begun in early January. Most investors realized that the American economy, and not gold, was the key to Wall Street happenings.

Today's economy is quite different from that of 1929, and there are institutional safeguards, most of them dating from the New Deal, to make certain that panic situations will not easily develop. For this reason, "another 1929" should probably not be a major fear, nor, for that matter, another 1914, 1907, 1901, 1893—and all the way back to 1792.

But this does not respond to the crucial question that many Americans were asking in the aftermath of the 1987 Crash: Will this panic, or any that might follow, necessarily mean we are in for a recession or depression?

For one answer, we might do well to recall Al Frank, that market-letter writer who was fully invested and margined on Labor Day 1987. Two months later he was refreshingly contrite. "I apologize," Frank told clients. "I did not foresee a potential correction in the market that even approached the magnitude of the unprecedented crash."

The operative word was *unprecedented*. It was of a magnitude never seen before. Did this mean it was unique, that knowledge of previous panics would be of little or no use as a guide? Perhaps so, but this should not have come as a surprise. After all, the 1987 Crash occurred fifty-eight years after the 1929 debacle. This is to suggest that some of those safeguards erected during the 1930s had become obsolete by the 1980s. How many laws retain their pertinence after more than half a century? Of course, mob psychology may be similar, and human nature did not undergo a revolution in this span, but the economies, trading methods, and scope were so different as to make comparisons worth little. The next panic—or further reverberations from this one—will require analysis of current problems and not specific, didactic references to Herbert Hoover and Franklin Roosevelt, or Ronald Reagan.

Some are fond of citing George Santayana, who said, "Those who cannot remember the past are condemned to repeat it." Remember, yes, but with caution when drawing "lessons." Most historians do not entertain notions of eternal return and the cyclical nature of experience. Worse than failing to understand history is to believe that it contains specific messages that, if applied, can resolve current problems favorably. Alas, there are no such magic formulas.

More useful is a comment by Robert Lovett uttered at a different time in different circumstances. The statesman reflected on just what it was we learned from the past. "Good judgment is usually the result of experience," he wrote, "and experience frequently is the result of bad judgment."

BIBLIOGRAPHY

Adams, Charles F., and Adams, Henry. *Chapters of Erie*. New York, 1871.

Allen, Frederick Lewis. *The Great Pierpont Morgan*. New York, 1949.

———. *The Lords of Creation*. New York, 1935.

———. *Only Yesterday*. New York, 1931.

Alexander, David. *Panic!* Evanston, 1960.

Alexander, Holmes. *The American Talleyrand*. New York, 1935.

Angley, Edward. *Oh, Yeah!* New York, 1930.

Andreades, Andreas. *History of the Bank of England, 1640–1903*. London, 1909.

Ansbacher, Max. *The New Stock Index Market*. New York, 1983.

Auletta, Ken. *Greed and Glory on Wall Street: The Fall of the House of Lehman*. New York, 1986.

Auerbach, Joseph, and Hayes, Samuel L. III. *Investment Banking and Diligence*. Boston, 1986.

Ayers, Leonard. *Turning Points in Business Cycles*. New York, 1939.

Badeau, Adam. *Grant in Peace*. Philadelphia, 1888.

Barnes, James. *John G. Carlisle: Financial Statesman*. New York, 1931.

Beckman, Robert. *The Downwave*. New York, 1983.

Benton, Thomas Hart. *Thirty Years' View*. 2 vols. New York, 1885.

Bird, Caroline. *The Invisible Scar*. New York, 1966.

Bladen, Ashby. *How to Cope with the Developing Financial Crisis*. New York, 1982.

Bleyer, Willard. *Main Currents in the History of American Journalism*. New York, 1927.

Boesky, Ivan. *Merger Mania*. New York, 1985.

Bolles, Albert. *Financial History of the United States*. 3 vols. New York, 1879–1884.

Bourne, Edward. *The History of the Surplus Revenue of 1837.* New York, 1885.

Boutwell, George. *Reminiscences of Sixty Years in Public Affairs.* New York, 1902.

Boyd, George. *Elias Boudinot: Patriot and Statesman.* Princeton, 1952.

Brooks, John. *The Takeover Game.* New York, 1987.

Bruchey, Stuart. *The Roots of American Economic Growth.* New York, 1965.

Bullock, Charles. *Finances of the United States, 1775–1789.* Madison, 1895.

Burr, Anna. *The Portrait of a Banker: James Stillman, 1850–1918.* New York, 1927.

Burton, Theodore. *John Sherman.* Boston, 1906.

Cantor, Eddie. *Caught Short! A Saga of Wailing Wall Street.* New York, 1929.

Carey, Henry. *Financial Crises: Their Causes and Effects.* Philadelphia, 1864.

———. *The Harmony of Interests.* New York, 1852.

Casey, Douglas. *Strategic Investing.* New York, 1982.

Catterall, Ralph. *The Second Bank of the United States.* Chicago, 1903.

Chambers, William. *Old Bullion Benton.* Boston, 1956.

Chandler, Lester. *Benjamin Strong: Central Banker.* Washington, 1958.

Clews, Henry. *Fifty Years in Wall Street.* New York, 1908.

———. *The American Business System: A Historical Perspective.* Cambridge, 1957.

Cole, A. C. *The Irrepressible Conflict! 1850–1865.* New York, 1934.

Collins, Frederick. *Money Town.* New York, 1946.

Collman, Charles. *Our Mysterious Panics, 1830–1930.* New York, 1931.

Conant, Charles. *A History of Modern Banks of Issue.* New York, 1915.

———. *Wall Street and the Country.* New York, 1904.

Crane, Burton. *The Sophisticated Investor.* New York, 1959.

Dallas, George. *Life and Writings of A. J. Dallas.* Philadelphia, 1871.

Davis, Joseph. *Essays in the Earlier History of American Corporations.* 2 vols. Cambridge, 1917.

Dewey, Davis. *Financial History of the United States.* New York, 1936.

———. *National Problems: 1885–1897.* New York, 1907.

Domett, Henry. *A History of the Bank of New York, 1784–1884.* New York, 1898.

Dos Passos, John. *A Treatise on the Law of Stock Brokers and Stock Exchanges.* New York, 1882.

Dreman, David. *The New Contrarian Investment Strategy*. New York, 1982.

Eames, Francis. *The New York Stock Exchange*. New York, 1894.

Edward, George. *The Evolution of Finance Capitalism*. New York, 1938.

Ellis, Charles. *The Second Crash*. New York, 1973.

Faulkner, Harold U. *From Versailles to the New Deal*. New Haven, 1950.

————. *Politics, Reform and Expansion, 1890–1900*. New York, 1959.

————. *The Decline of Laissez Faire, 1897–1917*. New York, 1951.

Ferris, Paul. *The Master Bankers*. New York, 1984.

Fisher, Irving. *The Stock Market Crash and After*. New York, 1930.

Foner, Philip. *Business and Slavery*. Chapel Hill, 1941.

Ford, Henry Jones. *The Cleveland Era*. New Haven, 1919.

Fosback, Norman. *Stock Market Logic*. Fort Lauderdale, Fla., 1981.

Fowler, W. Worthington. *Twenty Years of Inside Life in Wall Street*. New York, 1880.

Freeman, Douglas S. *George Washington, Patriot and President*, vol. 6. New York, 1954.

Friedman, Milton, and Schwartz, Anna. *A Monetary History of the United States, 1867–1960*. Princeton, 1963.

Fuess, Claude. *Daniel Webster*. 2 vols. Boston, 1930.

Fuller, Robert. *Jubilee Jim*. New York, 1938.

Galbraith, John K. *The Great Crash*. New York, 1954.

Garraty, John. *Right Hand Man: The Life of George W. Perkins*. New York, 1960.

Gates, Paul W. *The Illinois Central Railroad and Its Colonization Work*. Cambridge, 1934.

Gilbart, James. *The History of Banking in America*. London, 1837.

Ginger, Ray. *The Age of Excess*. New York, 1965.

Gouge, William. *A Short History of Paper Money and Banking in the United States*. Philadelphia, 1833.

Gould, Leslie. *The Manipulators*. Chicago, 1971.

Govan, Thomas. *Nicholas Biddle*. Chicago, 1959.

Grayson, Theodore. *Leaders and Periods of American Finance*. New York, 1932.

Greider, William. *Secrets of the Temple*. New York, 1987.

Grodinsky, Jules. *Jay Gould: His Business Career, 1867–1892*. Philadelphia, 1957.

Hamilton, John. *The Works of Alexander Hamilton*, vols. 6 and 7. New York, 1851.

Hammond, Bray. *Banks and Politics in America: From the Revolution to the Civil War*. Princeton, 1957.

————. "Jackson, Biddle, and the Bank of the United States." *Journal of Economic History* 7 (May 1947).

Harding, W. G. P. *The Formative Period of the Federal Reserve System.* New York, 1925.

Harris, Charles. *Memories of Manhattan in the Sixties and Seventies.* New York, 1884.

Harris, Seymour. *Economics of the Kennedy Years and a Look Ahead.* New York, 1964.

————. *Twenty Years of Federal Reserve Policy.* 2 vols. Cambridge, 1933.

Hedges, Joseph. *Commercial Banking and the Stock Market before 1863.* Baltimore, 1938.

Hepburn, A. Barton. *A History of Currency in the United States.* New York, 1915.

Hesseltine, William. *Ulysses S. Grant: Politician.* New York, 1935.

Hicks, Frederick, ed. *High Finance in the Sixties: Chapters from the Early History of the Erie Railway.* New Haven, 1929.

Hidy, Ralph. *The House of Baring in American Trade and Finance, 1763–1861.* Cambridge, 1949.

Hildreth, Richard. *The History of Banks.* London, 1837.

Hirst, Francis. *Six Panics and Other Essays.* London, 1913.

————. *The Stock Exchange.* London, 1911.

Hoffman, Paul. *The Dealmakers.* New York, 1980.

Hoffmann, Charles. "The Depression of the Nineties—An Economic History." Ph.D. diss., Columbia University, 1954.

————. "The Depression of the Nineties." *Journal of Economic History* 16 (June 1956).

Holbrook, Stewart. *The Age of the Moguls.* New York, 1954.

————. *The Story of American Railroads.* New York, 1947.

Holt, Thomas. *How to Survive and Grow Richer in the Tough Times Ahead.* New York, 1981.

Hoopes, Roy. *The Steel Crisis.* New York, 1963.

Hoyt, Edwin. *The House of Morgan.* New York, 1966.

James, Marquis. *Biography of a Business, 1792–1942: Insurance Company of North America.* New York, 1942.

Jenks, Leland. *The Migration of British Capital to 1875.* New York, 1938.

Josephson, Matthew. *An Infidel in the Temple.* New York, 1967.

————. *Life Among the Surrealists.* New York, 1962.

————. *The President Makers.* New York, 1940.

————. *The Robber Barons.* New York, 1934.

Juglar, Clement. *A Brief History of Panics.* Edited by DeCourcey W. Thom. London, 1915.

Kearny, John. *Sketch of American Finances, 1789–1835*. New York, 1887.

Kennan, George. *E. H. Harriman: A Biography*. 2 vols. Boston, 1922.

King, Norman. *The Money Messiahs*. New York, 1983.

Kinley, David. *Money*. New York, 1904.

Knox, John. *History of Banking in the United States*. New York, 1900.

Kuznets, Simon. *National Product Since 1869*. New York, 1946.

Lampert, Hope. *Till Death Do Us Part*. New York, 1983.

Lane, Wheaton. *Commodore Vanderbilt: An Epic of the Steam Age*. New York, 1942.

Lanier, Henry. *A Century of Banking in New York, 1822–1922*. New York, 1922.

Larson, Henrietta. *Jay Cooke, Private Banker*. Cambridge, 1936.

Lauck, William. *The Causes of the Panic of 1893*. New York, 1907.

Lawrence, Joseph. *Wall Street and Washington*. Princeton, 1929.

Lawson, Thomas. *Frenzied Finance: The Crime of Amalgamated*. London, 1906.

Lee, Maurice. *Economic Fluctuations: Growth and Stability*. Homewood, Ill., 1959.

Lefevre, Edwin. *Wall Street Stories*. New York, 1901.

Lightner, Otto. *The History of Business Depressions*. New York, 1922.

Lord, Walter. *The Good Years: From 1900 to the First World War*. New York, 1960.

McGrane, Reginald. *The Panic of 1837*. New York, 1936.

Mackay, Charles. *Extraordinary Popular Delusions and the Madness of Crowds*. New York, 1932.

Malkiel, Burton. *A Random Walk Down Wall Street*. New York, 1973.

Medbury, James. *Men and Mysteries of Wall Street*. Boston, 1870.

Merrill, Horace. *Bourbon Leader: Grover Cleveland and the Democratic Party*. Boston, 1957.

Miller, Harry. *Banking Theories in the United States before 1860*. Cambridge, 1927.

Miller, John. *The Federalist Era: 1789–1801*. New York, 1960.

Miller, Nathan. *The Enterprise of a Free People*. Ithaca, 1962.

Mitchell, Broadus. *Alexander Hamilton: The National Adventure*. New York, 1962.

Mitchell, Wesley. *Business Cycles: The Problem and Its Setting*. New York, 1927.

Moody, John. *The Masters of Capital*. New Haven, 1921.

Morris, Joe Alex. *What a Year!* New York, 1955.

Mowry, George, ed. *The Twenties: Fords, Flappers, and Fanatics*. New York, 1963.

Myers, Margaret. *The New York Money Market.* New York, 1939.

Nichols, Roy. *The Disruption of American Democracy.* New York, 1948.

Neill, Humphrey. *The Inside Story of the Stock Exchange.* New York, 1950.

Nevins, Allan, ed. *Diary of George Templeton Strong.* 4 vols. New York, 1952.

———. ed. *Diary of Philip Hone.* 2 vols. New York, 1927.

———. *The Emergence of Lincoln.* 2 vols. New York, 1950.

———. *Grover Cleveland: A Study in Courage.* New York, 1938.

———. ed. *Letters of Grover Cleveland, 1850–1908.* New York, 1933.

———. *Study in Power: John J. Rockefeller.* 2 vols. New York, 1953.

New York Stock Exchange. *The Stock Market Under Stress.* New York, 1963.

Noble, H. G. S. *The New York Stock Exchange in the Crisis of 1914.* New York, 1915.

North, Douglass. *Economic Growth in the United States, 1790–1860.* New York, 1961.

———. *Growth and Welfare in the American Past.* New York, 1966.

Noyes, Alexander Dana. *Financial Chapters of the War.* New York, 1916.

———. *Forty Years of American Finance.* New York, 1909.

———. *The Market Place.* Boston, 1938.

———. *The War Period of American Finance.* New York, 1927.

Nugent, Walter. *The Money Question During Reconstruction.* New York, 1967.

Oberholtzer, Ellis. *Jay Cooke: Financier of the Civil War.* 2 vols. New York, 1907.

O'Connor, Richard. *The Scandalous Mr. Bennett.* New York, 1962.

Parker, George. *Recollections of Grover Cleveland.* New York, 1909.

Philbrick, Frank. *The Mercantile Conditions of the Crisis of 1893.* Lincoln, Neb., 1902.

Pomerantz, Sidney. *New York: An American City, 1783–1803.* New York, 1938.

Powell, Ellis. *The Evolution of the Money Market, 1385–1915.* London, 1915.

Pyle, J. G. *The Life of James J. Hill.* New York, 1917.

Redlich, Fritz. *The Moulding of American Banking: Men and Ideas.* 3 vols. New York, 1947, 1951.

Regan, Donald. *A View from the Street.* New York, 1972.

Remini, Robert. *Andrew Jackson and the Bank War.* New York, 1967.

Rezneck, Samuel. "Distress, Relief, and Discontent in the United States During the Depression of 1873–78." *Journal of Political Economy* (December 1950).

―――. "The Depression of 1819–22, A Social History." *American Historical Review* (October 1933).

―――. "The Influence of Depressions upon American Opinion, 1857–1859." *Journal of Economic History* (May 1942).

―――. "Patterns of Thought and Action in an American Depression, 1882–1886." *American Historical Review* (January 1956).

―――. "The Social History of an American Depression, 1837–1843." *American Historical Review* (July 1935).

―――. "Unemployment, Unrest, and Relief in the United States During the Depression of 1893–97." *American Historical Review* (August 1953).

Richardson, Albert. *A Personal History of Ulysses S. Grant.* Hartford, 1885.

Robbins, Lionel. *The Great Depression.* London, 1934.

Rothbard, Murray. *The Panic of 1819.* New York, 1962.

Rowen, Hobart. *Kennedy, Johnson, and the Business Establishment.* New York, 1964.

Ruff, Howard. *How to Prosper During the Coming Bad Years.* New York 1979.

Samuels, Ernest. *Henry Adams: The Major Phase.* Cambridge, 1964.

Sarnoff, Paul. *Russell Sage: The Money King.* New York, 1965.

―――. *Speculator King: Jesse Livermore.* New York, 1967.

Satterlee, Herbert. *J. Pierpont Morgan: An Intimate Portrait.* New York, 1939.

Schlesinger, Arthur, Jr. *A Thousand Days: John F. Kennedy in the White House.* Boston, 1965.

―――. *The Age of Jackson.* Boston, 1953.

―――. *The Age of Roosevelt: The Crisis of the Old Order: 1919–1933.* New York, 1957.

Schultz, William, and Caine, M. R. *Financial Development of the United States.* New York, 1937.

Scroggs, William. *A Century of Banking Progress.* New York, 1924.

Seitz, Don. *The Dreadful Decade.* Indianapolis, 1926.

Sellers, Charles, Jr. *James K. Polk: Jacksonian.* Princeton, 1957.

Shannon, Fred. *The Farmer's Last Frontier.* New York, 1945.

Sherman, John. *Recollections of Forty Years.* Chicago, 1895.

Slosson, Preston. *The Great Crusade and After, 1914–1928.* New York, 1937.

Smith, Matthew. *Sunshine and Shadow in New York*. Hartford, 1893.

Smith, Walter. *Economic Aspects of the Second Bank of the United States*. Cambridge, 1953.

———, and Cole, Arthur. *Fluctuations in American Business, 1790–1860*. Cambridge, 1935.

Snyder, Carl. *American Railways as Investments*. New York, 1907.

Sobel, Robert. *The Big Board: A History of the New York Stock Market*. New York, 1960.

———. *The Great Bull Market: Wall Street in the 1920s*. New York, 1968.

———. *Inside Wall Street*. New York, 1977.

———. *The New Game on Wall Street*. New York, 1987.

Sorensen, Theodore. *Kennedy*. New York, 1965.

Soule, George. *Prosperity Decade*. New York, 1947.

Sparkling, Earl. *Mystery Men of Wall Street*. New York, 1930.

Sprague, O. M. W. *History of Crises Under the National Banking System*. Washington, 1910.

Stedman, E. C. *The New York Stock Exchange*. New York, 1905.

Stevens, Frank. *The Beginnings of the New York Central Railroad*. New York, 1926.

Stevens, Mark. *The Insiders: The Truth Behind the Scandal Rocking Wall Street*. New York, 1987.

Studenski, Paul, and Krooss, Herman. *Financial History of the United States*. New York, 1963.

Sullivan, Mark. *Our Times: The United States, 1900–1925*, vol. 3. New York, 1930.

Swanberg, W. A. *Jim Fisk: The Career of an Improbable Rascal*. New York, 1959.

Tarbell, Ida. *The Nationalizing of Business, 1878–1898*. New York, 1936.

Taus, Esther. *Central Banking Functions of the United States Treasury*. New York, 1943.

Taylor, George. *The Transportation Revolution, 1815–1860*. New York, 1951.

Thomas, Dana. *The Plungers and the Peacocks*. New York, 1967.

Timberlake, Richard. *Money, Banking, and Central Banking*. New York, 1965.

Train, George Washington. *Young America in Wall Street*. New York, 1857.

Twain, Mark (Samuel L. Clemens), and Warner, Charles Dudley. *The Gilded Age*. 2 vols. New York, 1929.

Turner, Frederick Jackson. *The United States: 1830–1850*. New York, 1935.

Unger, Irwin. *The Greenback Era*. Princeton, 1964.

United States. 41st Congress, 2nd Session, Committee on Banking and Currency, *Hearings on the Gold Panic of September 24, 1869.* Washington, 1870.

————. 88th Congress, 1st Session, *Report of the Special Study of Securities Markets of the Securities and Exchange Commission,* parts 1–6. Washington, 1963.

————. District Court of the United States for the Southern District of New York. *Corrected Opinion of February 4, 1954, in the case of H. S. Morgan et al., by Harold R. Medina, U.S.C.J.* New York, 1954.

————. *Economic Report of the President, Together with Annual Report of the Council of Economic Advisors, 1963.* Washington, 1963.

————. *Historical Statistics of the United States: Colonial Times to 1957.* Washington, 1958.

Van Deusen, Glyndon. *The Jacksonian Era, 1828–1849.* New York, 1959.

Van Vleck, George. *The Panic of 1857.* New York, 1943.

Walker, James. *The Epic of American Industry.* New York, 1957.

Wanniski, Jude. *The Way the World Works.* New York, 1978.

Weberg, Frank. *The Background of the Panic of 1893.* Washington, 1936.

Wecter, Dixon. *The Age of the Great Depression, 1929–1941.* New York, 1948.

Weiner, Neil. *Stock Index Futures.* New York, 1984.

Wells, David. *Practical Economics.* New York, 1885.

Whalen, Richard. *The Founding Father: The Story of Joseph P. Kennedy.* New York, 1964.

White, Bouck. *The Book of Daniel Drew.* New York, 1937.

White, William A. *A Puritan in Babylon.* New York, 1938.

Whitney, Richard. *The Work of the New York Stock Exchange in the Panic of 1929.* New York, 1930.

Wicker, Elmus. *Federal Reserve Monetary Policy, 1917–1933.* New York, 1966.

Wilburn, Jean. *Biddle's Bank: The Crucial Years.* New York, 1967.

Winans, R. Foster. *Trading Secrets: Seduction and Scandal at the Wall Street Journal.* New York, 1986.

Winkleman, Barnie. *Ten Years of Wall Street.* Philadelphia, 1932.

Winkler, John. *Morgan the Magnificent.* New York, 1930.

Woodward, W. E. *Meet General Grant.* New York, 1928.

Wycoff, Richard. *Wall Street Ventures and Adventures through Forty Years.* New York, 1930.

Zahorchak, Michael. *Favorable Executions: The Wall Street Specialist and the Auction Market.* New York, 1970.

INDEX